THE CAMBRIDGE COMPANION TO

THE STOICS

Each volume in this series of companions to major philosophers contains specially commissioned essays by an international team of scholars, together with a substantial bibliography, and will serve as a reference work for students and nonspecialists. One aim of the series is to dispel the intimidation such readers often feel when faced with the work of a difficult and challenging thinker.

The history of the school spans many centuries, from its foundation by Zeno c. 300 B.C. and consolidation by Chrysippus and his students in the third and second centuries B.C.; through the innovations of Panaetius and Posidonius; to the Roman period dominated by Seneca, Epictetus, and Marcus Aurelius.

This unique volume offers an odyssey through the ideas of the Stoics in three particular ways: first, through the historical trajectory of the school itself and its influence; second, through the recovery of the history of Stoic thought; and third, through the ongoing confrontation with Stoicism, showing how it refines philosophical traditions, challenges the imagination, and ultimately defines the kind of life one chooses to lead.

A distinguished roster of specialists has written an authoritative guide to the entire philosophical tradition. The first two chapters chart the history of the school in the ancient world, and are followed by chapters on the core themes of the Stoic system: epistemology, logic, natural philosophy, theology, determinism, and metaphysics. There are two chapters on what might be thought of as the heart and soul of the Stoic system: ethics. The volume also considers the Stoic influence outside philosophy in the fields of medicine, grammar and linguistics, and astronomy. The concluding chapters trace the influence of Stoicism through the early modern period.

New readers will find this the most convenient and accessible guide to the Stoics currently available. Advanced students and specialists will find a conspectus of recent developments in the interpretation of the Stoics.

Brad Inwood is Professor of Classics and Canada Research Chair in Ancient Philosophy, University of Toronto.

The Cambridge Companion to
THE STOICS

Edited by

Brad Inwood
University of Toronto

CAMBRIDGE
UNIVERSITY PRESS

PUBLISHED BY THE PRESS SYNDICATE OF THE UNIVERSITY OF CAMBRIDGE
The Pitt Building, Trumpington Street, Cambridge, United Kingdom

CAMBRIDGE UNIVERSITY PRESS
The Edinburgh Building, Cambridge CB2 2RU, UK
40 West 20th Street, New York, NY 10011-4211, USA
477 Williamstown Road, Port Melbourne, VIC 3207, Australia
Ruiz de Alarcón 13, 28014 Madrid, Spain
Dock House, The Waterfront, Cape Town 8001, South Africa

http://www.cambridge.org

First published 2003

Printed in the United States of America

Typeface Trump Medieval 10/13 pt.   *System* LaTeX 2_ε [TB]

A catalog record for this book is available from the British Library.

Library of Congress Cataloging in Publication Data
The Cambridge companion to the Stoics / edited by Brad Inwood.
　　p.　cm. – (Cambridge companions to philosophy)
　　Includes bibliographical references and index.
　　ISBN 0-521-77005-X – ISBN 0-521-77985-5 (pbk.)
　　1. Stoics.　I. Inwood, Brad.　II. Series.
　B528 .C26　2003
　188 – dc21　　　　　　　　　　　　　　　　2002031359

ISBN 0 521 77005 x hardback
ISBN 0 521 77985 5 paperback

CONTENTS

v

CONTRIBUTORS

KEIMPE ALGRA is Professor of Ancient and Medieval Philosophy at the University of Utrecht. He is the author of *Concepts of Space in Greek Thought* and co-editor of the *Cambridge History of Hellenistic Philosophy*.

CATHERINE ATHERTON is Adjunct Associate Professor of Classics and Philosophy at the University of California at Los Angeles. She is the author of *The Stoics on Ambiguity* (Cambridge 1993) and many articles on Hellenistic philosophy, ancient grammarians, and the history of the theory of language.

DAVID BLANK is Professor of Classics at the University of California at Los Angeles. He has held Humboldt, NEH, and Fulbright fellowships and has published widely on ancient grammar and philosophy. Current work includes an edition of the *Rhetoric* of Philodemus.

SUSANNE BOBZIEN is Professor of Philosophy at Yale University. She is the author of *Determinism and Freedom in Stoic Philosophy*, co-author of *Alexander of Aphrodisias: On Aristotle's Prior Analytics 1.1–7*, and has published on many aspects of ancient logic and ancient determinism.

TAD BRENNAN is Associate Professor of Philosophy at Yale University. He is the translator (with Charles Brittain) of Simplicius' commentary on Epictetus' *Enchiridion*. He has written on Plato, Aristotle, Sextus Empiricus and much of Hellenistic philosophy, especially Stoic ethics and psychology.

JACQUES BRUNSCHWIG is Professor Emeritus of Ancient Philosophy at the University of Paris-I. In addition to his considerable output in French, he has contributed to many collections or collective works in English, including *The Cambridge History of Hellenistic Philosophy*. A selection of his *Papers in Hellenistic Philosophy* was published by Cambridge University Press.

DOROTHEA FREDE is Professor of Philosophy at Hamburg University. She is the author of *Aristoteles und die Seeschlacht, Plato – Philebus, Translated with introduction and notes, Platon Philebos, Übersetzung mit Kommentar*, and *Platons Phaidon – der Traum von der Unsterblichkeit*.

CHRISTOPHER GILL is Professor of Ancient Thought at the University of Exeter. He is the author of *Personality in Greek Epic, Tragedy and Philosophy: The Self in Dialogue*, and is presently completing *The Structured Self in Hellenistic and Roman Thought*. He has edited several collections of essays on ancient thought and culture.

R. J. HANKINSON is Professor of Philosophy and Classics at the University of Texas at Austin. He is the author of *The Sceptics, Cause and Explanation in the Ancient Greek World* and many other works on various aspects of Greek philosophy and science.

BRAD INWOOD is Professor of Classics and Canada Research Chair in Ancient Philosophy at the University of Toronto. He is the author of *Ethics and Human Action in Early Stoicism* and *The Poem of Empedocles*, and the co-author of *Hellenistic Philosophy: Introductory Readings*.

T. H. IRWIN is Susan Linn Sage Professor of Philosophy and Humane Letters at Cornell University. Among his many books are translations with notes of *Plato's Gorgias* and *Aristotle's Nicomachean Ethics, Aristotle's First Principles, Classical Thought* and *Plato's Ethics*.

ALEXANDER JONES is Professor of Classics and the History and Philosophy of Science and Technology at the University of Toronto. Among his many publications on the ancient exact sciences are *Astronomical Papyri from Oxyrhynchus*, and (with J. L. Berggren), *Ptolemy's Geography: An Annotated Translation of the Theoretical Chapters*.

A. A. LONG is Professor of Classics and Irving Stone Professor of Literature at the University of California, Berkeley. His most recent books include *Stoic Studies*, *The Cambridge Companion to Early Greek Philosophy*, and *Epictetus: a Stoic and Socratic Guide of Life*.

MALCOLM SCHOFIELD is Professor of Ancient Philosophy at the University of Cambridge. His books include *An Essay on Anaxagoras*, *The Stoic Idea of the City*, and *Saving the City*. He is co-author with G. S. Kirk and J. E. Raven of the second edition of *The Presocratic Philosophers*. Of the many collected volumes he has co-edited the most recent is *The Cambridge History of Greek and Roman Political Thought*. He was editor of *Phronesis* from 1987–92.

DAVID SEDLEY is Laurence Professor of Ancient Philosophy at the University of Cambridge. He is author of *Lucretius and the Transformation of Greek Wisdom*, co-author with A. A. Long of *The Hellenistic Philosophers*, and editor of *The Cambridge Companion to Greek and Roman Philosophy*. He is the editor of *Oxford Studies in Ancient Philosophy*.

MICHAEL J. WHITE is Professor of Philosophy at Arizona State University. He is the author of *Agency and Integrality*, *The Continuous and the Discrete*, *Partisan or Neutral: The Futility of Public Political Theory*, and *Political Philosophy: A Short Introduction*.

Introduction: Stoicism, An Intellectual Odyssey

Stoicism has its roots in the philosophical activity of Socrates. But its historical journey began in the enrichment of that tradition with other influences by Zeno of Citium almost a century after Socrates' death, and it continued in the rise and decline of the school he founded. An apparently long pause followed during the Middle Ages, although it seems clear that its philosophical influence continued to be felt through a variety of channels, many of which are difficult to chart. In the early modern period, Stoicism again became a significant part of the philosophical scene and has remained an influential intellectual force ever since.

In the middle of the last century, Max Pohlenz, in a book whose value was always limited by the cultural forces of its time and place (Pohlenz 1948), described the school as an 'intellectual movement.' 'Intellectual movement' captured something of the longevity and protean variability of Stoicism. The dynamic connotations of that metaphor are apt, but I prefer the metaphor of a special kind of journey. An intellectual engagement with Stoicism is an odyssey in three ways. First, the historical trajectory of the school itself and its influence is replete with digressions, narrative ornament, and improbable connections, yet moving ultimately toward an intelligible conclusion. Second, the task of recovering the history of Stoic thought is an adventure in the history of philosophy. It can be a perilous journey for the novice, one requiring guides as varied in their skills and temperaments as was Odysseus, whose epithet *polutropos* ('man of many talents') indicates what is called for. And third, for those readers who find the central ideas of Stoicism appealing either in a purely intellectual way or in the moral imagination, the ongoing confrontation with Stoicism is one which refines philosophical intuitions, challenges both imagination and analytical talents, and leads ultimately to hard philosophical choices which, if taken seriously, define the kind of life one chooses to lead.

This *Companion* is intended as a resource for readers of various kinds as they approach Stoicism along any of these paths, whether they do so for the first time or after considerable prior experience. The authors contributing to this volume are all masters of their fields, but they are as different in their intellectual and literary styles as were the Stoics themselves. I hope that the variety of talents and approaches brought together in this *Companion* will serve the reader well.

Since this book is to serve as a guide to an entire philosophical tradition and not just to one philosopher, it has an unusual structure. It begins with two chapters that chart the history of the school in the ancient world. David Sedley (Chapter 1) takes us from the foundation of the school to the end of its institutional life as a school in the conventional ancient sense, and Christopher Gill (Chapter 2) picks up the story and takes it through the period of the Roman Empire, an era often thought to have been philosophically less creative but, paradoxically, the period which has given us our principal surviving texts written by ancient Stoics. It is therefore also the period which most decisively shaped the understanding of Stoicism in the early modern period, when philosophers did not yet have access to the historical reconstructions of early Stoicism on which we now rely.

The central part of the book is a series of chapters on major themes within the Stoic system. We begin with epistemology (Chapter 3, R. J. Hankinson) and logic (Chapter 4, Susanne Bobzien), two areas in which the philosophical influence of Stoicism has been particularly enduring. Ancient Stoicism produced the most influential (and controversial) version of empiricism in the ancient world, and the logic of Chrysippus, the third head of the school, was one of the great intellectual achievements of the school, though it was not until the modern development of sentential rather than term logic that its distinctive merits became visible. Natural philosophy is, of course, founded on cosmology and the analysis of material stuffs, so in Chapter 5 Michael J. White sets out the framework in which the following three chapters should be read. Theology (Chapter 6, Keimpe Algra), determinism (Chapter 7, Dorothea Frede), and metaphysics (Chapter 8,

Jacques Brunschwig) complete the cycle of topics in natural philosophy and open up, each in its own way, an area of philosophy in
which Stoicism set an agenda for centuries to follow. Yet it is ar-
guable that ethics is the heart and soul of the Stoic system (as one
might expect of a school whose traditions go back to Socrates); it is
covered in two chapters that take markedly different approaches to
the topic: 'Ethics' (Chapter 9, Malcolm Schofield) and 'Moral Psychology' (Chapter 10, Tad Brennan).

With that, one might regard the standard three-part account of
Stoic philosophy as being complete, since the main topics of logic,
physics, and ethics are covered. But Stoicism had a profound influence on intellectual life outside its own boundaries as well, and
three shorter chapters explore the relationships between Stoicism
and medicine (Chapter 11, R. J. Hankinson), ancient grammar and
linguistics (Chapter 12, David Blank and Catherine Atherton), and
the astronomical sciences (Chapter 13, Alexander Jones). In each case
some of the more extravagant claims of influence (in both directions)
are challenged, deflated, or modified in light of recent advances in
the understanding of Stoicism by authors who are expert historians
of the ancient sciences in question.

Finally, the *Companion* concludes with two chapters that aim to
give readers a small taste of what is possible in the way of future ex-
ploration. The influence of Stoicism on later thought has often been
discussed, yet in the last twenty-five years our understanding of ancient Stoicism has improved so fundamentally that much of what
used to be taken for granted must be reassessed. With medieval philosophy, the state of research is still too preliminary to permit a reliable guide to be written, but significant reassessments of the impact
of ancient Stoicism on modern philosophy are beginning to appear.
Chapter 14 ('Stoic Naturalism and its Critics', T. H. Irwin) offers a
sharply focused case study of the philosophical reaction to ethical
naturalism in the Stoic mode through to Butler in the early modern
period. Similar studies could be developed in other areas of philosophy as well, but one example must suffice. Chapter 15, 'Stoicism in
the Philosophical Tradition', by A. A. Long, provides a suitably broad
sense of where these possibilities might be found. Long's generous
assessment of the historical impact of Stoicism in the early modern period covers Spinoza, Lipsius, and Butler and sets the stage for
further study of the period down to Kant.

Throughout the *Companion*, the reader will find a wide variety of philosophical approaches, from the reflective explorations of ethics by Malcolm Schofield to the magisterial exposition of logic by Susanne Bobzien. Authors have been encouraged to write in the manner that best suits their topic, and the result is as varied as the paths taken by the Stoic tradition itself. Similarly, no attempt has been made to impose a unified set of philosophical or historical presuppositions on the authors, as is apparent in the differing assessments of Aristotle's influence on early Stoicism made by Sedley (who tends to minimize it) and by White and Frede, who see the early leaders of the school as reacting rather more directly to Aristotle's work. A similar variation will be found in the handling by various authors of some of the more specialized technical terms coined or used by the ancient Stoics, since the best translation of any such term is determined by the authors' interpretations. Take, for example, the term *kathêkon* in Stoic ethics. In Chapter 10, Brennan explains it without translating it; Sedley renders it 'proper action'; Gill as 'appropriate' or 'reasonable action'; Hankinson as 'fitting action'; and Brunschwig follows Long and Sedley (1987) in rendering the term 'proper function'. In such cases the authors have made clear the original technical term so that themes can be followed easily across the various chapters where it might occur. And the reader will certainly find significant overlap and intersection of themes in this *Companion*. The Stoic school in antiquity prided itself (rightly or wrongly) on its integration and internal consistency. The 'blended exposition' (DL 7.40) that characterized their teaching of the three parts of philosophy is bound to replicate itself in any modern discussion of their work.

The variety of interpretation found in this *Companion* is, the reader should be warned, typical of the current state of scholarship in the field. There is little orthodoxy among specialists in the study of ancient Stoicism – and that is wholly appropriate in view of the state of our evidence for the early centuries of the school's history. But although a standard 'line' is not available on most issues, there has developed a broad consensus on the most important factors that contribute to the study of Stoicism, as they do for any past philosophical movement: the sources for understanding it, the external history which affects it, and the leading topics to be dealt with. This growing consensus is reflected in a number of excellent works of which the reader of this book should be aware. Without pretending to provide a guide to further reading – a virtually impossible task – I merely indicate here some of the key resources about which any reader will want to know. Bibliographical details appear after Chapter 15.

A fuller and more authoritative account of the school during its Hellenistic phase is in the *Cambridge History of Hellenistic Philosophy* (Algra et al. 1999), in the context of a comprehensive account of other movements in the period. English translations of primary texts are scattered in various collections and other publications, many of which will be difficult to use for readers who are limited to English. But two particularly useful collections are Long and Sedley (1987), which includes extensive philosophical discussion, and Inwood and Gerson (1997). There have been several highly influential volumes of essays in the area of Hellenistic philosophy; for example, Schofield et al. (1980), Schofield and Striker (1986), and Brunschwig and Nussbaum (1993). Collections of papers by Brunschwig (1994a), Long (1996), and Striker (1996a) are also excellent sources for challenging detailed discussions. But, inevitably, the only way for a newcomer to find his or her way around the primary and secondary sources for Stoicism is to dive in – and this *Companion* aims to make that plunge more inviting and less hazardous than it would otherwise be.

I am hopeful that many readers will find this plunge worth taking; if they do, the labours of the authors and editor will not have been in vain. Stoic philosophy is a curious blend of intellectual challenges. It will reward those whose strongest interests are in the historical evolution of ideas, but it will bring an even greater reward to those whose concern with Stoicism lies in the wide range of still challenging philosophical problems they either broached for the first time or developed in a distinctive way. There are also rewards for those who, like Lawrence Becker (1998), are convinced that a fundamentally Stoic approach to the role of reason in human life is worth exploring and developing in the present millennium, just as it has been during the last three.

As editor, I have many debts to acknowledge. The first is to the authors of the chapters that follow. They have been genuinely companionable throughout the long gestation of this project, devoting time and thought to its overall well-being, often at the cost of personal and professional inconvenience. The expert assistance of Rodney Ast made it possible to prepare the final manuscript in far less time than I could otherwise have hoped for. Financial support for the editorial work has come from the Canada Research Chair programme of the Canadian government and from the Social Sciences and Research Council of Canada. I am particularly grateful to the Cambridge University Press for its patience and flexibility (and for permission to include the chapter by A. A. Long, which also appears in *Hellenistic and Early Modern Philosophy*).

But my greatest debt is to my family, especially to my wife, Niko Scharer. The compilation of this *Companion* took place during an unusually busy stretch of our life, one beset by more distractions and activities than are normally compatible with Stoic *tranquillitas*. Without her tolerance for an often-absent domestic companion, this Stoic *Companion* might never have been completed.

Brad Inwood
Toronto, June 2002

1   The School, from Zeno to Arius Didymus

I. PHASES

The history of the Stoic school is conventionally divided into three phases:

- Early Stoicism: from Zeno's foundation of the school, c. 300, to the late second century B.C.: the period which includes the headship of the greatest Stoic of them all, Chrysippus
- Middle Stoicism: the era of Panaetius and Posidonius
- Roman Stoicism: the Roman Imperial period, dominated by Seneca, Epictetus, and Marcus Aurelius

Although the Stoic tradition's continuity is at least as important as any resolution into distinct phases, the traditional divisions do reflect key changes which no school history can afford to ignore. The following account will, in fact, assume a rough division into five phases, despite acknowledgment of extensive overlaps between them:

1. the first generation
2. the era of the early Athenian scholarchs
3. the Platonising phase ('Middle Stoicism')
4. the first century B.C. decentralisation
5. the Imperial phase

The primary ground for separating these is that each represents, to some extent, a different perspective on what it is to be a Stoic – that is, on what allegiances and commitments are entailed by the chosen label.

2. ATHENS

The history of Stoicism in its first two centuries is that of a marriage between two worlds. The major figures who founded and led the Stoic school came, with remarkably few exceptions, from the eastern Mediterranean region. Yet the city that gave their school not just its physical location but its very identity was Athens, the cultural metropolis of mainland Greece.

According to Socrates in Plato's *Theaetetus* (173c–e), the true philosopher is blissfully unaware of his civic surroundings. Not only does he not know the way to the agora, he does not even know that he does not know it. Yet, paradoxically, it was Socrates himself, above all through Plato's brilliant literary portrayals, who created the indissoluble link between the philosophical life and the city of Athens. There the leading schools of philosophy were founded in the fourth and third centuries B.C. There the hub of philosophical activity remained until the first century B.C. And there, after two centuries of virtual exile, philosophy returned in the second century A.D. with the foundation of the Antonine chairs of philosophy, to remain in residence more or less continuously for the remainder of antiquity. During all this time, only one other city, Alexandria, was able to pose a sustained challenge to Athens' philosophical preeminence.[1]

The founder of Stoicism, Zeno, came to Athens from the town of Citium (modern Larnaca) in Cyprus. His successor Cleanthes was a native of Assos, in the Troad (western Turkey); and *his* successor, Chrysippus, the greatest of all the Stoics, came from Soli, in Cilicia (southern Turkey). In the generation after Chrysippus, the two leading figures and school heads were of similarly oriental origin: Diogenes of Babylon and Antipater of Tarsus. Nor does this pattern – which could be further exemplified at length – distinguish the Stoics from members of other schools, who were almost equally uniformly of eastern origin. Rather, it illustrates the cultural dynamics of the age. Alexander the Great's conquests had spread the influence of Greek culture to the entire eastern Mediterranean region and beyond. But among those thus influenced, anyone for whom the

---

[1] The many valuable studies relating to the history and nature of philosophical schools include (in chronological order) Nock (1933), Ch. XI, 'Conversion to philosophy'; Lynch (1972); Glucker (1978); Donini (1982); Natali (1996); and Dorandi (1999).

philosophical tradition inaugurated by Socrates held a special appeal was likely to be drawn to the streets and other public places of the city in which Socrates had so visibly lived his life of inquiry and self-scrutiny. (In this regard, philosophy stood apart from the sciences and literature, for both of which the patronage of the Ptolemaic dynasty in Alexandria offered a powerful rival attraction.) So deep was the bond between philosophy and Athens that when in the first century B.C. it was broken, as we shall see in Section 8, the entire nature of the philosophical enterprise was transformed.

3. ZENO

The early career of Zeno, the founder of Stoicism, eloquently conjures up the nature of the Hellenistic philosophical enterprise. He was born in (probably) 334 B.C. at Citium, a largely Hellenized city which did, however, retain a sufficient Phoenician component in its culture to earn Zeno the nickname 'the Phoenician'. Nothing can be safely inferred from this latter fact about Zeno's intellectual, ethnic, or cultural background, but what is clear is that, at least from his early twenties, he was passionately addicted to the philosophical traditions of Athens, encouraged, it was said, by books about Socrates that his father, a merchant, brought back from his travels. He migrated there at the age of twenty-two, and the next decade or so was one of study, entirely with philosophers who could be represented as the authentic living voices of Socrates' philosophy. If Stoicism emerged as, above all, a Socratic philosophy, this formative period in Zeno's life explains why.

His first studies are said to have been with the Cynic Crates, and Cynic ethics remained a dominant influence on Stoic thought. Crates and his philosopher wife, Hipparchia, were celebrated for their scandalous flouting of social norms. Zeno endorsed the implicitly Socratic motivation of this stand – the moral indifference of such conventional values as reputation and wealth. The most provocative of Zeno's own twenty-seven recorded works – reported also to be his earliest, and very possibly written at this time – was a utopian political tract, the *Republic*. In characteristically Cynic fashion, most civic institutions – temples, law courts, coinage, differential dress for the sexes, conventional education, marriage, and so forth – were to be abolished. What was presumably not yet in evidence, but was to become the key to Zeno's mature philosophy, was his attempt to rescue an ethical role for conventional values.

Polemo, the head of the Platonic Academy, and the Megaric philosopher Stilpo, both of them known above all for their ethical stances, were among Zeno's other teachers, and both will have helped him develop his own distinctive ethical orientation. Polemo defended the position of the Platonist and Aristotelian schools that there are bodily and external goods, albeit minor ones, in addition to the all-important mental goods. Stilpo's most celebrated doctrine was the self-sufficiency of the wise, maintained on the precisely opposite ground that nothing that befalls one's body or possessions can be in the least bit good or bad. Zeno sided with Stilpo's Cynicising view on this, but also seems to have inherited from Polemo, and developed, an ethical stance which associated moral advancement with 'conformity to nature'. In this synthesis of his two teachers' contrasting positions, we can already glimpse the makings of the most distinctive Stoic thesis of all. For according to Zeno and his successors, bodily and external advantages such as health and wealth are not goods – Stilpo was right about that – but they are, on the other hand, natural objects of pursuit. We should, therefore, in normal circumstances, seek to obtain them, not caring about them as if their possession would make our lives any better, but on the ground that by preferring them we are developing our skills at 'living in agreement with nature', the natural 'end' whose attainment amounts to perfect rationality, happiness, and a good life. In this way, Stoicism could underpin a thoroughly conventional set of social and personal choices, and was thereby enabled to commend itself more widely in the Hellenistic world than its essentially convention-defying forebear Cynicism.

Zeno's rejection of Platonic metaphysics, which marks a vital break from Polemo and his school, may also have been influenced by Stilpo. Finally, Diodorus Cronus, whose classes Zeno attended alongside the future logician Philo, represented the dialectical side of the Socratic tradition, offering Zeno a training in logic as well as in the study of sophisms.

It was around the turn of the century that Zeno formed his own philosophical group, at first known as 'Zenonians' but eventually dubbed 'Stoics' after the Painted Stoa (Stoa Poikilê) in which they used to congregate. Zeno remained in Athens until his death in 262, and the school he had founded was to become the dominant school of the Hellenistic Age.

Soon after the emergence of Zeno's school, the minor 'Socratic' movements headed by his teachers Stilpo (the 'Megarics') and Diodorus (the 'Dialecticians') seem to have vanished from the scene. The impression is that the Stoa, having absorbed their most important work, had now effectively supplanted them.[2] There is, in fact, evidence that the Stoics themselves were happy to be classed generically as 'Socratics'.[3] And with good reason: their ethical system, characterised by its intellectualist identification of goodness with wisdom and the consequent elimination of non-moral 'goods' as indifferent, was thoroughly Socratic in inspiration. True, the standard of perfection that they set for their idealised 'sage' was so rigorous that even Socrates himself did not quite qualify in their eyes. But there can be little doubt that, even so, the detailed portrayals of the sage's conduct which generation after generation of Stoics compiled owed much to the legend of Socrates. A prime example is the sage's all-important choice of a 'well-reasoned exit' from life, an ideal of which Socrates' own death was held up as the paradigm. Roman Stoics like the younger Cato and Seneca even modeled their own deaths on that of Socrates.

As for the Academy, Zeno's other main source of inspiration, within a few decades it had largely shelved its doctrinal agenda and, under the headship of Arcesilaus, become a primarily critical and sceptical school. The main target of this 'New Academy' was, by all accounts, none other than the Stoa, and the two schools' polemical interaction over the following two centuries is one of the most invigorating features of Hellenistic philosophical history. In Zeno's own day the Peripatetic school, founded by Aristotle and now maintained by his eminent successor Theophrastus, retained much of its prestige and influence, but for the remainder of the Hellenistic Age only the philosophically antithetical Epicurean school could compete with the Stoa as a doctrinal movement.

---

[2] Likewise another minor Socratic school, the hedonist Cyrenaics, was eclipsed by the Epicureans.

[3] Philodemus, *De Stoicis* XIII 3: the Stoics 'are willing (*thelousi*) also to be called Socratics'. This should not, as it sometimes is, be misinterpreted as expressing a positive preference on their part for 'Socratics' as a school title.

One apparent feature of early Stoicism that has caused controversy is the surprising rarity of engagement with the philosophy of
Aristotle. Even some of the most basic and widely valued tools of
Aristotelian philosophy, such as the distinction between potentiality and actuality, play virtually no part in Stoic thought. Although
there is little consensus about this,[4] the majority of scholars would
probably accept that, at the very least, considerably less direct response to Aristotelianism is detectable in early Stoicism than to
the various voices of the Socratic-Platonic tradition. It is not until the period of Middle Stoicism (see Section 7) that appreciation of
Aristotle's importance finally becomes unmistakable. Yet Aristotle
and his school were among the truly seminal thinkers of late-fourth-
century Athens and, in the eyes of many, Aristotle himself remains
the outstanding philosopher of the entire Western tradition. How
can a system created immediately in his wake show so little consciousness of his cardinal importance? One suggested explanation is
that Aristotle's school treatises, the brilliant but often very difficult
texts by which we know him today, were not at this date as widely
disseminated and studied as his more popularising works. But an alternative or perhaps complementary explanation lies in Zeno's positive commitment to Socratic philosophy, of which the Peripatetics
did not present themselves as voices. Either way, we must avoid the
unhistorical assumption that Aristotle's unique importance was as
obvious to his near-contemporaries as it is to us.

Zeno's philosophy was formally tripartite, consisting of ethics,
physics, and logic. His ethics has already been sketched above as
a socially respectable revision of Cynic morality. His physics –
stemming in large part from Plato's *Timaeus* but with an added role
for fire which appears to be of Heraclitean inspiration, and which
may reflect the input of his colleague Cleanthes – posits a single,
divinely governed world consisting of primary 'matter' infused by
an active force, 'god', both of them considered corporeal and indeed
depending on that property for their interactive causal powers. As
probably the one good and perfectly rational thing available to human inspection, this world is a vital object of study even for ethical

---

4 Views range from that of Sandbach (1985) that Aristotle's school treatises were all
but unknown to the early Stoics, to those of others, such as Hahm (1977), who give
Aristotelian philosophy a very significant role in the formation of Stoicism.

purposes. 'Logic', finally, includes not only the formal study of argument and other modes of discourse, but also what we would broadly call 'epistemology'. Here, in a clean break with his Platonist teacher, Zeno developed a fundamentally empiricist thesis according to which certain impressions, available to everybody through their ordinary sensory equipment, are an infallible guide to external truths and, therefore, the starting point for scientific understanding of the world.

Zeno appears to have been more an inspirational than a systematic philosophical writer, and it was left to later generations to set about formalising his philosophy (see especially Section 5).

4. THE FIRST-GENERATION SCHOOL

The temporary title 'Zenonians' must have reflected Zeno's intellectual dominance of the group gathered around him, more than any formal submission to his leadership on their part, or for that matter any official institutional structures (on which our sources are eloquently silent). For during Zeno's lifetime there is no sign of the phenomenon that, as we shall see, was to hold the Athenian school together after his death, namely, a formal commitment to his philosophical authority. His leading colleagues were a highly independent and heterogeneous group. It would be wrong to give the impression that *no* degree of doctrinal conformity was expected: when, for example, one of Zeno's eminent followers, Dionysius of Heracleia (later nicknamed 'Dionysius the Renegade'), was induced by an excruciating medical condition to reject the doctrine that physical pain is indifferent and so to espouse hedonism, he left the school altogether. Nevertheless, by contrast with later generations, it is the lack of conformity that stands out.

This difference should not cause surprise, since it reflects the broad pattern of philosophical allegiance in the ancient world. The evolution of a formal school around a leader was likely to be, as in Zeno's own case, a gradual process, during which emerging differences of opinion would continue to flourish. It was, typically, only after the founder's death that his thought and writings were canonised, so that school membership would come to entail some kind of implicit commitment to upholding them. Plato's school, the Academy, is an excellent illustration of this pattern. In Plato's own lifetime, it could house fundamental philosophical disagreements between Plato and his leading associates (including Aristotle). After his death, a commitment to upholding Plato's philosophy and to respecting the authority of his text becomes evident among his successors over many centuries, despite their widely divergent positions on what his philosophy amounted to (as we have seen, the New Academy regarded its essence as critical rather than doctrinal). A similar distinction between the first and subsequent generations can be detected even in the reputedly authoritarian Epicurean school.[5]

Among the first-generation Stoics, Zeno's most notable colleague was Aristo of Chios, who, if he ever tolerated the label 'Zenonian', did so in virtue of being a member of Zeno's circle, certainly not a devoted follower on doctrinal matters. He explicitly rejected the two nonethical parts of philosophy – physics and logic – endorsed by Zeno, and in ethical theory he stayed much closer to the recent Socratic-Cynic tradition than Zeno himself did, rejecting the latter's keynote doctrine that bodily and external advantages, although morally 'indifferent', can be ranked in terms of their natural preferability or lack of it. According to Aristo, the term 'indifferent' must be taken at face value: since health or wealth, if badly used, does more harm than illness or poverty, there is *nothing* intrinsically preferable about either, and typically Zenonian rules such as 'Other things being equal, try to stay healthy' damagingly obscure that indifference.

It was probably only after Zeno's death (262), with the consequent canonisation of his thought, that Aristo's independence began to look like heresy. It may well have been at this stage that he went so far as to set up his own school,[6] said to have been in the Cynosarges gymnasium outside the city walls of Athens. The later Stoic tradition chose to revere Zeno but not Aristo and, because history is written by the winners, Aristo has come to be seen with hindsight as a marginal and heretical figure. This was certainly not so in his own day, when his impact at Athens was enormous. For example, Arcesilaus, who led the Academy into its sceptical phase, appears to have engaged in debate with Aristo at least as much as with Zeno. Aristo's own pupils included a leading Stoic, Apollophanes, and the celebrated scientist, Eratosthenes.

[5] On this and other aspects of school allegiance, cf. Sedley (1989).
[6] DL VII 161.

There are signs of philosophical independence also in other figures of the first-generation school. Herillus of Carthage, who had
unorthodox views on the moral 'end', is specifically reported to have
included critiques of Zeno in his writings.[7] And Persaeus, himself a
native of Citium and undoubtedly a close associate of his fellow citizen Zeno, nevertheless wrote dialogues in which he portrayed himself arguing against him (Athenaeus 162d). The one first-generation
Stoic who clearly appears in the sources as committed to endorsing
Zeno's pronouncements is Cleanthes; and, for all we know, the evidence for this may entirely represent the period after Zeno's death in
262, when Cleanthes himself took over the headship of the school.
It is to that second phase that we now turn.

5. THE POST-ZENONIAN SCHOOL

Given what we will see (Section 6) to have been the apparent lack of
an elaborate institutional framework, it was perhaps inevitable that
the school's sense of identity should come from a continuing focus
on its founding figure, Zeno. Without his personal engagement in its
debates, teaching, and other activities, it may have been equally inevitable that his defining role should be prolonged by a new concern
with scrutinizing his writings and defending and elaborating his doctrines. At any rate, doctrinal debates between leading Stoics quickly
came to take the form of disputes about the correct interpretation
of Zeno's own words. Numerous disputes of this type are evident
between Cleanthes and Chrysippus, the latter of whom went so far
as to teach outside the Stoa before eventually returning to succeed
Cleanthes as school head on his death in 230. A typical case concerns the nature of *phantasiai* (i.e., 'impressions', 'presentations', or
'appearings').[8] Cleanthes took these to be pictorial likenesses of their
objects, imprinted on the soul, itself a corporeal part of the living
being. Chrysippus, insisting on the impossibility of the soul simultaneously retaining a plurality of these imprints, argued that they
were modifications of the soul but not literal imprints. What is significant in the present context is less the details of the debate than
its form. For Zeno, following a tradition inaugurated by the famous

---

[7] DL VII 165.
[8] S. E. *M* VII 227–41. Cf. Ch. 3, Hankinson, this volume.

image of the mind as a wax tablet in Plato's *Theaetetus*,[9] had defined impressions as mental 'imprints', and the respective positions
of Cleanthes and Chrysippus were presented and developed as rival
interpretations of Zeno's own words. Although there is no reason to
doubt that their competing arguments were in fact focused on the
philosophical merits of their respective cases, the formally exegetical character of the exchange speaks eloquently of the authority that
Zeno, once dead, came to exert in the school. Various other debates
seem likely to have taken on the same formal framework. Consider,
for instance, the controversy between (once again) Cleanthes and
Chrysippus about whether Zeno's definitions of each virtue as wisdom regarding a certain area of conduct made all the virtues identical with one and the same state of mind, wisdom – as Cleanthes
held – or left each – in line with Chrysippus' doctrine – as a distinct
branch of wisdom.[10] Even the most high-profile and enduring of all
Stoic debates – regarding the correct formulation of the moral 'end'
(*telos*) – seems to have started from Zeno's laconic wording of it as
'living in agreement' (although he may himself have subsequently
started the process of exegesis by adding 'with nature'), bequeathing
to his successors the unending task of spelling out its precise implications.[11] Even where intraschool disputes were not a factor and
the criticisms came from outside, Zeno's formal assertions and arguments had to be defended and vindicated. Thus, a number of his
extraordinarily daring syllogisms were defended against his critics.
Many of these were defences of theistic conclusions that no Stoic
would hesitate to endorse;[12] but one – his syllogistic defence of the
thesis that the rational mind is in the chest, not the head – had a
conclusion which itself became increasingly untenable in the light
of Hellenistic anatomical research – despite which Chrysippus and
other leading Stoics resolutely kept up their championship of it.[13]

   In all this, the actual source of authority was Zeno's writings,
now recast in the role of the school's gospels. Although the works
that were preserved under his name undoubtedly conveyed some

---

[9] Plato, *Tht.* 191–5.
[10] Plutarch, *Virt. mor.* 441a–c, *St. rep.* 1034c–e.
[11] See, e.g., Stobaeus *Ecl.* II 75–76.
[12] For these syllogisms, and later Stoic defences of them, see Schofield (1983).
[13] For Zeno's syllogism and the defensive reformulations of it by Chrysippus and
    Diogenes, see Galen, *PHP* II 5. See also on Posidonius, n. 16.

of the intellectual charisma which had won Zeno the leadership of his movement, it is equally apparent that they were far from systematic, leaving all the more room for exegetical debate. As for his first treatise, the *Republic*, with its endorsement of outrageously unconventional social practices, it became a celebrated source of embarrassment to later Stoics, some of whom resorted to bowdlerisation,[14] while others dismissed it as a folly of Zeno's youth – belonging, by good fortune, to his pre-Stoic phase. Others, however (almost certainly including Chrysippus) had the courage to defend its contentions against the critics.[15]

Chrysippus himself (school head c. 230–206) is universally recognized as the most important thinker in the history of the school; to a considerable extent, the Stoicism expounded in this volume is the Stoicism of Chrysippus. His preeminence should not be mistaken, as it often is, for a newly arrived 'Chrysippean orthodoxy', as if his authority now somehow supplanted Zeno's. Subsequent members of the Athenian school showed a healthy readiness to express disagreement with Chrysippus, whereas Zeno to all appearances continued to be above criticism.[16] His acknowledged importance is attributable rather to his encyclopedic elaboration and systematisation of Stoic thought, in a series of treatises running to an astonishing 705 volumes or more. Above all, the school's logic – today widely considered the jewel in the Stoic crown – is agreed to owe its development overwhelmingly to Chrysippus. His 'authority', such as it was, consisted in the uniquely high respect which his work had earned among his fellow Stoics, and did not depend on his formal standing in the school's history or institutional structure.

In the sixty or so years following Chrysippus' death, there were just two scholarchs: Zeno of Tarsus and Diogenes of Babylon. Not surprisingly after the Chrysippean overhaul, their own respective imprints on the Stoic system can seem relatively minor ones. Minimal information survives on Zeno, and Diogenes earns his appearance

---

[14] Cf. n. 57.
[15] The main evidence is discussed by Schofield (1991).
[16] A nice example is the way in which Posidonius, who openly challenged Chrysippus' version of Stoic monistic psychology (see Section 7) in favour of Plato's tripartition of the soul, nevertheless departed from Plato in locating all three soul parts in the chest (Galen, *PHP* VI 2.5 = F146 EK), in deference, undoubtedly, to Zeno's express argument for placing the rational mind here (see n. 13). For further critiques of Chrysippus by Posidonius, cf. T83, F34, 159, 164–6 EK.

in the school's history largely for his skillful handbook-style definitions of dialectical and ethical terms, and for his formal defences of
Zeno of Citium's controversial syllogisms. The main area in which
Diogenes can be seen to go beyond mere consolidation of the school's
achievements – and this may well be a sign of the intellectual fash-
ions of the day – is aesthetics: Philodemus preserves evidence of
major contributions by Diogenes to musical and rhetorical theory.

6. INSTITUTIONAL ASPECTS

Even less is known about the institutional character of the Stoa than
about that of other Athenian schools. We have no evidence that Zeno
bequeathed to his successor any kind of school property, financial
structure, or organisational hierarchy. What is well attested, however, is that – as in other philosophical schools – there was a formal
head (the 'scholarch'). Whether he was nominated by his predecessor or elected after his death is unknown but, once appointed, he certainly held the office for life.

Although the school's institutional structure remains obscure, the
question of finance clearly bulked large. Not all school adherents
were wealthy; Cleanthes in particular was reputedly impecunious
and is reported to have charged fees.[17] His successor Chrysippus
wrote in support of the practice, which he himself plainly adopted,[18]
as did at least one of his own successors, Diogenes of Babylon.[19] In
his work *On livelihoods*, Chrysippus enlarged the question, asking
in how many ways a philosopher might appropriately earn a living.
The only three acceptable means, he concluded, were serving a king
(if one could not oneself be a king), reliance on friends, and teaching. There is no evidence that Chrysippus adopted the first of these
practices, and Zeno was said to have explicitly declined invitations
to the Macedonian court.[20] Other leading Stoics did adopt it, however: Persaeus took up the invitation to Macedon in Zeno's stead,
and Sphaerus, a younger contemporary, had strong links with both
the Alexandrian and Spartan courts.

[17] Philodemus, *Ind. St.* 19 with Dorandi (1994) *ad loc.*
[18] Plut. *St. rep.* 1043b–1044a.
[19] Cic. *Acad.* II 98.
[20] DL VII 6.

Quite apart from financial considerations, some of these dynastic links were undoubtedly of considerable political significance for the long-term fortunes of the Stoa.[21] In Athens itself, too, the school's public standing seems to have been high. After the brief period in 307 during which the philosophers were exiled from the city (ironically, a symptom of their growing political importance), all the signs are that they enjoyed considerable public esteem. Although, other than Epicurus, virtually all the Hellenistic philosophers of whom we hear were non-Athenians, it seems clear that many were granted Athenian citizenship.[22] In addition to citizenship, other recognitions of eminence were conferred on philosophers. Zeno of Citium, for instance, although he is said to have refused the offer of citizenship out of respect for his native city, was formally honoured by the Athenians in a decree at the time of his death:[23]

Because Zeno of Citium spent many years philosophising in the city, and furthermore lived the life of a good man, and exhorted those young men who came to join him to virtue and self-discipline and encouraged them towards what is best, setting up as a model his own life, which was one in accordance with all the teachings on which he discoursed, the people decided – may it turn out well – to praise Zeno of Citium the son of Mnaseas and to crown him with a golden crown, as the law prescribes, for his virtue and self-discipline, and also to build him a tomb in the Kerameikos at public expense.

(The decree then continues with details of the commissioners appointed to oversee the work.)

It is from the mid second century onward that the philosophers' civic standing seems to have been at its most remarkable. In 155, the current heads of the Stoa (i.e., Diogenes of Babylon), the Academy, and the Peripatos were chosen as ambassadors to represent Athens in negotiations at Rome, pleading for remission of a fine imposed on

---

[21] This aspect is explored by Erskine (1990).

[22] Cf. Philodemus, *Hist. Acad.* XXXII 6–8 Dorandi (1991), where the Academic Charmadas, returning to Athens from Asia, 'easily obtained citizenship, and opened a school in the Ptolemaeum...' For the epigraphic evidence on this honorific practice, see Osborne (1981–3).

[23] DL VII 10–11. The decree was, rather pointedly, exhibited in both the Academy and the Lyceum.

the city for the sack of Oropus.[24] The occasion was of especial historical importance because of the packed lectures that the philosophers gave while in Rome, causing shock waves among the Roman establishment, but doing more than any other single event to ignite at Rome a fascination with philosophy which was to remain undiminished for the remainder of antiquity and to have special importance for the future fortunes of Stoicism.

7. THE INTEGRATION OF PLATONISM

From the mid second century B.C. onward, a new trend in the Stoic school's orientation becomes visible: a revised recognition of its Platonic heritage. Some have traced this trend back to Diogenes of Babylon (see Section 5), but the best evidence points to his successor Antipater of Tarsus (school head in the 150s and 140s B.C.) as its true instigator. Antipater, notable among other things for his innovative work in logic, wrote a treatise entitled *On Plato's doctrine that only what is virtuous is good* (SVF 3 [Antipater] 56), in which (we are told) he argued that a wide range of Stoic doctrines in fact constituted common ground with Plato. We do not know his motivation, but a plausible conjecture links the treatise to his well-attested engagement with his contemporary critic, Carneades, the greatest head of the sceptical Academy, with whom he fought a running battle over the coherence of the Stoic ethical 'end'. There were obvious tactical gains to be made by showing that Stoic ethical and other doctrines, under fire from the Academy, were in fact identical to the doctrines of the Academy's own founder.

Be that as it may, the new interest in exploring common ground with Plato[25] gathered pace in the late first century B.C. with Antipater's successor Panaetius (scholarch 129–110), and Panaetius' own eminent pupil Posidonius (lived c. 135–51 B.C.). By this stage, the motivation was certainly much more than polemical. Plato's *Timaeus* in particular had exerted a seminal influence on early Stoic

---

[24] The absence of an Epicurean representative among them attests the apolitical stance adopted and promoted by this school.

[25] One area where Antipater seems likely to have been doing just this is metaphysics: he is the first Stoic recorded (Simplicius, *In Ar. Cat.* 209.11ff., 217.9ff.) as writing about *hekta*, 'properties', a theme which here and elsewhere involves comparison between Platonic Forms and the entities equivalent to them in Stoicism.

cosmology, and Posidonius evidently made the *Timaeus* a special object of his own study and veneration. Most famously, in developing his disagreement with Chrysippus' analysis of moral failings ('passions'), he adopted a version of the tripartite psychology that Plato had developed in that dialogue, among others. In doing so, however, he was not seeking to set up Plato as the new patron saint of Stoicism. Nor, for that matter, was he merely using Plato's dialogues, in the way that previous Stoics had undoubtedly done, maintaining their distance from Plato's own thought[26] while plundering him as a historical source for the life and philosophy of Socrates, a uniquely revered figure in the school; for Socrates is not the principal speaker of the *Timaeus*. Rather, Posidonius was apparently relying on the traditional (and probably correct) identification of Plato's spokesman Timaeus as a Pythagorean, thereby using the dialogue as a step toward fathering his school's philosophy on that most august of all the early sages, Pythagoras.[27] So much for his formal stance; none of this is to deny that the close study of Plato (as well as of Aristotle) had a profound impact on Posidonius' style of philosophical thinking.

In adopting this Pythagoreanising mode, Posidonius was rewriting Stoicism's ancestry in a way which goes beyond anything we can plausibly attribute to Panaetius. The latter was already, like his pupil after him, an avid reader of Plato and his philosophical successors, but the evidence repeatedly suggests that the ultimate authority figure lying behind those thinkers was for him still Socrates. In addition to writing a treatise on Socrates, he is said to have branded Plato's *Phaedo* inauthentic because of its (un-Stoic) insistence on the soul's immortality, an indication that he regarded Plato's genuine Socratic dialogues as philosophically authoritative. Even what is often seen as his most striking philosophical innovation, the bipartition of the soul into rational and desiderative components,[28] could easily have been defended as authentically Socratic on the evidence of Plato's

---

[26] Examples of anti-Platonic works by early Stoics include Persaeus, *Against Plato's Laws* (DL VII 36) and Chrysippus, *On justice against Plato* (SVF 3.157, 288, 313, 455).

[27] Galen, *PHP* V 6.43. Pythagoras should not be thought of as supplanting Zeno's authority (cf. n. 16), but as underwriting it. Posidonius might have pointed to Zeno's own work, *Pythagorika*, about which we know nothing beyond its title (DL VII 4). On the growing importance attached, from around this time, to establishing an *ancient* pedigree, see Boys-Stones (2001).

[28] Panaetius 121–7 Alesse.

Gorgias.[29] It was Posidonius' *tri*partition of the soul that first clearly went beyond what the Stoics recognized as 'Socratic' and invoked an earlier, allegedly 'Pythagorean', tradition.[30]

Leaving aside this last development, most other features of Panaetius' and Posidonius' work show an impressive harmony of approach. Both, for example, are said to have made regular use of early Peripatetic as well as Platonist writings.[31] One way in which their Aristotelianism manifested itself was in an encyclopedic polymathy which had not been at all characteristic of their Stoic forerunners. Beyond the usual philosophical curriculum, both wrote widely on historical, geographical, and mathematical questions, among many others. Posidonius' history alone – it was a continuation of Polybius' – ran to fifty-two volumes. Both, but especially Posidonius, traveled widely in the Mediterranean region, and both became intimates of prominent Roman statesmen (Scipio the Younger in Panaetius' case, Pompey and Cicero in Posidonius').

There are a number of aspects in which this reorientated Stoicism points forward to the school's future character, as will become increasingly evident in the following discussion. It is also of vital relevance to the history of Stoicism to mention the impact of this new approach on the Academy. For what Panaetius and Posidonius had brought about was a pooling of philosophical resources among what could be seen as three branches of the Platonist tradition: early Platonism, Aristotelianism, and Stoicism. This 'syncretism', as it has come to be known, had a visible impact on a younger contemporary of Panaetius, Antiochus of Ascalon.[32] Antiochus was a member of the Academy – at this date still formally a sceptical school but increasingly interested in the development of positive doctrine. From his side of the divide, he came to share the Middle Stoa's recognition of a common heritage, differing only in that he reclaimed it – or at any rate all that was best in it, which for him excluded some central

[29] Cf. Plato, *Gorgias* 493a–d. Importantly, it could also be presented as the correct interpretation of Zeno of Citium, as indeed it was by Posidonius (Galen, *PHP* V 6.34–7 = F166 EK).

[30] In addition to these remarks on Posidonius and the *Timaeus*, note that Chrysippus already regarded tripartition as Plato's own contribution rather than Socrates' (Galen, *PHP* IV 1.6), and that at least one tradition (cf. Cic. *Tusc.* IV 10, DL VII 30) located the antecedents of Platonic tripartition in Pythagoras.

[31] For Panaetius, see Philodemus, *Ind. St.* 51, Cicero *Fin.* IV 79. For Posidonius, Strabo II 3.8 = Posidonius T85 EK.

[32] On Antiochus, see Barnes (1989) and Görler (1994).

aspects of Stoic ethics – for the Platonist school. How influential Antiochus was on the later history of Platonism is disputed, but what is not in doubt is that he became enormously influential in late republican Rome, where he won many followers, among them such leading intellectuals as Varro and Brutus. Cicero, too, knew him personally and, although probably never an Antiochean by formal allegiance, showed Antiochus' philosophy special favour in his own writings. Thus it is that a significant part of the influence that Stoic thought achieved at Rome in the first century B.C. arrived indirectly, through Antiocheanism. A symptom of this is that when Cicero in his *Academica* presents what to all intents and purposes is Stoic epistemology, its formal guise is as Antiochus' theory of knowledge. Similarly, Varro's surviving writings illustrate how Antiocheanism helped to establish in the intellectual bloodstream of the ancient world the fundamental contributions of Stoicism to linguistic theory. The syncretism that Panaetius had inaugurated became, in these and comparable ways, a vital factor in the broad dissemination of Stoicism.

It remains to ask whether this 'Middle Stoicism' marks a clean break from the preceding Stoic tradition. Panaetius did, it is true, abandon several of the older Stoic dogmas. Notably, he rejected the thesis of the world's periodic dissolution into divine, creative fire (the 'conflagration'), and instead advocated the Aristotelian thesis of the world's eternity. In doing so, he may have been consciously aligning himself with the Stoa's Platonist forerunners – for the thesis that the world is in fact eternal had been adopted by some of Plato's immediate successors as the correct reading of the *Timaeus*. But he was not thereby severing a link to the Stoic tradition. On the contrary, doubts about the conflagration had already been expressed by his predecessors Zeno of Tarsus and Diogenes of Babylon;[33] and, because the theory may well have originated as Cleanthes' Heraclitean importation to early Stoic cosmology, no doubt there were ways in which it could be rejected without formally repudiating the authority of the school's founder, Zeno himself.[34] At all events, Panaetius' view on

---

[33] For the plausible proposal that Antipater too had denied the conflagration, see Long (1990), 286–7. The apparent counter-evidence at DL VII 142, which Long considers, can be disarmed: it almost certainly refers to the scholarch's namesake, Antipater of Tyre (see *ibid.* 139; I am grateful to Thamer Backhouse for pointing this out). Long argues persuasively that Carneades' critiques influenced this Stoic retraction.

[34] Diogenes' strong commitment to defending Zeno's explicit arguments (see nn. 12–13), placed alongside his eventual rejection of the conflagration, strengthens the

the conflagration was in keeping with the thought of his immediate forerunners. Moreover, Posidonius appears – on this issue, as on at least one other of Panaetius' innovations, his reported doubts about divination – to have reverted to the older Stoic thesis, thus confirming that we are here witnessing nothing more than one of the familiar internal school divisions over individual points of doctrine.

It would be possible to make similar contextualising remarks about other innovations associated with Panaetius.[35] Overwhelmingly, the synoptic picture comes out as one of continuity rather than radical change. On the vast majority of philosophical issues, what we know of both Panaetius and Posidonius places them firmly within the main current of Stoic debate. Their innovatively hospitable attitude to Plato and Aristotle enables them to enrich and, to a limited extent, reorientate their inherited Stoicism, but, for all that, they remain palpably Stoics, working within the established tradition.

8. THE PHILOSOPHICAL DIASPORA

A vital watershed in philosophical history are the years 88–86 B.C., when first a Peripatetic philosopher, Athenion, and then an Epicurean, Aristion, briefly gained absolute power at Athens, both siding with Mithridates against the Romans.[36] Ironically, given the role played by philosophers, these were also the events – a product of the protracted Mithridatic War (89–84) – that finally destroyed Athens' standing as the centre of the philosophical world. It was during

suggestion that he did not regard the latter as inalienably Zenonian. And although DL VII 142 distinguishes Panaetius' assertion of the world's indestructibility from the destructibility attributed to it by many other Stoics, including both Zeno of Citium and Posidonius, it must be borne in mind that in one acknowledged sense of *kosmos* (the sum total of all world phases: SVF 2.528, 620) all Stoics agreed on the world's eternity, thus leaving a certain scope for reconciling apparent differences.

35 One innovation often attributed to Panaetius is a shift of ethical focus from the sage to the non-sage. But there is no evidence that his celebrated treatise *On proper action* (Cicero's main source or model for *Off.* I–II) involved any such shift. *All* Stoic treatises on this theme had been aimed primarily at offering advice to the non-wise, with the sage's conduct invoked as a paradigm. Panaetius' alleged innovation is inferred from an anecdote at Seneca. *Ep.* 116.5, in which he offers advice to a non-sage which, he admits, might not be applicable to a sage. If this anecdote is trustworthy (which cannot be assumed), the doctrinal novelty consists not in moving the spotlight to the nonsage, but in a new emphasis on possible differences between the conduct appropriate to the sage and to the nonsage.

36 The fullest discussion of these events is Ferrary (1988), 435–94.

Athenion's brief reign as tyrant that Athens suffered a crippling siege by Sulla's army, at the end of which the city was sacked.

It is unclear how much physical damage was done during the siege to the traditional public meeting places of the schools (both the Academy and the Lyceum, being outside the city walls, had been plundered for timber by Sulla).[37] It is possible that the war made it too difficult to recruit pupils, especially from abroad, and also that the philosophers' high political profile in these years made Athens too dangerous a place for some of them. But whatever the precise reasons may have been, after Sulla's capture of the city in 86 many if not most philosophers left, and the Athenian schools seem to have lost their institutional importance. We have, for example, little information on any successions of their scholarchs after this date. Philo of Larissa and Antiochus, who fought for Plato's mantle, conducted their battles from Rome and Alexandria, respectively, and it was primarily in these cities that new philosophical departures occurred in the following decades.

If the philosophical centre of gravity now shifted away from Athens, one possible explanation is the dispersion of the school libraries. Philodemus, who moved from Athens to Italy around this time, brought with him a fine old collection of Epicurus' own writings, possibly inherited from his master Zeno of Sidon.[38] It is conceivable that Philo, the current Academic scholarch, likewise brought the Academy's book collection with him when he moved to Rome. Sulla, at all events, probably carried more than one book collection back to Rome with him as part of his war booty (including, according to the story,[39] some long-lost copies of Aristotle's school treatises). Just as the Athenian Peripatos had gone into decline after Theophrastus, on his death c. 287, had bequeathed his books to Neleus of Scepsis, who promptly removed them from Athens, it is a tempting hypothesis that disruption of school libraries in the 80s B.C. was a leading cause of Athens' decline as a philosophical centre. What better explanation of the fact that Alexandria, with its magnificent library, was now to outshine it for many years? In

[37] Posidonius (ap. Athenaeus 213d) presents Athenion in 88 speaking of the gymnasia being in a squalid condition and the philosophical schools silent, but no causes are mentioned.

[38] See Dorandi (1997).

[39] Strabo XIII 1.54; Plut. *Sulla* 26.

the light of this pattern, we may legitimately suspect a similar hemorrhage of books from the Stoic school after Panaetius' death, when, as we shall see, its centre of gravity shifted from Athens to Rhodes.

The fate of the Stoic school during this era of decentralisation is a matter on which we lack solid information. From Cicero,[40] describing a nostalgic return to the Athenian schools in 79 B.C., we hear mainly of past glories, along with some indication of what few philosophical lectures and classes remain available. These include no mention of Stoic teaching, and there is every reason to assume that the Athenian Stoa was effectively defunct by this date.

As a matter of fact, it remains a strong possibility that its effective demise had occurred two decades earlier. There is no clear evidence of the Stoa's survival as an institution after the death of Panaetius in 110 B.C., and Panaetius' own frequent absences in Rome may well both reflect and help account for Athens' diminishing importance as a Stoic centre at this time. Philodemus' history of the Stoa (the fragmentary so-called *Index Stoicorum*) closes with the scholarchate of Panaetius and a survey of his pupils, and appears in an incomplete closing sentence to claim that *all* the successors to Zeno have now been covered. Posidonius, undoubtedly Panaetius' most distinguished pupil, never became head of the Athenian school but taught in Rhodes. Since Rhodes was Panaetius' but not Posidonius' native city, it is a reasonable guess that Panaetius – reported to have retained his Rhodian citizenship and even his family's priesthood in the Rhodian town of Lindos, and to have refused the offer of Athenian naturalisation[41] – had himself already been fostering the Stoic school there *in absentia*, especially if (as may be conjectured) he owned property in or around the city. To all appearances, this Rhodian school in effect now eclipsed or even replaced the Athenian one. For in addition to Hecato – another eminent Stoic of the day who, as a Rhodian, may be guessed to have been at least associated with the Rhodian school[42] – we can link at least two other individuals with it, neither of them a Rhodian. Paramonus of Tarsus, a follower of Panaetius,

---

[40] *Fin.* V 1–6.

[41] Fr. 10 Alesse.

[42] Other known Rhodian Stoics of the same generation are a certain Plato (DL III 109), Stratocles (Philodemus, *Ind. St.* 17), and possibly Leonides (Strabo XIV 2.13). For a valuable catalogue of philosophers associated with Rhodes (albeit lacking Paramonus), see Mygind (1999).

seems to have moved to Rhodes, as has been persuasively proposed on the evidence of a Rhodian statue base dedicated by him.[43] And the fully institutional character of the Rhodian school is further confirmed by the fact that Posidonius' own grandson, Jason of Nysa, eventually succeeded him as its head.[44] This presence in the early first-century B.C. Rhodian school of a non-Rhodian contingent is a striking feature, and suggests that what we are witnessing is not yet the *de*centralisation of philosophy that was to become the hallmark of philosophy in the Imperial Age, but rather its attempted *re*centralisation to a new headquarters, which at least for a while imitated the metropolitan role previously played by Athens. Although the choice of Rhodes for this role may be suspected to have depended at least in part on the geographical accident of Panaetius' birth, it is perhaps no coincidence that around the same time we hear of an Epicurean school in Rhodes, whose members showed a degree of independence from the school's Athenian headquarters sufficient to shock at least one of the latter's adherents.[45]

Meanwhile, the leading Stoics at Athens in this post-Panaetian period are named by Cicero as Mnesarchus and Dardanus.[46] Since these two were both born around 160 B.C.,[47] there is no reason why they should not between them have remained active until 88–86 B.C., the period of the great philosophical exodus from Athens. But there is no evidence that either, let alone both, became scholarch,[48] and the fact that they are named jointly in this way may even count against any such hypothesis (if one had been scholarch, we would expect Cicero to privilege him over the other). Their being, in Cicero's words, the leading Stoics *at Athens* must surely be linked to the further fact – hardly a coincidence – that both were in fact themselves Athenians, who therefore had personal motives for remaining in Athens even when others were leaving. This, along with the new prominence of the Rhodian school, is strong evidence that, as far as the Stoa is concerned, the process of regionalisation was already far advanced by the end of the second-century B.C.

---

43 Ferrary (1988), 461–2.
44 Posidonius T40 EK.
45 The evidence comes from Philodemus, *Rhetoric* II, and is presented in Sedley (1989).
46 They were '*principes Stoicorum*' at Athens at a time when Antiochus could, had he wished, have defected to them (Cic. *Acad.* II 69), which must certainly be after – perhaps twenty years after – the death of Panaetius.
47 Dorandi (1999), 41.
48 Ferrary (1988), 457–64, Dorandi (1994), 25.

If Panaetius had no formal successor at Athens, we do not know why. One hypothesised explanation, the advent of factional rifts within the school, is not adequately supported by the evidence.[49] An alternative conjecture would be that Posidonius formally inherited the headship but decided to exercise it at Rhodes, thus leaving the Athenian school leaderless and virtually defunct – especially if, as speculatively suggested above, he inherited and took with him the school's library.

Nevertheless, if the disruptions of 88–86 can still be viewed as marking the most decisive watershed in the school's history, it is because those years saw a wholesale decentralisation of philosophy in all the leading schools, changing the nature of the philosophical enterprise in its entirety. The metropolitan headquarters of the main schools at Athens either vanished or lost much of their importance. Relatively small local philosophical groups, of which there had already been a significant number in existence, now proliferated throughout the Greco-Roman world. Deprived of dialectical interaction in their school's authentic Athenian environment, but still well equipped with books, adherents turned above all to the study of its foundational texts.[50] Thus we see, from the mid-first century B.C. onward, the newly burgeoning industry of producing commentaries on the treatises of Aristotle and the dialogues of Plato. For Stoics, although writing or studying commentaries never became a habitual mode of philosophising, we have clear evidence from Epictetus that the exegesis of set passages from Chrysippus became a basic teaching tool.

An important change of attitude to the entire history of philosophy seems to start from this date. Philodemus' history of the Stoa, we have already seen, ends with the last generation of the Athenian school and does not, as it might have done, continue with its Rhodian counterpart. The same approach becomes endemic in the subsequent historical tradition, so that even much later doxographies and biographical histories of philosophy, including those of the Stoa, tend to stop with the thinkers of the early to mid-first century B.C. In the case

---

[49] Ferrary (1988), 457–64 (cf. Dorandi [1994], 25), believes that after the death of Panaetius the school broke up into rival factions, tied to the names of Diogenes, Antipater, and Panaetius. For a preferable interpretation of the evidence, see p. 29.

[50] See Hadot (1987). Further important remarks on this new style of philosophy can be found in Donini (1994). The move away from Athenocentric philosophy is especially well characterized by M. Frede (1999c), 790–3.

of the Stoa, Posidonius and other members of the Athenian school's last generation are usually the latest philosophers deemed worthy of inclusion. Although we know of numerous significant Stoics of later date, their doctrines are rarely ranked and discussed alongside those of the school's golden age. It is almost as if the history of philosophy was felt to have come to an end with the demise of the Athenian schools. Instead of continuing to take it forward, the primary task of the philosopher was now to interpret and understand it, and to enable others to do the same. The new pattern of philosophical teaching, involving the scholarly study of school texts, is an integral part of this picture. Needless to say, the tendency toward such an outlook did not in practice prevent the emergence of much significant new philosophical work, especially in the Platonist camp but also among later Stoics. Yet, even the most innovative thinkers more often than not saw their own work as that of recovering, understanding, and living the wisdom of the ancients.

Seneca is considerably less beholden to the ancients than most philosophical writers of his period, but there is little doubt that even for him, as for at least some approximately contemporary Stoics such as Cleomedes,[51] the philosophers of the Athenian school – especially its last major spokesman, Posidonius – remained objects of intense study. But there is reason to suspect that there were competing views as to which member of the Athenian school had really been its final, summative spokesman. I say this because Athenaeus,[52] writing in the second-century A.D., knows of rival Stoic clubs calling themselves 'Diogenists', 'Antipatrists', and 'Panaetiasts'. Since Diogenes, Antipater, and Panaetius had been the last three formal heads of the Athenian school, it is a tempting inference that the split between these groups represented differing views as to which authority represented the culmination of the Athenian Stoic tradition before its decline.[53] If that conjecture is correct,[54] it remains a matter for further

---

[51] See Ch. 13, Jones, this volume.
[52] Athenaeus 186a.
[53] This explanation is suggested by the analogous attitude of Antiochus, who, in order to present himself as heir to the early Academy, placed especial emphasis on the legacy of Polemo, not as the greatest of the early Academics, but as (to all intents and purposes) the last scholarch before the school deserted Plato, hence as its best summative spokesman.
[54] A recently discovered papyrus (PBerol. inv. 16545) which discusses Antipater's epistemological views (see Backhouse [2000]), even comparing variant readings of his manuscripts, could well be the work of an 'Antipatrist'.

speculation whether Posidonius, whose influence remained so strong in later generations, could have represented for some the figurehead of a fourth faction, or whether – more plausibly – he was appropriated by the Panaetists as an authentic spokesman for his mentor Panaetius. Unfortunately, we have too little evidence about the factional structure of imperial Stoicism for any such approach to be profitably pursued at present.

Whereas the new philosophical decentralisation had a dramatic impact on the great cultural centres – Athens, Alexandria, and to a lesser extent Rome – in the regional capitals the change was no doubt more gradual. A good illustration is offered by Tarsus in Cilicia. Strabo[55] judged that in his own time, the late first century B.C., the educational establishments at Tarsus, including the schools of philosophy, were outstripping those of Athens and Alexandria, even though he conceded that they differed from the latter two in attracting only local residents as pupils. As a matter of fact, the city had produced eminent Stoics for at least the previous two centuries – including two scholarchs: Zeno of Tarsus and Antipater of Tarsus (even the greatest of the Stoics, Chrysippus [see Section 5], was the son of a Tarsian father) – and it may well be that it had had its own Stoic school long before Strabo's day. But its new growth in importance as a philosophical centre does represent the changing intellectual world of the first century B.C. Further testimony to this growth, and to the high standing which such regional schools achieved, is Augustus' choice of two philosophers in succession, both natives of Tarsus and one of them (Athenodorus) a Stoic, to govern the city. Strabo is able to recite a long list of Tarsians, past and present and of various persuasions, who have become professional philosophers, and most of whom have ended up working abroad: Rome, he informs us, is packed with them.[56]

By the mid to late first century B.C., Rome had acquired what is probably as strong a claim as any city's to being a hub of Stoic activity. It is often remarked that the value system of patrician Romans made them natural Stoics. Admittedly, we know of surprisingly few Romans in this period who became Stoics, whereas these did include the most celebrated of all the Roman Stoics, Marcus Cato. We

---

[55] Strabo XIV 673.
[56] Strabo XIV 5.14–15.

actually know of somewhat more late republican Romans who were
Antiocheans, New Academics, or even Epicureans, than were Stoics.
At the same time, however, there can be no doubt that *Greek* Stoics
acquired a strong foothold in the city, especially around the time
of transition from the Republican to the Imperial age. Some leading Greek Stoics of the day seem to have had the ear of Augustus,
hence to have had the opportunity to become influential figures in
the Roman world.

Two of these in particular – Athenodorus and Arius Didymus –
should be mentioned, since they conveniently encapsulate the nature of Stoicism in the late first-century B.C. and, to that extent, may
provide an illuminating background to Seneca, the best-known Stoic
of the next generation. What we know of them suggests a synthesis
of practical counseling to a dynast and his family, and scholarship on
the history of philosophy – the latter by no means confined to study
of the Stoic tradition.

Athenodorus, having been appointed governor of his native Tarsus
by Augustus,[57] spent most of his career at Rome where, as the
emperor's moral counselor, he is reported to have been held by him
in high regard. His ethical work on the subject of 'nobility' was already known to Cicero, writing in 50 B.C.[58] Seneca too consulted
his ethical writings, critically discussing his views on the relative
merits of public and private life in *On Peace of Mind* (*De tran-
quillitate animi*). But his ethical writings were at least partly doxographical, since in 44 Cicero, when working on his philosophical
masterpiece *De officiis* (itself a basically Stoic treatise), is found obtaining from him his notes on Posidonius' teaching on 'duties'.[59]
In another related aspect of his *oeuvre*, Athenodorus joined in the
spate of critical commentary writing on the newly rediscovered or
revived *Categories* of Aristotle. Textual exegesis – interschool as well
as intraschool – and philosophising were becoming twin aspects of a
single enterprise.

---

[57] Athenodorus of Tarsus is unfortunately the name of two eminent Stoics – see
   Goulet *Dictionnaire* (1989), pp. 654–9 – but the following sketch applies, so far as
   the two can be distinguished, to the one nicknamed 'Calvus', also known as 'son of
   Sandon'. The approximately contemporary Athenodorus of Tarsus who, as director
   of the Pergamum library, expurgated the writings of Zeno of Citium (DL VII 34) is
   thought to be the other one, surnamed Cordylion.

[58] Cic. *Ad fam.* III 7.5.

[59] Cic. *Ad Att.* XVI 11.4.

Much the same can be said of Arius Didymus. Like Athenodorus a Stoic, and like him a court philosopher who gained Augustus' confidence, he achieved eminence as an exponent of practical moral philosophy. His consolation to Augustus' wife, Livia, on the death of her son Drusus is portrayed by Seneca[60] as a classic of emotional therapy, and other legends abounded concerning Augustus' deep trust in him. However, once again the roles of moral adviser and scholar of philosophy prove not to be mutually exclusive: Arius Didymus is widely, if controversially,[61] identified with the Arius whose *Epitome* – summarising large areas of Stoic, Peripatetic, Platonic, and other philosophy – is excerpted *in extenso* by Stobaeus. Such engagement by a leading Stoic in the compilation of philosophical history is another sign of the times (compare, in the Epicurean school, his older contemporary Philodemus, whose histories of philosophical schools were probably his best-known prose works). To some extent it may reflect the fact that probably already by this date, as certainly in subsequent centuries,[62] a full philosophical education was understood ideally to involve a training in all four of what were now recognised as the principal sects – Platonism, Aristotelianism, Stoicism, and Epicureanism. Although this need not in itself entail the fashion of philosophical 'eclecticism' that has sometimes been associated with the age,[63] it is at the very least symptomatic of a constructive softening of school boundaries.

It was in such a philosophical milieu – one in which someone could be simultaneously a scholar of philosophical history, an author of ethical treatises, and a counselor to dynasts, and in which narrow philosophical sectarianism was starting to look outmoded – that the 'Roman' phase of Stoicism began life.[64]

---

[60] Sen. *Ad Marc. de cons.* 4.2–6.1.

[61] Against, see Göransson (1995); cautiously in favour, Mansfeld and Runia (1997).

[62] Apollonius of Tyana (Philostratus, *Vit. Ap.* I 7), in the early to mid first century A.D., is said to have found for himself at nearby Aegae teachers of all four main philosophical systems, and for good measure a Pythagorean teacher too. Galen (*De cognoscendis curandisque animi morbis* 8 [*Scripta minora* 1.31.23ff.]), in the mid second century, was able to study with representatives of those same four schools at his native Pergamum.

[63] Dillon and Long (1988)

[64] My thanks to Brad Inwood for his valuable help in drafting this chapter.

2 The School in the Roman Imperial Period

I. THE STEREOTYPE

According to a stereotypical view, Stoicism in the period of the Roman Empire was philosophically uncreative. The 'school' had an ill-defined institutional status and there was a good deal of eclecticism and merging of different philosophies. The dominant theme was ethics, and the main surviving works consist of exercises in practical moralising based on ideas mapped out centuries before. Unsurprisingly, in the later part of this period, Stoicism was replaced as a living philosophy by a revived Platonism and by a form of Christianity that was increasingly more sophisticated and theoretically aware.

Like all stereotypes, this one contains an element of truth; but it obscures important respects in which Stoicism continued as an active philosophical force for at least the first two centuries A.D. Although there was no institutional 'school' as there was in the Hellenistic Age, there were numerous Stoic teachers, and the distinctive three-part Stoic educational curriculum was maintained, with important work continuing in all three areas (i.e., logic, ethics, and physics). As well as being the dominant philosophical movement in the period, Stoicism was also strongly embedded in Greco-Roman culture and, to some extent, in political life, and the ideal of living a properly Stoic life remained powerful. In the third and fourth centuries A.D. and later, Neoplatonic and Christian writers built on key Stoic ideas and absorbed them into their systems.

2. PHASES

It is not possible to demarcate distinct phases of institutional and intellectual development within this period as it is in the Hellenistic Age (see Chapter 1). However, we can highlight ways in which the different phases of imperial rule and cultural life influenced Stoic philosophical activity. This also serves to bring out the prominence of Stoicism in the political arena in the first two centuries A.D.

The Julio-Claudian era (from Augustus to Nero) was, in broad terms, a positive context for Stoic and other philosophical activity. As noted in Chapter 1, Augustus maintained two Stoic philosophers, Athenodorus of Tarsus and Arius Didymus, who combined the roles of moral adviser and philosophical scholar.[1] Under Nero, Seneca (1 B.C. – A.D. 65) also combined these roles but was a much more important figure politically and philosophically. Seneca was first tutor, then adviser, to the young Nero, and is thought to have been a key restraining influence on the emperor during the first, more successful, period of his realm (54–62)[2]. Subsequently, he fell out of favour, was suspected (with other Stoics, including his nephew Lucan) of organising a conspiracy against Nero, and committed suicide in 65. His death, vividly described by Tacitus (*Ann.* XV 62–4), and partly modeled on the death of Socrates, as presented in Plato's *Phaedo*, was conceived as a gesture of defiance and of heroic fortitude. During his life and especially in his years of retirement, Seneca was an immensely prolific writer of (largely) Stoic philosophical works, mainly on ethics but also on meteorology (*Natural Questions*). He also composed a series of tragedies, which show Stoic influence.[3]

Seneca's life encapsulates two striking features of the first century A.D. On the one hand, significant numbers of upper-class Romans found in Stoicism a guiding ethical framework for political involvement. On the other hand, Stoic ideals could also provide a theoretical basis for moral disapproval of a specific emperor or his actions and for principled disengagement or suicide.[4] This pattern can be found

---

[1] See Ch. 1, Section 8; the summary of Peripatetic ethics ascribed to 'Arius' in Stobaeus is discussed later in this chapter.

[2] All further dates A.D. unless otherwise indicated.

[3] See Rosenmeyer (1989).

[4] For some striking examples, see Plin. *Ep.* III 11, 16, Tac. *Ann.* XVI 25, XVI 34.3 (see André [1987], 24 and 37–8). On deaths inspired by Stoicism, see Griffin (1986). On Seneca as politician and philosopher, see Griffin (1976 [1992]) and (2000). Since

under the Flavian emperors (from Vespasian to Domitian) and their successors, as well as under the Julio-Claudians. Musonius Rufus (c. 30–100), a Roman 'knight' (i.e., member of the second-highest social class), was actively engaged in politics, especially in opposing what he saw as wrongdoing, under Vespasian, as well as Nero, and was twice exiled. He was also a Stoic teacher, whose students included Epictetus and Dio Chrysostom; his surviving writings fall wholly in the area of practical ethics. Epictetus (c. 50–130), an ex-slave from Phrygia, studied with Musonius at Rome before setting up his own school in Nicopolis (Western Greece). His oral ethical teachings, preserved by Arrian (the *Discourses*), constitute a major source for reconstructing Stoic patterns of education in this period. Although unable to engage in Roman politics directly, Epictetus provided advice to many upper-class Romans; his teachings reflect the type of thinking about principled involvement – or disengagement – that underlie the actions of Musonius or Seneca.[5]

The reign of Hadrian (117–138) and of the Antonine emperors (from Antoninus Pius to Commodus, 138–192) was highly favourable for literary and intellectual life in general. This period saw the zenith of the 'Second Sophistic', a flourishing of cultural activity throughout the Greco-Roman world, centred on declamation (rhetoric as performance) but embracing philosophical and technical studies. There was considerable imperial patronage: several emperors established chairs of rhetoric at Rome and elsewhere; Marcus Aurelius set up four chairs of philosophy at Athens (for Stoicism, Epicureanism, Aristotelianism, and Platonism).[6] The latter event marks the re-emergence of Athens as an intellectual centre, along with the Hellenistic capitals (i.e., Pergamon, Smyrna, Antioch, and Alexandria), of a re-animated Greco-Roman culture. The writings of authors such as Aulus Gellius (active c. 180), Lucian (born c. 120), and Athenaeus (active c. 200) display a cultural context with a high level of awareness of philosophy, including Stoicism, among other forms of intellectual and artistic life. Marcus Aurelius, emperor in 161–180, was strongly influenced by Stoicism. The *Meditations*, written in Greek, serves as a type of philosophical diary, in which the emperor drew

---

Stoicism did not teach that imperial rule as such is wrong, caution is needed about the idea of a 'Stoic opposition'.

[5] On Musonius and Epictetus, see Gill (2000), 601–3, 607–11.

[6] Dio Cassius LXXI 31.3; see further Lynch (1972), 190; André (1987), 53.

on (largely) Stoic principles to construct a framework to meet the challenges of human life as he experienced it.

It is more difficult to trace clear indications of Stoic activity in the third century, particularly in its second half. Diogenes Laertius, whose *Lives of the Philosophers* is a major source for ancient philosophy, including Stoicism, probably lived in the first half of the third century but discusses no thinker later than the second century. However, Stoicism, particularly as expressed in Epictetus' *Discourses*, remained influential in the thought of later antiquity and beyond. Plotinus (205–270) drew on Stoic as well as Aristotelian ideas in his version of Platonism, whereas the sixth-century Neoplatonist, Simplicius, wrote a massive commentary on Epictetus' *Handbook*. Epictetus' austere moralism attracted the interest of early church fathers, such as Clement of Alexandria and Origen – an interest that persisted among medieval Christian ascetics.[7]

3. BEING A STOIC TEACHER

What in this period did it mean for someone to be a 'Stoic teacher'? Clearly, in the absence of an institutional 'school', there is no question of a central authority accrediting teachers. To this extent, being a Stoic teacher is a matter of presenting oneself in that light and having others accept the claim. But there were some recognised defining characteristics. One was that Stoic teaching was based on a well-established canon of written treatises. Although Zeno continued to have a special status as the founder of the school, the substantial body of works by Chrysippus – the great systematic thinker of Stoicism – formed the core of the Stoic corpus in this period. It is clear from Epictetus, especially, that 'expounding Chrysippus' and 'being a Stoic teacher' had come to mean much the same thing.[8] The second key feature was the distinctive integrated three-part philosophical curriculum (i.e., logic, ethics, and physics). Although the Stoics we know about in this period did not necessarily take an equal interest

[7] On Epictetus' influence, see Spanneut (1962), esp. 633–67. On Neoplatonic and Christian responses to Stoicism, see below. See most recently Sorabji (2000).

[8] See, e.g., Epictetus, *Diss.* I 4.6–9, I 17.13–18. This partly reflects the emphasis in Epictetus' school on logic, in which Chrysippus' works were fundamental; see Long (1996), 89–106. On Chrysippus as the great systematizer of Stoicism, see Chapter 1, Section 5.

in all three areas,[9] the curriculum itself continued to be recognised as a special defining characteristic, with important theoretical implications.[10]

Not all the figures noted earlier as Stoics would have regarded themselves as Stoic 'teachers', at least not in the same sense. Musonius Rufus and Epictetus were well recognised as teachers with an identifiable body of students; in Epictetus' case, we can reconstruct a picture of an institution (at Nicopolis) with a determinate programme of studies.[11] Others were recognised teachers but operated primarily within a single household, as advisers to an emperor (as Athenodorus or Arius Didymus did for Augustus) or to Roman aristocrats.[12] Seneca was himself a Roman aristocrat at the centre of power; although he thought of himself as a Stoic and composed a series of important Stoic essays, he would not have characterised himself as a 'Stoic teacher'. Similarly, Marcus Aurelius (who studied under a Stoic teacher in his youth and continued his studies in adult life)[13] would not have regarded himself as a teacher but rather as someone who tried to apply the Stoic message to help him live a good life.

This variation of status has a bearing on the question (discussed in Section 6) of Stoic orthodoxy and eclecticism. A related point is the distinction between (1) formal exposition of Stoic texts in a curricular context; and (2) public lectures, speeches, or discussions based on Stoic doctrines but formulated in non-technical style, with audiences or participants who are not necessarily adherents of Stoicism. Epictetus' *Discourses* constitutes good evidence for this distinction and also provides a striking example of Stoic semi-public discourse.[14] Seneca's moral essays and letters represent written versions of the second type of activity. Although both types can be characterised as

[9] Seneca was dismissive of logic (*Ep.* 45.5, 49.5); Marcus had a limited grasp of logic and physics (*Meditations* I 17).

[10] On the three-part Stoic curriculum, see LS 26. There are various versions of the order of studies; the main point seems to be that they should be integrated. Middle Platonists adopted this view wholesale, Annas (1999), 108–12; Lucian (second century) parodied the linkage of ethics and logic (*Sale of Philosophies* 20–5).

[11] On the role of logic in his curriculum, see Long (1996), 104–6; Barnes (1997), Ch. 3; on the teaching-methods in general, see Hijmans (1959).

[12] See Donini (1982), 32–34.

[13] *Meditations* I 7–8; see further Birley (1987), Chs. 2–5.

[14] See, e.g., *Diss.* I 7., I 17, II 25, which underline the value of logic (in an integrated curriculum) but which do not set out to teach formal logic.

'Stoic teaching', it is important to recognise the difference in objective and in type of discourse.

4. TREATISES AND THEIR ORIGINALITY

One continuing mark of philosophical vitality is that Stoic treatises are still being produced in this period, in all three areas of the philosophical curriculum, some surviving intact or in large part (which is not true of any treatise from the Hellenistic Age). Hierocles, active around 120, wrote an *Elements of Ethics* of which we have extensive extracts. These extracts show him drawing out the importance of the idea of 'self-perception' in animal (including human) development and so illuminating the more elementary stages of *oikeiôsis* ('familiarisation' or 'appropriation').[15] Cornutus, active c. 50–65 in Rome and teacher of the poets Lucan and Persius, wrote one of the few complete surviving Stoic treatises from any period. His *Summary (Epidromê) of the Traditions of Greek Theology* is a collection of allegorical interpretations of Greek myth. It provides an important source of evidence for the allegorical treatment of etymology and presupposes the Stoic theory that language has 'natural' meaning and is not simply a set of conventional symbols.[16]

Hierocles' work falls within ethics; Cornutus' within physics, in the sense that theology, in Stoicism, belongs within the study of nature. There are two other (and more obviously 'physical') works from this era. Seneca's *Natural Questions* is a large work, though it is partly incomplete and there is continuing debate about the correct order of the surviving books. Although focused on specific topics within one of the more restricted and technical aspects of Stoic physics, the work has larger intellectual objectives. Broadly, the aim is to show that a rational (and in a sense 'naturalistic') analysis of phenomena such as meteors, storms, and earthquakes is compatible with the Stoic providential view of the universe.[17] Cleomedes, in the first or second century, wrote a shorter work, *Caelestia (Meteôra)*, on what were standard topics in Stoic physics: spherical astronomy and

---

[15] He also draws a distinction between four types of *oikeiôsis*, one to ourselves and three to externals; see further Long (1996), Ch. 11.

[16] See Most (1989); on Stoic etymology, LS, Vol. 1, p. 195; also Boys-Stones (2001), 49–59.

[17] See Codoñer (1989), Hine (1996), and Inwood (2002).

terrestrial geography. It provides access to types of argument (e.g., on the measurement of the earth) and on the epistemology of astronomy which are unknown to us from other Stoic sources.[18]

Can we tell whether these treatises merely provide access to areas of Stoic theory that had already been developed in earlier Stoic thinking or whether they are substantively original? What would 'originality' mean in this connection? The relevant kind of originality is not, I take it, putting forward a completely new set of ideas, but rather making a new and significant move in a continuing debate based on an existing (Stoic) framework of thought. The Stoic essays outlined differ in this respect. Cornutus' work is explicitly presented as a school text; it seems designed for young men in their late teens moving from literary and rhetorical studies to philosophical ones (as Cornutus' pupil, the poet Persius, did at sixteen). One would expect in such a work not originality but rather a clear and comprehensive exposition of existing Stoic thought on allegorical interpretation of myth. This is what we seem to find, even though the contents do not have exact parallels elsewhere.[19]

Cleomedes' work on astronomy, by contrast, is an essay or treatise, not a school text; it seems also to have a distinct theoretical position, developing Posidonius' view that the role of physics is to provide explanations for the data provided by specialist sciences such as astronomy. Cleomedes also uses the essay to engage in debate with other schools about conceptually demanding issues in physics. He debates with Peripatetics about the infinite void and the stability of the cosmos, and with Epicureans about the size of the sun and our knowledge of this. To this extent, the treatise seems to have a partially innovative aim, although the style of exposition is brief and schematic.[20] In Seneca's *Natural Questions*, the independence of approach and project is more evident, especially in Books VI–VII, I–II (which seems to be the correct order). Seneca sets out to show that phenomena such as earthquakes, meteors, and lightning – traditionally taken as indications of supernatural intervention by gods – are amenable to rational explanation based on careful analysis of empirical evidence. This line of argument seems virtually Epicurean, but

---

[18] See Ch. 13, Jones, this volume.
[19] See Most (1989), esp. 2023–34; there may be more innovation in the implied links with Neronian ideology (Most, 2034–44).
[20] See Todd (1989), 1367–71.

it has a fundamentally different objective. Whereas the Epicureans want to show that the natural universe is free from divine influence, Seneca wants to bring out the divinity of the world. The fact that the universe is rationally intelligible as a coherent nexus of cause and effect is precisely what makes it 'divine', in Stoic terms.[21]

Hierocles' *Elements of Ethics* seems also to be advancing fresh points within the ethical area. The analysis of animal development and psychophysical cohesion in terms of self-perception rather than self-awareness seems to be new. Also, we can detect within this analysis a considered attempt to meet objections, whether actual or imagined, to the explanation of animal development by self-perception.[22] Another area in which we seem to find innovation in this period is in Stoic thinking on fate and responsibility, a subject that embraces logic, ethics, and physics. A powerful recent treatment of this subject (Bobzien 1998) suggests that there are only two major Stoic theories on this topic: one deriving from Chrysippus, which dominated Stoic thinking for several centuries; and one emerging in the first or second century A.D., which Bobzien attributes to Philopator (active c. 80–120). The distinctive feature of the latter theory is a hierarchical analysis of types of natural motions, which is used as the basis of a new account of what it is about human actions that makes them 'depend on us'. Philopator has the same overall objective as Chrysippus: to demonstrate the compatibility of fate and human responsibility; however, he supports Chrysippus with this new form of analysis.[23]

5. PRACTICAL ETHICS

One area in which Stoic philosophy is clearly creative in this period is that of practical or applied ethics. The area itself is not new within Stoicism. Its origins lie in two crucial doctrinal moves made by Zeno, and adopted by Chrysippus but rejected by Aristo, in the formative years of the school. According to Zeno and Chrysippus, advantages such as health and wealth are naturally 'preferable', even though their value is substantively different from that of virtue, which alone can count as 'good'. A related distinction (again not adopted by Aristo) is that between the perfectly right actions (*katorthômata*)

[21] See refs. in n. 17, esp. Inwood (2002).
[22] See LS 53B, 57C; Inwood (1984), Long (1996), Ch. 11.
[23] Bobzien (1998), Ch. 8.

of the perfect wise person and the 'appropriate' or reasonable actions (*kathêkonta*) that can also be performed by imperfect, non-wise people.[24] These distinctions provided the basis both for extensive theoretical debate about these different types of value and for certain kinds of practical advice. The practical advice (directed at non-wise people who want to become wise) centred especially on determining what types of actions were, indeed, 'appropriate' and in determining, in one's life, the right relationship between gaining 'preferable' advantages and acting virtuously (at least, making progress toward virtue).

The richest source in the pre-Imperial period for this type of Stoic material is Cicero's *On Duties* (*De officiis* = about *kathêkonta*). This is substantially based on a book of Panaetius' on this topic, but it also draws on advice and casuistry (i.e., the analysis of key examples) going back at least to Diogenes and Antipater. A special feature of Panaetius' approach, reflected in Cicero, is the use of the theory of the four *personae* to differentiate our ethical and social roles, thereby providing the basis for more closely specified advice about what is 'appropriate' for us.[25] A second area of practical advice relates to the emotions or passions (*pathê*). These are understood in Stoicism as products of a specific kind of error; namely, that of treating merely 'preferable' advantages as if they were absolutely good, which only virtue is. This type of mistake produces intense reactions (passions), which constitute a disturbance of our natural psychophysical state. These disturbances are treated as 'sicknesses' that need to be 'cured' by analysis of their nature and origin and by advice. Cicero, again, is the best pre-Imperial source for this area of Stoic thought (in his *Tusculan Disputations* Books III–IV), which goes back to Chrysippus.

There are substantial works of practical ethics from the Imperial period, drawing on both these areas. For instance, Seneca's *On Benefits* and Musonius' diatribes (based on oral teaching) draw on Stoic advice about appropriate actions in specific types of situations, and Seneca's *On Anger* uses Stoic thinking about the nature and therapy

---

[24] LS sections 58–9 (LS translate *kathêkonta* as 'proper functions'), esp. Vol. 1. pp. 358–9; also Sedley (1999a), 130–3. In Ch. 1, n. 35, Sedley translates 'proper actions'. On Aristo's role in the development of the Stoa, Ch. 1, Section 4.

[25] Cicero, *Off.*, esp. I 107–21 (four-*personae* theory), III 51–7, 63 (Stoic casuistry); also Inwood (1999), 120–7.

of the passions.[26] Epictetus' *Discourses* and Marcus Aurelius' *Meditations* combine both areas in ways to be considered shortly. These Stoic-inspired works form part of a larger family of writings on practical ethics in the later Hellenistic and Imperial periods, drawing on different philosophical traditions (and sometimes merging them) and on more popular thought.[27]

What, if anything, is new about the Imperial versions of Stoic practical ethics? One (at least partial) innovation lies in thought about the main genres or types of practical ethics; this is also reflected in the kind of guidance offered in the works themselves. This subject also has pre-Imperial antecedents. For instance, Philo of Larisa (158–84 B.C.), of the Academic (Platonic) school, outlined a threefold typology of protreptic (i.e., encouragement to improving oneself), therapy, and advice.[28] Seneca offers an alternative threefold pattern of ethical guidance: (1) assessing the value of each thing, (2) adopting an appropriate and controlled impulse toward objects pursued, and (3) achieving consistency between impulse and action.[29] Epictetus' threefold pattern is similar but not identical. Topic 1 relates to desires and aversions, which depends on the evaluation of the objects desired or avoided. The satisfaction or frustration of our desires leads to the production or avoidance of the passions. Topic 2 relates to impulse and rejection; specifically, the impulse to perform actions that are or are not 'appropriate'; this topic is closely linked to social ethics. Topic 3 relates to infallibility, especially in giving 'assent' to 'impressions' (the terms reflect the Stoic analysis of action). The focus here seems to be on achieving complete consistency within one's belief system and between beliefs and action.[30] In Marcus Aurelius, we can find a version of Epictetus' typology, but modified in its order and with

---

[26] On Seneca's *On Benefits* (or *Favours*) and *On Anger*, see Cooper and Procopé (1995). *Aufstieg und Niedergang der römischen Welt* II 36.3 (1989) contains a series of essays on this side of Seneca's writing.

[27] This body of work has recently aroused increased interest, in part because it seems to anticipate contemporary concern with applied ethics and psychotherapy: see, e.g., Foucault (1986), Nussbaum (1994), Sihvola and Engberg-Pedersen (1998), Sorabji (2000).

[28] Stobaeus, II 39.20–41.25. See Brittain (2001) Ch. 6, esp. 277–280.

[29] *Ep.* 89.14. For a similar pattern, ascribed to the 'Middle Platonist' Eudorus (active c. 25 B.C.): (1) discourse about theory (about the ends or goals of life), (2) about impulse, and (3) about action, Stobaeus II 42.7–45.6.

[30] *Diss.*, III 2.1–15; also Bonhöffer (1890), 19–28; Dobbin (1998), 91–4; on the terminology, Inwood (1985), 116–19.

a stress on adopting what we might call 'the cosmic perspective' as part of the desired set of beliefs and attitudes.[31]

It is sometimes suggested that the threefold pattern in Epictetus represents a version of the complete Stoic curriculum (corresponding to the order, physics, ethics, and logic).[32] But it may be better to interpret all these typologies as subdivisions of ethics and, specifically, of applied or practical ethics. The relationship between ethical theory and practical advice was itself a subject of discussion in this period, notably by Seneca. Seneca stresses that both parts of ethics are distinct but interdependent, and he insists (in contradiction to Aristo, for instance) that both parts have their own validity.[33]

These indications of fresh thinking about genres of practical ethics go along with creativity in the forms of instruction, both literary and oral. For instance, Seneca's extended series of letters of ethical guidance to a single addressee (i.e., Lucilius) represents an original use of the letter genre, designed to display the lifelong shared quest of two philosophically minded adults for ethical perfection.[34] Epictetus' oral teachings, as preserved by Arrian, do not simply constitute (practical) lectures. Rather, whether couched in monologue or dialogue form, they serve as a means of directed discourse to lead the listener or interlocutor through the threefold ethical programme outlined previously. Epictetus' repeated stress on 'examining your impressions' and recognising what is and is not 'up to us' can be understood in the light of that programme. Epictetus uses these formulae to lead the interlocutor to (1) reexamine the overall goals of his desires; (2) adjust his impulse to action and his view of his social commitments in the light of thought about goals; and (3) aim at complete consistency in belief, attitude, and state of mind.[35] Epictetus' use of directed, systematic questioning is strongly reminiscent of Socrates (as presented in the early Platonic dialogues). Also Socratic is the conviction that seems to underlie his procedure, that such reexamination

---

[31] *Meditations* VIII 7, and III 11; also P. Hadot (1995), 195–6.

[32] See, e.g., P. Hadot (1995), 193–5.

[33] *Ep.* 94.2, 31, 50–1, 95.10–12, 61, 63–4 (= LS 66I–J); on Aristo's (absolutist) ethical position, see Ch. 1, Section 4. On subdivisions in Stoic ethics, see LS 56, 66.

[34] Seneca's usage is, presumably, partly inspired by Cicero's (real) series of letters to his friend Atticus. His *On Mercy (De clementia)* is also original in its focus on Nero; on distinctive features of this work and *Ben.*, see Griffin (2000), 535–43, 545–51.

[35] For these formulae, see, e.g., *Handbook* 1; for the three-fold programme, see above and n. 29.

of basic beliefs will lead any interlocutor to the same conclusion; namely, to the 'preconceptions' that underlie human thought and discourse.[36] In some ways still more remarkable is the form of Marcus' *Meditations*. Although apparently written for his eyes only, as a kind of notebook or diary, the work has a distinctive literary-philosophical character and power. Each of the isolated comments, evocative of the oracular fragments of the Presocratic thinker, Heraclitus, seeks to express a profound truth. In content, the sayings encapsulate the outcome of the (highly Stoic) programme of practical ethics noted previously. However, the style is informed by a range of less Stoic influences (including Cynic and Platonic colouring) by which Marcus conveys, in particular, a cosmic perspective on human life, including his own life.[37]

6. DOCTRINAL ORTHODOXY AND ECLECTICISM

In previous scholarship, it has been quite common to see the late Hellenistic and Imperial periods (when the great philosophical schools of Athens were defunct or scattered) as eras of widespread philosophical eclecticism. 'Eclecticism' has often been interpreted negatively, as suggesting a kind of individualistic 'pick-and-mix' approach to philosophy. However, as the thought of this period has been scrutinised more closely and as the concept of 'eclecticism' has itself been examined, scholars have become much more cautious about making this type of claim.[38] In this period as in others, most philosophically committed thinkers saw themselves as having a determinate intellectual position and (unless someone was himself the founder of a new movement) an allegiance to a specific school with its own founder and conceptual framework.[39] This is not to deny that someone might interpret what it meant to be a Stoic or Academic,

---

[36] Long (2002) stresses especially the quasi-Socratic project of many of the *Diss.*, e.g., I 17; see also Long (1996), Ch. 12; on 'preconceptions', see LS 40.

[37] On the form of the *Meditations*, see R. B. Rutherford (1989), esp. 143–7, 155–67; on the Heraclitean influence, see Long (1996), 56–7; on Marcus' philosophical position, see Section 6.

[38] See Dillon and Long (1988), esp. Introduction and Ch. 1.

[39] See Sedley (1989), also Ch. 1, Section 5. However, caution is needed to avoid over-assimilating allegiance to an ancient philosophical school to that to a modern monotheistic religion (to that degree, it is misleading to describe Zeno's works as the 'gospels' of Stoicism).

for instance, in broader terms than was normal, or might incorporate within the school's theory ideas drawn from other sources.[40] A further possible move was that of redescribing the position of one's own school in terms drawn from another position. For instance, the summary of Peripatetic ethics ascribed to 'Arius' in Stobaeus seems to reconceive ethical development in terms based on the influential Stoic theory of *oikeiôsis*, while retaining key features of the Peripatetic conceptual framework.[41] 'Eclecticism', in other words, insofar as it is a relevant notion in this period, refers to a more limited and considered kind of activity than has often been recognised.

How far can we see eclecticism in Stoic treatises and writings on practical ethics in this period? In the treatises outlined previously (see Section 4), this idea is of limited relevance. Although we have little basis for comparative assessment of the treatises of Cleomedes on cosmology and Cornutus on etymology, there is no indication of unorthodox treatment in these works. In the case of the later Stoic theory on determinism attributed by Bobzien to Philopator, although new concepts are introduced into the debate (relating to types of motion and degrees of responsibility), the theory remains in all essentials true to Chrysippus' approach.[42] The status of Seneca's *Natural Questions* is slightly more open; here and elsewhere, we need to be aware that he is not formally a Stoic teacher. The work is presented as having its own intellectual programme, and Seneca occasionally adopts an Epicurean view (about multiple possible explanations of phenomena, V 20), criticises Stoic thinkers, and commends Aristotle (VII 30.1–2). Nonetheless, taken as a whole, the project is Stoic in conception and in detail: although much more narrowly focused than Lucretius' *On the Nature of the Universe*, it is a kind of riposte to the Epicurean worldview offered there and, in particular, challenges its understanding of death.[43]

The question is more complex in the case of practical ethics. In addition to the variety of types of authors involved, there is the question

---

[40] On this move in Middle Platonism, see below and nn. 80–83.

[41] Stobaeus, II 116.21–152.25; cf. Annas (1990a), (1993), 279–87. On the question whether this 'Arius' should be identified with 'Arius Didymus', see Chapter 1, Section 8 and n. 61.

[42] This is so even though the sources for reconstructing the theory are Peripatetic (Alexander of Aphrodisias) and Platonic (Numenius); Bobzien (1998), Ch. 8, esp. 359–70.

[43] VI 32, contrast Lucretius III, esp. 830–911.

of the relationship between technical and non-technical discourse, and also that of the audience being addressed (and the further question of whether this makes a difference to the orthodoxy of the ethical content). I begin with the work of those who presented themselves explicitly as Stoic teachers. In the teachings of Musonius Rufus, a striking feature (and one of special interest to modern readers) is the high valuation he places on marriage and family life. For instance, he presents women as equally capable of virtue (and of philosophy) as men; he also criticises double standards about male and female sexual activity outside marriage. He presents marriage as a context for 'shared life' and mutual concern as well as child-rearing, and claims that marriage and child-rearing are compatible with doing philosophy. He also advises people to have large families rather than to dispose of unwanted children in infancy.[44] He combines this positive view of the institution of marriage, perhaps surprisingly, with commendation of the austere Cynic way of life. The marriage of two Cynics, Crates and Hipparchia, as well as that of Socrates and Xanthippe, are presented equally as exemplars of philosophy practised within marriage; there is also praise of the simple or austere life associated with Cynics as well as Socrates.[45]

These emphases, taken in isolation, might seem unorthodox and to reflect Musonius' personal views. But, in fact, the view of women as equally capable of virtue and the idea of marriage as a context for fully shared life have parallels in much earlier Stoic thinking.[46] Musonius' views on the value of women and family life have roots in such central Stoic ideas as that 'all human beings have the starting points of virtue' and that the parent-child relationship is a central paradigm of human sociability and of the desire to express virtue in action.[47] Similarly, the idealisation of the Cynic lifestyle has its foundation in the Cynic contribution to the origins of Stoicism (Crates was supposed to be one of Zeno's teachers), though this is also

---

[44] See *Diss.* 3–4, 12, 13A–B, 14–15; for text and translation, see Lutz (1947); also Gill (2000), 601–3.

[45] See *Diss.* 14 and 19.

[46] See, e.g., DL VII 175 (Cleanthes), and Stobaeus IV 503.18–512.7 (Antipater, and also Hierocles).

[47] See LS 61L (my translation) and LS 57F(1–2), also (8), on the wise person's natural desire for marriage and rearing children as well as for political engagement. See Geytenbeek (1963), 56–8, 64–5, 67.

a specially strong theme in first-century Roman culture.[48] Where Musonius is innovative is in developing these ideas and spelling out their implications for practical life in a way that is not fully paralleled in our other sources.

Epictetus' *Discourses* raises the issue of eclecticism in a more acute form. Bonhöffer, whose books were for many decades the most substantial studies of Epictetus (only recently augmented by Long, 2002), argued strongly that he presented a thoroughly orthodox version of Stoic ethics.[49] More recent scholars have been more inclined to see at least partial innovations, although within a consistently Stoic framework of thought. For instance, his special emphases on 'what is up to us' and on the human capacity for 'choice' or 'rational agency' (*prohairesis*) have been taken to imply a (more Aristotelian) indeterminist concept of free will or to anticipate the modern concept of 'will'.[50] In addition to underlining the quasi-Socratic method of at least some of the *Discourses*, Long also sees Epictetus as adopting a Socratic conception of god as one who urges humans to express 'the god within' by exercising their rational critical faculties.[51] One can also see Epictetus as the exponent of a particularly 'tough' version of Stoicism, which de-emphasizes the role of selecting 'preferable' advantages in ethical life and which favours the austere Cynic ideal rather than the practice of virtue within more conventional life-styles.[52]

In considering this question, it is important to keep in mind that the *Discourses* do not represent detailed, technical exposition of Stoic ethics (which Epictetus also offered within his school), but rather an attempt to spell out the core messages of Stoic ethics for a

---

[48] The linkage of Cynics and Socrates as ideals (Musonius 14 start) is paralleled in Epictetus; e.g., IV 1.114–16, 156–8, 159–69. On the Cynic role in the origins of Stoicism, see above, and on the Cynic ideal in the first century A.D. see nn. 52, 56, and 76–9.

[49] Bonhöffer 1890 and 1894 (now translated as 1996).

[50] For these views, see, respectively, Dobbin (1991) and Kahn (1988); also Inwood (1985), 116–19, on innovations in Epictetus' psychological terminology.

[51] Long (2002); see, e.g., *Diss.* I 3, I 14.11–14, II 8.12, 22; also Plato, *Apology* 28e, 30a–b (Socrates' mission to promote rational enquiry presented as a 'divine' one), 40 a–b (the *daimonion* or inner divine voice).

[52] Epictetus' dismissive attitude to 'externals', such as health and wealth (e.g., *Diss.* I 1, *Handbook* 1) might seem to suggest the position of Aristo, rather than Zeno or Chrysippus (Chapter 1, Section 4 above); for the idealisation of the Cynic life-style, see, e.g., III 22, III 24.

more general audience. Epictetus' reiterated contrast between what is and is not 'up to us' and on exercising our *prohairesis* (rather than being concerned with our body and 'externals') may best be understood as a way of conveying these messages. What he is underlining, perhaps, is the importance of shaping your life around the search for virtue (which is, in principle, 'up to us') rather than around trying to obtain 'preferables' (something which is not 'up to us').[53] His use of the term *prohairesis* (not a standard one in Stoic terminology) need not carry any psychological significance not already implied in Stoic thinking about human rationality and agency.[54] Bobzien, considering Epictetus within the history of Stoic thinking about determinism, finds no clear indications in the *Discourses* of an Aristotelian concept of indeterminist freedom of choice. 'Freedom' for Epictetus, and in Stoicism generally, is, rather, a moral ideal.[55] Epictetus' use of the Cynic teacher (especially Diogenes, the founder of Cynicism) as an ideal is certainly an index of a relatively 'tough' or radical version of Stoicism. But this can be paralleled in a number of other first-century Stoic-inspired thinkers, as well as in the Stoic tradition more generally. It is combined with the theme, prominent in Musonius too, that the search for virtue can also be practised while maintaining conventional social and family roles.[56]

So it may be that what are sometimes seen as innovative or heterodox ideas are better interpreted as accessible ways of encapsulating key standard themes of Stoic ethics. This is not incompatible with signaling the kind of version of Stoic ethics being adopted; in this case, a relatively tough and uncompromising one.[57] It is to be noted that, in Epictetus and other writers on practical ethics in this period, the objective seems to be to reach out to a more general audience without diluting the fundamentals of Stoic ethics; for

[53] Cf. the first topic in the three-fold programme of practical ethics, outlined above.
[54] Stoic theory implies a highly unified view of human psychology, in which emotions are integrally linked with beliefs and reasoning; hence, if *prohairesis* suggests 'will', this need not be a new idea in Stoicism.
[55] Bobzien (1998), Ch. 7; contrast Dobbin (1991).
[56] See Griffin (1976 [1992]), 111–12, on admiration in Stoic circles, including that of Seneca, for the Cynic Demetrius; on Dio's combination of Cynicism and Stoicism, see below. On Epictetus' commendation of the virtuous maintenance of conventional roles, see, e.g., *Diss.* I 2, II 10.
[57] See Gill (1988), 187–94, contrasting Epictetus' way of using the idea of roles from Cicero's more conventionalist approach; also Gill (1995), xxi–iii.

instance, regarding the radical difference in value between virtue and indifferents.

In considering from this standpoint Seneca's writings on practical ethics, there is the further fact that he does not present himself as a Stoic teacher, and also sometimes asserts his doctrinal independence; he can be quite blunt about this, as at *Natural Questions* VII 22.1: 'I do not agree with the views of our school.' Also, in the *Letters* particularly, he frequently refers with a level of interest and tolerance bordering on favour to the ideas of other schools, notably those of Epicureans.[58] Even so, there are grounds for seeing Seneca's practical writings as, on the whole, strongly shaped by Stoic principles. One example from *On Anger* brings out a number of important considerations. This work is, in general, the vehicle of an emphatically Stoic view about the need to extirpate rather than simply moderate passions such as anger.[59] At one point (II 4), Seneca offers an account of the process by which passions occur which is in some respects unfamiliar. He introduces the notion of 'pre-passion' and includes the idea that an emotion, once formed, makes one determined to act in a given way 'at all costs' (whether right or wrong). Is Seneca offering his own innovative view of the formation of a passion? One of the unfamiliar elements, the idea of a 'pre-passion' (i.e., an instinctive or impulsive reaction not yet rationally adopted) may go back to Posidonius, and has some parallels elsewhere in Stoic sources.[60] Also, as Inwood (1993) suggests, other factors may be at work. Seneca seems to be taking the essence of the orthodox Stoic view of emotions – that they depend on the rational assent of the person involved but that, once formed, they can outrun rational control – and to be recasting it in his own vivid, nontechnical terms.[61] This is part of a larger point not always appreciated, brought out by Inwood (1995a). Whereas thinkers such as Cicero and Lucretius in the late Republican period focused on finding exact Latin equivalents for Greek technical philosophical terms, Seneca seems to be animated by a different

[58] However, his aim in doing so is consistently to show that Epicurean insights support the (more systematic and convincing) Stoic view.
[59] See, e.g., I 9–10, 17, III 3.
[60] See Cooper (1998), who argues that Posidonius' ideas about 'emotional movements' are much more in line with orthodox Stoic thinking on emotions than is usually supposed; also LS 65Y.
[61] On the question of Seneca's orthodoxy or innovation, see also Pohlenz (1948), 305–9, Grimal (1989), Rist (1989), Sorabji (2000), Chs. 3–4.

aim: thinking out philosophical ideas *in Latin*, including rethinking the terminology and imagery.[62] This is not 'eclecticism', exactly, but it may give the impression of being so.

How much of a Stoic is Marcus Aurelius in his *Meditations*? On the one hand, apart from his explicit allegiance to Stoicism (e.g., I 7–8), the dominating themes are strongly Stoic and there are clear signs of the influence of Epictetus' ethical programme. On the other hand, the style is idiosyncratic, with strong Heraclitean, Cynic, and Platonic colouring.[63] His psychological language seems to reflect a version of Platonic dualism rather than the orthodox stress on psychological unity.[64] Most puzzling of all, despite his frequent adoption of a cosmic perspective on ethical life, he sometimes expresses indifference about which worldview is correct: the Stoic providential one or the Epicurean view that the universe is a fortuitous collection of atoms. In Marcus' case, there is no *a priori* reason to demand doctrinal consistency. But we can explain these features in a way that makes sense within his predominantly Stoic standpoint. The contrast between mind (or ruling divinity) and body can be taken, like some comparable language in Epictetus, as an expression of the central Stoic ethical theme of the importance of pursuing virtue rather than bodily advantages.[65] The 'providence or atoms' theme is more puzzling, though in some passages the question seems more open than in others.[66] But it may be important that Marcus acknowledges, in *Meditations* I 17, that he has not himself actually completed the three-part Stoic curriculum (including logic and physics) that would yield the cosmic understanding he seeks to apply to his own life. Hence, the Stoic worldview has to be, in this respect, taken on trust (though Marcus overwhelmingly does take it on trust) – a fact perhaps acknowledged in his use of the 'providence or atoms' theme.[67]

---

[62] This process may generate what some see as internal tensions in Seneca's writings (e.g., between using violent or militaristic language and aiming to extirpate the passions); see Nussbaum (1994), Ch. 11, and Wilson (1997).

[63] See n. 37.

[64] The division is, roughly, between mind, soul (or breath), and body; see, e.g., *Meditations* II 2, III 16, VI 32, XIII 3.

[65] Cf. Gill (1997a), xi–xii.

[66] In *Meditations* IV 27, X 6, XI 18, the question (though posed) seems to presuppose a providential (Stoic) answer; elsewhere (e.g., II 11, VI 10, VII 32), the question is left more open.

[67] See Annas (forthcoming); for other approaches, Rist (1983), 29–30, Asmis (1989), 2250–1; for a survey of the question, Gill (1997a), 181–200.

7. RELATIONS WITH OTHER SCHOOLS

Questions of orthodoxy and eclecticism lead naturally to that of relations with other schools. Two aspects are explored here: active debate and controversy, and the assimilation of Stoic thought by members of other schools. The fact that there was controversy about Stoic ideas is evidence of their continued significance in the intellectual life of the period; it also shows that Stoic theory had clearly defined boundaries on certain issues. The adoption of Stoic ideas by thinkers of different allegiance highlights a more fluid side of intellectual life at this time, but this need not be taken to mean that allegiance is meaningless or that boundaries have vanished entirely.

One important area of debate in this period concerns the emotions or passions and, more broadly, ethical psychology.[68] Three questions tend to be linked in this debate: whether emotions should be moderated or 'extirpated', whether human psychology is to be understood as a combination of rational and non-rational aspects or as fundamentally unified and shaped by rationality, and whether ethical development is brought about by a combination of habituation and teaching or only by rational means. On these issues, thinkers with a Platonic or Peripatetic affiliation tend to adopt the first of these two positions and Stoics the second.[69] Plutarch's essay, *On Moral Virtue*, encapsulates this debate; Plutarch articulates the first (Platonic-Aristotelian) position and criticises the Stoic one. This view is, on the whole, characteristic of Plutarch (c. 45–125), who regards himself as a Platonist, although a more Stoic view on the passions is sometimes adopted elsewhere.[70]

Galen takes a broadly similar line to Plutarch in Books IV–V of *On the Doctrines of Hippocrates and Plato*, but explores the issues more thoroughly, thereby providing the main primary source for the Stoic theory of the passions (see Chapter 10, Brennan). In Books

---

[68] See Sihvola and Engberg-Pedersen (1998), on Hellenistic philosophy of emotions and the continuation of this in the Imperial period.

[69] For a similar contrast between positions, but here expressing the Stoic side and criticising the Peripatetic, see Cicero, *Tusc.* III 22, IV 39–46; Seneca, *On Anger* I 7–14. However, Platonic and Stoic positions were sometimes linked, for instance, by Eudorus and Philo.

[70] For instance, in less doctrinaire essays, such as *On Peace of Mind* and *On Freedom from Anger*, Plutarch sometimes praises the (Stoic ideal) of *apatheia* (freedom from passions) rather than moderation of the passions. See Dillon (1977 [1996]), 189, 193–8; also Babut (1979), 298–301, 316–17, 321–33.

I–III of that work, Galen takes up the related question of the contrast between a tripartite psychological model, in which the brain, heart, and liver are regarded as distinct motivational sources, with different locations; the Stoic unified model, centred on the heart, is treated as the locus of rationality as well as emotions. Galen (129–c. 215) was a philosophically minded doctor who aimed to reconcile the philosophies of Plato and Aristotle with the findings of medical science, including the Alexandrian discovery of the anatomic and psychological role of the brain and nerves.[71] On ethical development, he advocated a combination of rational and nonrational methods.[72]

In this debate, the Stoic positions attacked are long-standing ones; for Galen, the target is, specifically, Chrysippus.[73] But sometimes a revised Stoic position emerges. Thus, according to Bobzien's reconstruction of the debate on determinism, the modified Stoic position of Philopator (active between 80 and 140) emerges in response to the focus on mental events (as well as actions) in Middle Platonist and Peripatetic discussions.[74] It also seems that Philopator's contribution aroused a specific type of Peripatetic response; namely, that of Alexander of Aphrodisias (second and third centuries), the Aristotelian commentator who is also a prime source for Philopator's theory. The Stoic theory was a key influence in generating what Bobzien sees as a new form of indeterminism, which is based on the Aristotelian idea that choosing agents are capable of alternative actions in a given situation, but which anticipates Christian and modern ideas of 'free will'. But Philopator's own position remains firmly based on Chrysippus' compatibilism and denies the possibility of alternative actions by a given agent in a given situation. Thus, Stoic involvement in debate on this point does not lead to unorthodox positions.[75]

Continuing debate represents one aspect of Stoic relations with other schools in this period. Another is the adoption of Stoic ideas

---

[71] On Galen's criticisms of Chrysippus, see Mansfeld (1991), Tielemann, (1996), Gill (1998).

[72] See, e.g., *On the Passions and Errors of the Soul*; also Hankinson (1993) Ch. 11, this volume.

[73] Galen (perhaps misleadingly) maintains that Posidonius (c. 135–51 B.C.) had a more Platonic position; see Cooper (1998), Gill (1998).

[74] Bobzien (1998), 359.

[75] See further Bobzien (1998), Ch. 8, esp. 396–412.

by those whose primary allegiance lies elsewhere. An intermediate case, taken first, is that of a thinker who probably regarded himself as a Stoic, but whose formulation of this embraces Cynic and Platonic themes. Dio Cocceianus of Prusa (later called 'Chrysostom', the 'golden tongue', c. 40 – c. 110) is a complex and enigmatic figure whose career embraced both rhetoric and philosophy. He studied with Musonius in the 60s; later he repudiated and publicly criticised his former teacher. When banished from Rome and Bithynia by Domitian (c. 82), he presented his exile as bringing about a 'conversion' to philosophy (Oration 13) and traveled around the Eastern Empire as a Cynic-Stoic teacher. Subsequently, he became an intellectual adviser to the emperors Nerva and Trajan, and resumed his former position as a wealthy leading provincial.[76]

Many of his eighty surviving speeches have philosophical themes. The dominant position is a type of Cynic-Stoic one, of a kind that is broadly similar to that of Musonius and Epictetus but which also incorporates Platonic ideas. For instance, in the fourth Kingship Oration (couched as a dialogue between Diogenes the Cynic and Alexander the Great), Dio argues for a thesis with Cynic, Stoic, and Platonic resonance: that kingship depends not only on status, but also on the possession of kingly qualities, including mastery over self.[77] A dialogue on slavery argues for an idea with similar connotations: that real 'freedom' is only conferred by virtue and, hence, even great kings are not 'free' to act as they wish.[78] In a third speech (36), Dio defines the ideal state by reference to two models: one, primarily Platonic, is that in which the rulers alone are wise (21); the other (more Stoic) is 'governed by a king according to law in complete friendship and harmony' (31). The king, in the latter model, seems to derive from a fusion of the Platonic ideal monarch with the Stoic idea of the universe as unified by reason, identified with Zeus (35–6). The overall moral seems not to be advocacy of Roman imperial monarchy but rather the idea that any state (even in the remote city of Olbia where the speech is set) should be governed by objective, universal standards.[79]

---

[76] See further Jones (1978), Ch. 6; Moles (1978); Russell (1992), 4–6.
[77] Oration 4.44–75; cf. Moles (1990).
[78] Oration 14; cf. Plato, *Gorgias* 467a–471e, *Republic* 579b–e, Epictetus, *Diss.* IV 1.
[79] For a fuller summary, see Gill (2000), 606–7; on the background in Stoic political thought, see LS 67; Schofield (1991), Ch. 3.

Dio does not offer a theoretical justification of the kind of fusion he offers, but we can find more explication of this type of move in the thinkers associated with 'Middle Platonism'.[80] The prototype is offered by the Academic (sometimes regarded as the first Middle Platonic thinker), Antiochus of Ascalon (130–69 B.C.). Although claiming to be reviving the original form of Platonism, he actually introduces substantial Stoic, as well as Peripatetic, elements. His justification was that Aristotle and Zeno were simply developing ideas that were implicit in Plato's dialogues.[81] This kind of view was adopted by two Platonic thinkers in Alexandria: Eudorus (active c. 25 B.C.) and Philo (c. 20 B.C. – 45 A.D.). Eudorus made a further move, taken up by some later thinkers, of presenting Plato's thought as a development of that of Pythagoras (a move accompanied by the growth of pseudo-Pythagorean documents[82]). Philo further expands the lineage, claiming that Pythagoras gained his wisdom from followers of Moses. This legitimated the interpretation of the first five books of the Old Testament in Platonic-Stoic terms, in part through the extensive use of Stoic allegorical interpretation.[83] These moves may seem bizarre or disingenuous and to reduce to absurdity the notion of philosophical allegiance to an original founder (Sedley [1989]). But they imply an idea associated in modern philosophy with the suggestion that various thinkers or thought systems, despite their different starting points, may 'converge on the truth'.[84]

The dominant themes in Middle Platonism are, unsurprisingly, more Platonic than Stoic. They include the idea of God as thinking himself (or the Forms), as a unified or perfect intellect, as a demiurge or the *logos*; in ethics, there is a preference for the Antiochean conception of perfect happiness (as including external goods) and for the moderation rather than extirpation of passions.[85] But some Platonic thinkers favour Stoic versions of these theses; Atticus (150–200),

---

[80] That is, Platonism between the period of strongly institutional life (the Old and New Academy), ending with Philo (in 88 B.C.) and the Neoplatonism of Plotinus (204–69).

[81] See, e.g., Cicero, *Fin.* IV 3, V 22. The Stoic ideas adopted include that of active and passive principles in the universe, that of the goal as 'life according to nature', and of development as 'appropriation' (*oikeiôsis*). See Dillon (1977 [1996]), Ch. 2.

[82] See Sedley, Chapter 1, Section 7.

[83] Dillon (1977 [1996]), 117–21, 143–4.

[84] See further, Williams (1985), Ch. 8.

[85] See Dillon, 'Platonism' in Zeyl (1997), 416–17.

for instance, adopts the Stoic view that virtue is self-sufficient for happiness, rather than the Antiochean view.[86] Philo's theses also come close to Stoicism; but even when they do not, he adopts a highly Stoic conceptual vocabulary, so that his texts are widely used as sources for Stoic terminology. The idea that philosophy consists of an integrated system of ethics, logic, and physics was widely accepted by Middle Platonists.[87] The tendency of Platonism to absorb Stoic themes and language leads to the appearance of these in works of popular philosophising with (broadly) Platonic roots, such as the *Dialexeis* (lectures) of Maximus of Tyre (second century) and the *Tablet* of Cebes (first century B.C. or A.D.).[88]

The tendency of Platonic philosophers to absorb elements of Stoicism persists in Neoplatonism, at a period when Stoicism seems to have stopped being a living philosophy. Thus, Plotinus shared with Stoicism the idea that a rational force unifies and organises matter, but identifies this force with the world soul of Plato's *Timaeus* and analyzes it in terms of Aristotle's hierarchy of natural functions.[89] In one of the most elaborate of such appropriations, a long commentary on Epictetus' *Handbook*, Simplicius (c. 490–560) presents this summary of key themes of Stoic practical ethics as an introduction for students new to philosophy of the complex system of Neoplatonic metaphysics.[90] Middle Platonism had a strong influence on the evolution of Christian doctrine, from Clement of Alexandria (c. 200) onward, and through that route Christian thinkers absorbed Stoic ideas such as the cosmic role of *logos* (reason) and the sufficiency of virtue, but understood in Middle Platonic terms.[91] This process was accompanied by the adoption by Christian thinkers of the view propagated by Philo, that philosophy simply provides the means of interpreting authoritative texts which embody divine wisdom.[92]

---

[86] See Dillon (1977 [1996]), 251–2.

[87] See Dillon (1977 [1996]), index, 'philosophy, divisions of', and Annas (1999), 109–12. This tripartition was itself borrowed by Stoics from the early Platonist Xenocrates (Sextus *M* VII 16).

[88] On Stoic touches in these works, see Trapp (1997), 1948, n. 12, and (1997a), 170–1.

[89] O'Meara, 'Plotinus', in Zeyl (1997), 423.

[90] I. Hadot (2001), Chs. 3–4.

[91] On Christian responses to Stoic thinking on the passions, see Sorabji (2000), Chs. 22–6.

[92] Bos, 'Christianity' in Zeyl (1997), esp. 130–1. See also Boys-Stones (2001), Chs. 8–9, who sees this process starting in Stoicism.

8. STOICISM AND ROMAN POETRY

One of the striking features of the Imperial period is the influence
that philosophy, particularly Stoicism, had on Roman literature, including poetry – a feature without parallel in other eras of antiquity.
By the late Republican period, philosophy had come to play a significant part in the education of upper-class Greeks and Romans. In
Roman literature, the presence of philosophy, including Stoicism, is
marked in poetry, as well as prose from the end of the first century
B.C. and throughout the first century A.D.[93]

But how deep does this influence go? The answer, of course, varies
in different cases; the question is, inevitably, a complex one. The focus here is on satire, epic, and Senecan tragedy. The language and concepts of Stoicism constitute a presence in all three Roman satirists.
But in Horace and Juvenal, the use of Stoicism is localised and op-
portunistic. Horace (65–5 B.C.) is quite capable of using, as targets of
satire, key Stoic concepts, such as the perfection of the sage and the
folly and irrationality of everyone else, or the idea that only the sage
is free (Satires II 3, 7). But he is also capable in his 'Roman Odes' of
fusing Stoic themes with patriotic attitudes to create powerful lyric
poetry.[94] Similarly, Juvenal (active early second century A.D.) is prepared to adopt a quasi-Stoic view of the vanity of all nonvirtuous
human desires in Satire 10 (especially 346–66) or to make reference
to the Stoic therapy of the emotions (Satire 13). But he does so, it
seems, only for negative satiric effect.[95] The situation is totally different with Persius (34–62 A.D.), who studied Stoicism with Cornutus
from the age of sixteen and was closely linked with Stoics such as
Seneca and Lucan. Persius' Satires serves as the vehicle of his commitment to Stoic ethics, expressed positively in his tribute to his
teacher Cornutus (Satire 5) or indirectly through critical dialogue
(Satire 4). In Satire 1, he justifies his writing of satire by a brilliant
portrayal of contemporary decadence, which weaves together (in a

[93] For a very systematic treatment of the influence of Stoicism on Roman prose, as
well as poetry, see Colish (1985); the possible influence of Stoicism on Roman law
is treated in her Ch. 6 (see also Johnston [2000], 622–3, 630–3).

[94] Odes III 2–3, 5. On the question whether it makes any sense to attribute to Horace
a philosophical position, see Colish (1985), 160–8.

[95] On Satire 13, see Braund (1997); see further Braund (1988) on Juvenal's attitude to
anger and indignation in his satires as a whole.

way that is deeply Stoic) the expression of vice in psychological, bodily, and social styles.[96]

The question of Stoicism and Roman epic poetry is more complex. There is little question that for Virgil, Lucan, Silius Italicus, and possibly Statius, Stoicism helps to shape the conceptual framework of the poems. But to what extent can we say that the poetic vision of any of these poems directly reflects the Stoic world-view? In all the poems, there are two main possible points of contact: the picture of divine-human causation of events (including the role of Fate), and the ethical and psychological portrayal of the characters.

In Virgil's *Aeneid*, elements that evoke Stoicism include the emphasis on Fate (which is, as in Stoicism, compatible with and brought about by human actions); also Stoic is the stress on accepting Fate as a key part of the virtuous response. Another important factor is the characterisation of key figures in terms of the contrast between virtue (or reason) and passion. An important strand in this mode of portrayal is the presentation of the surrender to passion as bringing about a descent into a kind of madness, a strand that forms part of the portrayal of Dido and Turnus as well as Aeneas. But does this mean that the poetic vision of the poem is essentially Stoic? Some scholars argue that the psychology and ethics are to be understood as Aristotelian or Homeric rather than Stoic. We should remember that Euripides' *Medea* also embodies this theme and, for that very reason, caught the interest of Chrysippus. It is perhaps futile to ask whether Virgil's use of the idea owes more to literary or philosophical sources. Moreover, even if we see the conceptual language of the *Aeneid* as strongly coloured by Stoicism, there remains a question of whether a poem whose vision is, for many readers, deeply tragic can express the (ultimately positive) world view of Stoicism.[97]

Similar though less profound questions are raised by the other epics. Lucan (39–65) was Seneca's nephew and another of Cornutus' students; like his uncle, he died because of his supposed involvement in the Pisonian conspiracy against Nero. His *Pharsalia*, describing the civil war that ended the Roman republic, is deeply political. Its Stoic colour comes out mainly in the presentation of Cato as an

[96] See Colish (1985), 194–203, and, for a penetrating study of *Satire* 1, Bramble (1974).
[97] See Colish (1985), 225–52, Gill (1983), Gill (1997), with references to other relevant studies.

embodied Stoic sage and in the strongly ethical picture of Pompey and Caesar. The view of Fate as an arbitrary and capricious force, however, reflects his view of historical events rather than Stoicism. Although the *Thebaid* of Statius (c. 45 – c. 96) has sometimes been seen as Stoic, the thoroughly negative view of human and divine or fated action makes this difficult to sustain. The most plausible candidate for being a Stoic motif is probably the presentation of the passions as powerfully harmful and irrational forces that eventually lead to a kind of madness and self-destruction. The *Punic Wars* of Silius Italicus (26–101) seems to be much more shaped by Stoicism, notably in the contrasted and strongly ethical characterisation of the main Carthaginian and Roman generals.[98]

Finally, there is the question of how far Seneca's tragedies reflect the Stoicism that is so important to him in other ways.[99] The main Stoic motifs are the presentation of uncontrolled passion as generating madness, destruction and self-destruction, and the idea that this process has a cosmic as well as ethical dimension. More difficult to locate in a Stoic world-view is the portrayal of Fate (a powerful but rather negative presence in the plays) and the bleak, violent overall vision. However, to bring home the full force of the impact of Stoicism in this period, we should bear in mind that Lucan's *Pharsalia*, Persius' *Satires*, and perhaps Seneca's tragedies are all products of the brief but intensely charged cultural atmosphere of Nero's Rome.[100]

[98] See Colish (1985), 252–89; also (on Statius), Fantham (1997), (on Silius) Billerbeck (1985 and 1986).

[99] Rosenmeyer (1989).

[100] The precise date of composition of Seneca's tragedies is not known.

3   Stoic Epistemology

Stoic Sages never make mistakes. Secure in their understanding of the providential structure of the world, which is identical with fate, which in turn is identical with the will of Zeus (DL VII 135, =SVF 2.580; Plutarch, *St. rep.* 1049f, 1056c = SVF 2.937; cf. 2.931, 2.1076), Sages order their lives in accordance with it, assimilating their will to the will of Zeus, living in accordance with nature, and so achieving the smooth flow of life, the *eurhoia biou* so devoutly to be wished for (DL VII 87, =SVF 3.4; Cicero, *Fin.* III 31, IV 14–15, =SVF 3.15, 3.13; cf. 3.4–9, 3.12–16).

It seems clear enough that if the Sage is to be anything more than an unattainable, regulative ideal (and that is a big 'if'), the Stoics need powerful reasons, in the form of a powerful epistemology, for supposing that such practical infallibility can ever actually be attainable. And even if the Sage is supposed only to be an ideal figure (and the Stoics were doubtful whether such a superhuman ethical cognizer ever had existed: Sextus, *M* IX 133, =54D LS; Alexander, *Fat.* 199.16, =SVF 3.658, =61N LS), still, for the ideal to function as anything more than a piece of remote wishful thinking, it had better be possible at least to approach that ideal; and the Stoics did indeed set great store by the notion of *prokopē*, moral and cognitive progress (Stobaeus V 906.18–907.5, =SVF 3.510, =59I LS).

But again, if we are to be confident that such an approach is possible, we need to be confident that we can, as a matter of fact, refine and perfect our understanding of the world, replacing our formerly false opinions with true ones. Even if that end is more modest than that of Sagehood, it still requires some serious epistemological underpinning of a sort that will necessarily open the Stoics to sceptical attack. It is the purpose of this chapter to limn the origins of the Stoics' epistemology and to assess its resilience and to trace its development under sceptical fire.

Numenius, a first-century A.D. Platonist (reported in Eusebius' *Preparation for the Gospel*: XIV 6.13, =68G LS), wrote that 'both the doctrine of the cataleptic impression (*kataleptikê phantasia*) and its name, which he [i.e., Zeno of Citium, founder of the Stoic school] had been the first to discover, were highly regarded in Athens'.

But what, precisely, is this 'cataleptic impression'?[1] According to Diogenes Laertius, the Stoics held that

> there are two types of impression, one cataleptic, the other noncataleptic; the cataleptic, which they hold to be the criterion of matters, is that which comes from something existent and is in accordance with the existent thing itself, and has been stamped and imprinted (*enapesphragismenên kai enapomemagmenên*);[2] the noncataleptic either comes from something non-existent, or if from something existent then not in accordance with the existent thing; and it is neither clear (*enargês*), nor distinct. (1: DL VII 46, =SVF 2.53, =40C LS; cf. DL VII 49–51, =SVF 2.52, 55, 61, =39A LS; *M* VII 248, =SVF 2.65, =40E LS)

So the Stoics do not hold that all perceptions are true, as notoriously do the Epicureans (DL X 31–2, =16B LS; Lucretius IV 469–521, =16A LS; Sextus, *M* VII 206–10, =16E LS; and see 11 below), whatever precisely that is supposed to mean.[3] A cataleptic impression,

---

[1] I transliterate the *kataleptikê* of *kataleptikê phantasia*, in preference to any of the several possible translations. *kataleptikê* is the verbal adjective from *katalambanein*, grasp or get a grip on, and it is the impression which gets a grip on reality. For this reason 'graspable impression', preferred by some, seems to get the causal sense wrong – it is not the impression which we can grasp, but rather the impression *with which* we can grasp: 'grasping' might be better, if it did not suggest greed. *katalambanein* is also used to mean 'apprehend', in the sense of apprehending a criminal; and this has suggested 'apprehensive impression'; but that, too, sits ill in English, with its obvious connotations of poltroonery. LS render it as 'cognitive impression', but that seems a little too strong, and to have unwanted connotations of internality. At all events, however we render it, it is a term of art – and its various definitions need always to be borne in mind. Indeed, 'impression' is perhaps an over-translation of *phantasia*, more literally to be rendered as 'appearance'; but that is now hallowed by modern critical usage.

[2] The literal sense of these complex passive participles is worth attention: *en* 'in' plus *apo* 'out of or from' prefixed to the perfect participles 'sealed' or 'stamped' and 'impressed' or ' wiped upon'; the combination of the prepositions in each case suggesting internal location of the affection and its external cause.

[3] For discussion of the doctrine and its interpretation, see Long and Sedley (1987) i, 83–6; Taylor (1980); Everson (1990b).

then, satisfies the following conditions:

CIi: it derives from an existent object;

CIii: it accurately represents that object;

and

CIiii: it is 'stamped and imprinted' on the sensoria.[4]

Taken together, CIi–iii represent Zeno's first definition (D[1]) of the notion of a cataleptic impression. As regards CIi, 'many impressions strike us from what does not exist, as in the case of madmen, and these are not cataleptic' (*M* VII 249, =SVF 2.65, =40E LS). As for CIii, 'some are such that, although they come from an existent object, they do not represent that object, as in the case of the mad Orestes' (*ibid.*).[5] In the case of CIiii, they hold that 'it is stamped artistically with all the object's peculiar qualities (*idiômata*)' (*ibid.*), i.e., 'so that all the peculiar qualities of the objects represented are stamped artistically' (*M* VII 250, =SVF 2.65, =40E LS) – that is with the precision and attention to detail one expects from a craftsman.

But the idea of an impression itself still needs some further elucidation. CIiii goes some way toward specifying its mode of production and serves to distinguish it from a mere figment, a *phantasma*, which, according to Diocles of Magnesia, is 'a supposition of thought, such as occurs in dreams' (DL VII 50, =SVF 2.55, =39A(3) LS), a product of the imagination (*phantastikon*), 'an empty attraction, an affection (*pathos*) of the soul without an impressor (*phantaston*)' (Aëtius, IV 12.4, =SVF 2.54, =39B LS). Thus, an impression, as opposed to a figment, is actually imprinted on the percipient, in some causally suitable fashion, by the external object (i.e., both CIi and CIiii are satisfied). Indeed, according to Aëtius, it 'reveals both itself and what produced it'. But, of course, not every impression satisfies CIii; hence, not every impression is cataleptic.

---

[4] It is worth stressing that not all impressions are sense-impressions: some impressions will be purely intellectual in content (DL VII 51, =SVF 2.61, =39A LS), such as our notion of God; furthermore, other texts give as the content of impressions such conditionals as 'if it is day, the sun is not above the earth' (an example of an 'unpersuasive impression'), and 'undecidable propositions' such as 'the number of stars is even' (*M* VII 243–4, =SVF 2.65, =39G LS). But, given the Stoics' empiricism, sensory impressions are the most important.

[5] The case of Orestes, who supposes that his sister Electra is one of the Furies pursuing him to avenge his murder of his mother (Euripides, *Orestes* 256–64), was a commonplace of these epistemological debates: *M* VII 244–5, VII 259, VIII 57, VIII 63, VIII 67.

Diogenes, in line with the implications of CIiii, defines an impression as

an imprinting (*tupôsis*) on the soul, the name having been appropriately borrowed from the imprints made by the seal in wax. (2: DL VII 45; cf. VII 50, =SVF 2.55, =39A(3) LS; and 4 below)

But how literally this image is to be taken was itself a matter for dispute among the Stoics themselves. Zeno, followed by Cleanthes, took it at face value (no doubt influenced by the 'wax-block model' of Plato's *Theaetetus*: 191c–195a). But Chrysippus took issue with this, on the grounds that a wax block can hold at most one impression. Any subsequent impressing ruins the original and renders the accumulation of impressions impossible, which in turn would preclude memory and skill (*technê*, defined by the Stoics as a 'system of jointly exercised impressions': *M* I 75, II 10, VII 109, etc.). For this reason, he preferred the neutral (and explanatorily unhelpful) term *heteroiôsis*, or alteration (*M* VII 230, =SVF 1.58; VII 227–30, VII 372–3, =SVF 2.56).

Chrysippus' insistence on the importance of absorbing multiple impressions is, however, well founded. For the Stoics do indeed make such accumulations of impressions central to their account of concept-formation:

the Stoics say: when a man is born, he has the controlling (*hêgemonikon*) part of his soul like paper well prepared for writing on. On this he inscribes (*enapographetai*)[6] each one of his conceptions (*ennoiai*). The first kind of inscription is that by way of the senses. For in sensing something as white, they have a memory of it when it has gone away. And when many memories of the same type have occurred, then we say that we have experience (*empeiria*), since experience is a multitude of impressions similar in type. Of the conceptions, some occur naturally by means of the aforementioned modalities and without conscious effort, while others come about by our instruction and attention. These latter are called conceptions only, but the former are called preconceptions (*prolêpseis*) as well ... A concept (*ennoêma*) is an image (*phantasma*)[7] in the mind of a rational animal; for when the image comes to the rational soul, it is called a concept, taking its name

---

[6] Note again the combination of '*en*' and '*apo*': 'writing-on-out of'.

[7] Note here that Aëtius does not reserve *phantasma* for a mere figment, as he does in the passage immediately following (IV 12.1–5), and as does Diocles of Magnesia: DL VII 50.

from the mind (*nous*). For this reason, what comes to irrational animals are images only; while those which come to us and to the gods are generically images but specifically concepts. (3: Aëtius IV 11.1–6, =SVF 2.83, =39E LS; cf. Cicero, *Acad.* II 20–2, II 30–1)

That report clearly echoes in some respects the sketchy account of concept-formation offered by Aristotle at *Post. An.* II 19 and *Meta.* I 1, where perceptions result in memory, and then (in man) in *empeiria*, and finally, for the fortunate, in technical ability and knowledge (compare here the Stoic definition of *technê* as a 'system of jointly exercised impressions'), in which the raw content of the preconceptions (*prolêpseis*: a term also used, in a roughly similar sense, by the Epicureans: DL X 33, =17D LS) is spelled out and given articulate conceptual shape.

Moreover, it follows Aristotle in being broadly empiricist in flavour (there is no room for Platonic innate ideas in the neonate: rather, it is a perfect Lockean *tabula rasa*) and also, in my view, in its causal emphasis. Concepts are not acquired by some rational process of inductive inference; rather, they are simply built up in the soul by a suitable accretion of perceptual impressions:

conception is a kind of impression, and impression is an imprint on the soul . . . they [sc. the Stoics] define conceptions as a kind of stored-away thoughts, memories as steady and stable imprints, while they fix scientific understandings (*epistêmai*) as possessing complete unchangeability and firmness. (4: Plutarch, *Comm. not.* 47, 1084f–1085a, =SVF 2.847, =39F LS; cf. Cicero, *Acad.* I 41, =SVF 1.60–1; II 145, =SVF 1.66, =41A LS)

Further conceptual machinery is developed, again in good empiricist fashion (the empiricist of record here being Hume: *Enquiry Concerning Human Understanding*, Section II):

of the things we conceive, some are conceived by confrontation (*periptôsis*), some by similarity (*homoiotês*), some by analogy (*analogia*), some by transposition (*metathesis*), some by composition (*sunthesis*), and some by opposition (*enantiôsis*). (5: DL VII 53, =SVF 2.87, =39D LS; cf. *M* VIII 58–60)

This too derives from Diocles of Magnesia; the succeeding lines flesh it out. Sense objects are conceived by confrontation; similarity leads us to form an image of Socrates on the basis of a likeness of him; analogy helps us to form concepts by augmentation or diminution, and to conceive of the centre of the earth by analogy with other spheres whose structures we can directly investigate. Transposition allows us to imagine 'eyes on the chest', composition such monstrosities as centaurs, opposition concepts like death (DL VII 53, =SVF 2.87, =39D LS). And even this list is not exhaustive:

> furthermore, some things are conceived by transition (*metabasis*), like meanings (*lekta*) and place; good and bad are conceived naturally (*phusikôs*);[8] and some things by privation (*sterêsis*), like the handless. (6: DL VII 53, =SVF 2.87, =39D LS)

Moreover, Sextus ascribes to them the following soundly empiricist slogan: 'every conceiving (*noêsis*) occurs either from perception (*aisthêsis*) or not without perception, that is to say either from an encounter or not without an encounter' (*M* VIII 56, =SVF 2.88): *nil in intellectu quod non prius in sensibus*. This also is a recognizable extension (or perhaps reinterpretation) of a well-known Aristotelian dictum: thinking is either imagination (*phantasia*) or not without imagination (*DeAnima* I 1, 403a8–9; III 7, 431a16–17); Aristotle's sense of *phantasia* is not the Stoics' one of an impression – but that makes the borrowing (and the reinterpretation) all the more pointed.

So the cataleptic impression does not yet amount to knowledge. In fact, Zeno

> placed apprehension [*comprehensio*: Cicero's rendering of the Greek *katalêpsis*] between knowledge and ignorance, numbering it neither among the good things nor the bad, but holding that it was trustworthy on its own. For this reason he ascribed reliability to the senses, because, as I said earlier, apprehension produced in the senses seemed to him to be both true and faithful, not because it apprehended everything in the object, but because it omitted nothing that might confront it, and because nature had provided it as a sort of yardstick for scientific understanding (*scientia*) and as the source of itself from which subsequently the conceptions of things were imprinted in the mind, and from which not only first principles but also certain broader roads for the discovery of reason were opened up. But error, rashness, ignorance, opinion, and suspicion, and in a word everything inconsistent with firm and stable assent, he disassociated from virtue and wisdom. (7: Cicero, *Acad.* I 42, =SVF 1.60, =41B LS)

---

[8] This is the closest the Stoics get to allowing innate conceptual machinery; what they have in mind is their notion of *oikeiôsis* or appropriation, the natural, instinctual drive of animals to seek out what is advantageous to them: see Brunschwig (1986); and Hankinson (1997), 191–2, 198.

Sextus concurs:

they [sc. the Stoics] say that there are three of them interrelated to each other, knowledge, opinion, with apprehension lying between the two of them; and of these knowledge is the secure and firm apprehension unalterable by reason, opinion is weak [and false][9] assent, while apprehension is intermediate between these, being assent to a cataleptic impression. According to these people, a cataleptic impression is one which is true and such that it could not be false. (8: *M* VII 150–2, =41C LS)

Assent to a cataleptic impression, or *katalêpsis*, is not yet knowledge, which must be more stable and structured (see **4** above; Zeno compared an impression to an open palm, assent to a slight curling of the fingers, *katalêpsis* to the hand clenched in a fist, and knowledge to that fist grasped tightly in the other hand: *Acad.* II 145, =SVF 1.66, =41A LS). But it is better than mere opinion, which they define as 'assent to what is not apprehended' (*M* VII 156), and which no true Sage will ever tolerate (Stobaeus, II 111.18–112.8, =41G LS; and see **10** below); indeed, as **7** suggests, there is no real distinction between opinion and ignorance. Opinion may happen to be true – but merely happening to be true is not good enough, at least for anyone with pretensions to put their actions on a soundly virtuous footing.

The impressions must be assented to before they can function as sources of impulse (in the case of impressions involving evaluations of things) or of apprehension. According to Cicero, this insistence on the mediation of assent[10] is one of Zeno's innovations:

to these things, which are impressions and received, as it were, by the senses, he adds the assent of the mind, which he holds to be located within us and voluntary. (**9**: Cicero, *Acad.* I 40, =SVF 1.61, =40B LS)

The cataleptic impression merely presents itself as worthy of endorsement; it is still up to the mind whether to accept its credentials.

But what precisely are those credentials? If the cataleptic impression is to be (at any rate partially; there was subsequent disagreement in the school: DL VII 54, =SVF 2.105, =40A LS) the Stoic criterion of truth, we had better, one might think, be able to recognize it is as such. On the face of it, it doesn't look as though it will be enough simply to say that a cataleptic impression is one that meets

---

[9] The words in brackets are almost certainly a copyist's error: see Maconi (1988), 240 n. 26; Hankinson (1998c), Ch. V, n. 13.

[10] Which is also crucial to Stoic action-theory: see Inwood (1985).

conditions CIi–iii: for it to be criterial, the cognizer must know that he cognizes. But where is the source for such a guarantee? The last sentence of **1** suggests that a cataleptic impression will be marked by its clarity and distinctness – but those notions themselves are no more clear and distinct here than they are in Descartes' more famous, and famously opaque, deployment of them.

The sceptical point is relatively simply put: If clarity and distinctness are internal characteristics of the impressions themselves, then what reason do we have for supposing that, simply in virtue of these phenomenal features, they are telling us the truth (i.e., that CIi–iii are satisfied)? Alternatively, if these terms refer to some objective, external fact about the impression's provenance (it really does come from a real object in the appropriate manner), how are we to recognize that it has them? The last sentence of **8** hints at an attempted answer: A cataleptic impression is (CIiv) such that it could not be false. But that simply reformulates the problem: How can we know when CIiv is satisfied?

It is, then, not surprising that the sceptical Academy of Arcesilaus (c. 315–240 B.C.) found ample scope for deploying its weapons of mass dogma-destruction in this context; and it is likely that CIiv was invoked by the Stoics as the first stage in their counterattack against the sceptical onslaught.

Arcesilaus became head of the Academy in 272 B.C., but had no doubt been plying his particular version of the Socratic refuter's trade for some time prior to that. Although ready to take issue with any positive doctrine (that, indeed, was his method: assert any proposition *p* and Arcesilaus will argue for not-*p*: DL IV 37; *Index Academicus* 20.2–4; Cicero, *Fin.* II 2, V 10, =68J–K LS),[11] the sources make him out as particularly engaged with Stoicism, perhaps because the Stoics were offering the most philosophically interesting and attractive doctrines (we need not accept Numenius' claim that he attacked Zeno out of jealousy of his fame: the fame itself would be spur enough).

---

[11] I will not here take sides on the vexed question of whether Arcesilaus, or his successors in the sceptical Academy, propounded any positive doctrines over and above their commitment to universal refutation (in Arcesilaus' case) and argument *pro* and *contra* (in that of Carneades); although I am inclined to suppose that they did (see Hankinson [1998c], Chs. V and VI; and forthcoming).

For the next two hundred years, the philosophical destinies of both the Stoic and the Academic schools are intimately intertwined. Chrysippus (c. 280–205 B.C.) sought to defend and rehabilitate Stoic doctrines damaged by sceptical argument: 'if Chrysippus had not existed, neither would the Stoa', ran a later Stoic slogan (DL VII 183, =SVF 2.6), which Carneades pointedly adopted, suitably amended: 'if Chrysippus had not existed, neither would I' (DL IV 62). Most of the remainder of this chapter will attempt to tease out this symbiotic history of dialectical interaction.

Arcesilaus, Cicero writes,

(1) perhaps asked Zeno what would happen if the Sage could not apprehend anything, and if it was also the mark of the Sage not to form opinions. (2) Zeno, I imagine, replied that he [i.e., the Sage] would not form opinions because he could apprehend something. (3) What sort of thing? An impression, I suppose. (4) What sort of impression? An impression that was impressed, sealed, and moulded from something which is, just as it is. (5) Arcesilaus then asked if this held even if there were a true impression exactly the same in form as a false one. (6) Here Zeno was acute enough to see that if an impression proceeding from something existent was such that there could be an impression of something non-existent of exactly the same form, then no impression could be apprehended. (7) Arcesilaus agreed that this addition to the definition was justified, since one could not apprehend an impression if a true one were such as a false one could be. (8) However he argued forcefully in order to show that no impression of something existent was such that there could not be an impression of something non-existent of the same form. (10: *Acad.* II 77, =SVF 1.59, =40D LS)

Sextus fills this out a little:

(1) they added 'of such a type as could not come from something non-existent' because the Academics did not suppose, as the Stoics did, that an impression could not be found in all respects similar to it. (2) For the Stoics assert that he who has the apprehensive impression fastens on the objective difference of things with the skill of a craftsman, since an impression of this kind has a special characteristic of its own compared with other impressions, like horned serpents as compared with all other serpents; (3) while the Academics hold that a false impression could be found that was indistinguishable (*aparallaktos*) from the apprehensive one. (11: *M* VII 252, =SVF 2.65, =40E LS; cf. *M* VII 152, VII 163, VII 248, VII 416, VII 426)

Thus, under pressure from Arcesilaus, Zeno modifies definition D^I by the addition of a new clause CIv 'of such a type as could not come from something non-existent' (cf. DL VII 50), which is presumably a further specification of CIiv. Arcesilaus' challenge is clear enough: Even if we grant, for the sake of argument, that there are impressions meeting conditions CIi–iii, as long as it is possible that, for any impression I which satisfies CIi–iii, there can be another impression I^* which is indistinguishable from it in terms of its contours, and yet which does not satisfy the definition (it comes from some other object, or from no object at all, being a mere figment), then the Stoics' definition of the cataleptic impression cannot be criterial. We can never know, simply by inspecting the impression itself, whether or not it meets the conditions.[12]

Cicero, speaking as an Academic sceptic, summarises:

there are four general premises which conclude to the position that nothing can be known, apprehended, or comprehended, around which the whole debate centres: [A](i) that some false impression exists; (ii) that this cannot be apprehended; (iii) that in the case of impressions among which there is no difference it is not possible that some of them can be apprehended while others cannot; (iv) that there is no true impression deriving from the senses to which there does not correspond another impression which does not differ from it and cannot be apprehended. Of these four, everybody admits (ii) and (iii); Epicurus does not grant (i), but you [sc. the Stoics and their followers] with whom we are arguing allow this too; the whole conflict concerns (iv). (12: *Acad.* II 83, =40J LS [part]; cf. II 40–1)

[A] is the Academics' argument. The Epicureans reject Ai, and with it the rest of the argument. The Stoics accept Ai–iii, but reject Aiv. But how are they to do so?

The Academic method of supporting Aiv was by example: there are myriad cases of people being deceived into thinking they are seeing one of a pair of identical twins, when in fact they are seeing the other; and no one can tell two sufficiently similar eggs apart (*M* VII 409–10; *Acad.* II 20, II 5–6, II 58–9, II 84–6). But if this is so, consider a particular case of veridical impression forming – I see one of two identical twins (Castor, say), and assent to the impression (as it happens correct) that it is Castor. But for all I can tell from simply

---

[12] These and subsequent issues are dealt with in more detail in Hankinson (1997), 168–83.

inspecting the impression, it *might* have been Pollux (this can, of course, be true even when I have no idea that Castor has an identical twin; indeed, it is precisely under those circumstances that I might rashly commit myself to its being Castor); so Aiv is justified. As Cicero puts it, 'there was no mark to discern a true impression from a false one' (*Acad.* II 84; cf. II 33–4).

The Stoics fight back: 'you say that there is no such degree of similitude in the nature of things' (*Acad.* II 84). It is a consequence of the Stoics' Leibnizian metaphysics that no two things can be exactly alike (see, e.g., Plutarch, *Comm. not.* 1077c–e, =28O LS),[13] and that is supposedly true for impressions as well. Moreover, as we saw, a cataleptic impression is supposed to be one which 'artistically reproduces the peculiar qualities (*idiômata*) of its object' (*M* VII 248, 250, =SVF 2.65, =40E LS).

But the Academics are unimpressed:

let us grant that: there certainly *seems* as though there is, and so it will deceive the sense; but if one such similitude is deceptive, everything will be thrown into doubt. For, with the removal of that appropriate criterion of recognition, even if the one you see is the same as the one you think you see, you will not make that judgment, as you say you ought, by means of a mark (*nota*) which is such that no false one could be of the same kind. (**13**: *Acad.* II 84, =40J LS [part])

Sextus, arguing against the Stoic criterion at *M* VII 402–35, seeks first to show that false impressions can be found that do not differ from true ones 'in respect of the clear and intense characteristic (*idiôma*)', and then that false impressions can be found that do not differ from true ones 'in respect of stamp and imprint' (i.e., their internal contours: in Descartes' sense, they are not distinct).

But the Stoics here will retort that cataleptic impressions accurately represent the distinguishing characteristics, the *idiômata*, of the object (*M* VII 250–1); the object's particular *idiômata* directly produce the *idiôma* of the particular type of cataleptic impression (*M* VII 252). Thus, cataleptic impressions are made so by the essential

---

[13] The reason, roughly, is that particular properties are the determinants of identity, hence, if qualitatively identical attributes were instantiated in distinct spatiotemporal substrates, the same thing would, absurdly, exist in distinct places. Plutarch remarks, dismissively, that it's harder to accept that there have been no distinct but indiscernible items than it is to reject the metaphysics that gives rise to such a conclusion.

natures of the object they represent, which in turn entails that cataleptic impressions of the same object will share content.[14]

But the issue between the Stoics and their opponents is precisely whether, and if so how, two distinct impressions may share contents. A little more precision is needed. Let us treat an impression as a particular perceptual-event token – so defined, every impression is *sui generis*, and no impression can recur. But surely impressions of the same type can recur – the issue between the schools is how and under what circumstances this should be said to happen. Let us now characterize the *internal content* (C_I) of an impression I as involving its representational structure.[15] We can now say that the set S of impressions $\{I_1, I_2, I_3, \ldots I_n\}$, where the C_I of all the I_i's is indiscernible, is a set of impressions of the same type.

The issue between Stoic and sceptic can now be sharply posed: Can there be a set S of type-identical, internal content-sharing impressions, which is nonetheless such that not all of the I's are impressions of the same object? If the answer is 'yes', the sceptics are vindicated; if not, the Stoics live to fight another day. But even if the answer is 'no', the sceptics will still retort that what matters are not sets like S, where the impressions are as a matter of fact indiscernible with respect to internal content; rather, all that is at issue is whether there can be a set S^*, where the impressions are indistinguishable to the individual whose impressions there are – if there can, then the Stoics are still in trouble (*Acad.* II 85, =40J LS, and text 8).

And yet, the Stoics will reply, that is not enough to make out the sceptical case. The world is full of fools, poor cognizers, who are chock-full of sets of impressions like S^*; but that just shows that none of their impressions (or at least none of the ones which fall into such sets) are cataleptic. The Stoics, after all, do not require

---

[14] I do not mean to suggest that the impression brings you face to face, as it were, with the internal, essential nature of the thing – after all, the impression itself reproduces only what 'confronts' it. But it is because the thing is the (particular) thing that it is; i.e., because of its essential individuality, that it will, for the Stoics, reveal in its impression a unique phenomenal face.

[15] I put things this way, since content had better not be individuated simply by the phenomenological nature of the impression, otherwise my impression of you at noon in a good light will differ in content from my impression of you in the evening in a dim one; I leave things this vague, since precision is difficult to achieve in this area, and, at least in this case, is not (I think) requisite for clarity. For a modern attempt to make similar distinctions, see Goldman (1977).

that everyone be capable of such feats of discernment – only that the cognitively progressive should be.

There now appears to be something of a standoff. The sceptics are committed, after all (at any rate, for the sake of the argument), to Aiv; and that seems rather a strong claim. Is it really plausible to suppose that absolutely every true impression might have an indistinguishably similar false congener? Surely, if I'm wide awake and it's broad daylight, it is simply idle to suppose that the impression I'm now receiving might not be one of my computer. It won't be enough, if this is right, simply to point to the existence of cases of delusion; rather, it has to be the case that we might all be deluded about absolutely anything.[16] And yet, it seems that the sceptics need this to ward off the Stoics' claim that it is only in regard to some impressions that they suppose that the no-false-siblings condition applies.

On the other hand, the Stoics still apparently owe us an account of how the paradigm criterial cases of cataleptic impression can be recognized as such by their subjects. It clearly will not be enough to say that in these cases the subjects are certain that their impressions meet all the conditions CIi–v, since subjective certainty on its own is not, for good sceptical reasons, an infallible guide; many people are certain of things that turn out false. But if there is a special kind of internal certainty, then the Stoics owe us an account of what it is like, and how we can infallibly recognize it as such when we have it.

It is worth pointing out here that they do not need to claim that no one can be mistaken about an impression's cataleptic status; nor do they even need to claim (as in fact they did not: see **15**) that no one in receipt of a cataleptic impression can fail to recognize it as such and assent to it.

This is an important distinction, often overlooked in sceptical argument: It is one thing to hold (i) that you can falsely suppose yourself to be in a certain condition C when you are not; quite another to claim (ii) that when you are in C, you can falsely suppose that you are not. For at least some values of C, (i) seems clearly possible, but (ii) clearly (or at any rate arguably) not. At least, the mere fact that

---

[16] Not, note, that everybody might be deluded about absolutely everything (i.e., $\Diamond(x)(p)$(if x supposes that p, then $\neg p$) – the sceptics do not need that very strong possibility of global delusion to generate their claim – rather, anybody might be deluded about anything ($\neg(\exists x)(\exists p)\neg\Diamond(x$ supposes that p, and $\neg p$); but the claim is still strong enough, perhaps too strong to be intrinsically plausible.

type (i) conditions sometimes – perhaps even regularly – hold does not in itself have any tendency to show that type (ii) cases must also be likely to hold. Consider 'being awake' as a substituend for C: the fact that I can falsely suppose myself to be awake when I'm not (i.e., when I'm dreaming) does not show that I can falsely suppose myself not to be awake when I am. All they need is for there to be some cases where cataleptic impressions are had, are recognized as such, and assented to, and that in *those* cases there is no room for doubt.

It is for this reason precisely that the Academics sought to make out that there was absolutely no impression that met condition CIv. To this end, they employed examples the types of which were to become stocks-in-trade of later epistemological argument. The Stoics stressed the motivational force of clear and distinct impressions (their Humean force and vivacity, if you like), but the Academics were not impressed:

so if impressions are cataleptic to the extent to which they draw us on to assent and to adjoin to them the corresponding action, then since false ones are also of such a kind, we must say that non-cataleptic impressions are indistinguishable (*aparallaktoi*) from the cataleptic. Furthermore, the hero [sc. Heracles] grasped the impression from his own children that they were the children of Eurystheus in the same way as from the arrows (that they were arrows).[17] So since both moved him equally, it must be conceded that the one is indistinguishable from the other. (**14**: *M* VII 405–7; cf. *M* VIII 67, *Acad.* II 38, II 90; Plutarch, *Col.* 1121e, 1122c)

Sextus is discussing the case of the madness of Heracles in which he slew his own children mistaking them for those of his enemy Eurystheus. Heracles' (false, and hence evidently non-cataleptic) impression that the children before him are those of his enemy, Sextus suggests (almost certainly here, as elsewhere, relying on originally Academic arguments), differs not at all in terms of internal or motivational characteristics from the perfectly clear and distinct impression he has of his arrows; but one of them is false – so, although he might have had a veridical impression of Eurystheus' children, he could not have had one which met CIv; hence, he can have had no cataleptic impression of anything.

Here again the Stoics may reply that, although Heracles perhaps supposed his impression to be cataleptic, it wasn't; and it is no part of their doctrine that every apparently cataleptic impression must be

---

[17] Accepting Heintz's plausible supplement '*hôs toxôn*'.

one. So the standoff continues. The Academics, in effect, must claim that no matter how 'good' the impression seems to be, it might still be false; the Stoics must hold that every case of a delusive impression will, on closer inspection, be found to fall short in respect of the clarity and distinctness requisite for genuine *katalêpsis*. And it is hard to see how either side can make their case by pursuing these types of argument.

At this point, we should consider an alternative possibility, raised by Frede (1983) in an influential article. On Frede's view, what distinguishes the cataleptic impression is not some internal marker of infallibility, by means of which it can be recognized for what it is; rather, what marks it out is a causal feature of its causal origin, in virtue of which it has a particularly motivating force.

The claim, then, is that there are certain impressions which do arise in the appropriate way, and just because they do, they have a greater tendency to earn our assent: 'it seems that the differentiating mark of cognitive impressions is a causal feature rather than a phenomenological character to be detected by introspection' (Frede, 1983, 85). Clause CIv would now refer to this causal feature (as would Cicero's '*nota*': see **13**); and Frede points to the causal flavour of the first sentence of **14**, and similar passages (see also **17**).

The problem with this interpretation is that, if correct, it renders much Academic criticism beside the point.[18] Lucullus, the spokesman for Antiochean Stoicizing epistemology in Cicero's *Academica*, repeatedly insists that we must know individual facts, and know that we know them, in order to explain our ability to get around in the world (*Acad.* II 23–6, II 27–9, II 30–2, II 33–6, II 37–9). Moreover, it would make the criterion something that we could possess without being aware that we possess it, which, although not fatal to the view, at least seems to run against the general thrust of the Stoic conception of wisdom and even of approaching wisdom.

We shall return to this point later. But whatever we think about the causal suggestion, it is clear that the Stoics were forced into another strategic retreat under the weight of sceptical fire:

whereas the older Stoics declare that this cataleptic impression is the criterion of truth, the more recent ones added the clause 'provided that there is no obstacle (*enstêma*)'. For there are times when a cataleptic impression

---

[18] And as Annas (1990), 195 n. 25, points out, if this is right 'it is hard to see how the Stoic-sceptic debate lasted as long as it did'.

occurs, yet it is incredible (*apistos*) because of the external circumstances. (**15**: Sextus, *M* VII 253–4, =40K LS; cf. **17**)

The suitable mythological cases here are those of Admetus, being presented by Heracles with his wife Alcestis brought back from the dead, and Menelaus being confronted by the real Helen at the house of Proteus, after he has left the phantom Helen – whom he believes to be the real one – onboard his ship. Both received impressions that met the conditions for being cataleptic (*M* VII 254–5, =40K LS), yet neither believed them, for perfectly good reasons:

Admetus reasoned that Alcestis was dead, and the dead do not rise again, while certain demons do wander about from time to time; and Menelaus reflected that he had left Helen under guard on the ship, and that it was not implausible (*apithanon*) that what he had found at Pharos was not Helen but some supernatural phantom. (**16**: *M* VII 256, =40K LS; cf. *M* VII 180; *PH* I 228)

The Stoic response is simple:

the cataleptic impression is not unconditionally the criterion of truth, but only when there is no obstacle to it. For in this latter case, being evident and striking, takes hold of us, as they say, practically by the hair and drags us to assent. (**17**: Sextus, *M* VII 257; cf. **8**)

In other words, we can fail to realize that a cataleptic impression is cataleptic, not in virtue of any deficiency in the impression itself (it still meets conditions CIi–v), but rather because the force of other commitments we have is such as to make us reject even the clear evidence of the senses.

At *M* VII 424 (=40L LS), Sextus says that, according to the Stoics, five things need to 'concur' in order for the impression to command assent: the sense organ, the object perceived, the environment, the manner, and the intellect; if any one of these fails, then it will not do so: 'hence some held that the cataleptic impression is not a criterion in all cases, but only when there is no obstacle to it'.

But for the criterion to function transparently for us, we need to know that those conditions do indeed concur: and how can we do that in the face of familiar sceptical objections? The Menelaus case (**16**) is particularly *à propos* here, since Menelaus is doubly deceived, mistaking a noncataleptic impression for a cataleptic one and vice versa. Just what is going wrong in the case of his original acceptance of the fake Helen as genuine? He is not, presumably, out of his mind or sensorily deranged (although he is deluded), and the only thing wrong with the object (in terms of its physical characteristics) is that it is not the right one. Not surprisingly, Sextus complains that the notions of cataleptic impression and of real object are interdefined, allowing us no independent purchase on either (*M* VII 426).

But presumably, as the Alcestis case shows, the idea is that the existence of other deeply held beliefs makes it impossible to assent to the given impression. And other sources do indeed suggest that one way in which impressions commend themselves to us is in terms of their fit with other impressions and other beliefs. Now, this criterion, as a matter of practicality, is clearly defeasible – the question is, are the Stoics right to insist that with suitable practice and application, we can make ourselves into better cognizers (cf. *Acad.* II 20, II 56–8, II 86)?

The important thing is that the Stoics are still committed to truth. Intriguingly, Carneades the Academic made use of the Alcestis case in developing his own epistemology of plausibility.[19] Impressions can be merely plausible (i.e., *prima facie* persuasive); plausible and tested (*diexôdeumenai*); or plausible, tested, and unreversed (*aperispastoi*). They are tested by comparison with the reports of other sense modalities (e.g., touching it to see if it feels solid as well as looking solid) and by improving the conditions of the original impression (e.g., getting closer, turning on the light): *M* VII 158–75, =69DE LS; *PH* I 227–9. What Carneades does, effectively, is to allow[20] that persuasiveness, suitably tested for confirmation and consistency, is a perfectly workable guide to acceptance and action; what he rejects is that it needs any metaphysical underpinning by reference to the truth, or that it is sufficient for knowledge.

So far, we concentrated on the cataleptic impression as the Stoic criterion of truth. But a text of Diogenes gives evidence of disagreement within the school on the subject of the criterion:

they say that the cataleptic impression is the criterion of truth . . . ; so says Chrysippus in Book II of his *Physics*, and Antipater and Apollodorus. Boethus

---

[19] Whether he did so in his own right or merely as part of the dialectical battle with the Stoics is a question beyond the scope of this inquiry, although I hold to the former interpretation: Hankinson (1998c), Chs. V and VI; Hankinson (forthcoming); but see also Allen (1994 and 1997).

[20] Again either in his own voice, or on behalf of the Stoics.

admits more criteria: intellect and sensation and desire and scientific under-standing. And Chrysippus, contradicting himself in the first book of his *On Reason*, says that sensation and preconception are criteria (preconception being a natural concept of the universal). And some of the older Stoics ad-mit right reason (*orthos logos*) as a criterion, as Posidonius says in his *On the Criterion* (**18**: DL VII 54, =SVF 2.105, 1.631 =40A LS, =Fr 42 EK)

This short report has prompted much critical discussion,[21] and it is by no means clear how reliable it is. But the conclusion seems in-escapable that there was at least some debate in the school about the nature of the criterion that probably went back at least to Chrysippus and, if the vague Posidonian reference in the last sentence is taken seriously, perhaps earlier still.[22]

The situation is further muddied by the protean nature of the no-tion of a criterion itself. Sextus distinguishes three main senses of the term (agent, instrument, and mechanism), and proceeds to show that dogmatic disputes about all of them render the notion inappre-hensible (*PH* II 18–79). In *M* VII 29, he first distinguishes two generic types of criterion (of action and of truth); he then subdivides the lat-ter into three species (general, special or technical, and particular: *M* VII 31–3), the last of which, 'the rational criteria', are then treated according to the divisions of *PH* II 21 (*M* VII 34–7); and all of the rest of *M* VII is concerned with destructive criteriology.

Two things stand out from text **18**, however. First, it seems that some Stoics, at any rate, were prepared to allow reason, in one form or another, a criterial role. The idea that both the senses and the intellect are criterial in some sense was to become a commonplace,[23] and is prominent in Cicero's presentation of Antiochus' Stoicizing epistemology in *Acad.* But reason is not presented as an independent criterion: rather, it goes to work on material already supplied by the senses, in proper empiricist fashion (II 19–20, II 31, II 43–4, II 45).

And this brings us to the second point. Chrysippus brings in preconception as a further criterion. But preconception is precisely

---

[21] See, e.g., Pohlenz (1938); Annas (1980); Kidd (1989).

[22] Kidd (1989), 143–5, argues that Posidonius' ascription of the right reason criterion to the 'older Stoics' is mistaken.

[23] Sextus (*M* VII 217–18) fathers it on the Peripatetics, in particular Theophrastus, and although that attribution is often questioned, I agree with Long (1988), 199, n. 59, that there is no obvious reason why it should be.

the pre-theoretical, indeed even pre-articulate, 'natural' conceptu-
alizing of a universal (e.g., 'whiteness' or 'animal'): they 'occur
naturally... and without conscious effort (see 3)'. The point is that,
for Chrysippus at least, all the criterial work is being done prior to
any intellectual unpacking we may do of the concepts so derived.
This appears to be at odds with the suggestion of 18 that other Stoics
saw a more fundamental role for reason.

But at bottom, this dispute may amount to no more than a disagreement over the proper scope of the notion of a criterion. Should it
be restricted to what is foundational, the bedrock upon which the rest
of the epistemic structure is to be erected? Or can it be stretched to
include the mechanisms by which that edifice is to be constructed?
As we have seen from Sextus, the Greek notion of a criterion is certainly elastic enough to serve either function; and, if one adopts the
general Stoic position, then in order for one to arrive at the final
understanding of things on the basis of deductions and abstractions
from one's impressions and preconceptions, then one's equipment
for making such moves had better be in proper working order:

hence the mind utilizes the senses, and creates the technical abilities (artes)
as secondary senses, as it were, and strengthens philosophy itself to the point
where it creates virtue, from which thing alone the whole of life can be made
appropriate. (19: Cicero, Acad. II 31)

Although the speaker here is the Antiochean Lucullus, there is no
reason to doubt that this was also the view of contemporary Stoicism.

But there is, of course, one other function the mind or reason may
accomplish in the area of the cataleptic impression. Once you allow
that it will function as the criterion of truth only when there is no
overriding obstacle to its being accepted as such (15, 17), then specifically mental operations of comparing and contrasting the content
of the candidate impression with other impressions and with other
commitments come into play. Of course, as the examples show, this
sometimes leads us to reject impressions that are in fact cataleptic, misled by mistaken further beliefs. But it is also reasonable to
suppose that such a process will also, and perhaps rather more frequently, force us to reject initially convincing impressions which are
not in fact cataleptic, on the grounds of their inconcinnity with our
other commitments.

If this is right, then it is tempting to suppose that later Stoics at any rate, after absorbing heavy sceptical punishment, sought to make coherence among a set of mental contents (beliefs, impressions, memories, conceptions) in some sense criterial. Annas (1980) goes as far as to call this the 'coherence view' of the Stoic criterion, which she detects in the Stoic texts, and which she contrasts with what she calls (rather unhappily) the 'correspondence view'; namely, the idea that individual cataleptic impressions, because of their direct representative connection with reality, are on their own criterial.

Annas allows that the term 'correspondence' is not particularly felicitous here; and it is worth stressing that the Stoics (like all the ancients) are firmly committed to a correspondence theory of truth: propositions are true just in case they mirror actual states of affairs. There is no hint in them, or in any other ancient theorist for that matter, of the view that coherence is itself sufficient for – indeed, constitutive of – truth. By the same token, the most they can possibly espouse is a coherence theory of knowledge, or perhaps rather of justification – but of course such a theory is perfectly compatible with a correspondence theory of truth.

But did the Stoics actually hold any such theory? There is little or no direct evidence to suggest that they did. Those who argue for it do so on the basis of general features of Stoic metaphysics, stressing in particular their providential determinism and their belief in the sympathetic interconnectedness of everything. And of course what the Stoic sage accomplishes, by bringing his nature into perfect accord with the structure of Nature as a whole, and by having only desires which are, in the ineluctable course of things, capable of realization (and hence in accord with the will of Zeus, Fate itself), is an understanding of the total structure of that Nature (which is where we came in).

But that fact does not in itself tell in favour of the Stoics' admitting considerations of coherence into their account of knowledge, understanding, or justification, other than in the trivial sense that total understanding, *epistême*, of things, the hand grasped around the closed fist, will be of a totality of facts which is at least mutually coherent.

One might also here invoke the Stoic conception of demonstration as a type of inference to the best explanation, designed to lead us from phenomenal facts to their hidden explanations (*PH* II 142, II 169–70, II 179).[24] The world is such that it will guide the diligent and practised inquirer from evident facts, by means of logically impeccable inferences, to the non-perceptible states of affairs that must obtain if the phenomena are to be as they are. This is the epistemology of the *sêmeion endeiktikon*, the indicative sign, a notion that not surprisingly also came under heavy and sustained sceptical fire (*PH* II 97–133; *M* VIII 141–299).[25]

The Stoics argued, for example, that the evident fact of sweating was enough to show that the skin was perforated with invisible pores (*PH* II 140; *M* VIII 306; DL IX 89); this inference is buttressed, among other things, by the axiom that nothing physical can penetrate a solid physical body (*M* VIII 309). But all this shows is that we need to invoke other aspects of our physical picture of the world (in this case, one supposedly secured by *a priori* reason alone) in order to make the appropriate inferences, not that the fact that they all hang together is itself a reason for supposing them to be true.

But one other text needs to be considered in this context:

the action of Sphaerus, a colleague of Chrysippus' as pupil of Cleanthes, was not without wit: having been summoned to Alexandria by King Ptolemy, on arrival there, he was presented at dinner on one occasion with birds made of wax and when he stretched out his hands to grasp them, he was charged by the King with having assented to something false. But he cleverly replied that he had not assented to the claim that they were birds, but rather that it was reasonable (*eulogon*) that they were birds; for the cataleptic impression differs from the reasonable one, in that the former is infallible, while the reasonable may turn out otherwise. (20: Athenaeus, VIII 354e, =SVF 1.624; cf. DL VII 177, =SVF 1.625, =40A LS)[26]

As 20 indicates, Sphaerus was an early Stoic: and this is the only text which provides some support for Posidonius' claim that the early

---

[24] On this, see Barnes (1980); and also Brunschwig (1980).

[25] Aenesidemus, who refounded Pyrrhonism in disgust at the increasingly dogmatic tendencies of the Academy under Philo and Antiochus, argued, in one of his eight modes against the purveyors of causal explanation (*PH* I 180–6), that no set of phenomena could entail a unique explanation (*PH* I 181), anticipating Duhem and Quine on the underdetermination of theory by data.

[26] The report in Diogenes is close enough verbally to show that they both derive from a common source – however, in Diogenes' version, Sphaerus is presented with wax pomegranates rather than birds; nothing of course of significance turns on this difference.

Stoics employed right reason as a partial criterion (see **18**). The story
was clearly well known in later antiquity, although that of course
does not vouch for its accuracy. But tales of this sort, while in one
sense clearly apocryphal, are often trustworthy (after some discount-
ing for sectarian bias) regarding the philosophical point they are supposed to illustrate. And so, with some reservations, I am prepared to
accept that **20** does illustrate a genuine Stoic manoeuvre.

At first sight, the retreat to the reasonable may seem to be more
of a capitulation than a strategic withdrawal; it certainly appears to
abandon the claim that any (first-order) impression can be in and
of itself criterial, self-warrantingly true, and acceptable. In this, the
move parallels that made by the Stoics in the practical arena, when
confronted with Arcesilaus' argument to the effect that, since on the
Stoics' own account the sage has no mere opinions, and since the
cataleptic impression is unavailable or, at any rate, cannot infallibly
reveal itself as such, then the sage ought to suspend judgment (*M* VII
151–7, =41C LS).

The Stoics respond, in part, by saying that all of the desires, impulses, and beliefs about the future of the Stoic in progress toward
sagehood will be hedged around with a mental 'reservation', *hupexairesis* (Stobaeus II 115.5–9, =SVF 3.564, =65W LS; Seneca, *Ben.* IV
34, =SVF 2.565): I want to go to the market today only if God wills
it so.[27] Similarly, they make use of the notion of the reasonable, *eulogon*, in action contexts. Philodemus reports Diogenes of Babylon,
the Stoic contemporary of Carneades, as saying:

> it is sufficient, concerning these things and those which derive from ex-
> perience, for us to be convinced in accordance with the reasonable, just as
> when we set sail in summer we are convinced we will arrive safely. (**21**:
> Philodemus, *Sign.* 7.32–8, =42J LS)

Only the sage will get everything correct all of the time on the
basis of proper understanding – his actions will be righteous ones
(*katorthômata*). By contrast, someone who is only progressing will
perform *kathêkonta*, fitting actions, which are defined as 'being con-
sequential in life, something which, when done, has a reasonable justification'[28] (Stobaeus, II 85.13–86.4, =SVF 3.494, =59A LS; cf. DL
VII 107, =SVF 3.493).

---

[27] The subject of *hupexairesis* is difficult and controversial: see Inwood (1985) 119–
126, 165–175, 210–215; Brennan 2000; Brunschwig forthcoming.

[28] Or perhaps 'defence': *apologia*.

Arcesilaus also deployed this criterion of *ex post facto* reasonable justification, in his account of how someone who suspends judgment about everything can nonetheless go on living, and thus evade the '*apraxia* argument' (*M* VII 158, =69B LS).[29] Interestingly, he describes such actions as *katorthômata*, the Stoics' term for the perfect actions of the sage, which will not need any such defence. It is possible that *katorthôma* had not yet acquired its technical Stoic sense at the time of Arcesilaus' argument (see Ioppolo [1981], 147–51). But perhaps Arcesilaus' language is deliberately pointed: such reasoned actions are, in the nature of things, the best we can hope to come up with, but they are still sufficient for ordinary life.[30]

In any event, the Stoic will now apparently act on the basis of what seems reasonable, knowing that such actions may turn out to be fruitless and the beliefs associated with them false. As good Stoics, they will accept that result with equanimity – the universe could not have gone any differently anyway. There is no room for regret in the Stoic universe (cf. Seneca, *Ben.* IV 34, =SVF 3.565).

One further feature of 20 deserves notice. Sphaerus did not assent to the impression 'those are birds'; but he allegedly agreed that he assented to something; namely, that it was reasonable that the things were real birds. Since he assented, *that* content ('it is reasonable to suppose that those are birds') must take the form of a cataleptic impression: it is this which meets conditions CIi–v, and which bears its nature on its sleeve (although can it really be said to represent an object?). But of course the embedded content is fallible, indeed false.

It is easy to characterize this retreat to second-order contents as fraudulent, a way of getting infallibility on the cheap. Moreover, the more such concessions the Stoics make, the harder it becomes to distinguish them from the sceptics, while the post-Carneadean Academy under Philo and Antiochus apparently became too dogmatic in tone for hardliners like Aenesidemus. It is not an accident that the Academy ceases to exist as a practising school at some time around the 80s B.C.,[31] when Philo produces his new epistemology (Cicero, *Acad.* II 18), and Antiochus reacts violently against it.

---

[29] For the '*apraxia* argument', to the effect that a sceptic, having no beliefs, will be rendered unable to act, see Plutarch, *Col.* 1122a–f, =69A LS; see also Hankinson (1998c), 87–9. See Ch. 7, Section 5, Frede, this volume.

[30] See also Maconi, 1988; Hankinson (1998c), 86–91.

[31] For the later history of the Academy, see in particular Glucker (1978) and Barnes (1989).

This is not the place to assess Philo's epistemological innovations:[32] but it is clear from Cicero that he rejected the Stoic cataleptic
criterion, while maintaining that knowledge was possible. It was this
that scandalized Antiochus, who held that knowledge could be guaranteed only by accepting the Stoic criterion, which in turn suggests
that this was still standard Stoic doctrine in his day.

The question, of course, is what, precisely, does this doctrine now
amount to? Antiochus still holds to all of CIi–v; Philo rejects CIv,
but claims we may still know things. Antiochus argues that, unless
there are cataleptic impressions, there cannot be certainty in the arts
and sciences, as there evidently is. Indeed, he retails a form of natu-
ralized epistemology. The Stoics were wont to appeal to the natural
instincts of all creatures for their own preservation as an indication
of the providential structure of the world that of *oikeiôsis*, appropriation, the seeking out of what is in fact suited to one's particular
constitution (cf. DL VII 85–6; Seneca *Ep.* 121.6–15; Hierocles *Elements of Ethics*, 1.34–2.9). Antiochus himself argues (*Acad.* II 24–5)
that we need cataleptic impressions in order to act, or we will not
be able to initiate actions on the basis of impulses (*hormai*) in accordance with our own natures:

that which moves someone must first be seen and believed in by him, which
cannot be done if the object of vision cannot be distinguished from a false
one. But how can the mind be moved to appetition if the object of vision
is not perceived as being in accordance with its nature or foreign to it? (**22**:
Acad. II 25)

Appeals to nature also pepper Antiochus' syncretist, but heavily
Stoicizing ethics, reported in Cicero, *Fin.* V 9–74 (see V 24–6, V 27,
V 31, V 33, V 34–7, V 39–40, V 41–3, V 44, V 46–7, V 55, V 58–9, V 61,
V 66). At V 36, the senses are extolled as being naturally capable of
perceiving their objects, while

Nature ... perfected the mind with its remaining requirements just as it did
the body: for it adorned it with senses suited to the perception of things,
requiring little or no assistance for their verification. (**23**: *Fin.* V 59)

All of this would be equally at home in the Peripatetic tradition;
but then so, as we saw earlier (see 3), would much of the traditional
Stoic epistemology have been.

---

[32] See Barnes (1989); Hankinson (1997), 183–96; (1998c), 116–20; Striker (1997);
Brittain 2001.

This picture is reinforced in *Acad.*: the senses are as good as we could desire (II 19, a claim later controverted by Cicero: II 81–2), and can be sharpened with practice (II 20). They generate the common conceptions (*koinai ennoiai*), the general concepts in virtue of which we order our universe (II 21–2) first by abstracting general properties, such as whiteness and sweetness, from particular instances; then combining them to produce nominal concepts of substances, such as man and horse; and finally proceeding therefrom to their real definitions, which are the source of all scientific inquiry (see 3 and 4). But

> if there were such false notions, or ones impressed upon the mind by impressions such as could not be distinguished from true ones, how could we make any use of them? And how could we tell what was consistent with any particular thing and what inconsistent with it? (24: *Acad.* II 22)

Memory too would fall, and the whole of scientific knowledge (*ibid.* II 22).

So our natural capacities entail that we have cataleptic impressions, a position Antiochus sticks to, as presumably did contemporary Stoics, against all sceptical objections, even while having allowed that we may mistake non-cataleptic impressions for cataleptic ones and, even more damagingly, vice versa (see 16 and 17). There will still be cases when all of the circumstances are favourable and their cataleptic quality shines through: we will then know on the basis of them, and know that we know them.

This is precisely what Philo denies. If I am right, he accepts that we can know things, and that to know something is for us (a) to believe it, for it (b) to be true, and for us (c) to stand in the right cognitive relation to it. But that is all. These impressions need not – indeed, cannot – be such as to meet CIv. All that matters is that (a)–(c) are somehow satisfied: we can never know for sure that they are. Philo, then, is an externalist as well as a reliabilist. Numenius writes:

> but as time went by and his *epochê* began to fade as a result of ordinary life, he no longer remained firm in his convictions about these things, but the clarity (*enargeia*) and agreement (*homologia*) of his experiences turned him around. (25: in Eusebius, *Pr. ev.* XIV 9.2)

Although Numenius' hostility is evident, the testimony is clear enough. Philo became impressed by the stability of his perceptual experience, its generally mutually confirmatory tendencies (*homologia*); this disposes him to suppose that some – perhaps very many, perhaps even the majority – of his sense impressions are true, and satisfy condition (a)–(c) on knowledge. Of course, he can never know for sure which of them are true – and this is what gets up Antiochus' nose. Only if we can be absolutely certain, for some set of impressions, that they reveal the truth, he thinks, are we entitled to claim knowledge. This latter, I take it, formed the non-negotiable core to the Stoic notion of the cataleptic impression – one which they were not, even under the most stringent sceptical attack, prepared to abandon.

4   Logic[1]

Stoic logic is in its core a propositional logic. Stoic inference concerns the relations between items that have the structure of propositions. These items are the assertibles (*axiômata*). They are the primary bearers of truth-values. Accordingly, Stoic logic falls into two main parts: the theory of arguments and the theory of assertibles, which are the components from which the arguments are built.

I. SAYABLES AND ASSERTIBLES

What is an assertible? According to the Stoic standard definition, it is

a self-complete sayable that can be stated as far as itself is concerned (S. E. *PH* II 104).

This definition places the assertible in the genus of self-complete sayables, and so everything that holds in general for sayables and for self-complete sayables holds equally for assertibles. Sayables (*lekta*) are items placed between mere vocal sounds on the one hand and the world on the other. They are, very roughly, meanings: 'what we say are things, which in fact are sayables' (DL VII 57). Sayables are the underlying meanings in everything we say or think; they underlie

---

[1] This chapter is a modified and much shortened version of Bobzien (1999b), where more details and more textual evidence on all the topics treated here can be found, accessible for readers without Greek or Latin. Other useful and fairly comprehensive treatments of Stoic logic are Frede (1974) and Mates (1953) (although the latter is outdated in part). Still worth reading are also Kneale and Kneale (1962), Ch. 3. The surviving textual evidence on Stoic logic is collected in FDS. There are two collections of articles: Brunschwig (1978) and Döring and Ebert (1993).

any rational presentation we have (S. E. *M* VIII 70). But they generally also subsist when no one actually says or thinks them.[2] The Stoics hold further that

> of sayables some are self-complete (*autotelê*), others deficient (*ellipê*). Deficient are those which have an unfinished expression, e.g.: 'writes', for we ask: who? Self-complete are those which have a finished expression, e.g.: 'Socrates writes' (DL VII 63).

Self-complete sayables include assertibles, questions, inquiries, imperativals, oaths, invocations, assertible-likes, puzzlements, curses, and hypotheses (DL VII 65–8). Of these, besides the assertibles, only the hypotheses and imperativals seem to have been considered in the context of logic in the narrow sense; that is, the logic of inference.[3]

What marks off assertibles from other self-complete sayables is that (i) they can be stated (ii) as far as they themselves are concerned. Assertibles can be stated, but they are not themselves statements. They subsist independently of their being stated, in a similar way in which sayables in general subsist independently of their being said. This notwithstanding, it is the characteristic primary function of assertibles to be stated. On the one hand, they are the only entities we can use for making statements: no statements without assertibles; on the other, assertibles have no other primary function than their being stated. A second account determines an assertible as

> that by saying which we make a statement (DL VII 66).

'Saying' here signifies the primary function of the assertible: one cannot genuinely say an assertible without stating it. To say an assertible is more than just to utter a sentence that expresses it. For instance, 'If Dio walks, Dio moves' is a complex assertible, more precisely a conditional, that is composed of two simple assertibles, 'Dio walks' and 'Dio moves'. Now, when I utter the sentence, 'If Dio walks, Dio moves', I make use of all three assertibles. However, the only one I actually assert is the conditional, and the only thing I genuinely say is that if Dio walks, Dio moves.

---

[2] Cf. Barnes (1993), (1999), M. Frede (1994a), Schubert (1994). For an alternative view, see LS.

[3] Cf. Barnes (1986) on Stoic logic of imperatives and Bobzien (1997) on Stoic logic of hypotheses.

Thus understood, phrase (i) of the definition ('can be stated') suffices to delimit assertibles from the other kinds of self-complete sayables. What is the function of phrase (ii) 'as far as itself is concerned'? It isn't meant to narrow down the class of assertibles further, but to preempt a misinterpretation: the locution 'can be asserted' could have been understood as potentially excluding some items which for the Stoics were assertibles. For two things are needed for stating an assertible: first, the assertible itself, and second, someone to state it. According to Stoic doctrine, that someone would need to have a rational presentation in accordance with which the assertible subsists. But many assertibles subsist without anyone having a corresponding presentation. In such cases, one of the necessary conditions for the 'statability' of an assertible is unfulfilled. Here the qualification 'as far as the assertible itself is concerned' comes in. It cuts out this external condition. For something's being an assertible it is irrelevant whether there actually is someone who could state it.

There is a further Stoic account of 'assertible'; it suggests that their 'statability' was associated with their having a truth-value:

an assertible is that which is either true or false (DL VII 65).

Thus truth and falsehood are properties of assertibles, and being true or false – in a nonderivative sense – is both a necessary and a sufficient condition for something's being an assertible. Moreover, we can assume that one can only state something that has a truth-value.

Assertibles resemble Fregean propositions in various respects. There are, however, important differences. The most far-reaching one is that truth and falsehood are temporal properties of assertibles. They can belong to an assertible at one time but not at another. This is exemplified by the way in which the truth-conditions are given: the assertible 'It is day' is true when it is day (DL VII 65). Thus, when the Stoics say, '"Dio walks" is true', *we* have to understand '... is true now', and that it makes sense to ask: 'Will it still be true later?' For the assertible now concerns Dio's walking now; but uttered tomorrow, it will concern Dio's walking tomorrow, and so on. This 'temporality' of (the truth-values of) assertibles has a number of consequences for Stoic logic. In particular, assertibles can in principle change their truth-value: the assertible 'It is day' is true now, false later, and true again tomorrow. The Stoics called assertibles that (can) change their truth-value 'changing assertibles' (*metapiptonta*). Most Stoic examples belong to this kind.

2. SIMPLE ASSERTIBLES

The most fundamental distinction among assertibles (analogous to the modern one between atomic and molecular propositions) was that between simple and non-simple ones. Non-simple assertibles are composed of more than one assertible (see Section 3). Simple assertibles are defined negatively as those assertibles which are not non-simple. There were various kinds of simple and non-simple assertibles. We are nowhere told the ultimate criteria for the distinctions. But we should remember that the Stoics weren't after giving a grammatical classification of sentences. Rather, the classification is of assertibles, and the criteria for their types are at heart logical. This leads to the following complication: The only access there is to assertibles is via language; but there is no one-to-one correspondence between assertibles and declarative sentences. One and the same sentence (of a certain type) may express self-complete sayables that belong to different classes. Equally, two sentences of different grammatical structure may express the same assertible. How then can we know which assertible a sentence expresses? Here the Stoics seem to have proceeded as follows: Aiming at the elimination of (structural) ambiguities, they embarked upon a programme of regimentation of language such that the form of a sentence would unambiguously determine the type of assertible expressed by it. The advantage of such a procedure is that once one has agreed to stick to certain standardizations of language use, it becomes possible to discern logical properties of assertibles and their compounds by examining the linguistic expressions used.

Now to the various types of simple assertibles.[4] Our sources provide us (i) with three affirmative types: predicative or middle ones, catagoreutical or definite ones, and indefinite ones; and (ii) with three negative types: negations, denials, and privations (DL VII 69–70, S. E. *M* VIII 96–100). Each time the first word of the sentence indicates to what type a simple assertible belongs.

---

[4] Cf. also Ebert (1993), Brunschwig (1994).

Examples of the predicative (*katêgorika*) or middle assertibles are of two kinds: 'Socrates sits' and '(A) man walks'. They are defined as assertibles that consist of a nominative 'case', like 'Dio', and a predicate, like 'walks' (DL VII 70). The name 'middle' is based on the fact that these assertibles are neither indefinite (they define their object) nor definite (they are not deictic) (S. E. *M* VII 97). Assertibles of the type '(A) man walks' are extremely rare in Stoic logic.

The definite (*hôrismena*) or catagoreutical (*katagoreutika*) assertibles have in their standard linguistic form a demonstrative pronoun as subject expression.[5] A typical example is 'This one walks'. They are defined as assertibles uttered along with *deixis* (S. E. *M* VIII 96). What do the Stoics mean by '*deixis*'? In one place, Chrysippus talks about the *deixis* with which we accompany our saying 'I', which can be either a pointing at the object of *deixis* (ourselves in this case) or a gesture with one's head in its direction (Galen *PHP* II 2.9–11). So ordinary *deixis* seems to be a non-verbal, physical act of indicating something, simultaneous with the utterance of the sentence with the pronoun.

How are definite assertibles individuated? The sentence (type) by which a definite assertible is expressed does clearly not suffice for its identification: Someone who utters the sentence 'This one walks' pointing at Theo expresses a different assertible from the one they would assert pointing at Dio. However, when I now utter 'This one walks', pointing at Dio, and then utter the same sentence again tomorrow, again pointing at Dio, the Stoics regarded these as two statements of the same assertible. Thus, one way to understand the individuation of definite assertibles is to conceive of a distinction between, as it were, *deixis* type and *deixis* token: a *deixis* type is determined by the object of the *deixis* (and is independent of who performs an act of *deixis* when and where): same object, same *deixis*. By contrast, *deixis* tokens are the particular utterances of 'this one' accompanied by the physical acts of pointing at the object. Hence, there is one assertible 'This one walks' for Theo (with the *deixis* type pointing-at-Theo), one for Dio (with the *deixis* type pointing-at-Dio), and so forth.

But how then does a definite assertible differ from the corresponding predicative one – for example, 'This one walks' (pointing at Dio)

---

[5] On definite assertibles, see also Denyer (1988).

from 'Dio walks'? Are they not rather two ways of expressing the same assertible? Not for the Stoics. We know from a passage on Chrysippus' modal theory that in the case of the assertibles, 'Dio is dead' and 'This one is dead' (pointing at Dio) uttered at the same time one could be true, the other not (Alex. *In Ar. An. pr.* 177.25–178.4). For the latter assertible is said to be false while Dio is alive but destroyed once Dio is dead, whereas the former simply changes its truth-value from false to true at the moment of Dio's death. The reason given for the destruction of the definite assertible is that once Dio is dead the object of the *deixis*, Dio, no longer exists. Now, for an assertible destruction can only mean that it ceases to subsist, and hence no longer satisfies all the conditions for being an assertible. And this should have something to do with the *deixis*. So perhaps in the case of definite assertibles, statability becomes in part point-at-ability, and Stoic point-at-ability requires intrinsically the existence of the object pointed at. This is not only a condition of actual statability in particular situations – as is the presence of an asserter; rather, it is a condition of identifiability of the assertible, of its being this assertible.

The indefinite (*aorista*) assertibles are defined as assertibles that are governed by an indefinite particle (S. E. *M* VIII 97).[6] They are composed of one or more indefinite particles and a predicate (DL VII 70). Such particles are 'someone' or 'something'. An example is 'Someone sits'. This assertible is said to be true when a corresponding definite assertible ('This one sits') is true, since if no particular person is sitting, it isn't the case that someone is sitting (S. E. *M* VIII 98).

The most important kind of negative assertible is the negation (*apophatikon*). For the Stoics, a negation is formed by prefixing to an assertible the negation particle 'not:', as for instance in 'Not: Diotima walks'. In this way an ambiguity is avoided regarding existential import in ordinary language formulations, such as 'Diotima doesn't walk': 'Diotima doesn't walk' counts as an affirmation, which – unlike 'Not: Diotima walks' – presupposes for its truth Diotima's existence (Apul. *De int.* 177.22–31, Alex. *In Ar. An. pr.* 402.8–12).[7] Stoic negation is truth-functional: the negation particle, if added to true

[6] On indefinite assertibles, see also Crivelli (1994).
[7] Cf. A. C. Lloyd (1978a).

assertibles, makes them false; if added to false ones makes them true (S. E. *M* VIII 103). Every negation is the negation of an assertible; namely, of the assertible from which it has been constructed by prefixing 'not:'. Thus 'Not: it is day' is the negation of 'It is day'. An assertible and its negation form a pair of contradictories (*antikeimena*):

> Contradictories are those (assertibles) of which the one exceeds the other by a negation particle, such as 'It is day' – 'Not: it is day'. (S. E. *M* VIII 89)

This implies that an assertible is the contradictory of another if it is one of a pair of assertibles in which one is the negation of the other (cf. DL VII 73). Of contradictory assertibles, precisely one is true and the other false.

The Stoics also prefixed the negation particle to non-simple assertibles in order to form complex negations. The negation of a simple assertible is itself simple; that of a non-simple assertible non-simple. Thus, the addition of the negative doesn't make a simple assertible non-simple. The negation particle 'not:' isn't a Stoic connective (*syndesmos*), for such connectives bind together parts of speech and the negation particle doesn't do that.

A special case of the negation is the so-called super-negation (*hyperapophatikon*) or, as we would say, 'double negation'. This is the negation of a negation, for instance, 'Not: not: it is day'; it is still a simple assertible. Its truth-conditions are the same as those for 'It is day' (DL VII 69).

The second type of negative assertible, the denial (*arnêtikon*), consists of a denying particle and a predicate. An example is 'No-one walks' (DL VII 70). This type of assertible has a compound negative as subject term. Unlike the negation particle, this negative can form a complete assertible if combined with a predicate. The truth-conditions of denials have not been handed down, but they seem obvious: 'No-one φ's' should be true precisely if it isn't the case that someone φ's. Denials must have been the contradictories of simple indefinite assertibles of the kind 'Someone φ's'. Finally, the privative (*sterêtikon*) assertible is determined as a simple assertible composed of a privative particle and a potential assertible, like 'This one is unkind' (DL VII 70, literally 'Unkind is this one', a word order presumably chosen to have the negative element at the front of the sentence). The privative particle is the alpha privativum 'α-' ('un-').

3. NON-SIMPLE ASSERTIBLES

Non-simple assertibles are those that are composed of more than one assertible or of one assertible taken twice (DL VII 68–9) or more often. These constituent assertibles are combined by one or more propositional connectives. A connective is an indeclinable part of speech that connects parts of speech (DL VII 58). An example of the first type of non-simple assertibles is 'Either it is day, or it is night'; one of the second type is 'If it is day, it is day.'

Concerning the identification of non-simple assertibles of a particular kind, the Stoics took what one may call a 'formalistic' approach. In their definitions of the different kinds of non-simple assertibles they mention the characteristic propositional connectives, which can have one or more parts, and determine their position in (the sentence that expresses) the non-simple assertibles. The place of the connectives relative to (the sentences expressing) the constituent assertibles is strictly regulated in such a way that the first word of the assertible is indicative of the type of non-simple assertible it belongs to, and – mostly – the scope of the connectives is disambiguated.

Non-simple assertibles can be composed of more than two simple constituent assertibles (Plut. *St. rep.* 1047c–e). This is possible in two ways. The first has a parallel in modern logic: the definition of the non-simple assertible allows that its constituent assertibles are themselves non-simple. An example of such an assertible is 'If both it is day and the sun is above the earth, it is light.' The type of non-simple assertible to which such a complex assertible belongs is determined by the overall form of the assertible. Thus the above example is a conditional. The second type of assertible with more than two constituent assertibles is quite different. Conjunctive and disjunctive connectives were conceived of not as two-place functors, but – in line with ordinary language – as two-or-more-place functors. So we find disjunctions with three disjuncts: 'Either wealth is good or ⟨wealth⟩ is evil or ⟨wealth is⟩ indifferent' (S. E. *M* VIII 434).

All non-simple assertibles have their connective, or one part of it, prefixed to the first constituent assertible. As in the case of the negation, the primary ground for this must have been to avoid ambiguity. Consider the statement

p and q or r.

In Stoic 'regimented' formulation, this becomes either

Both p and either q or r.

or

Either both p and q or r.

The ambiguity of the original statement is thus removed. Moreover, like Polish notation, the Stoic method of prefixing connectives can in general perform the function that brackets have in modern logic. Avoidance of ambiguity may also have been behind the Stoic practice of eliminating cross-references in non-simple assertibles. Thus, where ordinary discourse has 'If Plato walks, he moves', the Stoics repeated the subject term: '...Plato moves'.

The truth-conditions for non-simple assertibles suggest that the Stoics weren't aiming at fully covering the connotations of the connective particles in ordinary language. Rather, it seems, the Stoics attempted to filter out the essential formal characteristics of the connectives. Leaving aside the negation – which can be simple – only one type of non-simple assertible, the conjunction, is truth-functional. In the remaining cases, modal relations (like incompatibility), partial truth-functionality, and basic relations like symmetry and asymmetry, in various combinations, serve as truth-criteria.

For Chrysippus we know of only three types of non-simple assertibles: conditionals, conjunctions, and exclusive-cum-exhaustive disjunctive assertibles. Later Stoics added further kinds of non-simple assertibles: a pseudo-conditional and a causal assertible, two types of pseudo-disjunctions, and two types of comparative assertibles. Possibly, the main reason for adding these was logical, in the sense that they would allow the formulation of valid inferences which Chrysippus' system couldn't accommodate. A certain grammatical interest may also have entered in.

The conjunction (*sumpeplegmenon, sumplokê*) was defined as 'an assertible that is conjoined by certain conjunctive connective particles; for example, 'Both it is day and it is light'' (DL VII 72). Like modern conjunction, the Stoic one connects whole assertibles: it is 'Both Plato walks and Plato talks', not 'Plato walks and talks'. Unlike modern conjunction, the conjunctive assertible is defined in such a way that more than two conjuncts can be put together on a par (cf. Gellius XVI 8.10). The standard form has a two-or-more part connective: 'both...and...and... ...'. The truth-conditions, too, are formulated in such a way as to include conjunctions with two or more conjuncts: a Stoic conjunction is true when all its constituent assertibles are true, and otherwise false (S. E. *M* VIII 125, 128); it is thus truth-functional.

The conditional (*sunêmmenon*) was defined as the assertible that is formed with the linking connective 'if' (DL VII 71). Its standard-ized form is 'If p, q'. In Chrysippus' time, the debate about the truth-conditions of the conditional – which had been initiated by the logicians Philo and Diodorus – was still going on.[8] There was agreement that a conditional 'announces' a relation of consequence; namely, that its consequent follows (from) its antecedent (*ibid.*). Under debate were what it is to 'follow' and the associated truth-conditions. A minimal consensus seems to have been this: the 'announcement' of following suggests that a true conditional, if its antecedent is true, has a true consequent. Given the acceptance of the principle of bivalence, this amounts to the minimal requirement for the truth of a conditional that it must not be the case that the antecedent is true and the consequent false – a requirement we find also explicitly in our sources (DL VII 81). It is equivalent to Philo's criterion.

Chrysippus offered a truth-criterion that differed from Philo's and Diodorus' (Cic. *Acad.* II 143, DL VII 73, Cic. *Fat.* 12). It was also described as the criterion of those who introduce a connection (*sunartêsis*) (S. E. *PH* II 111); this connection can only be that which holds between the antecedent and the consequent. The requirement of some such connection must have been introduced to avoid the 'paradoxes' that arose from Philo's and Diodorus' positions. In the truth-criterion itself, the connection in question is determined indi-rectly, based on the notion of conflict or incompatibility (*machê*): a conditional is true precisely if its antecedent and the contradictory of its consequent conflict (DL VII 73). Consequently, the example 'If the earth flies, Axiothea philosophises' – which would be true for both Philo and Diodorus – is no longer true. It is perfectly pos-sible that both the earth flies and Axiothea doesn't philosophise. For a full understanding of Chrysippus' criterion, we need to know what sort of conflict he had in mind. But here our sources offer little

---

[8] For Philo's and Diodorus' logic, see Bobzien (1999b).

information. Some later texts state that two assertibles conflict if they cannot be true together. This confirms that the conflict is some sort of incompatibility.

It is historically inappropriate to ask whether Chrysippus intended empirical, analytical, or formal logical conflict, given that a conceptual framework which could accommodate such distinctions is absent in Hellenistic logic. Still, we can be confident that what we may call formal incompatibility would have counted as conflict for Chrysippus: Assertibles like 'If it is light, it is light' were regarded as true (Cic. *Acad.* II 98) – presumably because contradictoriness was the strongest possible conflict between two assertibles. Equally, some cases that some may describe as analytical incompatibility were covered: for instance 'If Plato walks, Plato moves' was regarded as true. And it seems that some instances of cases of what we might label 'empirical incompatibility' were accepted by some Stoics: so conditionals with causal connections of the kind 'If Theognis has a wound in the heart, Theognis will die' were probably considered true (S. E. *M* VIII 254–5). On the other hand, the connection expressed in divinatory theorems ('If you are born under the Dog-star, you won't die at sea') seems to have been an exception. Chrysippus denied that such theorems would make true conditionals, but held that they would make true (indefinite) negations of conjunctions with a negated second conjunct (Cic. *Fat.* 11–15).[9]

Some Stoics introduced two further kinds of non-simple assertibles, grounded on the concept of the conditional (DL VII 71–4). Both were probably added only after Chrysippus. The first, called 'pseudo-conditional' (*parasunêmmenon*), is testified at the earliest for Crinis and has the standardized form 'Since p, q'. The truth-criterion for such assertibles is that (i) the 'consequent' must follow (from) the 'antecedent', and (ii) the 'antecedent' must be true. The second kind is entitled 'causal assertible' (*aitiôdes*) and has the standard form 'Because p, q'. The name is explained by the remark that p is, as it were, the cause/ground (*aition*) of q. The truth-condition for the causal assertible adds simply a further condition to those for the pseudo-conditional; namely (iii), that if p is the ground/cause for q, q cannot be the ground/cause for p, which in particular implies that 'Because p, p' is false.

---

[9] Cf. Bobzien (1998), Ch. 4.2.

The Greek word for 'or' (ê) has several different functions as a connective particle, which are distinct in other languages. It covers both the Latin *aut* and the Latin *vel*, and also both the English 'or' and the English 'than'. It plays a role as a connective in at least three different types of non-simple assertibles.

The early Stoics seem to have concentrated on one type of disjunctive relation only: the exhaustive and exclusive disjunctive relation, called '*diezeugmenon*', here rendered 'disjunction'. This is the only disjunctive that figures in Chrysippus' syllogistic. It is defined as 'an assertible that is disjoined by the disjunctive connective "either", like "Either it is day or it is night"' (DL VII 72). The disjunctive connective could take more than two disjuncts, and there are examples of such disjunctions (S. E. *PH* I 69). Thus, the connective was 'either...or...or......' with its first part ('either') prefixed to the first disjunct. One source presents the truth-conditions for disjunctions as follows:

...(i) all the disjuncts must be in conflict with each other and (ii) their contradictories...must be contrary to each other. (iii) Of all the disjuncts one must be true, the remaining ones false. (Gellius XVI 8.13)

Here, first a non-truth-functional criterion is given ((i) and (ii)); this is followed by a truth-functional criterion (iii). I take (iii) to be an uncontested minimal requirement as we had it in the case of the conditional. For it certainly was a necessary condition for the truth of a disjunction that precisely one of its disjuncts had to be true, but most sources imply that this was not sufficient. The truth-condition they state is stricter and typically involves the term 'conflict' already familiar from the conditionals. It is a conjunction of the two conditions (i) and (ii). First, the disjuncts must conflict with each other; this entails that, at most, one is true. Second, the contradictories of the disjuncts must all be contrary to each other; this ensures that not all of the contradictories are true, and hence that at least one of the original disjuncts is true. The two conditions combined mean that 'necessarily precisely one of the disjuncts must be true'. As in the case of the conditional, a full understanding of the truth-criterion would require one to know what kind of conflict the Stoics had in mind.

Some Stoics distinguished two kinds of a so-called pseudo-disjunction (*paradiezeugmenon*) (Gellius XVI 8.13–14). Regarding their standard form, most examples are formed with 'either...or...' or, occasionally, just with '...or...'; some have more than two pseudo-disjuncts. Thus, the two types of pseudo-disjunctions seem indistinguishable in their linguistic form from disjunctions (and from each other). Their truth-criteria are simply the two halves of the truth-condition for the genuine disjunction. One kind is true if its pseudo-disjuncts conflict with each other, which entails that, at most, one of them is true. The other is true if the contradictories of its pseudo-disjuncts are contrary to each other, which entails that at least one of the pseudo-disjuncts is true.

As mentioned previously, the Greek word for 'or' serves another purpose: that of the English word 'than'. Accordingly, we sometimes find a further kind of non-simple assertible discussed in the context of the disjunctives, the comparative assertible, formed by using a comparative (*diasaphêtikos*) connective.[10] Two types are known (DL VII 72–73), with the connectives 'It's rather that...than that...' and 'It's less that...than that...'. These are two-part connectives, again with the characteristic part prefixed to the first constituent assertible, thus allowing the identification of the type of assertible. The truth-conditions have not survived.

The definition of the non-simple assertibles implies that they take any kind of simple assertibles as constituents, and that by combining connectives and simple assertibles in a correct, 'well-formed' way, all Stoic non-simple assertibles can be generated. But apparently this isn't so: non-simple assertibles that are composed of simple indefinite ones raise special problems. Unlike the case of definite and middle assertibles, one can conceive of two different ways of linking indefinite ones.

First, following Stoic formation rules to the letter, by combining two simple indefinite assertibles into a conjunction or a conditional, one obtains assertibles like the following:

If someone breathes, someone is alive.
Both someone walks and someone talks.

According to Stoic criteria these would be true, respectively, if 'Someone is breathing' and 'Not: someone is alive' are incompatible and if 'Someone (e.g., Diotima) walks' is true and 'Someone (e.g.,

---

[10] Cf. Sluiter (1988).

Theognis) talks' is true. However, complex assertibles with indefinite pronouns as grammatical subject more commonly tend to be of the following kind:

If someone breathes, that one (he, she) is alive.
Someone walks and that one talks.

Here the truth-conditions are different, since the second 'constituent assertible' isn't independent of the first. In fact, we find no Stoic examples of the first type of combinations of indefinite assertibles but quite a few of the second (e.g., DL VII 75; 82). It was explicitly dealt with by the Stoics and it seems that the terms 'indefinite conjunction' and 'indefinite conditional' were reserved for it. In order to express the cross-reference in the second 'constituent assertible' to the indefinite particle of the first, 'that one' (*ekeinos*) was standardly used.

The Stoics were right to single out these types of assertibles as a special category. Plainly, the general problem they are confronted with is that of quantification. The modern way of wording and formalizing such statements, which brings out the fact that their grammatical subject expressions do not have a reference ('For anything, if it is F, it is G') didn't occur to the Stoics. We do not know how far they 'understood' such quantification as lying behind their standard formulation; but we know that they suggested that sentences of the kind 'All S are P' be reformulated as 'If something is S, that thing is P' (S. E. *M* XI 8–9).

The Stoic accounts of assertibles reveal many similarities to modern propositional logic, and there can be little doubt that the Stoics attempted to systematize their logic. However, their system is quite different from the propositional calculus. In particular, Stoic logic is a logic of the validity of arguments, not a system of logical theorems or logical truths. Of course, the Stoics did recognise some logical principles which correspond to theorems of the propositional calculus. But, although they had a clear notion of the difference between meta- and object language, logical principles that express logical truths were apparently not assigned a special status, different from logical meta-principles. A survey of the principles concerning assertibles may be useful. First, there is the principle of bivalence (Cic. *Fat.* 20), which is a logical meta-principle. Then, corresponding to logical truths, we find:

- a principle of double negation, expressed by saying that a double-negation (Not: not: p) is equivalent to the assertible that is doubly negated (p) (DL VII 69)
- the principle that all conditionals that are formed by using the same assertible twice (like 'If p, p') are true (Cic. *Acad.* II 98)
- the principle that all disjunctions formed by a contradiction (like 'Either p or not: p') are true (S. E. *M* VIII 282)

Moreover, some Stoics may have dealt with relations like commutativity and contraposition via the concepts of inversion (*anastrophê*) and conversion (*antistrophê*) of assertibles (Galen *Institutio logica* VI 4). Inversion is the change of place of the constituent assertibles in a non-simple assertible with two constituents. Commutativity could thus have been expressed by saying that for conjunctions and disjunctions, inversion is sound. In a conversion, the two constituent assertibles are not simply exchanged, but each is also replaced by the contradictory of the other. The Stoics seem to have recognized that conversion holds for conditionals; that is, they seem to have accepted the principle of contraposition (cf. DL VII 194).

Finally, regarding the interdefinability of connectives, there is no evidence that the Stoics took an interest in reducing the connectives to a minimal number. For the early Stoics, we also have no evidence that they attempted to give an account of one connective in terms of other connectives, or that they stated logical equivalences of that kind.

4. MODALITY[11]

As the previous sections have illustrated, the Stoics distinguished many different types of assertibles, which were generally identifiable by their linguistic form. In addition, the Stoics classified assertibles with respect to certain of their properties which weren't part of their form. The most prominent ones, after truth and falsehood, were the modal properties possibility, necessity, impossibility, and non-necessity. Two further such properties were plausibility and

---

[11] Cf. Bobzien (1986), (1993), and (1998), Ch. 3.1.

probability (DL VII 75–6): An assertible is plausible (*pithanon*) if it induces assent to it (even if it is false); an assertible is probable or reasonable (*eulogon*) if it has higher chances of being true than false.

Stoic modal logic is not a logic of modal propositions (e.g., propositions of the type 'It is possible that it is day' or 'It is possibly true that it is day') formed with modal operators which qualify states of affairs or propositions. Instead, their modal theory was about non-modalized propositions like 'It is day', insofar as they are possible, necessary, and so forth. The modalities were considered – primarily – as properties of assertibles and, like truth and falsehood, they belonged to the assertibles at a time; consequently, an assertible can in principle change its modal value. Like his precursors in Hellenistic logic, Philo and Diodorus, Chrysippus distinguished four modal concepts: possibility, impossibility, necessity, and non-necessity.

The Stoic set of modal definitions can be restored with some plausibility from several incomplete passages (DL VII 75, Boeth. *Int.* II 234.27–235.4). We can be confident that these definitions were Chrysippus' (cf. Plut. *St. rep.* 1055df). Like the modal notions of Philo and Diodorus, they fit the four requirements of normal modal logic that (1) every necessary proposition is true and every true proposition possible; every impossible proposition is false and every false proposition non-necessary; (2) the accounts of possibility and impossibility and those of necessity and non-necessity are contradictory to each other; (3) necessity and possibility are interdefinable in the sense that a proposition is necessary precisely if its contradictory is not possible; and (4) every proposition is either necessary or impossible or both possible and non-necessary:

A possible assertible is one which (A) is capable of being true and (B) is not hindered by external things from being true;

an impossible assertible is one which (A') is not capable of being true ⟨or (B') is capable of being true, but hindered by external things from being true⟩;

a necessary assertible is one which (A'), being true, is not capable of being false or (B') is capable of being false, but hindered by external things from being false;

a non-necessary assertible is one which (A) is capable of being false and (B) is not hindered by external things ⟨from being false⟩.

In the cases of possibility and non-necessity, two conditions (A and B) have to be fulfilled. In the cases of necessity and impossibility, one of two alternative conditions has to be satisfied (A′ or B′), leading to two types of necessity and impossibility. The first parts of the definitions (A, A′) are almost identical with Philo's modal definitions. The second parts (B, B′) feature 'external things' which must or must not prevent the assertibles from having a certain truth-value. We have no examples of such external things, but they should be external to the logical subject of the assertible. For instance, things that prevent truth should include ordinary, physical hindrances: a storm or a wall or chains that prevent you from getting somewhere.

The accounts leave us in the dark about another aspect of the hindrances; namely, *when* they need to be present (or absent). Knowledge of this is essential for an adequate understanding of the modalities. One text (Alex. *In Ar. An. pr.* 177–178) suggests that for the possibility of an assertible, the requirement of absence of hindrances covers present-plus-future time – relative to the utterance of the assertion. For we learn that for Chrysippus 'Dio is dead' is possible (now) if it can be true at some time; equally, that 'this one is dead [pointing at Dio]', which is impossible, wouldn't be impossible (now) if, although being false now, it could be true at some later time. If one reads 'can be true' as short for Chrysippus' requirement 'is capable of being true and not prevented from being true', it seems that an assertible is possible for Chrysippus if (A) it is capable of truth, and (B) there is some time later than now when it will not be hindered from being true. For instance, 'Sappho is reading' is Chrysippean possible, as long as Sappho isn't continuously prevented from reading from now on. Correspondingly, an assertible falls under the second part of the definiens of the impossible if (B′) it is capable of being true, but is from now on prevented from being true – as in the above example, if Sappho were suddenly struck by incurable blindness or died. Chrysippean necessity of the second type (B′) would require continuous prevention of falsehood; non-necessity, at least temporary absence of such prevention.

5. ARGUMENTS

The second main part of Stoic logic is their theory of arguments. Arguments (*logoi*) form another subclass of complete sayables (DL VII 63); they are neither thought processes nor beliefs, nor linguistic expressions; rather, like assertibles, they are meaningful, incorporeal

entities (S. E. *PH* III 52). However, they are not assertibles, but compounds of them.

An argument is defined as a compound or system of premisses
and a conclusion (DL VII 45). These are self-complete sayables, standardly assertibles, which I shall call the 'component assertibles' of
the argument. The following is a typical Stoic argument:

P₁   If it is day, it is light.
P₂   But it is day.
C   Therefore, it is light.

It has a non-simple assertible (P₁) as one premiss and a simple assertible (P₂) as the other. The non-simple premiss, usually put first,
was referred to as 'leading premiss' (*hêgemonikon lêmma*). The other
premiss was called the 'co-assumption' (*proslêpsis*). It is usually simple; when it is non-simple, it contains fewer constituent assertibles
than the leading premiss. It was introduced by 'but' or 'now', and
the conclusion by 'therefore'. It was the orthodox Stoic view that an
argument must have more than one premiss.

A passage in Sextus defines 'premisses' and 'conclusion': the premisses of an argument are the assertibles that are adopted by agreement for the establishing of the conclusion; the conclusion is the
assertible established by the premisses (S. E. *M* VIII 302). A difficulty with this account is that it seems that something only counts
as an argument if the premisses – at the very least – appear true to the
discussants. This rules out arguments with evidently false premisses
such as reductions to the absurd and arguments with premisses the
truth of which isn't (yet) known, such as arguments concerning future courses of actions.

Difficulties like these may have given rise to the development
of the Stoic device of hypothesis and hypothetical arguments: the
Stoics thought that occasionally one must postulate some hypothesis as a sort of stepping-stone for the subsequent argument (Epict.
Diss. I 7.22). Thus, one or more premisses of an argument could be
such a hypothesis in lieu of an assertible; and it seems that hypothetical arguments were arguments with such hypotheses among their
premisses. These were apparently phrased as 'Suppose it is night' instead of 'It is night' (Epict. *Diss.* I 25.11–13). They could be agreed
upon *qua* hypotheses; that is, the interlocutors agree – as it were – to
enter a non-actual 'world' built on the relevant assumption, but they

remain aware of the fact that this assumption and any conclusions drawn hold only relative to the fact that this assumption has been made.[12]

The most important distinction among arguments is that between valid and invalid ones. The Stoic general criterion was that an argument is valid if the corresponding conditional formed with the conjunction of the premisses as antecedent and the conclusion as consequent is correct (S. E. *PH* II 137). If the assertible 'If (both P_1 and...and P_n), then C' is true, then the argument 'P_1;...P_n; therefore C' is valid. It seems that the criterion for the correctness of the conditional was the Chrysippean one: An argument is valid provided that the contradictory of the conclusion is incompatible with the conjunction of the premisses (DL VII 77). Thus, the Stoic concept of validity resembles our modern one (see also the end of Section 6). But one should recall that the conditional has to be true according to Chrysippus' criterion, which isn't necessarily restricted to logical consequence. This brings out a shortcoming of the Stoic concept of validity, since what is needed is precisely *logical* consequence. It is unfortunate to have the same concept of consequence for both the antecedent-consequent relation in a conditional and the premisses-conclusion relation in an argument. In any event, the concept of conflict seems too vague to suffice as a proper criterion for validity.

In addition to validity, the Stoics assumed that arguments had the properties of truth and falsehood. An argument is true (we would say 'sound') if, besides being valid, it has true premisses; it is false if it is invalid or has a false premiss (DL VII 79). The predicates of truth and falsehood are here based on the truth of assertibles but are used in a derivative sense. The relevance of truth and falsehood of arguments is epistemic: Only a true argument warrants the truth of the conclusion.

Since the concept of truth of arguments is based on that of truth of assertibles, and the latter can change their truth-value, so can arguments. For instance, the argument given above will be true at daytime but false at night. It seems that arguments with premisses that did (or could) change truth-value were called 'changing arguments' (*metapiptontes logoi*) (Epict. *Diss.* I 7.1).

---

[12] Cf. Bobzien (1997).

The Stoics also assumed that arguments could be possible, impossible, necessary, and non-necessary (DL VII 79). These modal predicates, too, would be used in a derivative sense. With Chrysippus' modal accounts, a necessary argument would then be one that either cannot be false or can be false but is hindered by external circumstances from being false, and similarly for the three remaining modalities.

6. SYLLOGISTIC[13]

More important for logic proper are the divisions of valid arguments. These are based primarily on the form of the arguments. The most general distinction is that between syllogistic arguments or syllogisms and those called 'valid in the specific sense' (*perantikoi eidikôs*). The latter are concludent (i.e., they satisfy the general criterion of validity), but not syllogistically so (DL VII 78). Syllogisms are, first, the indemonstrable arguments; and second, those arguments that can be reduced to indemonstrable arguments.

The indemonstrable syllogisms are called 'indemonstrable' (*anapodeiktoi*) because they are not in need of proof or demonstration (DL VII 79), given that their validity is obvious in itself (S. E. *M* II 223). The talk of five indemonstrables alludes to classes of argument, each class characterized by a particular basic argument form in virtue of which the arguments of that class are understood to be valid. Chrysippus distinguished five such classes; later Stoics, up to seven.

The Stoics defined the different kinds of indemonstrables by describing the form of an argument of that kind. The five Chrysippean types were described as follows (S. E. *M* VIII 224–5; DL VII 80–1). A first indemonstrable is an argument that is composed of a conditional and its antecedent as premisses, having the consequent of the conditional as conclusion. The following is an example:

If it is day, it is light.
It is day.
Therefore it is light.

A second indemonstrable is an argument composed of a conditional and the contradictory of its consequent as premisses, having

---

[13] For a detailed discussion of Stoic syllogistic, see Bobzien (1996).

the contradictory of its antecedent as conclusion; for example:

If it is day, it is light.
Not: it is day.
Therefore not: it is light.

A third indemonstrable is an argument composed of a negated conjunction and one of its conjuncts as premises, having the contradictory of the other conjunct as conclusion; for example:

Not: both Plato is dead and Plato is alive.
Plato is dead.
Therefore not: Plato is alive.

A fourth indemonstrable is an argument composed of a disjunctive assertible and one of its disjuncts as premises, having the contradictory of the remaining disjunct as conclusion; for example:

Either it is day or it is night.
It is day.
Therefore not: it is night.

A fifth indemonstrable, finally, is an argument composed of a disjunctive assertible and the contradictory of one of its disjuncts as premises, having the remaining disjunct as conclusion; for example:

Either it is day or it is night.
Not: it is day.
Therefore it is night.

Each of the five types of indemonstrables thus consists – in the simplest case – of a non-simple assertible as leading premiss and a simple assertible as co-assumption, having another simple assertible as conclusion. The leading premisses use all and only the connectives that Chrysippus distinguished.

The descriptions of the indemonstrables encompass many more arguments than the examples suggest, and this for three reasons. First, in the case of the third, fourth, and fifth indemonstrables, the descriptions of the argument form provide for 'commutativity' in the sense that it is left open which constituent assertible or contradictory of a constituent assertible is taken as co-assumption.

Second, the descriptions are all given in terms of assertibles and their contradictories, not in terms of affirmative and negative assertibles. In all five cases, the first premiss can have any of the four combinations of affirmative and negative assertibles: for instance, in the case of the first and second indemonstrable (if we symbolize affirmative assertibles by p, q, negative ones by 'not: p', 'not: q'):

if p, q   if not: p, q   if p, not: q   if not: p, not: q.

Combining these two points, we obtain four subtypes under the first and second descriptions of indemonstrables and eight in the case of the third, fourth, and fifth (i.e., thirty-two subtypes in all).

The third reason for the multitude of kinds of indemonstrables is the fact that the descriptions, as formulated, permit the constituent assertibles of the leading premisses to be themselves non-simple. And indeed, we have an example that is called a second indemonstrable and that is of the kind:

If both p and q, r; now not:r; therefore not: ⟨both p and⟩ q.

In addition to describing the five types of indemonstrables at the meta-level, the Stoics employed another way of determining their basic forms; namely, by virtue of modes (*tropoi*). A mode is defined as 'a sort of scheme of an argument' (DL VII 76). An example of the (or a) mode of the first indemonstrable would be:

If the first, the second; now the first; therefore the second.

It differs from a first indemonstrable in that ordinal numbers have taken the place of the antecedent and consequent of the leading premiss, and the same ordinals are re-used where the antecedent and consequent assertibles recur in co-assumption and conclusion. A mode is syllogistic when a corresponding argument with the same form is a syllogism. It seems that the modes, and parts of modes, performed at least three functions in the Stoic theory of arguments.

First, the modes functioned as forms in which the different indemonstrables – and other arguments – were propounded (S. E. *M* VIII 227). If, for instance, one wants to propound a first indemonstrable, the mode provides a syntactic standard form in which one has (ideally) to couch it. When employed in this way, the modes resemble argument forms: the ordinals do not stand in for particular assertibles; rather, their function resembles that of schematic letters. So, any argument that is propounded in a particular syllogistic mode is a valid argument, but the mode itself isn't an argument. The logical form presented by a syllogistic mode is the reason for the particular argument's formal validity. In this function, the modes can be used to check the validity of arguments.

In the two other ways in which modes and ordinal numbers are employed, the ordinals seem to stand in for assertibles and the modes are used as abbreviations of particular arguments rather than as argument forms. Thus, in the analysis of complex syllogisms (discussed later in this section), for purposes of simplicity and lucidity, ordinals may stand in for simple assertibles, in the sequence of their occurrence in the argument (S. E. *M* VIII 235–7). And in the so-called mode-arguments (*logotropoi*), the constituent assertibles are given in full when first occurring, but are then replaced by ordinal numbers, as in the following:

If it is day, it is light.
Now the first.
Therefore the second (DL VII 77).

In which respects then are all and only the indemonstrables basic and evident? We can infer from the presentation of the types of indemonstrables that their validity is grounded on their form. We can also list some ways of being basic and evident which Chrysippus cannot have had in mind. First, it seems that Chrysippus was not entertaining the idea of minimizing connectives (see Section 3, p. 99). Second, Chrysippus cannot have been concerned to minimize the number of types of indemonstrables: for, with the help of the first *thema*, second indemonstrables can be reduced to first ones (and vice versa), and fifth to fourth ones (and vice versa), and this can hardly have escaped his attention. Third, Chrysippus seems not to have aimed at deducing the conclusions from premises of the minimum possible strength. For any conclusion one can draw from a first or second indemonstrable (with a leading premiss 'If p, q'), one could also draw from a corresponding third indemonstrable (with a leading premiss 'Not: both p and not:q'). The extra requirement in the truth-criterion for the conditional – compared with the negated conjunction – i.e., the element of conflict, seems irrelevant to the conclusions one can draw.

What could have been Chrysippus' positive criteria for choosing the indemonstrables? In the indemonstrables – and consequently in all syllogisms – all and only the Chrysippean connectives ('and', 'if',

'or') and the negation ('not') are used to construct non-simple assertibles. Among these non-simple assertibles, Chrysippus distinguished
a particular class entitled 'mode-forming assertibles' (*tropika
axiômata*). These were apparently conditionals, disjunctions, and
negations of conjunctions. All indemonstrables have as leading premiss such a 'mode-forming assertible', and perhaps the deductive
power of the indemonstrables was thought to be somehow grounded
on these. Perhaps the thought was that the validity of the indemonstrables could not reasonably be doubted, because understanding the
mode-forming premisses implies knowing the validity of the corresponding forms of the indemonstrables. (Understanding 'Not: both p
and q' implies knowing that if one of them holds, the other doesn't;
understanding 'If p, q' implies knowing that (i) if p holds, so does
q, and (ii) if q doesn't hold, neither does p; and so on.) This kind
of criterion would, for instance, fail the following candidate for in-
demonstrability, although it is simple and evident in some way:

p, q, therefore p and q.

It wouldn't rank as an indemonstrable since understanding p
doesn't imply knowing that if q then 'p and q'.

The situation is complicated by the fact that Chrysippus also recognized fifth indemonstrables with several ⟨disjuncts⟩ (S. E. *PH* I 69).
They are of the following kind:

Either p or q or r
Now, neither p nor q
Therefore r.

Their form obviously differs from that of the fifth indemonstrables as given above. Such arguments cannot be reduced to some
combination of indemonstrables, and this could be why Chrysippus
regarded them as indemonstrables. However, as the name implies,
he did not introduce them as 'sixth indemonstrables'; rather, they
are a special version of the fifth – that is, they are fifth indemonstrables. If we take this seriously, we have to revise our understanding
of the fifth indemonstrable. We should assume that the leading premiss in a fifth indemonstrable has two *or more* disjuncts, and that
the 'basic idea' which one grasps when one understands the disjunctive connective is 'necessarily precisely one out of several' rather
than '... out of two'. As a consequence, one also has to modify one's

understanding of the co-assumption: its description 'the contradictory of one of its disjuncts' becomes a special case of 'the contradictory of one *or more* of its disjuncts', the added possibility coming down to 'the conjunction of the negation of all but one of them'. Such co-assumptions were standardly expressed with 'neither ... nor ...' (e.g., S. E. *PH* I 69).

In some Latin authors we find lists of seven basic syllogisms which may be of Stoic origin (e.g., Cic. *Topics* 53–57; Martianus Capella IV 414–421). The lists vary slightly from one source to another, but the first five types always correspond closely to Chrysippus' indemonstrables. Perhaps the sixth and seventh types were intended to have pseudo-disjunctions as leading premises, but the texts are unclear on this point.

Not all Stoic syllogisms are indemonstrables. Non-indemonstrable syllogisms can be more complex than indemonstrables in that they have more than two premises, but they can also have just two premises. For example, in our sources we find Stoic non-indemonstrable syllogisms of the following kinds:

If both p and q, r; not r; p; therefore not:q.
If p, p; if not:p, p; either p or not:p; therefore p.
If p, if p, q; p; therefore q.

The Stoics distinguished and discussed several special cases of syllogisms, both indemonstrable and non-indemonstrable. First, there are the indifferently concluding arguments (*adiaphorôs perainontes*), such as:

Either it is day or it is light.
Now it is day.
Therefore it is day. (Alex. *In Ar. Top.* 10.10–12)

This argument is of the kind:

Either p or q; p; therefore p.

The name of these arguments is presumably based on the fact that it is irrelevant for their validity what comes in as second disjunct. Often mentioned in tandem with the indifferently concluding arguments are the so-called duplicated arguments (*diaphoroumenoi logoi*) (Alex. *In Ar. Top.* 10.7–10). It seems that their name rests on the fact that their leading premiss is a 'duplicated assertible'; that is, composed of the same simple assertible, used twice or several times (cf. DL VII 68–9). The standard example is:

If it is day, it is day.
Now it is day.
Therefore it is day.

It is a special case of the first indemonstrable.

A third type of syllogism was those with two mode-forming premisses; that is, arguments composed of two mode-forming assertibles as premisses and a simple assertible as conclusion: our examples are of this kind:

If p, q; if p, not:q; therefore not:p.

The following is a Stoic example:

If you know you are dead, you are dead.
If you know you are dead, not: you are dead.
Therefore not: you know you are dead. (Orig. *Contra Celsum* VII 15)

It is likely that the Stoics distinguished further types of syllogisms (Alex. *In Ar. An. pr.* 164.27–31).

Arguments of all these kinds were syllogisms. And, since all syllogisms are either indemonstrable or can be reduced to indemonstrables, these arguments, too – if they are not indemonstrables themselves – should be reducible to indemonstrables. The Stoic expression for reducing arguments was to analyze them into indemonstrables (DL VII 195). What is the purpose of such an analysis? It is a method of proving that certain arguments are formally valid by showing how they stand in a certain relation to indemonstrables. This relation between the argument-to-be-analyzed and the indemonstrables is basically either that the argument is a composite of several indemonstrables, or that it is a conversion of an indemonstrable, or that it is a mixture of both. The analysis was carried out with certain logical meta-rules, called '*themata*', which determined these relations. They were argumental rules; that is, rules that can only be applied to arguments. They reduce arguments to arguments, not (say) assertibles to assertibles. Our sources suggest that there were four of them (Alex. *In Ar. An. pr.* 284.13–17; Galen *PHP* II 3.188). We know further that the Stoics had some logical meta-rules, called '*theorems*', which were relevant for the analysis of arguments (DL VII 195; S. E. *M* VIII 231). Since the *themata* were regarded as sufficient for the analysis of all non-indemonstrable syllogisms, the function of some of the theorems was presumably to facilitate the analysis.

Stoic analysis is strictly an upwards method (to the indemonstrables) rather than a downwards method (from the indemonstrables). Analysis always starts with a given non-indemonstrable argument, and with the question whether it can be analyzed into indemonstrables by means of the *themata*. There are no signs that the Stoics ever tried to establish systematically what kinds of formally valid non-indemonstrable arguments could be deduced or derived from their set of indemonstrables with the *themata*.

Related to this point is the fact that Stoic analysis was carried through with the arguments themselves, not with argument forms – although, of course, the analysis depends precisely on the form of the arguments. This appears to imply that analysis had to be carried out again and again from scratch, each time the (formal) validity of a non-indemonstrable argument was in question. But this need not have been so: the Stoics seem to have introduced certain meta-rules, which would state that if an argument is of such and such a form, it is a syllogism or can be analysed into indemonstrables in such and such a way (S. E. *PH* II 3 together with Orig. *Contra Celsum* VII 15.166–7). Moreover, sometimes the modes were employed in order to facilitate the reduction; that is, ordinal numbers were used as abbreviations for constituent assertibles (S. E. *M* VIII 234–6). Such abbreviation brings out the form of the argument and makes it easier to recognize which *thema* can be used.

How did Stoic analysis work in detail?[14] How were the *themata* and theorems applied to arguments? Let us look first at the first *thema*:

When from two (assertibles) a third follows, then from either of them together with the contradictory of the conclusion the contradictory of the other follows (Apul. *De int.* 191.6–10).

The wording of the rule leaves the premiss order undetermined. It can be presented formally as:

(T1) $P_1, P_2 \mid\!\!- P_3$

P_1, ctrd $P_3 \mid\!\!-$ ctrd P_2

[14] Warning: On the following pages the discussion gets a little more technical.

'ctrd' stands for 'contradictory', '|-' for 'therefore'; P_1, P_2 ... mark places for assertibles. In an application of the rule, the argument-to-be-analysed would occupy the bottom line, the syllogism into which it is analysed the top line. For instance, if we have a non-indemonstrable argument of the kind

p; not:q; therefore not: if p, q

this can be reduced to a first indemonstrable of the kind

If p, q; p; therefore q

by employing the first *thema* as follows: When from 'p' and 'if p, q' 'q' follows (this being the indemonstrable), then from 'p' and 'not: q' 'not: if p, q' follows (this being the non-indemonstrable argument). Or formalized:

$$\frac{\text{If p, q; p |- q}}{\text{p; not:q |- not: if p, q}}\ (T1)$$

Whenever this procedure leads to one of the five indemonstrables, the argument-to-be-analysed is a syllogism. Application of the rule to all possible kinds of simple non-indemonstrable arguments leads thus to the reduction of syllogisms of four further types. As we will see, the first *thema* can also be employed several times in the same reduction, or in combination with one or more of the other rules of analysis.

It is helpful to consider the meta-rule known as a 'dialectical theorem' before discussing the remaining three *themata*:

When we have (the) premisses which deduce some conclusion, we poten-tially have that conclusion too in those premisses, even if it isn't expressly stated. (S. E. *M* VIII 231)

This theorem presumably did the same work as the second, third, and fourth *themata* together. Plainly, as it stands, it doesn't fully determine a method of analysis. It is only a general presentation of a principle. But a passage in Sextus (S. E. *M* VIII 230–8) illustrates how the analysis works, by applying it to two arguments. In the second example, the analysis is carried out first with the mode of the argument, then by employing the argument itself. Let us look at the former, which begins by presenting the mode of the argument-to-be-analysed:

For this type of argument is composed of a second and a third indemonstrable, as one can learn from its analysis, which will become clearer if we use the mode for our exposition, which runs as follows:

If the first and the second, the third.
But not the third.
Moreover, the first.
Therefore not: the second.

For since we have a conditional with the conjunction of the first and the second as antecedent and with the third as consequent, and we also have the contradictory of the consequent, 'Not: the third', we will also deduce the contradictory of the antecedent, 'Therefore not: the first and the second', by a second indemonstrable. But in fact, this very proposition is contained potentially in the argument, since we have the premisses from which it can be deduced, although in the presentation of the argument it is omitted. By combining it with the remaining premiss, the first, we will have deduced the conclusion 'Therefore not: the second' by a third indemonstrable. Hence there are two indemonstrables, one of this kind

If the first and the second, the third.
But not: the third.
Therefore not: the first and the second.

which is a second indemonstrable; the other, which is a third indemonstrable, runs like this:

Not: the first and the second.
But the first.
Therefore not: the second.

Such is the analysis in the case of the mode, and there is an analogous analysis in the case of the argument (S. E. *M* VIII 235–7).

The general procedure of reduction with the dialectical theorem is then as follows: take any two of the premisses of the argument-to-be-analysed and try to deduce a conclusion from them, by forming with them an indemonstrable. Then take that 'potential' conclusion and look whether by adding any of the premisses, you can deduce another conclusion, again by forming an indemonstrable. (The old premisses are still in the game and can be taken again, if required, as is plain from Sextus' first example: S. E. *M* VIII 232–3.) Proceed in this manner until all premisses have been used at least once and the last assertible deduced is the original conclusion. In that case, you have shown that the argument-to-be-analysed is a syllogism.

Thus, the dialectical theorem turns out to be a rule for chain-arguments by which a complex non-indemonstrable is split into two component arguments. The theorem should suffice to analyse all composite arguments; that is, all arguments with any of the following as underlying or 'hidden' structures. (A triangle gives the form of a simple two-premiss argument with the letter at the bottom giving the place of the conclusion. $P_1 \ldots P_n$ give the places of the premisses; C that of the conclusion of the argument-to-be-analysed; P_n^* that of a premiss that is a 'potential conclusion' and hence doesn't show in the argument-to-be-analysed. The type of argument-to-be-analysed has been added underneath each time.)

Type (1)   (three premiss arguments)

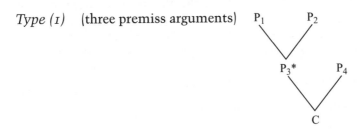

$P_1, P_2, P_4 \vdash C$

The argument in the above quotation, for instance, is of this type.

Type (2)   (four premiss arguments)

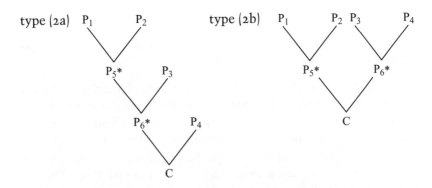

$P_1, P_2, P_3, P_4 \vdash C$

Expansions of these types are gained by inserting two-premiss arguments into the original argument in such a way that their conclusion is one of the formerly unasterisked premisses. These

conclusions then count as 'potential'; that is, do not appear in the
argument-to-be-analysed; they accordingly get an '*'. As is clear from
Sextus' first example of analysis (S. E. *M* VIII 232–3), the dialectical
theorem also covers inferences in which the same premiss is implicitly used more than once, but occurs only once in the original
argument. The most basic type of these is:

Type (3)

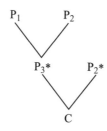

$P_1, P_2 \vdash C$
Sextus' first example, which is of the kind 'If p, if p, q; p ⊢ q', is of
this type. A more complex case is:

Type (4)

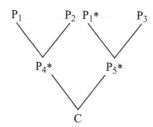

$P_1, P_2, P_3 \vdash C$
Again, all expansions and variations of these types, and moreover
all their combinations with Type (1), can be analysed by repeated
use of the theorem. If one takes together the first *thema* and the
dialectical theorem, with their help all non-indemonstrable Stoic
syllogisms of which we know can be analysed into Stoic indemonstrables.

   Next are the second, third, and fourth Stoic *themata*. Formulations of the third *thema* have survived in two sources (Simp. *Cael.*
237.2–4; Alex. *In Ar. An. pr.* 278.12–14). The second and fourth are
not handed down. However, a tentative reconstruction of them and
of the general method of analysis with the *themata* is possible since

there are a number of requirements that these three *themata* have to satisfy:

- The second, third, and fourth *themata* together should cover the same ground as the dialectical theorem.
- The *themata* have to be applicable, in the sense that by using them one can find out whether an argument is a syllogism.
- They have to be simple enough to be formulated in ordinary Greek.
- The second *thema*, possibly in tandem with the first, must reduce the indifferently concluding arguments and the arguments with two mode-premisses.
- The third and fourth *themata* should show some similarity or should be used together in some analyses (Galen *PHP* II 3.188).

The following is a reconstruction that satisfies these requirements.[15] One source presents the third *thema* thus:

When from two ⟨assertibles⟩ a third follows, and from the one that follows ⟨i.e., the third⟩ together with another, external assumption, another follows, then this other follows from the first two and the externally co-assumed one. (Simp. *Cael.* 237.2–4)

Thus, like the dialectical theorem, the third *thema* is a kind of chain-argument rule which allows one to break up a complex argument into two component arguments. Or formally: (P_1, P_2, ... give the places for non-external premisses; E, E_1, E_2 ... for external premisses; C for the conclusion of the argument-to-be-analysed).

$$\frac{P_1, P_2 \mid\text{-} P_3 \qquad P_3, E \mid\text{-} C}{P_1, P_2, E \mid\text{-} C}$$

For the analysis of arguments with more than three premisses, one needs an expanded version of the third *thema* in which one of the component arguments has more than two premisses. One obtains this if one modifies Simplicius' version in such a way that the second component argument can have more than one 'external premiss'. The expanded version then runs:

---

[15] This reconstruction is based on Bobzien (1996). For alternative reconstructions, see Mueller (1979), Ierodiakonou (1990), Mignucci (1993).

When from two assertibles a third follows, and from the third and one or more external assertibles another follows, then this other follows from the first two and those external(s).

Or formalized: (T3) $P_1P_2 \vdash P_3$ $P_3, E_1 \ldots E_n \vdash C$

$$P_1, P_2, E_1 \ldots E_n \vdash C$$

There are two types of composite arguments the reduction of which isn't covered by the third *thema*: first, those in which there are no 'external' premisses, but instead one of the premisses used in the first component argument is used again in the second component argument; second, those in which both a premiss of the first component argument and one or more external premisses are used in the second component argument. I conjecture that the remaining two *themata* covered these two cases. They hence could have run:

When from two assertibles a third follows, and from the third and one (or both) of the two another follows, then this other follows from the first two.

Formalized: (T2) $P_1, P_2 \vdash P_3$ $P_1, (P_2,) P_3 \vdash C$

$$P_1, P_2 \vdash C$$

And:

When from two assertibles a third follows, and from the third and one (or both) of the two and one (or more) external assertible(s) another follows, then this other follows from the first two and the external(s).

Formalized: (T4) $P_1, P_2 \vdash P_3$ $P_3, P_1, (P_2,) E_1 \ldots E_n \vdash C$

$$P_1, P_2, E_1 \ldots E_n \vdash C$$

Each of the second to fourth *themata* thus has a typical kind of argument to which it applies; but they can also be used in combination or more than once in one reduction. Going back to the types of arguments distinguished when discussing the dialectical theorem, one can see that arguments of Type (1) take the third *thema* once; those of Types (2a) and (2b) take it twice. More complex ones – without implicitly multiplied premisses – take it more often. Arguments of Type (3) take the second *thema* once; those of Type (4) take the fourth and third each once. More complex arguments may take combinations of the second, third, and fourth *themata*. Occasionally, the first *thema* is needed in addition. Taken together, the second, third, and fourth *themata* cover precisely the range of the dialectical theorem.

How were the *themata* applied? Before I describe the general method of analysis, here are a few examples. First, take again the second example from the Sextus passage (S. E. *M* VIII 230–8). The argument-to-be-analysed is of the following kind:

If both p and q, r; not:r; p |- not:q.

It has three premisses and takes the third *thema* once. By simply 'inserting' this argument into the *thema* we obtain:

When from two assertibles
[i.e., If both p and q, r; not:r]
a third follows
[i.e., not: both p and q (by a second indemonstrable)]
and from the third and an external one
[i.e., p]
another follows
[i.e., not: q (by a third indemonstrable)]
then this other
[i.e., not: q]
also follows from the two assertibles and the external one.

Or, using the formalized *thema*:

$$\frac{\text{If both p and q, r; not:r |- not:both p and q} \quad \text{Not:both p and q; p |- not:q}}{\text{If both p and q, r; not:r; p |- not:q}} \text{(T3)}$$

We obtain examples of the use of the second *thema* from some of the special types of non-indemonstrable arguments. Indifferently concluding arguments like:

Either p or q; p |- p

use the second *thema* once and reduce to one fourth and one fifth indemonstrable:

$$\frac{\text{Either p or q; p |- not:q} \quad \text{Either p or q; not:q |- p}}{\text{Either p or q; p |- p}} \text{(T2)}$$

Syllogisms with two mode-premisses like those of the kind:

If p, q; If p, not:q; therefore not:p

take the first *thema* twice, the second once and reduce to two first indemonstrables. The analysis works again step by step from the bottom line (a) to the top line (d):

(d) p; if p, not:q |- not:q
$$\overline{\hspace{6cm}} \ (T_1)$$

(c) If p, q; p |- q   p, q |- not: if p, not:q
$$\overline{\hspace{6cm}} \ (T_2)$$

(b) If p, q; p |- not: if p, not:q
$$\overline{\hspace{4.5cm}} \ (T_1)$$

(a) If p, q; If p, not:q |- not:p

The *general method* of analysis into indemonstrables by *themata* appears then to have worked as follows: In a very first step, you check whether the argument-to-be-analysed is an indemonstrable. If so, it is valid. If not, you next try to choose from the set of premisses of the argument-to-be-analysed two from which a conclusion can be deduced by forming an indemonstrable with them. If the argument-to-be-analysed is a syllogism, this conclusion, together with the remaining premiss(es) (if there are any), and/or one or both of the premisses that have been used already, entails the original conclusion – either by forming an indemonstrable or by forming an argument that by use of the four *themata* can be analysed into one or more indemonstrables. Next you see whether one of the remaining premisses plus this conclusion yields the premisses to another indemonstrable (in which case you apply the third *thema*); if there are no remaining premisses, or none of them works, you find out whether one of the premisses already used in the first step is such a premiss (in which case you apply the second or fourth *thema*). If the second component argument thus formed is an indemonstrable too, and all premisses have been used at least once and the last conclusion is the original conclusion, the analysis is finished, the argument-to-be-analysed a syllogism. If not, the same procedure is repeated with the argument which isn't an indemonstrable (i.e., the second component argument, which has the original conclusion as conclusion); and so forth until the premisses of the second component argument imply the original conclusion by forming an indemonstrable with it. If at any point in the analysis no indemonstrable can be formed, the first *thema* might help: namely, if the negation of the conclusion would produce a premiss you need; that is, a premiss that together with one of the available premisses makes up a pair of premisses for an indemonstrable. If at any step the application of none of the *themata* leads to two premisses that can be used in an indemonstrable, the argument is not a syllogism.

This method of reduction is practicable and easy. All one has to know is the *themata* and the five types of indemonstrables, plus those four types of simple arguments which can be reduced to indemonstrables by the first *thema*. The number of steps one has to go through is finite; they are not very many, even in complex cases. The method appears to be effective.

Stoic syllogistic is a system consisting of five basic types of syllogisms and four argumental rules by which all other syllogisms can be reduced to those of the basic types (DL VII 78, cf. S. E. *PH* II 156–7; 194). The Stoics didn't explicitly claim any completeness for their system, but their claim of the reducability of all non-indemonstrable syllogisms can be taken as a statement of completeness of sorts. It is also plausible to assume that the Stoics endorsed some pretechnical notion of syllogismhood, and that the indemonstrables plus *themata* were understood to 'capture' this notion; perhaps also to make it more precise. This leaves us with the problem of how we can find the independent Stoic criteria for syllogismhood; that is, how we can decide which features of the Stoic system preceded their choice of logical rules and which are simply a result of their introducing these rules. However, there is little evidence about what was the Stoic pretechnical notion of syllogismhood, and we cannot hope to decide whether the Stoics achieved completeness on their own terms. All we can do is determine some features of the Stoic system that are relevant to its completeness.

The Stoic system shared the following condition of validity with modern semantic interpretations of formal logic: It is necessary for the validity of an argument that it isn't the case that its premisses are true and its conclusion is false. Accordingly, it is a necessary condition for formal validity (i.e., syllogismhood) that no syllogism or argument of a valid form has true premisses and a false conclusion. To this we can add a couple of necessary conditions for Stoic syllogismhood which are not requirements for formal validity in the modern sense, and which show that the class of Stoic syllogisms can at most be a proper subclass of valid arguments in the modern sense.

First, there is a formal condition which restricts the class of syllogisms not by denying validity to certain arguments, but by denying the status of argumenthood to certain compounds of assertibles: The Stoic concept of argument is narrower than that of modern logic in that an argument must have a minimum of two premisses and a conclusion. Stoic syllogistic considers only arguments of the form

Δ ⊢ A

in which Δ is a set of premisses with at least two (distinct) elements. Stoic syllogistic doesn't deal with arguments of the forms

⊢ A   A ⊢ B   or Δ ⊢.

There is also no one-to-one correspondence between valid arguments and logically true conditionals. Such a correspondence exists only between a proper subclass of the latter – those which have the form 'If both A and B and…, then C' – and valid arguments.

Second, there is a restriction of validity through the requirement of non-redundancy of the premisses: An argument is invalid owing to redundancy if it has one or more premisses that are added to it from outside and superfluously (S. E. *M* II 431). For cases of non-indemonstrable arguments, one may interpret the clause 'from outside and superfluously' as meaning that there is no deduction in which this premiss, together with the others of the argument, entails the conclusion. The requirement of non-redundancy means that the following kinds of arguments count as invalid:

p; q; therefore p
If p, q; p; r; therefore q

although they are valid in all standard propositional calculi.

We can now show that the Stoic system of syllogisms captures the pretechnical elements of syllogismhood as determined by the requirements stated. First, no one- or zero-premiss arguments are reducible, since every indemonstrable has two premisses; and every *thema* can be applied only to arguments with two or more premisses. Second, redundant arguments cannot be reduced: The indemonstrables have no 'redundant' premisses, and the *themata* require that all premisses of the argument-to-be-analysed are components of the indemonstrables into which it is analyzed – either as premiss or as negation of a conclusion. So far then, at least, Stoic syllogistic coincides with what may have been their pretechnical notion of syllogismhood.

7. ARGUMENTS VALID IN THE SPECIFIC SENSE

Finally, we come to the second group of valid arguments distinguished by the Stoics, those called 'valid in the specific sense' (DL VII 78–9). The surviving information on these arguments is sparse and many details are under dispute. At least two subclasses were distinguished. One was the subsyllogistic arguments (*hyposyllogistikoi logoi*), another was the arguments named 'unmethodically concluding' (*amethodôs perainontes*); there may have been others. The Stoics held that all valid arguments were constructed by means of the indemonstrable syllogisms (*ibid.*). If we take this at face value, the validity of the specifically valid arguments may have been justified by the validity of syllogisms. One would expect this justification to vary from subclass to subclass.

Subsyllogistic arguments differ from the corresponding syllogisms only in that one (or more) of their component assertibles, although being equivalent to those in the syllogism, diverge from them in their linguistic form (Galen *Institutio logica* XIX 6). Examples are of the following type:

'p' follows from 'q'; but p; therefore q

instead of a first indemonstrable. We may assume that the reason why subsyllogistic arguments weren't syllogisms was that they didn't share their canonical form. This distinction displays an awareness of the difference between object- and meta-language: A conditional is indeed not the same as a statement that one assertible follows from another. The validity of a subsyllogistic argument may have been established by constructing a corresponding syllogism and pointing out the equivalence.

The following is a Stoic example for an unmethodically concluding argument:

You say that it is day.
But you speak truly.
Therefore it is day. (Galen *Institutio logica* XVII 2)

This isn't a syllogism. It is neither an indemonstrable nor can it be reduced to one, since it contains no non-simple assertible as component. What was the reason for the validity of such arguments? Perhaps they were dubbed 'unmethodically concluding' because there is no formal method of showing their validity; but even then their validity should have been justified somehow – and if we take the remark at DL VII 79 seriously, these justifications should have involved some suitably related syllogisms. But we have no direct evidence that suggests a way of detecting 'corresponding syllogisms', as in the case of the subsyllogisticals.

Several other arguments were considered valid by some Stoics; some of these may have counted as specifically valid arguments. First, the single-premiss arguments (*monolêmmatoi*): The orthodox Stoic view was that arguments must have at least two premisses. However, Antipater admitted single-premiss arguments, and he presumably regarded at least some as valid. If we trust Apuleius, Antipater adduced arguments like the following:

You see.
Therefore you are alive. (Apul. *De int.* 184.16–23)

What reasons he had for admitting these, we are not told. It is unlikely that Antipater proposed that they were syllogisms. For they are not formally valid. Antipater may have regarded them as unmethodically concluding, perhaps with a nonexplicit assumption of the kind 'If someone sees, that one is alive.' Second, there are the arguments with an indefinite leading premiss and a definite co-assumption mentioned previously in the context of non-simple assertibles. A typical example is:

If someone walks that one moves.
This person walks.
Therefore this person moves.

Despite the similarity, this isn't a straightforward first indemonstrable. How did the Stoics justify their validity? Presumably by referring to the truth-conditions of the leading premiss. Since its truth implies the truth of all subordinated assertibles, one can always derive the particular conditional one needs ('If this one walks, this one moves') and thus form the needed syllogism – in this case, a first indemonstrable. This relation between the indefinite conditional and the corresponding definite ones may have counted as an implicit assumption by which validity was justified (but which, if added, wouldn't make the argument formally valid).

5 Stoic Natural Philosophy (Physics and Cosmology)

I. INTRODUCTION

According to Diogenes Laertius, most of the Stoics – beginning with Zeno of Citium – divided philosophical doctrine into three parts: one physical, one ethical, and one logical. Diogenes also reports three homely similes concerning the relation among these parts of philosophy: (1) philosophy is like an animal, with logic corresponding to the bones and sinews, ethics to the more fleshy parts, and physics to the soul; (2) philosophy is like an egg, with logic corresponding to 'the outside' (shell), ethics to 'what is in between' (the white), and physics to 'the innermost part' (yolk); and (3) philosophy is like a productive field, with logic corresponding to the enclosing fence, ethics to the crop, and physics to the earth or trees.[1]

Whatever the precise import of these similes might have been, it seems clear that the Stoics held that physical doctrine stands in an intimate relation to ethics. For the Stoics, the end of human life is 'to live conformably with nature' (*to homologoumenon têi phusei zên*).[2] Consequently, physics – that part of philosophy that pertains to nature and that reveals the import of living 'conformably with nature' – obviously has ethical import. Logically distinct from this aspect of the relation of physical doctrine to ethics is a second point of connection between the two: the common contemporary assumption that it is both possible and desirable to undertake a 'value-neutral' investigation of nature is quite foreign to Stoic thought. Indeed, it is common to find what might be termed large-scale Stoic philosophical themes influencing physical doctrine – including some

[1] DL VII 40.
[2] DL VII 87.

124

of the rather technical aspects of Stoic physical doctrine. In particular, the Stoic themes of the unity and cohesion of the cosmos and
of an all-encompassing divine reason controlling the cosmos are of
fundamental importance to Stoic physics.

2. WHAT PHYSICS IS

Diogenes reports that the Stoics divided their physical doctrine into
topics pertaining to bodies, principles (*archai*), elements (*stoicheia*),
gods, boundaries or limits (*perata*), place, and void. This, he says, was
a 'specific' classification of physical topics. A 'generic' classification
distinguished physical topics pertaining to the cosmos, those pertaining to the elements (*stoicheia* again), and those pertaining to the
investigation of causes (*aitiologia*).[3] It is thus clear that the Stoics
conceived of physics or natural philosophy more broadly than one
characterization of it by Aristotle – that is, the conceptual investigation of *kinêsis* (motion or change) and of whatever is implied by
change (e.g., magnitude, place, and time).[4] As a major subdivision of
philosophy, Stoic physics includes not only what later came to be
called 'natural philosophy', but also cosmology and topics in 'first
philosophy' or metaphysics.

With respect to the former, 'specific' classificatory schema, the
distinction between principles and elements may initially seem puzzling since '*archai*' and '*stoicheia*' are not infrequently used as synonyms – as in Aristotle's frequent characterization of the Presocratic
philosophers' quest for *archai kai stoicheia* and in the geometrical
sense of 'elements' (*stoicheia*). It is widely attested that the two Stoic
archai – which will be discussed more later – were an active principle
(*to poioun*) identified with reason and god (*inter alia*), and a passive
principle (*to paschon*) identified with unqualified substance (*apoios
ousia*) or matter. Diogenes reports that the principal distinction that

---

[3] DL VII 132. The import of the distinction between the 'specific' and 'generic'
classification is far from obvious. In Ch. 8 of this volume, Brunschwig suggests
that perhaps the specific classification 'considers physics as a self-contained *eidos*,
whereas the [generic classification] considers it as part of a broader *genos*,' and thus
envisions that 'some of the topics in the 'generic' division, e.g., cosmology and aitiol-
ogy, are shared among physics and other disciplines, like astronomy and medicine'.
I certainly have not been able to come up with a more plausible account of the
distinction.

[4] See Aristotle, *Phys.* III 4.202b30–1.

the Stoics drew between *archai* and *stoicheia* is that whereas the former principles are ungenerated and indestructible, the latter elements – which are identified in terms of the traditional categories of fire, water, air, and earth – are destroyed in the world conflagration or *ekpurôsis*.[5] Principles, in common Stoic usage, are the more basic ontological concepts, whereas elements occupy a more derivative cosmological (and cosmogonical) position. But there are a number of problems, discussed in a later section, with respect to the relation between principles and elements.

The Stoics also recognized a distinction between cosmological issues of legitimate concern to mathematicians; that is, issues of what might be termed mathematical astronomy on the one hand[6] and cosmological issues properly investigated by physicists as such on the other: for example, what the 'substance' (*ousia*) of the cosmos is, whether the sun and stars are constituted of matter and form, whether or not the cosmos is generated, whether or not it is ensouled, whether or not it is destructible, and whether it is providentially directed.[7] A similar distinction between a mathematical and a non-mathematical investigation of causes is reported by Diogenes. Optics, catoptrics, and investigation of the causes of clouds, thunder, rainbows, halos, and comets are adduced as examples of the former.[8] It is not known whether 'mathematical physics' was practiced among the Stoic philosophers themselves earlier than Posidonius. We do have considerable evidence that Posidonius, in the first half of the first-century B.C., was involved in an extraordinarily wide variety of scholarly, historical, and mathematical and scientific pursuits.[9]

That bodies, principles, elements, gods, place, and void should have been regarded as principal topics in Stoic physics is not surprising. These are all topics having either a self-evident importance or a well-established pedigree in the natural philosophy of Greek

[5] DL VII 134.
[6] See Ch. 13, Jones, this volume.
[7] DL VII 132–133.
[8] DL VII 133.
[9] Among many other accomplishments, Posidonius wrote a book in defense of Euclidean geometry against the attacks on geometry by the Epicurean Zeno of Sidon. With respect to Posidonius' lost book *On Ocean*, I. G. Kidd comments that 'Posidonius' book appears to have covered an astonishing span, not only in content but also in form, ranging from mathematical theory to the vivid narrative of Eudoxus' (Kidd [1988] vol. II(i), 219–220).

antiquity (or both). However, it is perhaps surprising or even puzzling that *perata* (limits or boundaries) should be accorded such prominence. There is more discussion on this matter toward the end of this chapter.

3. THE ROLE OF PRIOR COMMITMENTS IN STOIC PHYSICS

The Stoic themes of the unity and cohesion of the cosmos and of an all-encompassing divine reason controlling that cosmos may be regarded as the principal controlling 'prior commitments' of Stoic physics, to borrow a concept that Lang applies to Aristotle's physics.[10] These themes do much, in other words, to shape the types of issues and problems that Stoic physics takes to be important, as well as the substance of what the Stoics have to say about these issues and problems. Of course, this influence is not a matter of completely setting the agenda of Stoic physics. But a case can be made that prior commitments are even more important for Stoic physics than they are for the physics of Aristotle.

For Aristotle, not only human (sense) experience in the form of *ta phainomena*, but also *ta endoxa* (how 'we', the many, as well as the few wise ones among us, think and talk about the world around us) exercise an important regulative function in natural philosophy. The Stoics, however, apparently were much more ready to depart from customary modes of thought and speech. Critics from outside the school, such as Plutarch, make much of the views of the Stoics that contradict 'common conceptions'. Cicero notes that certain Stoic doctrines, which he calls '*admirabilia contraque opinionem omnium*' ('astonishing and contrary to the beliefs of all people'), are termed '*paradoxa*' by the Stoics themselves.[11] While the *paradoxa* discussed by Cicero are ethical and epistemological, there is certainly evidence for a similar approach by the Stoics to physical topics – for example, Chrysippus' claim, in connection with the doctrine of total blending (*krasis di' holôn*), that a little wine thrown into the sea will interpenetrate with the whole sea.[12] In fact, Plutarch's spokesperson, Diadumenus in *De communibus notitiis adversus*

[10] Lang (1998), 280 *et passim*.
[11] Cicero, *Paradoxa Stoicorum* 4.
[12] Plutarch, *Comm. not.* 1078e.

Stoicos, emphasizes that the physical doctrines of the Stoics are fully as much at odds with 'common conceptions' (*koinai prolêpseis*) as are their ethical doctrines.[13] It is not clear that the Stoics, such as Chrysippus, who are Plutarch's targets, would have agreed with this assessment. However, a case can be made that one consequence of the relative detachment by the Stoics of physical inquiry from common conceptions is the enlargement of the role of prior commitments in natural philosophy. Moreover, an additional factor that could heighten the influence of prior commitments in the investigation of nature is the fact that, for the Stoics, knowledge of the natural world is not sought as an end in itself, but rather as enabling us to live in conformity with nature.

Following is a discussion on this influence with respect to certain key features of Stoic physical doctrine. This is certainly not the only way to approach Stoic physics. Nor, perhaps, is it the most discriminating approach: some subtleties and difficulties are glossed over, as are some significant differences among the doctrines of individual Stoic philosophers. But it is hoped that the method is particularly useful for a brief introductory and protreptic discussion such as the present one.

4. CORPOREALISM AND VITALISM

Hahm begins the first chapter of his *The Origins of Stoic Cosmology* with the observation that 'no idea is more deeply ingrained in Stoic philosophy than the conviction that everything real is corporeal'.[14] This seems quite correct, but two qualifications probably should be added. The first is that 'everything real' here designates what exists (*ta onta*). The Stoics had a wider category of 'something' (*ti*) that included, in addition to what exists (bodies), incorporeals or 'subsistents' (*ta huphestôta*) such as void, place, time, and what is 'sayable' (*ta lekta*: meanings).[15] The second qualification is that the Stoic conception of the corporeality of the cosmos does not at all connote the corporeal world of inert matter of seventeenth- and eighteenth-century natural philosophy, aptly described by Randall as a world consisting solely of 'solid, hard, massy particles, of

---

[13] *Comm. not.* 1073d.
[14] Hahm (1977), 3.
[15] See Ch. 8, Brunschwig, this volume.

substances connected by mechanical causation.'[16] The Stoics, on the contrary, followed the precedent of various Presocratics and of Plato in holding that the 'whole cosmos is a living being (or animal: zôion), ensouled and rational, having as its ruling principle (hêgemonikon) aether [typically equated with fire by the Stoics]'.[17] According to Chrysippus and Posidonius, 'reason (nous) extends to every part of it, just as soul does with respect to us'.[18] Also quite unremarkable is the Stoic doctrine that the cosmos is one, limited, and spherical. Like Aristotle, they held that it contains no void. But they adduced as the reason for this the 'conspiration' or 'breathing together' (sumpnoia) and 'tension' (suntonia) binding together heavenly and terrestrial things.[19]

What is most remarkable about this 'vitalism' is that the Stoics evidently insisted that the active, life-giving, rational, creative, and directive principle of the cosmos is just as corporeal as is the passive, 'material' principle. According to the report of Aristocles (itself reported by Eusebius), Zeno of Citium (like Heraclitus) held that fire is the *stoicheion* of everything, and (like Plato) he held that the *archai* of fire are matter and god; 'but he [Zeno] says that both are bodies, the active and the passive principle, while [Plato] says that the first active cause is immaterial'.[20] Origen also comments on the corporeality of the 'god of the Stoics', attributing to the Stoics the doctrine that, during the periodic conflagration (ekpurôsis) of the cosmos, 'the ruling part [i.e., god] is the whole substance', but during the intervening cosmic cycle (diakosmêsis) the ruling part 'exists in a part of it'.[21] Origen here refers to the distinctive Stoic doctrine of cosmic cycles. According to Diogenes Laertius, god, 'being the "demiurge" of the cosmic cycle, in certain periods of time consumes the whole substance [sc., of the cosmos] into himself and then again brings it forth from himself'.[22] Thus, god as *dêmiourgos* or craftsman is immanent in the cosmos as its active, rational, *and corporeal* principle, and is particularly identified with the creative fire (pur technikon)

---

[16] Randall (1962), Vol. 1, 60.
[17] DL VII 139.
[18] DL VII 138.
[19] DL VII 140.
[20] Aristocles *apud* Eusebius, *Praeparatio evangelica* XV = SVF 1.98.
[21] Origen, *Contra Celsum* IV 14 = SVF 2.1052.
[22] DL VII 137.

from which the world cycle arises and into which it periodically returns.

The Stoic conception of the active principle of the cosmos as corporeal elicited strong objections from later philosophers. According to one such objection, versions of which are found in Plutarch and Plotinus, the Stoics' identification of god with 'intellectual body' or '*nous* in matter' makes god into a composite of form and matter and thus compromises the status of God as a simple *first* principle, or *archê*.[23] Thus, Plutarch concludes that

if reason and matter are one and the same, [the Stoics] have not correctly defined matter as irrational. But if they are different, god would be a sort of trustee of both and not simple but a composite thing – corporeality from matter added to rationality.[24]

As Plotinus' version of the argument makes clear, the underlying assumption is that 'body comes to be from matter and form'.[25] However, there is little reason to believe that the Stoics would have accepted this presupposition.[26] The common Stoic definitions of a body, 'that which is extended in the three dimensions of length, breadth, and depth'[27] and 'extension in three dimensions along with resistance (*antitupia*)',[28] do not appear to imply hylomorphism in anything like the Aristotelian sense. In fact, the Stoics argued – in the words of Hahm – that 'if the constituent material of a thing is a body, the thing itself is a body'.[29] They seem to have employed this principle to conclude that qualities of corporeal things are themselves corporeal.[30]

[23] Plutarch, *Comm. not.* 1085b.
[24] *Comm. not.* 1085c.
[25] Plotinus, *Enneades* VI 1.26.12.
[26] In the words of M. Lapidge, 'the inseparability of *theos* and *hulê* is a feature of Stoic cosmology which cannot be too strongly emphasized: it is asserted by Alexander of Aphrodisias, Origen, Proclus, and Syrianus. Calcidius too emphasizes this feature of Stoic monism at length' (Lapidge [1973], 243–4).
[27] DL VII 135.
[28] Galen, *Quod qualitates incorporeae sint* 10 = SVF 2.381.
[29] Hahm (1977), 4.
[30] There is some evidence (e.g., SVF 2.376 and 379) for a Stoic doctrine according to which a quality is 'matter existing or being disposed in a certain way' (*hulê pôs echousa*). However, as Brunschwig has emphasized to me, the former passage (from Plotinus) is quite polemical and the latter (from Alexander of Aphrodisias) is ambivalent about whether the Stoic doctrine is that quality is *hulê pôs echousa* or is that quality is *pneuma pôs echon*. A problem here is that Simplicius (*In Ar. Cat.*

Similar considerations apply to an argument against an unending chain of movers attributed to the Stoics by Sextus Empiricus. The consequence of this argument is that there is a 'power that is, in itself, self-moving – which would be divine and eternal...So the power that moves matter and imposes on it, in an orderly way, generations and changes is eternal. Consequently, it would be god'.[31] Notable in its absence is any hint of the Aristotelian claim that a self-moving mover cannot be an *ultimate* mover. In the *Physics* Aristotle argues that

it is necessary, therefore, that what which moves itself consist of (i) an un-moved mover, and (ii) what is moved but not necessarily a mover, both of which are in contact the one with the other.[32]

And in *Metaphysics* XII, he draws the conclusion that an argument against an unending chain of movers has as a consequence that 'there exists some substance that is eternal, unmoved, and separate (*kechôrismenê*) from sensible things...It has been shown that this substance cannot have any magnitude but, rather, is partless and indivisible'.[33]

From the Stoic perspective, the '*kechôrismenê*' ('separate') would be especially crucial here. The Stoics surely would have resisted any argument for a first mover that is *kechôrismenon* from the cosmos, just as they would have resisted the arguments by Plutarch and Plotinus that would entail that god – or the form or *hêgemonikon* of god – exists, in the words of Plotinus, as an 'incorporeal creator' (*to poiêtikon asômaton*).[34] The reason for this resistance lies in the Stoic conviction that something incorporeal cannot act nor be acted upon. Cicero reports that Zeno denied that 'anything could be acted upon by that which is incorporeal – as Xenocrates and other older thinkers as well had said of the soul; rather, it is not at all possible

66–67 = SVF 2.369) reports a Stoic schema of categories that appears to distinguish qualities from *pôs echonta* (dispositions) and *pros ti pôs echonta* (relative dispositions). On the other hand, Simplicius (*In Ar. Cat.* 214 = SVF 2.391) also reports that the Stoics refer to qualities as '*hekta*' which, of course, comes from the same verb (*echein*) as does 'disposition' or 'being disposed is such-and-such a way' (*pôs echon*). The principal point, I believe, is the refusal of the Stoics to admit an 'ontological separation' between the corporeal 'subject' of a quality and the 'quality itself'.

[31] S. E., *M* IX 76 = SVF 2.311.
[32] Aristotle, *Phys.* VIII 5.258a18–21.
[33] Aristotle, *Meta.* XII 7.1073a3–7.
[34] Plotinus, *Enn.* VI 1.26.14–15.

for what is not body to act upon anything or to be acted upon'.[35] This stricture, in fact, becomes a common Stoic characterization of the corporeal, 'that which either acts or is acted upon', which Hahm rightly characterizes as 'the most important' Stoic account of body.[36]

Although the evidence is by no means conclusive, it seems likely that the Stoics had taken to heart Peripatetic worries about the causal efficacy of 'separate' Platonic forms. But an Aristotelian *incorporeal* unmoved mover that is *kechôrismenon* from what it moves might well seem to generate a similar problem, particularly if Aristotle's explanation, '[a final cause] moves as the object of desire but other things move by being moved',[37] is not deemed to constitute a satisfactory account of the causal action of something.

The history of non-monistic ontologies, such as the development of various dualisms in the seventeenth and eighteenth centuries, records the difficulties of adequately explaining the interaction of two *toto caelo* different kinds of entity. In fact, developments such as Malebranche's occasionalism suggest that such a dualism tends to issue not in a picture of a *single* world order, but rather that of multiple coexistent world orders more or less detached from one another. If Aristotle is thought to have attempted to unify the separate world orders of Platonic dualism, it is easy to interpret the Stoics as beginning with the assumption that Aristotelianism had not gone far enough in this direction. Hahm comments that

obviously, what the Stoics have done is . . . to distribute [Aristotle's] four causes between two entities, assigning the material cause to one entity [the passive *archê*], and motive, formal, and final causes to the other [the active *archê*].[38]

Since the active principle is corporeal, the Stoic prior commitment to the unity and cohesion of the cosmos is preserved. There are no 'separate' principles or causes the connection of which to the material world order might prove problematic.

The causal efficacy of the active principle is certainly exercised locally, not merely by 'superficial' contact but by a sort of total permeation and pervasion. According to Alexander of Aphrodisias, the

---

[35] Cicero, *Acad.* I 39.
[36] Hahm (1977), 11. See Brunschwig, Ch. 8, this volume.
[37] Aristotle, *Meta.* XII 7 1072b3-4 (translating the emendation of Ross).
[38] Hahm (1977), 44.

Stoics say that 'god is mixed with matter, permeating (*dihêkonta*) through all of it, shaping and forming it, and in this way making the cosmos'.[39] And Chrysippus is described by Diogenes Laertius as holding that '*nous* permeates (*dihêkontos*) through every part of [the cosmos], just as the soul does with respect to us, although more in some places and less in others'.[40] As the paradigm of corporeal causation, then, the action of the active, productive principle is local and, in a sense, 'by contact.' But the contact is 'contact throughout' and is not the 'mechanical' efficient causation associated with seventeenth- and eighteenth-century conceptions of corporeal causation: one billiard ball colliding with another or the intermeshing gears of a clock. A biological rather than a mechanical picture of corporeal causation is a more appropriate illustration of the Stoic concept: the corporeal and local but pervasive action of the bodily humors or fluids as described, for example, in the Hippocratic treatise *De natura hominis*.[41]

5. PRINCIPLES, ELEMENTS, GOD, AND WORLD CYCLES

The fundamental prior commitment to cosmic unity and cohesion is certainly manifest in the Stoic account of the constituents of the cosmos. However, there are opposing tensions which, in combination with the dearth of fragmentary evidence we possess concerning Stoic physical doctrine, give rise to interpretive problems.

Several problems arise, to begin with, concerning the relation between the apparently more ontologically fundamental principles (*archai*) and the apparently less ontologically fundamental elements (*stoicheia*). One obvious problem pertains to the status of fire. It is sometimes identified with the active principle or god and designated 'creative fire' (*pur technikon*). Plutarch quotes from the first book of Chrysippus' *On Providence*:

When the cosmos is fiery throughout, it is simply its own soul and controlling principle (*hêgemonikon*). But when it has changed into water and the soul that is retained in it, it in a certain way has changed into body and soul so as to be compounded of them; then it has another structure.[42]

---

[39] Alexander of Aphrodisas, *Mixt.* 11 = SVF 2.310.
[40] DL VII 138.
[41] *Oeuvres Complètes d'Hippocrate*, ed. É. Littré, Vol. 6 (1849; repr. 1962), 32–68.
[42] Plutarch, *St. rep.* 1053b = SVF 2.605.

Similarly, Origen reports that 'the god of the Stoics has the whole of substance (*tên holên ousian*) as its controlling principle, whenever there is the conflagration. But when there is the world cycle (*diakosmêsis*), he comes to be in part of it'.[43] The problem is that other sources indicate that god or the active principle 'generated, first of all, the four elements fire, water, air, and earth'.[44] As a created and apparently destructible element, fire would then have a subsidiary ontological and cosmogonical status. A distinction reported in Stobaeus seems to be intended to deal with the problem: 'there are two kinds of fire: one is uncreative and changes its nourishment [i.e., fuel] into itself; the other is creative, the cause of growth and preservation, as it does in plants and animals, where it is their "nature" (*phusis*) and soul. This is the sort of fire that is the substance of the stars'.[45]

A further problem with respect to the role of principles versus elements is that 'breath' or *pneuma* is frequently accorded an active, directive function with respect to natural processes. *Pneuma* is frequently characterized as constituted of the elements of fire and air. According to one account, it is identified with the 'stable condition' (*hexis*) that constitutes the characteristic nature of inanimate things – also with the 'nature' or *phusis* of plants, with the soul of animals, and with the rational soul of humans.[46] In an account given by Nemesius, this is explicated in terms of a 'tensile motion' (*tonikê kinêsis*) 'which moves simultaneously inwards and outwards, the outward movement producing quantities and qualities and the inward one unity and substance'.[47] In his *Physics of the Stoics*, Sambursky has interpreted this Stoic concept as an anticipation of the later conception of 'force field' in Western physics,[48] a reading that has not received universal approbation. But Sambursky is surely correct in emphasizing the cosmological role of the 'pneumalike *tonos* [in making] the cosmos into a single cohesive unit'.[49]

---

[43] Origen, *Contra Celsum* IV 14 = SVF 2.1052.
[44] DL VII 136.
[45] Stobaeus, *Ecl.* I 25.3 = SVF 1.120.
[46] See Philo of Alexandria, *Quod deus sit immutabilis* 35 = SVF 2.458.
[47] Nemesius of Emesa, *De natura hominis* 70–71 (in translation of Long and Sedley [1987], Vol. 1, 47J, 283).
[48] Sambursky (1959), 31–32.
[49] Sambursky (1959), 5. See Clement of Alexandria, *Strom.* V 8 = SVF 2.447; and Alexander of Aphrodisias, *Mixt.* 10 = SVF 2.441.

Although the details are probably forever lost, it seems clear that the Stoic *pneumatikos tonos* functions, in part, as a technical expression of the fundamental Stoic prior commitment to cosmic unity and coherence.

However, the problem remains that *pneuma* seems often to function in much the way that the active principle (creative fire or god) does – whereas its ontological status appears to be not even that of an element, but rather a synthesis of elements. Part of the problem here – as with respect to the ontological status of fire – may be the exiguous quantity and polemical quality of our evidence. Part of the problem may be differences, now difficult to reconstruct accurately, among various Stoic thinkers. Yet it seems reasonable to suppose that a third part of the problem is that of assimilating pre-existing traditions of natural philosophy and physical explanation into the monistic ontological framework demanded by fundamental Stoic commitments to cosmic unity and cohesion.

One such earlier tradition is that of the four elements or 'roots' – fire, air, water, and earth. For the Stoics, these are certainly not 'elemental' in the sense that each is a fundamental, *sui generis* kind of matter, which is incapable of being transformed into or coming-to-be out of any of the other four elements. But neither were the elements 'elemental', in this rather strong sense, for either Plato or Aristotle. According to the doctrine of Aristotle's *De generatione et corruptione* II 3, each of the four elements is the combination of one each of the opposing pairs of qualities, cold/hot and wet/dry: earth is cold and dry, water cold and wet, air hot and wet, and fire hot and dry. In *Meteorologica* IV, Aristotle characterizes hot and cold as active, wet and dry as passive qualities, commenting that the 'congealing' (*sunkritikon*) for which the hot and the cold are responsible is a way of being active.[50]

According to Diogenes Laertius, the Stoics associated fire with 'the hot', water with 'the wet', air with 'the cold', and earth with 'the dry'.[51] They too apparently distinguished active (*drastika*) and passive elements: air and fire are active, earth and water are passive.[52] It transpires that, in terms of the Stoic pairings of the qualitative opposites with the elements, this schema makes cold and hot active, wet

---

[50] *Meteor.* IV 1.378b21–23.
[51] DL VII 136.
[52] Nemesius, *De nat. hom.* 164 = SVF 2.418.

and dry passive – just as Aristotle had done in the *Meteorologica*. According to Aristotle's more complex pairings between qualities and elements, active and passive qualities are distributed over all four elements. The change made by the Stoics allows them to associate the active principles of cold and hot – which, as Galen points out, are particularly appropriate active principles if one tends to think of change in terms of alteration of density or rarefaction and contraction[53] – with the elements fire and air, of which *pneuma* or 'hot breath' is constituted. It seems plausible that the Stoics adapted Aristotelian element theory to make it better conform to the doctrine of the agency of *pneumatikos tonos*. However, the relation between *pneuma* and 'creative fire' remains obscure. It may be that, as Lapidge has suggested, the former actually replaced the latter as an account of the cosmic active principle or aspect.[54] Whatever the case, it seems clear that, despite the disdain of their critics, the Stoics wished to maintain the corporeality of the cosmic active principle.

As the Eleatics had demonstrated, it is exceptionally difficult to 'do cosmology' with a rigorously monistic vocabulary – whether or not the monism in question is materialistic. This difficulty might call into question the very coherence of the enterprise. But the Stoics did not seem to worry too much about the issue and chose, instead, to conscript the dualistic or pluralistic vocabulary of traditional Greek cosmology, medicine, and theology. Once one, as a Stoic, has come to understand the essential unity and cohesion of 'the whole', it might seem considerably less significant which of the following terms one uses to designate the 'active aspect' of that essentially corporeal whole: *pur, to hêgemonikon, pneuma, theos, nous, sperma, hexis,* or *tonikê kinêsis*. Although there are contextual differences, subtle or not so subtle, among these terms, there is a sense in which one is referring to the same (corporeal) thing or 'stuff' by all of them; and one is connoting that stuff under its active aspect.[55]

---

[53] Galen, *De naturalibus facultatibus* 106 = SVF 2.406.

[54] Lapidge suggests that Chrysippus introduced *pneuma* as active principle or 'aspect' of the cosmos, perhaps partly to resolve cosmological problems in the thought of Zeno and Cleanthes: 'It will be seen at once that the adoption of *pneuma* as central agent in the Stoic cosmology would cause the distinctions we have been considering – that between *archê* and *stoicheion*, and that between *pur technikon* and *pur atechnon* – to be abandoned' (Lapidge [1973], 273).

[55] This is a feature of what some contemporary scholars have termed Stoic 'nominalism'. In particular, Stoic monistic materialism virtually guarantees that, in many

Another illustration of Stoic accommodation of ontological monism to more conventional ways of thinking and speaking about reality is found in one feature of the Stoic doctrine of cosmic cycles. For a monist such as Spinoza, the identity of god and nature is axiomatic.[56] For orthodox Stoics, the doctrine of cosmic cycles allows them to 'qualify' this identity to a degree. During the phase of conflagration or *ekpurôsis* within a cosmic cycle, god may be regarded as completely existing 'in himself', so to speak. As a passage from Origen, quoted previously, puts it, 'the god of the Stoics has the whole of substance (*tên holên ousian*) as its controlling principle, whenever there is the conflagration'.[57] Plutarch indicates that within this phase, deity exists in its purest form: during the conflagration 'no evil whatsoever remains, but the whole is then sagacious and wise'.[58] This 'god-phase' of the cosmic cycle imparts a quasi-transcendence to god and allows the Stoics more naturally to speak of deity as the *creator* of the world order – as the 'creative fire that proceeds systematically to the creation of the cosmos encompassing all the seminal principles (*spermatikous logous*) according to which everything comes about by fate'[59] and as 'a sort of seed, which possesses the principles of all things and the causes of all things that have occurred, are occurring, and will occur – the interweaving and ordering of which is fate, knowledge, truth, and a certain inevitable and inescapable law of the things that exist'.[60]

During the remainder of the world cycle, however, god is immanent in the cosmos as its soul or rational, controlling principle. According to Plutarch's report, Chrysippus claims that 'the soul of the cosmos is not separated but continuously grows until it consumes its matter into itself'.[61] At this juncture, the conflagrational god-phase of the world cycle apparently recurs. Thus, the temporal phases of the world cycle permit the orthodox Stoics to maintain their monistic commitment to the unity and cohesion of what

instances, a difference in linguistic expressions does not correspond to a difference in the *referents* of those expressions.

[56] See A. A. Long, Ch. 15, this volume.
[57] Origen, *Contra Celsum* IV 14 = SVF 2.1052.
[58] Plutarch, *Comm. not.* 1067a = SVF 2.606.
[59] Aëtius, *Placita* I 7 = SVF 2.1027.
[60] Aristocles in Eusebius, *Pr. ev.* XV = SVF 1.98.
[61] Plutarch, *St. rep.* 1052c = SVF 2.604.

exists by identifying god and cosmos, while allotting to god a phase where he is manifested in quasi-transcendental perfection.

6. CAUSATION AND COSMIC COHESION

As we have seen, the unity and cohesion of the cosmos is a function of the active principle, god or creative fire; and the action of the latter is typically identified with fate (*heimarmenê*). In Cicero's *De fato*, fate is identified with 'antecedent causes' ('natural and antecedent causes' or 'external and antecedent causes'), which are characterized as 'assisting and proximate causes' (*causae adiuvantes et proximae*) and distinguished from 'complete and principal causes' (*causae perfectae et principales*). One aim of Chrysippus in making these distinctions appears to have been the development of a form of 'soft-determinist' compatibilism, a topic discussed in Chapter 7.

In this chapter, however, the concern is more with the determinism Chrysippus evidently associated with his concept of antecedent causes. At *De fato* 20–21, Chrysippus is portrayed as arguing by *modus tollens* from the premises that every proposition (*axiôma*) is true or false and that if there is motion without a cause (*motus sine causa*), then not every proposition will be true or false to the conclusion that there is no motion without a cause. He then infers that everything that happens happens by preceding causes (*causis fiunt antegressis*) and, consequently, that everything happens by fate. It is clear that an important assumption of Chrysippus' argument is that the truth or falsity of propositions with future signification entails the existence of antecedent causes that bring about (or preclude, respectively) the states of affairs that would make those propositions true (or false, respectively).

The Stoic account of fate as a 'chain of causes (i.e., an unalterable ordering and concatenation')[62] is characterized by Quintus Cicero, the Stoic spokesperson in Cicero's *De divinatione*, as being a matter of physics, not superstition.[63] A passage in Alexander of Aphrodisias' relates the Stoic conception of an all-encompassing causal nexus quite directly to Stoic concern with the unity and cohesion of the cosmos:

---

[62] Aëtius, *Placita* I 28 = SVF 2. 917.
[63] Cicero, *Div.* I 126.

Nothing comes to be in the universe in such a way that there is not something else which follows it with no alternative and is attached to it as to a cause; nor, on the other hand, can any of the things which come to be subsequently be disconnected from the things which have come to be previously, so as not to follow one of them as if bound to it. But everything which has come to be is followed by something else which of necessity depends on it as a cause, and everything which comes to be has something preceding it to which it is connected as a cause. For nothing either is or comes to be in the universe without a cause, because there is nothing of the things in it that is separated and disconnected (*apolelumenon te kai kechôrismenon*) from all the things that have preceded. For the universe would be torn apart and divided and not remain single forever, organized according to a single order and organization, if any causeless motion were introduced; and it would be introduced, if all the things that are and come to be did not have causes which have come to be beforehand (*progegonota = antecedentes*) [and] which they follow of necessity.[64]

A few lines later, Alexander states the fundamental principle of Stoic determinism:

It is equally true with respect to all [of the sorts of cause that the Stoics distinguish], they say, that it is impossible, when all the circumstances surrounding (*periestêkotôn*) both the cause and that of which it is a cause are the same, that things should *not* turn out a certain way on one occasion but that they *should* turn out that way on some other occasion. If this were to be the case, [they say that] there would be some uncaused motion.[65]

Such a principle has become virtually paradigmatic as a statement of causal determinism. It is regarded by the Stoics as a corollary of their commitments to the unity and cohesion of the cosmos and to an all-encompassing divine reason controlling that cosmos. And the principle of determinism itself has as corollaries two significant Stoic physical doctrines: 'nonevident', 'obscure', or 'hidden' (*adêla*) causal factors, and the eternal recurrence of the world order.

It is a plain fact that this principle of universal causal determinism does not *seem* to be true without exception: that is, it does not seem to be *universally* the case that when all the relevant causal factors are the 'same', there is always the same outcome. A very obvious move, for those such as the Stoics whose prior commitments lead

---

[64] Alexander of Aphrodisias, *Fat* 192, 3–14 (in the translation of Sharples [1983] 70–71).

[65] *Fat.* 192, 22–25.

them to embrace the principle in a strictly universal form, is to introduce the concept of causal features that are difficult (or practically
impossible) to detect but are sufficiently significant to produce different effects depending on their presence or absence. That the
Stoics adopted such an account of chance (tuchê) is attested by a
number of citations taken from von Arnim's collection, *Stoicorum
Veterum Fragmenta*: chance is a 'cause nonevident to human calcula-
tion/thought/reason' (*aitia adêlos anthrôpinôi logismôi/anthrôpinêi
dianoiâi/anthrôpinôi logôi*).[66] In his *De Stoicorum repugnantiis*,
Plutarch makes it clear that Chrysippus appealed to such nonevident causes within the context of his strict causal determinism. Just
as nonevident causes effect different outcomes with respect to the
behavior of balances and scales, 'we do not notice them when they
direct our own impulse one way or the other'.[67] It is essentially these
same *aitiai adêloi* that reappear in the phenomena with which contemporary chaos theory is concerned, where minute differences in
'initial conditions' – that is, 'causal noise' – can yield great differences
in effects. With respect to many of the Stoics, one consequence of
the doctrine of nonevident causes seems to have been a certain reticence about the development of causal explanations of *particular*
natural phenomena. Commenting on a remark of Strabo pertaining
to Posidonius ('With him [sc. Posidonius] we find a lot of aetiology
and a lot of Aristotelizing which members of our school shy away
from because of the obscurity of the causes'[68]), Frede comments that
'according to Strabo, then, the Stoics in general are hesitant to engage in aetiology because the real causes are so hidden and obscure;
Posidonius is an exception, and in this respect he is rather more
like a Peripatetic'.[69] Frede further notes that a 'recurring complaint'
against Chrysippus in Galen's *De placitis Hippocratis et Platonis* is
that he 'fails to state the cause or claims that the true explanation is
uncertain or too difficult to figure out'.[70]

Although, according to Chrysippus, it may be quite difficult to
work out the aetiology of particular events and states of affairs,
the commitment to cosmic unity and coherence in the form of the

[66] See SVF 2.965, 2.966, 2.967, 2.970, and 2.971.
[67] Plutarch, *St. rep.* 1045c.
[68] Strabo, *Geographica* II 3.8.23–25.
[69] Frede (1987), 130.
[70] Frede (1987), 131.

fundamental principle of determinism entails that there is such an aetiology. Insofar as we can determine, commitment to this general physical principle, as an expression of cosmic unity and coherence, was much more important to most Stoics than the limitations imposed on the explanation of particular physical phenomena by the existence of 'hidden' causes. This feature of Stoic physical thought underlines the general point that what the Stoics expected from physics, as a principal subdivision of philosophy, is not the same ideal of 'explanation of nature' attached to many classical modern and contemporary conceptions of physics: a nomic-deductive picture according to which the 'covering laws' of physics plus a complete description of an instantaneous world-state allows an omniscient observer to *predict* the subsequent history of the world to the finest detail.

Also intimately related to the fundamental principle of determinism is a Stoic doctrine we have previously encountered: eternally recurring world orders or cosmic cycles. In one classical form, the doctrine seems to have been that of exact eternal recurrence: that, as Nemesius puts it, 'there will be nothing different in comparison to what has happened before, but everything will occur in just the same way and indistinguishably, even to the least details'.[71] This form of the doctrine may well have been the most orthodox one because of the fact that it is the form that seems to respect most rigorously the Stoic principle of causal determinism. Although the principle of determinism does not entail this doctrine of exact recurrence, the principle would seem to entail that *if* there occurs a 'total state' y of the cosmos, indistinguishable in all detail from a prior total cosmic state x, there will be an eternal recycling of cosmic history in between. It seems likely that the Stoics appealed to the common ancient doctrine of the 'great year' (*annus magnus* or *perfectus*) to support their assumption that the antecedent of the conditional is satisfied. This doctrine, mentioned in Plato's *Timaeus* (39d) and Cicero's *De natura deorum* (II 20), is that of the return of the heavenly bodies to their exact relative positions. At *Contra Celsum* V 21, Origen attributes such a doctrine to the 'Platonists and Pythagoreans' in the context of a sort of astrological determinism: 'for when in certain fixed cycles the stars adopt the same configurations and relationships to each

---

[71] Nemesius, *De nat. hom.* 38 = SVF 2.625.

other, they say that everything on earth is in the same position as it was at the last time when the relationship of the stars in the universe to one another was the same'.[72] The same passage from Nemesius cited previously suggests that the Stoics appropriated the doctrine of the great year to their own use:

The Stoics say that when the planets return to the same position, with respect to inclination and declination, to where each was at the beginning when the cosmos was first established, at specified periods of time they bring about the conflagration and destruction of things. And when again the cosmos returns from the beginning to the same state, and when again the heavenly bodies are similarly disposed, each thing that occurred in the former period will come to pass indistinguishably [sc., from its past occurrence].[73]

As a number of contemporary commentators have noted, there were several variants of the Stoic doctrine of eternal recurrence. One variant apparently was derived from consideration of the identity of individuals, events, and so forth across cosmic cycles. Simplicius reports that the Stoics 'reasonably ask whether the I [that exists] now and the I [that existed] then are one in number, or whether I am fragmented (diaphoroumai) by the ordering of cosmic cycles one to the next'.[74] So a variant of the orthodox doctrine of exact recurrence reported by Origen is that an individual such as Socrates 'does not come to be again but an indistinguishable counterpart (aparallaktos) of Socrates, who will marry an indistinguishable counterpart of Xanthippe, and will be prosecuted by indistinguishable counterparts of Anytus and Meletus'.[75] As Barnes has pointed out, this variant appears to conflict with a principle of identity of indiscernibles accepted by most Stoics.[76] Plotinus seems to suggest restriction of the principle of identity of indiscernibles to single cosmic cycles,[77] but we do not know whether any Stoics adopted such a solution. We also do not know whether any Stoics entertained the distinction between a 'conception of time as *circular* [with just one world cycle

---

[72] Origen, *Contra Celsum* V 21 (in the translation of Chadwick [repr. 1965] 280).
[73] Nemesius, *De nat. hom.* 38 = SVF 2.625. See Ch. 1, Sedley, this volume, on other Pythagoreanizing aspects of Stoicism.
[74] Simplicius, *In Ar. Phys.* 886.13–16 = SVF 2.627.
[75] Origen, *Contra Celsum* IV 68 = SVF 2.626.
[76] Barnes (1978), 10–11.
[77] Plotinus, *Enn.* V 7.2 21–23.

'joined' at beginning and end by the *ekpurôsis*] and a conception of time as linear ... but in which a certain sequence of events/states of affairs is exactly and eternally repeated'.[78]

Although these issues are rather rarefied, there is one further attested variant of the doctrine of recurrence that strikes at the heart of Stoic natural philosophy. This is a doctrine, reported by Origen at *Contra Celsum* V 20, that allows some small differences from cycle to cycle. Not surprisingly, Alexander interprets this doctrine in Aristotelian terms – as allowing some variation from cycle to cycle with respect to 'accidental' attributes.[79] Barnes is surely correct in noting that such a variant would amount to abandoning causal determinism. Also plausible is his suggestion that, since determinism is so central to Stoic natural philosophy, such a heterodox doctrine could only have been maintained by a minor figure in the school's history (*'par un personnage de peu d'importance dans l'histoire du stoïcisme'*).[80]

With respect to the relation between eternal recurrence and determinism, it is worth reemphasizing the point that both doctrines were considered by the Stoics as manifestations of the all-encompassing divine reason controlling the cosmos. In the words of Long and Sedley,

> It would be a mistake, however, to think of everlasting recurrence as a purely mechanical consequence of Stoic determinism. God is a supremely rational agent, and the most interesting fact about the conflagration is its omnipresent instantiation of his providence ... In his own identity god is the causal nexus ...; hence the sequence of cause and effect is an enactment of divine rationality and providence. Since every previous world has been excellent ..., god can have no reason to modify any succeeding world.[81]

The Stoics' commitment to the unity and coherence of the cosmos as controlled by providential divine reason results in a deemphasis on human autonomy, insofar as such autonomy would compromise the cohesiveness of the universe and the hegemony of divine reason. However, it seems that most Stoics wanted to allow some conception of human responsibility. The consequence is one of the first

[78] White (1985), 174.
[79] Alexander of Aphrodisias, *In Ar. An. pr.* 181.25–31 = SVF 2.626.
[80] Barnes (1978), 10.
[81] Long and Sedley (1987), Vol. I, 311.

explicit occurrences of soft determinism in Western thought – that is, the affirmation of the principle of causal determinism together with a conception of 'what is up to us' (*to eph' hêmin*) considered to be compatible with determinism. Cicero reports that Chrysippus wished to 'strike a middle position' between those who hold 'all things happen by fate in such a way that fate bears the force of necessity' and those who hold that the 'motions of minds are voluntary and without any fate'.[82] It is not clear whether Chrysippus or other Stoics developed more than one strategy for staking out a soft-determinist middle ground. But it is clear that Cicero believed that Chrysippus' most important strategy involved distinguishing types of cause: 'since Chrysippus both rejected necessity and wished nothing to transpire without preestablished causes (*praepositis causis*), he distinguished kinds of causes so that he might escape necessity but retain fate'.[83]

The Stoics were famous (or notorious) for distinguishing what Alexander calls a whole 'swarm of causes' (*smênos aitiôn*),[84] and it seems likely that the principal motivation behind the Stoic 'investigation into causes' or *aitiologia* was to work out their soft determinism, which permits them to maintain their commitment to cosmic unity in the form of a principle of universal causal determinism without entirely sacrificing the commonsensical idea that human agents, at least on some occasions, are responsible for their actions. Despite considerable clarification provided by contemporary commentators, the details of the various Stoic causal schemata remain controversial.[85] Nonetheless, Cicero makes it clear that the distinction between 'complete and principal' (*perfectae et principales*) causes and 'antecedent' causes that are said to be 'assisting and proximate' (*adiuvantes et proximae*) is crucial to (one version of) Chrysippean soft determinism. The principal and perfect causes seem to be the same thing as the distinctively Stoic 'sustaining' (*sunhektika*) causes, which Clement also refers to as 'complete' (*autotelê*).[86] A synektic or sustaining cause apparently (1) necessitates its result; (2) is temporally coincidental with its result; and (3) is, in the words of Frede,

---

[82] Cicero, *Fat.* 39.
[83] *Fat.* 18.41.
[84] Alexander of Aphrodisias, *Fat.* 192, 18.
[85] See, in particular, Bobzien (1998).
[86] Clement of Alexandria, *Strom.* VIII 9 = SVF 2.351.

regarded by the Stoics as a '*vis* on the inside [of the thing possessing it], ... something active, something which exerts a force' that brings about its effect.[87] There are several illustrations attributed by Cicero to Chrysippus: whereas a cylinder and a top 'cannot begin to move without being pushed, but when this happens, he thinks that the cylinder continues to roll and the top to spin by their own nature (*suapte natura*)'.[88] It is this 'nature' that is the synektic cause of the behavior of cylinder and top. And this nature is conceived by the Stoics to be something more than a mere passive, necessary 'standing condition'.

It is perhaps possible to regard a Stoic synektic cause as something analogous to a Peripatetic formal cause, something that accounts for the characteristic behavior or 'way of being' of its possessor – although, of course, it is conceived by the Stoics as an active, *corporeal* principle. In the case of human behavior, Cicero depicts Chrysippus as maintaining that acts of 'assent' require antecedent causes in the form of sense impressions, but that such sense impressions are not synektic causes of the acts of assent. Thus, the act of assent 'will be in our power' (*sed assensio nostra erit in potestate*) because of its being the effect of some synektic cause apparently expressing our rational nature – 'in the way that it was explained that, with respect to the cylinder, although it was pushed from without, it nonetheless moves by its own force and nature'.[89]

Stoic accounts of 'freedom and responsibility' are discussed in Chapter 7. My present interest is limited to its connection with the Stoic commitment to cosmic unity and cohesion. Whereas a non-Stoic incompatibilist such as Alexander is committed to locating human responsibility in a certain degree of 'causal separation' of the agent from the rest of the cosmos, it is clear that the Stoic commitment to cosmic cohesion and its corollary, an all-encompassing providential cosmic reason, will not allow for a similar maneuver. Like subsequent determinists such as Spinoza, orthodox Stoics shift the emphasis from human responsibility to human worth and dignity – or reinterpret human responsibility in terms of worth and dignity. It seems plausible to claim that human dignity or worth *need* not require any sort of causal separation of humans from the rest of the

[87] Frede (1987), 140.
[88] Cicero, *Fat.* 42.
[89] *Fat.* 44.

cosmos. As rational agents, 'fragments' of divine reason, we can think of ourselves as ministers of the divine reason constituting the ruling principle or *to hēgemonikon* of the cosmos. In fact, Chrysippus is depicted by Cicero as arguing from the dignity and worth of man (by implicit appeal to the Stoic premise that a whole cannot be 'inferior' to any of its parts) to the conclusion that god exists:

for in [man] alone there is reason, than which there is nothing more excellent that can exist. But for there to be some man who believes that there is nothing in all the world that is better than himself is foolish arrogance. Therefore, god certainly exists.[90]

7. ANTICORPUSCULARIANISM AND COSMIC COHESION

At the time of the founding of the Stoa, Aristotle had worked out a detailed conceptual account of change. But since appeal to incorporeal forms was central to the Aristotelian account (as were such distinctively Aristotelian metaphysical notions as potentiality and actuality), such an account likely would not have found favor with the early Stoics. The materialist account of change on offer was corpuscularian – that of the Presocratic and Epicurean atomists. But this sort of account, too, would seem to violate fundamental Stoic commitments concerning the unity and cohesion of the cosmos. Since each corpuscle (atom) is quite separate and self-contained, separated from other atoms by void, there is a very literal sense in which the constituents of the cosmos do not constitute a cohesive unity. The Stoic response was to develop an anti-corpuscularian form of materialism, in which the body constituting the cosmos is characterized by a seamless, radical continuity. One well-attested corollary of Stoic anticorpuscularianism was the peculiar Stoic doctrine of total blending (*krasis di' holōn*). Another, for which the evidence is much more speculative, is the elimination of 'sharp divisions' in the form of limits such as surfaces from the cosmos.

The former doctrine of total blending is criticized as paradoxical by Alexander of Aphrodisias in his *De mixtione* and by Plutarch in *De communibus notitiis adversus Stoicos*. Alexander associates it with the Stoic doctrine of the radical continuity of matter – with those

[90] Cicero, *ND* II 16.

'who say that matter is completely unified and who hold that it is one and the same for all those things that come to be'.[91] According to Alexander, there is some difference of opinion among the Stoics pertaining to mixture. He proceeds to concentrate on the doctrine of Chrysippus, reporting that although Chrysippus holds that all of the cosmos or substance (*ousia*) is unified because of the *pneuma* (mixture of fire and air) permeating through all of it, he nevertheless distinguishes three kinds of mixture of bodies within the cosmos. One kind is simply the juxtaposition (*parathesis*) of sizeable 'chunks' of different stuffs (beans and grains of wheat, in Chrysippus' example), which Chrysippus says occurs by 'fitting together' or juncture (*harmê*) and in which each constituent preserves its proper nature and quality. Of course, from an atomist perspective, *all* mixture, and hence all change, occurs by such corpuscularian juxtaposition. Another sort of mixture is total combination (*sunkrisis di' holôn*), in which the constituent substances and the qualities they contain are altogether destroyed in order to produce something qualitatively distinct from the constituents. Alexander does not accord this type of Chrysippean mixture much attention, but it must have been conceived by the Stoics as the total replacement, in a given material substratum, of one set of qualitative determinations by another – where 'qualitative determination' is itself conceived in corporeal terms (e.g., as different degrees of 'tension' of matter). The third type of mixture is total blending (*krasis di' holôn*) or blending proper, the 'interpenetration of two or more bodies in such a way that each preserves its own proper nature and own qualities in the mixture'.[92]

It is this last kind of mixture, total blending, that both Alexander and Plutarch criticize as particularly paradoxical. Alexander reports what may well have been Chrysippus' account of total blending:

the commingled bodies go through one another (*chôrountôn di' allêlon*) in such a way that there is no part of them that does not partake of everything in such a blended mixture. If this were not the case, then the result would no longer be a blending (*krasin*) but rather a juxtaposition (*parathesin*).[93]

The idea seems to be that, no matter how small a three-dimensional spatial area occupied by such a total blending one

[91] Alexander of Aphrodisias, *Mixt.* 216, 1–2. = SVF 2.470.
[92] *Mixt.* 216, 28–31 = SVF 2.473.
[93] *Mixt.* 217, 10–13 = SVF 2.473.

considers, such an area is occupied by *all* the constituents of the mixture. Consequently, such a total blending cannot be conceived as being constituted of very small but separated corpuscles, bits, globules, or droplets of the original blended elements. For if there were within the blend such corpuscles, each with its own surface, of the original blended elements, there would be a certain three-dimensional spatial magnitude below which the elements would *not* be commingled. Alexander points out that a consequence of this view is that no part of the original constituents in the blending can have its own surface (*epiphaneia*). He argues that this fact entails that the original constituents in the blend would not be preserved and would not be capable of being separated out – as Chrysippus had claimed – but would be 'jointly fused and destroyed'.[94] In these arguments against the intelligibility of the Stoic doctrine of total blending, it is claimed that the idea of the existence of surfaces (of supposed corpuscles of constituent elements or bodies) in a mixture is inconsistent with the Stoic conception of total blending. Perhaps one radical Stoic response to such criticism would have been to do away with the 'physical reality' of surfaces altogether, an issue to which I shall soon return.

However, it seems that, among the various criticisms of the Stoic doctrine of total blending, the principal one is that it contradicts quantitative facts about mixing substances together. The doctrine of total blending apparently implies that each constituent stuff or body be the receptacle of the other. Critics of the doctrine assume that this means that the spatial *volume* of each constituent quantity of stuff be the receptacle of the other. So, as Plutarch puts it, if one ladle of wine is to be *totally* blended with two of water, the wine will have both the volume of one ladle (because that is what one begins with) but also the volume of two ladles 'by equalization of blending' (*tês kraseôs exisôsei*), because that is the volume of the water which supposedly becomes the receptacle of the wine that is totally blended with it.[95] Plutarch takes this to be a paradoxical consequence of the doctrine of those who 'stuff bodies into body'.[96] Plotinus reports a similar criticism. The fact that a mixture (typically) occupies more space than that of either of its constituent stuffs – namely, that of the sum of the spaces of its constituents – tells against the Stoic doctrine

[94] *Mixt.* 220, 37–221, 15.
[95] Plutarch, *Comm. not.* 1078a.
[96] *Comm. not.* 1078b.

of total blending. For if there were total blending, the space occupied by the totally blended compound should remain the same as that of the constituent stuff – but which one?[97]

Although there is no record of any Stoic response to this sort of criticism, a possible response emphasizes the distinction between two conceptions of quantity. In one sense of 'quantity', something like the contemporary sense of 'mass', the quantity of a body or stuff remains constant through various changes. In another sense of 'quantity', something like the sense of 'volume', quantity is quite variable: the same mass of stuff (e.g., of H_2O) can assume, in undergoing various processes of change, quite different spatial volumes (e.g., as ice, water, and steam). As I have previously suggested, it is open to Chrysippus to maintain that total blending is one such process of change that can result in the same mass assuming different spatial volumes. So it is not *a priori* absurd to argue that

before a total blending a quantity (mass sense) of wine possesses a certain volume (viz., a drop). After being totally blended with the ocean water, the same quantity (mass sense) of wine possesses a much greater volume (viz., one equal to that of the ocean water and also to that of the totally blended ocean water-and-wine).[98]

We are inclined to assume that the volume of two quantities of stuff that have been blended should simply be the numerical sum of the volumes of the two quantities of stuff before being blended. But there is no *a priori* reason why this assumption should be true. The existence of such a common belief is no doubt the result of experience. But, as Sharvy has pointed out, experience sometimes falsifies this assumption: mixing 10 cc. of water with 10 cc. of alcohol yields about 19 cc. of mixture.[99]

Accustomed as we are to physical theories that assume some quantum structure or other of matter, Stoic anticorpuscularianism – the doctrine that material stuffs have a radically continuous structure – may strike us as a peculiar and, perhaps, unpromising basis for physics. However, it is far from clear that such an assumption yields internal inconsistencies that can lead to its *a priori* rejection in the ways suggested by Alexander, Plutarch, and Plotinus. And,

[97] Plotinus, *Enneades* II 7.1 = SVF 2.478.
[98] White (1986), 386.
[99] Sharvy (1983), 451.

for the Stoics, anti-corpuscularianism was surely an important manifestation of their commitment to cosmic unity and cohesion.

It is also possible that a Stoic doctrine pertaining to limits (e.g., surfaces, edges, and boundaries) was closely linked to their commitment to cosmic cohesion and to their anti-corpscularianism. There is a fair amount of evidence for a Stoic doctrine which denied that limits possess corporeal status. Proclus reports that the Stoics held that limits 'subsist in mere thought' (*kat' epinoian psilên huphestanai*).[100] Plutarch evidently interprets this doctrine as implying that limits belong to the Stoic ontological category of incorporeals (*asômata*), and consequently are not to be reckoned among the things that exist.[101] However, Diogenes Laertius mentions that Posidonius maintained that surface (*epiphaneia*) exists 'both in thought and in reality' (*kai kat' epinoian kai kath' hupostasin*),[102] and seems to suggest that, in contrast, the more orthodox Stoic view was that surfaces and other such limits exist only *in intellectu*. Long and Sedley speculate that 'the Stoics regarded limits as mental constructs ... , and as such they may well have seen them as falling altogether outside the corporeal-incorporeal dichotomy'.[103] In fact, they suggest that limits belong in their own Stoic ontological category, which also includes fictional entities.[104] It is surely possible to interpret the Stoic doctrine of surfaces and such limits as no more than the obvious and not very portentous claim that, since such entities lack one or more of the three dimensions characterizing bodies, they cannot be corporeal and hence (according to the Stoic identification of what is corporeal with what exists) do not exist. However, both Long and Sedley and I have entertained the stronger hypothesis of a Stoic doctrine according to which limit entities, as 'mental constructs', are 'geometers' fictions, and hence involve a degree of *mis*representation' of physical reality.[105] Brunschwig has suggested yet another possibility, that limits belong outside of the category of 'something' altogether. They 'could be considered as purely mental constructions with no objective reality, that is to say, as NSTs [not somethings]'.[106]

---

[100] Proclus, *In primum Euclidis elementorum librum commentarii* 89.16.
[101] Plutarch, *Comm. not.* 1080e.
[102] DL VII 135.
[103] Long and Sedley (1987), Vol. 1, 301.
[104] See the 'stemma' of Stoic ontological distinctions in Long and Sedley (1987), Vol. 1, 163.
[105] White (1992), 286.
[106] Brunschwig (1994a), 97.

I have elsewhere attempted to develop in somewhat greater detail an account of the physical implications of an interpretation of limits that minimizes or denies their reality. That account uses some basic concepts drawn from contemporary 'fuzzy' point-set topology.[107] From a relatively nontechnical perspective,

the Stoic removal of limit entities from the physical world results in a sort of intuitive or 'pre-analytical continuity' of *to holon*, the entire physical cosmos. One physical object is so topologically interconnected with its environment that there are no joints, so to speak, between them; they insensibly blend into one another... [C]ontinuity in this intuitive sense is to be thought of not just as an epistemic limitation but as an ontological fact deriving from the removal of limit entities from the physical world and the ontological indeterminacy introduced by the elimination of such limits *kath' hupostasin*.[108]

Of course, such an interpretation of the Stoic doctrine of limits is highly speculative. However, as noted toward the beginning of this chapter, the importance accorded by Diogenes Laertius to 'limits' (*perata*) in his account of Stoic taxonomy of the subdivisions of physics suggests that *something* fairly important and perhaps extraordinary was going on with respect to the Stoic conception of limits. The conception of all such limit entities as geometrical fictions, in the sense that has just been specified, would certainly seem to be a rather important and extraordinary conception. If, in fact, such a conception was developed by the Stoics, there is little doubt that it was yet another manifestation of Stoic commitment to cosmic unity and cohesion. In that regard I heartily concur with the rationale given by Brunschwig for his placing of limits in the 'category' of 'not something': such an account, he says, 'is the one that seems the most plausible, bearing in mind the Stoics' fundamentally continuistic conception of the physical universe'.[109]

8. CONCLUSION

Much of the evidence that we possess concerning Stoic physics or natural philosophy comes from hostile sources, the purpose of which, in many cases, is to make Stoic doctrine appear to be either internally

[107] See White (1992), Ch. 7.
[108] White (1992), 324–325.
[109] Brunschwig (1994a), 97.

incoherent or at odds with common sense. The enduring exegetical problem, then, is whether this evidence, despite its obviously prejudicial character, is to be interpreted as a more or less accurate account of Stoic doctrine or whether it is usually a distortion or misrepresentation of Stoic doctrine. It seems unlikely that this issue can ever be completely adequately resolved, even with respect to a single source such as Plutarch or Alexander of Aphrodisias or Origen. Thus, we are left with an exegetical choice.

If we elect, at least initially, not to appeal to the hypothesis of thoroughgoing misunderstanding or misrepresentation of Stoic natural philosophy, we must still deal with what often will strike us as counterintuitive or strange doctrines in what these sources tell us about Stoic physical doctrines. Placing such doctrines within the context of fundamental Stoic 'prior commitments' frequently has the effect of mitigating their peculiarity. It seems particularly important to remind ourselves frequently that, as Hellenistic thinkers, the Stoics held that *all* human knowledge is ultimately 'practical' in the sense of informing us of the best way to live our lives. 'Physics' or natural philosophy is in no way to be excluded from this claim.

6   Stoic Theology

I.

The object of Stoic theology was the governing principle of the cosmos, insofar as this could also be labeled 'god'. The Stoics accordingly regarded theology as part of physics, more specifically as that part which does not focus on the details and the purely physical aspects of cosmic processes, but rather on their overall coherence, teleology, and providential design, as well as on the question of how this cosmic theology relates to popular forms of belief and worship.[1] Issues covered by Stoic theology include the nature of the divine principle of the cosmos, the existence and nature of the other gods, our proper attitude toward the gods – that is, the virtue of piety (*eusebeia*) and the opposite vice of impiety (*asebeia*), including our attitude toward traditional myth and ritual – and issues relating to fate and providence, including the way the providential ordering of the cosmos can be known by mankind by means of oracles and divination.

Whereas the founding father of the school, Zeno of Citium, still appears to have published his theological views in the context of his main cosmological work *On the whole*,[2] his successors accorded a more prominent position to theology as a subject in its own right. Cleanthes explicitly set off theology from the rest of physics, or from physics in the narrow sense (DL VII 41), and wrote a separate work *On the gods*. Persaeus wrote a work *On impiety*. Sphaerus appears

---

[1] For an overview of Stoic theology in the context of Hellenistic thought, see Mansfeld (1999). General surveys of ancient philosophical theology Babut (1974) and Gerson (1990).

[2] On Zeno's contribution to Stoic physics, see Algra (forthcoming).

to have been the first Stoic to have written a separate work *On divination*. Chrysippus published not only an *On the gods* and an *On Zeus*, but also works specifically devoted to fate, providence, divination, and oracles. He appears to have followed in Cleanthes' footsteps in treating theology as a separate subdiscipline. At any rate he claimed that it was the part of physics that was to be treated last, thus putting it at the final stage of the curriculum (the study of physics as a whole coming after logic and ethics). He even claimed that for this reason theology had rightly been said to be a kind of 'initiation' (*teletê*; Plutarch *St. rep.* 1035 A–B).[3] As one of our sources puts it:

the theories about the gods have to be the last thing to be taught, on top of everything else, when the soul is fortified and strong and able to remain silent in front of the uninitiated. For it is quite a struggle to hear the right things about the gods and to get a hold of them (Etymologicum Magnum *s.v. teletê* = SVF 2.1008).

Chrysippus' pupil Antipater of Tarsus not only discussed general theological issues in the seventh and eighth books of his *On the cosmos* (DL VII 148, 139), but also wrote a work, in two books, *On divination* (Cicero *Div.* I 6). Panaetius appears to have been to some extent an exception. He declared talk about the gods 'nugatory' and no positive views on theological details are recorded of him, whereas he seriously doubted the feasibility of divination. Yet even he wrote a work *On providence*.[4] Posidonius wrote an *On the gods*, a work *On heroes and daemons*, and works entitled *On fate* and *On divination*. The great Stoics of the Imperial Age, finally, discussed aspects of theology in the course of their predominantly ethical writings, whereas

---

[3] The comparison of the cosmos with the mysteries is also ascribed to Cleanthes (Epiphanius *Adv. Her.* III, 2, 9 = SVF I, 538). It recurs in Seneca *NQ* VII 30.6.

[4] Cicero *Ep. Att.* XIII 8 = fr. 33 Van Straaten = fr. 18 Alesse. On Panaetius' theological views, and in particular on the interpretation of Epiphanius' testimony on theology being nugatory (fr. 68 Van Straaten = fr. 134 Alesse), see the well-balanced discussion in Dragona-Monachou (1976) 269–278. There is no reason to assume that Panaetius rejected the pantheistic core of Stoic theology (he apparently did believe in providence). He may have doubted the possibility of knowledge about the details of god's working (which would explain his doubts concerning both the eventual conflagration and divination – on which see fr. 70–74 Van Straaten = fr. 136–140 Alesse). Or perhaps he simply wanted theology to be first and foremost *philosophical* theology, while regarding as 'nugatory' any attempt to link this philosophical theology to elements of traditional religion (such as polytheism and divination).

Seneca, as might be expected, also broaches theological issues in his *Naturales Quaestiones*.

As part of physics in the broad sense, theology shared in the at first sight somewhat ambiguous status of this part of Stoic philosophy. From a didactic point of view, physics appears to have represented the culmination of the philosophical curriculum, being an area which is the proper object of study for the advanced philosopher only, in the most proper sense perhaps even only for the virtuous (i.e., the wise). As we saw, this view was already defended by Chrysippus, but it recurs in such later authors as Cleomedes and Seneca.[5] On the other hand, physics, including theology, was supposed to provide the basis for the rest of Stoic philosophy, in particular ethics.[6] The latter point is made quite clear by Plutarch, who stresses that just as those who move public decrees prefix the phrase 'Good Fortune', Chrysippus, virtually prefixed 'Zeus, Destiny, Providence, and the statement that the universe, being one and finite, is held together by a single power'.[7] Plutarch is able to support this claim by *verbatim* quotations from Chrysippus' *On the Gods* and from his *Physical propositions* (Plutarch *St. rep.* 1035 B–C). The account of Stoic ethics in Cicero's *On Ends* winds up by making the same point (*Fin.* III, 73):

Nor again can anyone judge truly of things good and evil, save by a knowledge of the whole plan of nature and even of the life of the gods.

Both as the culmination of the philosophical curriculum and a basis of sorts for ethics, Stoic theology was apparently regarded as of central importance to the philosophical system as a whole, and the book titles quoted previously show that theological issues were prominent on the agenda of most Stoics.

[5] Cleomedes *Cael.* II, 1, 410–412 Todd; Seneca *NQ* I 6.

[6] The sequence ethics-physics (with logic put before ethics) is attributed to the Stoics as a didactic sequence in Sextus as well (*M* VII, 22–23). On the other hand, the thesis 'physics first' is ascribed to Panaetius and Posidonius in DL VII 41, and is also in general presupposed by the famous similes, in which the parts of philosophy, and the way they interrelate, are compared to the parts of an orchard or an egg (DL VII 40 and Sextus *M* VII 17).

[7] This list of items does not in itself suggest that Chrysippus thought that one should have a complete command of physics before being able to embark on ethics. It just embodies the claim – which is obviously correct – that Stoic ethics is based on a general conception of the world as teleologically ordered, and as governed by fate and providence. See also Brunschwig (1991).

II.

The Stoics were not the first ancient thinkers to approach questions concerning the existence and nature of the divine from a philosophical point of view. Elements of what may be called philosophical theology had been present in Greek philosophy right from its earliest stages. The Ionian cosmologists, focusing their attention on nature and the cosmos, endowed the physical principles governing this cosmos with attributes traditionally belonging to the divine (i.e., life, eternity, and power). Other thinkers chose to focus directly on the nature of god, or the gods, to try to determine this nature on the basis of philosophical arguments and to show, accordingly, that in some (or most) aspects, traditional myth and religion were on the wrong track. Thus, Xenophanes presented on the one hand a *reductio ad absurdum* of traditional anthropomorphism, while trying on the other hand to determine some of the characteristics of god (at any rate, his immobility) by examining what is fitting (*epiprepei*) for such a being (fr. B 26 Diels-Kranz). In the work of Plato, the cosmological approach and the more strictly theological approach co-exist, the former being more prominent, for example, in his discussion of the visible and generated 'cosmic' gods in the *Timaeus*, the latter in those passages in the *Republic* in which god is said to be good, and as such cause of the good only, and to be simple and unchanging, with the implication that he cannot deceive.[8]

Both the theological and the cosmological approaches gave rise to new forms of 'enlightened' piety.[9] In the course of the fifth century, however, yet a different approach appeared on the stage. This psychological or aetiological approach focused on the origins of religious beliefs, locating these origins in the fear of physical phenomena like thunder and lightning (Democritus, fr. A 75 Diels-Kranz); or in the gratitude of primitive man for the things that nourish and benefit us and for the people who discovered useful things for human civilization (a position defended by Prodicus, fr. B 5 Diels-Kranz, and later, in the fourth century, by Euhemerus); or on gods as a useful device for governments to ensure a supernatural sanction for good behaviour

---

[8] Plato *Republic* 377 b–383 c.

[9] For an overview of forms of cosmic theology in Xenophon, Plato, Aristotle, the Stoics, and Cicero, see Festugière (1949) 75–340.

(a view expressed in the so-called Sisyphus-fragment).[10] Such views could easily involve the suggestion that the traditional gods were no more than a human invention – which indeed amounts to a form of atheism.

In Stoic theology we find traces of all three approaches just discussed. We find the cosmological approach in several of the so-called proofs of the existence of god, which often amount to hardly more than the inference that the cosmos is ensouled and rational. On the other hand, we witness the Stoic counterpart of Xenophanes' more strictly theological approach in the attempt to determine the proper attributes of the divine on the basis of the general concept of god. Yet where Xenophanes appears to have started out from a concept of god that was seemingly independent of any empirical or cosmological considerations, the Stoics – at any rate, from Chrysippus onward – took their starting point in the 'preconception' (*prolêpsis*) of god, which in their view was formed in the minds of men on the basis of repeated experience of the world around them and its structure.[11]

A preconception was defined as 'a natural conception of the general characteristics of a thing'.[12] Here the word 'natural' indicates that, given the fact that human minds are all structured alike and work in the same way, preconceptions are the general conceptions we will all arrive at, if and insofar as we manage to stay unaffected by wrong reasoning and external ideological influences and derive our conceptions instead, without special mental attention, but through a 'natural', simple, and unconscious mental operation, from the data provided by experience.[13] It appears that according to the Stoics, our preconception of god included not only his eternity and

---

[10] On the Sisyphus-fragment (Critias fr. B 25 Diels-Kranz), its ascription (Euripides or Critias), and its *Sitz im Leben* in the context of Greek rational theology, see Kahn (1997).

[11] Even if it may have been Chrysippus who actually introduced the term '*prolêpsis*', our sources on Zeno also speak of certain *notiones* formed on the basis of experience, which could be the starting point for further enquiry (Cicero *Acad.* I 42; for this position of *notiones* as 'starting points' one may compare Plutarch *Comm. not.* 1060 A, according to whom preconceptions are the things from which the whole system can grow up as from seeds). Also Cleanthes appears to have explicitly referred to the natural formation of the *concept* (*notio*) of god, on which see Cicero *ND* II 13. The epistemological status of 'preconceptions' is discussed in Ch. 3, this volume.

[12] DL VII, 54: *ennoia phusikê tôn katholou*.

[13] See Sandbach (1971b) 26.

indestructibility (Antipater *ap.* Plutarch *St. rep.* 1051 F), but also and most importantly his providential and beneficent nature (Chrysippus *ap.* Plutarch *St. rep.* 1051 E). As Plutarch (*St. rep.* 1051 D–E) observes, the latter element was especially stressed by Chrysippus against Epicurus who, while recognizing the theological importance of our natural preconception of god, allegedly misconstrued this preconception by leaving out the element of providence.

The Stoics' commitment to the supposed 'natural' origin of our preconception of God helps to explain why at least some of them also practiced the third, psychological or aetiological, approach outlined previously, albeit of course without endorsing atheistic conclusions of any kind. In their view, apparently, this approach proved useful in showing that, and how, primitive man had at least partially developed the right preconception. Thus we know that Persaeus declared 'not improbable what Prodicus wrote', viz. that men of old considered as gods those who had discovered what was useful, as well as the things that nourish and benefit us themselves.[14] Whereas Prodicus' argument probably intended, or could at any rate easily be taken as intending, to weaken the claims of traditional religion, we may surmise that in the Stoic context of Persaeus' work, this argument was given a more positive twist. Persaeus presumably believed that in giving divine names to what is useful, these early people grasped an essential aspect of the way god manifests himself to humans: as a providential physical force.[15] Treating inventors and inventions as gods could thus be regarded as a way of expressing this particular element of the *prolêpsis* of god.

In a similar way, Cleanthes (Cicero *ND* II 14) appears to have re-applied the explanation of religion from fear of cosmic events which, as we saw, had also been put forward by Democritus. But whereas we may presume that for Democritus the bottom line was that the phenomena that triggered these religious feelings could and should in the end be explained naturalistically – that is, *without* taking recourse to divine causes – Cleanthes believed that they led early man toward the notion of a divine cosmic, or at least celestial, power. Some scholars have criticized Cleanthes for recycling this particular traditional argument. After all, its unrestricted application might

[14] Philodemus *Piet.*, col. II, 28–III, 11, text in Henrichs (1974) 13–14; and Cicero *ND* I 38; see also II 62.

[15] For the connection between utility and the divine, see also Cicero *ND* II 70.

seem to saddle god with some attributes which should in fact not, on the Stoic view, apply to him, viz. being terrible and harmful.[16] However, just as Persaeus' reference to Prodicus need not imply that he agreed with *every* aspect of Prodicus' position, so also Cleanthes may well have thought that the old argument about the primitive fear of celestial phenomena contained *some* elements of truth, without thereby being committed to the view that the fear itself of which the argument speaks was justified. That Cleanthes' reference to this primitive attitude indeed did not involve an endorsement of that attitude *in toto* is precisely what Cicero, our source, suggests. According to Cicero, the relevant aspect of this intuition of primitive man was that it 'suggested to mankind the idea of the existence of some celestial and divine power',[17] an idea which of course was perfectly acceptable to a Stoic. We know that the second-century Stoic Antipater could claim that those philosophers who divested the gods of beneficence were in *partial* (*apo merous*) conflict with our preconception of them.[18] Similarly, it must have been possible for the early Stoics to explain certain primitive views as *partial* adumbrations of the right preconception.

III.

Our most extensive sources on Stoic theology, Cicero and Sextus, each in their own way set out to examine their subject from a sceptical point of view. Accordingly, these texts examine how the Stoics themselves thought they could substantiate their theological claims.[19] It is to these Stoic 'proofs' of the existence of god, or the gods, that we shall now turn.

We should note, to begin with, that we are dealing with several interconnected issues. According to Cicero (*ND* II 3), the Stoics recognized four main questions in theology:

First they prove that the gods exist, next they explain their nature, then they show that the world is governed by them, and lastly that they care for the fortunes of mankind.

---

[16] See Sandbach (1971b) 31, and Dragona-Monachou (1976) 82–88.
[17] Cicero *ND* II 14: *vim quandam esse caelestem et divinam suspicati sunt.*
[18] Antipater *ap.* Plutarch *St. rep.* 1052 B.
[19] On sceptical arguments in the area of theology, see Burnyeat (1982) and Long (1990).

It is true that Cicero's own account in *ND* II is neatly structured according to these four questions, but in Stoic philosophical practice these questions were interrelated. Stoic proofs of the existence of god or gods as a rule involved an answer to the question of the *nature* of these gods as well, for the simple reason that usually what they set out to prove was that the gods *as conceived by the Stoics* exist. This means that the existence of god involves the fact that he governs, or rather *is*, the cosmos, which explains why some of the proofs for the existence of god simply amount to proofs that the cosmos itself is a rationally ordered living being. In the arguments from divination, on the other hand, the questions of divine existence and of providence appear to be intertwined as well. The existence of divination is both a proof that the gods exist (for 'if there are persons who interpret the will of certain beings, these beings must exist', *ND* II 12) and a proof of their providential care insofar as it shows that 'signs of future events are manifested by the gods' (*ND* II 12; 162–163). In addition, because of the importance of the preconception of god in Stoic theology, proofs of the existence of the gods are sometimes connected with questions concerning the *genesis* of the *concept* of god as well. Cleanthes, for example, is said to have offered four causal factors which could be held responsible for the formation in men's minds of the concept of god or gods (*ND* II 13–15): (1) the foreknowledge of future events; (2) the abundance of benefits which nature bestows on us; (3) our fear and awe when faced with impressive natural phenomena; and (4) the uniform motion of the heavens. Of these explanations of the genesis of the concept of god, at least (1) and (4) are elsewhere presented as straightforward arguments for the existence of the gods. Written out as *arguments* that are intended to induce our conscious assent, they thus express in a more explicit and articulate way what has already come to be present *in nuce*, and through an unconscious process, in our natural preconception of god. There is no real tension, in other words, between the Stoic appeal to the evidence of the universal preconception of god on the one hand and their elaborate 'proofs' on the other. The latter may be seen as articulating how the evident preconceptions can have originated in the first place.[20]

Sextus (*M* IX 60) and Cicero (*ND* II 4–12) preface their discussions of proofs of the existence of gods by a list of four main *types*

[20] See also Schofield (1980), 305.

of arguments (*tropoi*, as they are called by Sextus).[21] The two lists
are different, however, and Cicero's classification contains elements
which are unlikely to be orthodox, and which were probably tailored
to fit the specific Roman setting (and readership) of the dialogue.[22] In
the context of our present discussion, we do better to adopt Sextus'
list. The first three types of argument listed by him indeed offer a
useful classificatory framework which is able to account for most
of the Stoic arguments that have been preserved.[23] The first type
adduces the alleged fact that people always and everywhere have believed that there are gods: religion appears to be a universal human
phenomenon. This is what later became known as the argument *e
consensu omnium*. As we have seen, it was certainly already used
by Cleanthes, and it is also attested for Chrysippus (SVF 2.1019).

The second type is the argument from design. It detects the working of god in the rational and ordered structure of the cosmos – in
particular, but by no means exclusively, in the regular motions of the
stars. It is what was later called the argument *ex operibus dei*. Many
specific arguments by Zeno, Cleanthes, and Chrysippus have been
recorded that take this cosmological and teleological perspective. In
general, it is claimed that although god is not directly perceptible, his
existence can be inferred, on some minimal reflection, from the orderly, beautiful, and beneficent structure of the world. By thus being
able to accommodate feelings of wonder and religious awe *vis-à-vis*
nature, these Stoic arguments could have a more direct appeal than
the Aristotelian cosmological argument (i.e., the argument for a first
unmoved mover, presented in *Phys.* VIII and *Meta.* Λ, and famously

---

[21] A useful survey of Stoic arguments for the existence (and providence) of the gods
is in Dragona-Monachou (1976).

[22] Cicero *ND* II 4–12 mentions the following four reasons: (1) the orderly motion of the
heavens, (2) the consensus of mankind, (3) the recorded epiphanies of the gods, and
(4) divination. Cicero's item (3), which records such epiphanies of gods as allegedly
took place at various occasions in Roman history, seems particularly tailored to
the Roman setting of his dialogue and is hard to square with the orthodox Stoic
position according to which the traditional anthropomorphic conceptions of gods
are in need of reinterpretation. Also the way Cicero works out (4) has a strongly
Roman flavour.

[23] The fourth *tropos* listed by Sextus concerns the attempt to show that the arguments
of the opponents (i.e., the atheists) do not hold water. Insofar as I can see it plays
no role in Sextus' subsequent exposition (and refutation), presumably because in
Sextus' strategy negative arguments against other (atheist) dogmatists needed no
refutation.

worked out and articulated by Aquinas in various contexts). According to Aristotle, god's existence is not so much to be inferred directly from the way the cosmos presents itself to us, but rather is proved on the basis of the more theoretical claim that an infinite series of causes is inconceivable.[24]

The third type draws attention to the fact that the opposite position (i.e., atheism) entails consequences that are unacceptable. Thus it involves that a number of generally accepted phenomena, such as religious practices and divination, become utterly meaningless. The phenomenon of divination was adduced, as we saw, by Cleanthes, and the argument from divination also figures, without ascription in Sextus (M IX 132). Another absurd consequence of the denial of the existence of the gods, signalled by Chrysippus (Cicero, ND II 16) would be the implication that in that case there is nothing left in nature that is superior to man. In a different form, the argument is ascribed to Cleanthes by Sextus (M IX 88–91): If (as experience teaches us) some living beings are better than others, there must be (if we are to avoid an infinite series) one that is best. Now since experience suggests that man (being vulnerable, mortal, prone to wickedness, and so forth) is not the best, there must be some living being better than man (i.e., god). This argument later became known as the argument *ex gradibus entium*.[25]

A number of the preserved arguments – notably those by Zeno, but also some of Chrysippus' – were couched in a characteristically syllogistic form, whereas many others do not display any fixed formal structure. It is perhaps safe to assume that the recorded syllogisms were devised as poignant and compressed statements of arguments that could also be presented at greater length. This, at least, is how they are presented by Cicero.[26] The prominence of these syllogisms

[24] One may also compare the way in which Plato *Leg.* X 'proves' the existence of god by arguing for the existence of a world soul as a self-mover and hence as a first cause of cosmic motion (esp. 894d–895a). The Platonic argument is briefly referred to in the Stoic account at Cicero ND II 32, but in general, the Stoic cosmological arguments appear to focus on god as a cause of order rather than of motion.

[25] See also Aristotle in his *On Philosophy* (fr. 16 Ross). Scholars have claimed that the Cleanthean argument prefigures the ontological arguments presented by Descartes and Leibniz (see, e.g., Dragona-Monachou [1976] 96), to which we may object that it does not straightforwardly proceed on the assumption that perfection entails existence.

[26] Cicero ND II 20: 'The thoughts which we expound at length Zeno used to compress into this form (*sic premebat*)'. On the possibility that Zeno opted for the syllogistic form for dialectical reasons, see Schofield (1983) 49–57.

in our sources and the seriousness with which they were defended suggest that they represented more than a *jeu d'esprit*. Yet they do not appear to have particularly strengthened the Stoic case. They were rather vulnerable to criticisms insofar as they arguably presented as rigid demonstrations what were basically, at most, arguments from plausibility. At any rate, Cicero's Stoic spokesman Balbus complains that these brief syllogisms are much easier to combat and less persuasive than longer and more rhetorically embellished expositions of the same arguments (*ND* II 20). Indeed, we know that opponents – in particular the dialectician Alexinus – ridiculed the Zenonian syllogisms by devising 'parallels' (*parabolai*); that is, arguments of the same logical structure which would clearly turn out to be invalid on the Stoics' own presuppositions.

One Zenonian syllogistic argument has become rather famous among modern students of Stoicism, primarily because it has sometimes been claimed that it (or at any rate the way it was reformulated and defended by Diogenes of Babylon) prefigures Anselm of Canterbury's 'ontological' argument. Our source (Sextus *M* IX 133–136) has not only preserved Zeno's original syllogism but also the sceptical *parabolê*, as well as two later Stoic attempts to defend Zeno's original syllogism against this *parabolê*. Zeno's original syllogism can be written out as follows:

(a1) A man may reasonably honour the gods.
(a2) Those who are non-existent a man may not reasonably honour.
(a3) Therefore the gods exist.

It is not clear why precisely premiss (a1) is thought to be true; that is, why it is thought that honouring the gods is something one will *reasonably* (*eulogôs*) do.[27] But I take it that premisses (a1) and (a2) may be seen as related to the argument *e consensu omnium*. In that case, the reason to assume that (a1) is true is the fact that belief in the gods is very common if not universal; (a2) then shows why this fact is relevant to the question of the existence of the gods. However this may be, the *parabolê*, which is anonymous but may well have been devised by Alexinus,[28] seizes upon what is clearly the weak

[27] See on this problem Schofield (1983) 38–39 and Brunschwig (1994) 175–176.
[28] See Schofield (1983) 38–40 for a possible reconstruction of the history of the *parabolai* and the way they were collected and discussed by Diogenes of Babylon.

spot in the argument – viz. the inference, presupposed by premiss (a2), from the gods' being honoured on reasonable grounds (whatever those grounds may be) to their actual existence – by showing that it does not work even on the Stoics' own premises. For, the *parabolê* claims, one might as well say:

(b1) A man may reasonably honour the sages.
(b2) Those who are non-existent a man may not reasonably hon-
     our.
(b3) Therefore sages exist.

Here the conclusion (b3) would be unacceptable even to a Stoic because, as Sextus puts it, 'the wise man has been undiscovered till now'.

Sextus records two attempts to rescue the Zenonian argument. The first of these, which is the one that concerns us here, is ascribed to Diogenes of Babylon.[29] According to Diogenes, 'those who are non-existent' in (a2) should be glossed 'those who are not of such a nature as to exist', where 'being of such a nature as to exist' apparently means 'being capable of existing' in the physical sense of 'being bound to exist at *some* time'.[30] By thus giving a new sense to (a2) and (a3), and also to (b2) and (b3), this interpretation defuses the *parabolê* by showing that it does not yield an objectionable conclusion after all. For although the sage may not exist *now*, the Stoics did think that he might *at some point* come into existence. Diogenes goes on to show that this new and weaker version of (a3) (i.e., the gods are of such a nature as to exist) can be converted into the desired stronger version ('the gods exist'), whereas no such conversion is possible in the case of (b3). The crucial difference, according to Diogenes, between the sage and the gods is that for the latter to exist *at some point* in time would immediately imply their existing *now*, because it is part and parcel of the concept (*ennoia*) of god to be ungenerated

---

[29] For a more elaborate analysis of the argument, which is in some respects different from the one I here offer but to which I am much indebted, see Brunschwig (1994).

[30] It is clear that 'is of such a nature as to exist' should here not be taken as referring to possible existence in the strict sense of 'logical possibility' (which in Stoic modal logic covers events that will never actually happen, so that an inference from 'is of such a nature as to exist' to 'exists' would be illegitimate), nor as referring to necessary existence (for in that case no additional steps would be needed to complete the inference from 'is of such a nature as to exist' to 'exists'); see on this Brunschwig (1994) 181.

and indestructible. So if the gods exist *at some point* in time, they exist eternally, and hence they exist *now*. The same story does not hold for the sage.[31] Diogenes, in other words, tries to show that the *parabolê* is harmless in that the revised version of (b3), 'the sage is of such a nature as to exist', is perfectly acceptable in itself. The only thing that matters is that, contrary to the revised version of (a3), (b3) does not allow a further inference to the *actual existence* of the sage.

We may now see that this argument is in the relevant respects crucially different from the kind of 'ontological' argument, which, couched in the form of a prayer, is found in Anselm's *Proslogion*. According to this ontological argument, the existence of god is necessary in virtue of the very nature of the concept of god: the essence of god, who is defined as 'that than which nothing greater can be conceived',[32] involves his existence. Neither in the case of Diogenes of Babylon, nor in Zeno's original syllogism, are we dealing with an argument where existence is in this way included in the very essence of god as an immediate and evident truth. The claim that the gods are of such a nature as to exist is first itself inferred from the fact that they are the kind of beings that one may reasonably honour. Their actual existence is then inferred from the combination of (1) the fact that they are of such a nature to exist, and (2) the fact that if they exist, they are eternal.

IV.

The Stoic answer to the question of the nature of god, or the gods, is rather complex and can be characterized as an at first sight perhaps surprising mixture of pantheism, theism, and polytheism.[33] According to a famous common Stoic description of god (DL VII 147), god is

---

[31] Note that in Stoic logic, truth is a *temporal* property of an assertible. Hence 'sages exist' is true only if sages exist *now*; i.e., at the moment of utterance. See on this Bobzien (1999a) 95.

[32] Although this formula has its parallels in ancient texts (e.g., Cicero *ND* II 18 and Seneca *NQ* I *Praef.*, 13), the way it is put to use by Anselm was new.

[33] In the ancient context, the juxtaposition of monotheistic and polytheistic elements is less odd than it would seem to be to us. On 'henotheism' (the theory that there is one main god, but that this does not rule out the existence of many minor gods), see West (1999), Frede (1999a), and Versnel (1990).

an immortal living being, rational, perfect and thinking in happiness, un-receptive of anything bad and provident with regard to the cosmos and the things therein. But he is not of human form. He is the demiurge of the whole and as it were the father of all things, both in general and insofar as the part of him is concerned which pervades all things, and which is called by many names, corresponding to its powers.

The first part of this description is clearly tailored to fit a monothe-istic conception of a single cosmic god. The last sentence, however, makes room for a form of polytheism as well, in allowing also the visible partial manifestations of this one god to be called by many names. Indeed, Zeno already appears to have argued that the stars, but also years and months – in short, spatial and temporal parts of the one and eternal god – may be considered as gods (Cicero, *ND* I, 36). This explains why in Stoicism 'god' or 'the gods' are in many contexts interchangeable. According to Plutarch, both Cleanthes and Chrysippus declared the crucial difference between the one god and his many parts or manifestations to be the fact that the latter are perishable – after all, the parts of the cosmos will all be destroyed in the conflagration that will end this particular world order (discussed later) – whereas Zeus, the one god, is eternal.[34]

If we confine ourselves for the moment to the way in which the Stoics characterized their *single* cosmic god, we may add the follow-ing features. He is material (after all, he is to be identified as creative fire or *pneuma*; SVF 2. 614, 1133, 1134)[35] and finite, insofar as the cosmos is finite (Aetius I, 6 = SVF 2.528). Yet the doxographical re-port in Aetius adds that he is without any particular form of his own – a curious statement, which we may take to be a slightly garbled ver-sion of either the claim that he is not of *human* form (see the previous quotation from Diogenes), or to represent the claim that he 'assumes' a form as soon as he interacts with matter and thus gives rise to the cosmos and its parts.[36] In either case, it need not surprise us that Cicero's Stoic spokesman rather prefers to credit god with the actual form of the cosmos, describing him as 'rotating and round' (*volubilis et rotundus*) despite the ridicule of the Epicureans (*ND* II 46).

[34] Plutarch *Comm. not.* 1066 A.
[35] On the corporeality of god as a first principle (*archê*), see Ch. 5 and 8, White and Brunschwig, in this volume.
[36] Cf. the claim in DL VII 134 that the *archai* are *amorphoi*.

Both Zeno and Chrysippus are said to have claimed that the cosmos is the 'substance of god' (DL VII 148). Elsewhere, an even more straightforward identification of cosmos and god is ascribed to Chrysippus (Cicero *ND* I 39), and this identification can also be found in some reports of the common Stoic view in Arius Didymus (fr. 29 = SVF 2.428; fr. 31 = SVF 2.527). Yet the Stoics also could refer to God as the active principle, or formative *pneuma*, which is at work *in* the cosmos (Aetius I 7.33 = SVF 2.1027). This shows that even their basically pantheistic conception of a *single* god could take different forms, accordingly as the monistic or the dualistic perspective was predominant. Although the Stoic system is usually labeled 'monistic' insofar as it claims that there is only this one cosmos, insofar as matter and divine form are inextricably linked together, and insofar as any form of transcendent reality is rejected, it does exhibit dualistic features in distinguishing god from matter and treating god as clearly the highest principle, as a principle with an altogether different status from that of matter.[37] Moreover, god could be said to be present in various degrees in various parts of the physical world, but most strongly in the 'governing part' (*hêgemonikon*) of the cosmos (i.e., in the aether [DL VII 138]) or, according to Cleanthes, in the sun (Arius Didymus fr. 29 = SVF 1.499). The latter perspective could give rise to what comes close to a form of astral religion, such as we witness in the 'hymn to the sun' in the work of the later Stoic Cleomedes (*Cael.* II 1.336–403 Todd), as well as to the feeling that God, in his purest form, is somewhere 'high up there', and so in a way transcending the world of mortals. The dualistic perspective as such could easily generate such statements as we find in Seneca, to the extent that god – both *qua* mind of the cosmos and *qua* human rationality – has 'descended into' bodies (*Ep.* 41.5) or that, unlike human beings, god is 'pure soul' (*NQ* I *Praef.* 14). One should not regard such remarks in later Stoics as Platonizing *intrusions*;

---

[37] The monistic strand allowed a creative adaptation of Heraclitus, on which see Long (1975/1976), 45–46. The dualistic elements are probably due to the (diffuse) influence of the Academy (see the comparison between Xenocrates and Stoicism in Aetius I 7.30; general comparison between Platonic world soul and Stoic immanent god in Sextus *M* IX 107) and Peripatetic hylomorphism. For the Academic and Peripatetic background, see in general Hahm (1977) 29–56. Some notes on the possible influence of the *Timaeus* and the Academy are in Reydams-Schils (1999) 41–82.

they reflect a strand that had been present in orthodox Stoicism all along.[38]

So much for the 'two faces' (monistic and dualistic) of Stoic pantheism. Other aspects of the Stoic god rather appear to have favoured a yet different, more strictly theistic approach. As an immanent formative principle, god is said to be the one 'according to whom' a particular cosmic ordering comes to be and is perfected (Arius Didymus fr. 31), and since at the beginning of each cosmic cycle this creative process starts out from god himself, he may also be called the 'Demiurge' or 'Craftsman' of the cosmos (DL VII 137). As Zeno is claimed to have put it, the all-embracing rational nature is not just 'craftsmanlike', but also actually 'a craftsman' (Cicero ND II 58). Also when the Stoics spoke of god as a 'father', as 'blessed', 'happy', and 'beneficial', and when they identified providence with 'the will of Zeus' (Calcidius In Tim. 144), they were taking what looks like a theistic point of view. Behind all this lies the firm conviction that god's rationality – or, for that matter, the rationality of the cosmos – does not differ in kind from human rationality, so that to some extent god can be viewed as a 'person' with purposes and intentions. Interestingly, this is a point on which Spinoza, whose pantheism in some respects resembles Stoicism, radically parts company. In the famous appendix to the first part of his *Ethica*, he argues that the introduction of the wrongheaded ideas of cosmic teleology and providence has been the result of an all-too-human view of how god (i.e., the cosmos) actually works.[39] Anyway, it is worth noting that insofar as a later Stoic like Epictetus predominantly speaks of god in a theistic fashion, he is taking up a strand of Stoic theology which has been present right from the start.[40]

We now come to the polytheistic aspect of Stoic theology. The fact that the Stoics flatly rejected the traditional anthropomorphic Greek pantheon represents only one aspect of their attitude *vis-à-vis* the tradition. Their belief that the parts of the cosmos – the stars

---

[38] That there are Platonizing tendencies at work in Seneca's conception of the divine, and of the cosmic hierarchy, has been argued by Bonhöffer (1890) 78 and more generally by Donini (1979).

[39] On Spinoza and Stoicism, see Ch. 15, A. A. Long, in this volume.

[40] Ascribing such theistic utterances in Epictetus to the particular 'ferveur' of his 'piété' (cf. Jagu (1989) 2176–2177) tends to obscure the continuity between Epictetus and his predecessors in this respect.

and the sun in particular, but also the elements and so on – could be labeled divine also allowed the Stoics to make sense of various elements of traditional polytheistic myth by re-interpreting these in a cosmological sense. Thus Zeno of Citium already provided physical interpretations of elements of Greek myth as they can be found in Hesiod's *Theogony*. Although this practice of what is usually called 'allegorical interpretation' was certainly not new,[41] Zeno appears to have had his own agenda. His purpose was clearly not to defend the (consistency of the) ancient poet, nor to provide a sophisticated and enlightened version of traditional religion, but merely to 'appropriate' *some* elements of Hesiodic myth and to use these in support of his own Stoic cosmology and cosmogony.[42] In other words, we are only dealing with a partial and qualified acceptance of traditional polytheism. Similar practices are attested for Cleanthes, Chrysippus, Diogenes of Babylon, and – on a more systematic scale – the later Stoic Cornutus.[43] Of course, also here the Stoics could rely on their conviction (referred to in previous sections) that the myths and beliefs of the people of old contained elements of truth insofar as these people had at the very least formed a partial adumbration of the right preconception of god.[44]

It appears, then, that one of the most striking features of Stoic theology was its rather fluid conception of god. This did not go unnoticed. The Epicureans already found fault with it, as can again be inferred from the critique expressed by Velleius in the first book of the *De natura deorum*. Velleius criticizes Cleanthes for having at one moment said that the world itself is god, but at another for having given this name to the mind of the world, or to aether, or to

[41] A brief survey of the history of the practice in Algra (2001), n. 1.
[42] This procedure of 'appropriation' (*sunoikeioun*) is explicitly ascribed to Cleanthes and Chrysippus in Philodemus *Piet.*, PHerc.1428, col. vi, 16–26 (text in Henrichs [1974] 17). An equivalent term (*accommodare*) is used, with reference to Chrysippus, by Cicero *ND* I 41 (the texts of Cicero and Philodemus are to be traced back to a common source, possibly Zeno of Sidon).
[43] For a convenient survey of the evidence concerning Cleanthes, Chrysippus and Diogenes of Babylon, see Steinmetz (1986) 23–28; on Chrysippus and etymology, see Tieleman (1996) 196–203; on Cornutus, see Most (1989).
[44] The Epicurean opponents strongly disagreed. Velleius in the first book of Cicero's *De natura deorum* claims that it is precisely by re-interpreting the mythical gods and divesting them of their anthropomorphic features that Zeno took leave of the tradition (*ND* I 36), ending up with a cosmic god that was far removed from the right preconception (*ibid.* 37).

the stars (*ND* I 37). Similar criticisms are leveled against Zeno and Chrysippus (*ND* I 36–41).[45] They reappear in such later writers as Lactantius and Plutarch.[46] It would be wrong to view these varying Stoic conceptions of god as the result of incoherent and unconnected concessions to the tradition. In fact, the Stoics took great pains to account for the juxtaposition of what we might call pantheistic and polytheistic elements in their theology, by 'appropriating' and re-interpreting some aspects of traditional polytheism, while clearly rejecting others. Moreover, as I have tried to show, the various ways in which they could present their pantheism, and the *juxtaposition* of pantheism and theism, can all be explained by reference to the peculiar characteristics of Stoic physics and metaphysics.

V.

We may finally turn to the identification of the Stoic god with fate and providence and to some of the problems involved. According to the Stoics, god as fate determines everything. At the same time, as nature, he also sets the standard for what is morally good, a norm for humans to follow. Together these *prima facie* conflicting claims con-stitute the problem of 'free will' and moral responsibility, a subject discussed elsewhere in this volume.[47] But Stoic determinism also generates a problem of a more strictly theological nature: if god, *qua* fate, determines everything, and if, *qua* providence, he is at the same time intrinsically good, how are we to account for the existence of evil in the world? This question becomes all the more acute since providence, according to the Stoics, is not just a matter of cosmic teleology, of securing that the world as a whole is a beautiful and well-organised thing, or rather animal (Cicero *ND* II 58, and 71–153). Providence crucially extends to the position of man: the world is said to be there for the sake of gods and men (Cicero *ND* II 154–167). Why then do men suffer in a world in which everything is supposed to be for the best and tailored to human needs?

This is the problem of theodicy. In order to be able to sketch the Stoic answers, we should first of all make a distinction between the

---

[45] Cicero is here probably drawing on the arguments of his one-time Epicurean teacher, Zeno of Sidon.

[46] Cf. Lactantius *Div. inst.* VII 3 (SVF 2.1041); Plutarch *Comm. not.* 1085 B–C.

[47] See Ch. 7, Frede, in this volume.

causes of moral evil on the one hand and those of cosmic evil on the other. Moral evil, in the Stoic theory, is attributable to man himself. It is a matter of people making irrational choices and assenting to the wrong propositions. Insofar as this answer brings us back to the question of moral responsibility and determinism, we need not further discuss it in this chapter. Let us just note that the later Stoic Epictetus claims on almost every page that this is the kind of evil that really counts (because its elimination is 'up to us'). Yet even Epictetus has to acknowledge that there is also the question of the existence of cosmic evil and its relation to providence. The problem appears to have been addressed rather at length by Chrysippus in the fourth book of his *On providence* (Aulus Gellius *NA* VII 1.1–13 = SVF 2.1169 and 1170). Let us have a look at the way or rather, ways, in which he thought to be able to answer this question.

His first answer claims that, as opposites, good and evil are interdependent, both epistemically (we cannot conceive of the good without evil) and ontologically (the good apparently cannot exist without evil). The second answer is of a physical nature, although it proceeds along similar lines as (and, according to Gellius, is related to) the first answer: the good and purposive workings of providence inevitably involve some concomitant evils, as a form of 'collateral damage'.[48] Two further Chrysippean answers have been recorded by Plutarch (*St. rep.* 1051 B–C), but it is not clear to what extent Chrysippus was actually positively committed to them (the phrasing suggests that he may have merely presented them as suggestions in a dialectical context). Evil may be due to some simple oversights, just as in a good household a little wheat may sometimes be lost.[49] Or such mishaps may be due to bad daemons.[50] Finally, in his *On nature*, Chrysippus also

---

[48] In the Stoic god, as the governing principle of the cosmos, we thus find as it were 'telescoped' together what Plato's *Timaeus* (e.g., 46 e–47 c) attributed to the activity of the Demiurge on the one hand and to Necessity (with its 'co-causes') on the other. The example which, according to Gellius, *loc. cit.*, Chrysippus gave of necessary 'concomitances' (the fragility of the human skull, inevitable for the enhancement of our rationality, for with a fleshy and thick skull there would not be room enough for the senory organs) appears to have been imported from *Tim.* 75 a–c.

[49] A solution that had been emphatically rejected by Plato *Leg.* X 901 b–903 b.

[50] Little is known of the Stoic view on daemons. The term *daimôn* could be used to denote the human rational soul (cf. DL VII, 88, and Posidonius fr. 187 EK), but there is some evidence (DL VII, 151; Plutarch *Is.* 260 E, *Def. Or.* 419 A), which suggests that prominent Stoics like Chrysippus and Posidonius also believed in the existence of independent daemons, beings which were traditionally credited with

claimed that some apparent evils can simply be explained away by showing that on closer view they are goods: wars may drain off surplus population (Plutarch *St. rep.* 1049 B, quotation from Chrysippus' *On the gods*) and, on a smaller scale, bedbugs wake us up and mice encourage us not to be untidy (Plutarch *St. rep.* 1044 D).

It would be otiose to evaluate these arguments here. I want to note that especially the first two show that in a sense, the powers of the Stoic god are, perhaps surprisingly, limited. His workings do entail a degree of imperfection and are bound by certain constraints. It is true that as a formative force he guarantees the teleology and the ordering for the good which is to be found in the cosmos (in a way which a random disposition of atoms along the lines of Epicurean physics never could achieve, according to the Stoics). Yet, as a rational principle, he incorporates the laws of rationality, where opposites may be said to entail each other, and as a physical force he incorporates the laws of physics, according to which some things cannot be created without a certain amount of waste.[51] He is clearly not a transcendent factor of mere bliss. In this respect, the Stoic conception of god is much closer to Heraclitus than to either the Neoplatonic or the Judaeo-Christian conceptions of god.[52]

Related to the problem of cosmic evil is the question of how the theorem of the periodic conflagration of the cosmos – another inevitable concomitant of god's physical nature, for as fire or *pneuma* he has to consume his fuel (i.e., cosmic matter)[53] – could be fitted

an intermediary status between men and gods. As independent 'psychic' entities that were stronger than men, but possessed a divinity which was not unalloyed, such demigods could apparently be either good or bad. In the former case they were thought to figure as guardians over human affairs (DL VII, 151). In the latter case they could do harm – a fact which was apparently thought to be just as compatible with the overall providential design of the cosmos as the existence of moral evil among men. For the evidence on Posidonius' work *On Heroes and Daemons*, see frs. 24 and 108 EK.

51 This may be why Cleanthes claimed that some things which come about by fate are nonetheless not the product of providence (Calcidius *in Tim.* 144). He may, however, also have been thinking of moral evil (which is 'up to us' and hence not attributable to god). That god, as a physical force, is limited by certain constraints is also suggested by Epictetus *Diss.* I 1.7–13 and II 5.27.

52 This may serve to counter the notorious suggestion of Pohlenz (1948), 96 and 100 (and elsewhere) that the Stoic conception of god was basically un-Greek and more closely akin to the 'Semitic' conception of a transcendent divinity.

53 See Zeno's argument in Alexander of Lycopolis 19, 2–4 (not in SVF; text in LS 46 I); see further Van der Horst and Mansfeld (1974).

into the providential ordering of the cosmos.[54] How can an immanent and providential god be responsible for the destruction of the
cosmos? Chrysippus discussed this subject in the first book of his *On
providence* (see the text printed as SVF 2.604, 605, 623, and 1049).
His main line of defense appears to have been to claim that the cosmos does not really die (hence in a sense is not really destroyed)
in the act of conflagration. For the conflagration is not the death –
in the strict sense of the *separation* of body and soul – of the cosmos. God, the soul, rather *consumes* the body of the cosmos, only
to renew it by turning into primeval moisture again (SVF 2.604). In
a relevant sense, then, the cosmos is not destroyed but lives on to be
eternal.

Apart from the problem of theodicy, the identification of god with
both providence and fate also involved the need to redefine the relation between god and man as traditionally conceived, in particular
the way in which gods communicates to man (divination) and man
communicates to god (prayer). Epicurus ridiculed the idea of a (theistically conceived) god waiting for the occurrence of signs in order
to take the appropriate action (*Letter to Pythocles* 115). The Stoics
tried to avoid similar absurdities by explaining divination, in a pantheistic rather than a theistic way, as not involving any specific and
intentional course of action on the part of god but as something made
possible by the providentially ordered sequence of causes and effects
in the cosmos:

The gods are not directly responsible for every fissure in the liver or for every
song of a bird, since, manifestly, that would not be seemly or proper in a god,
and furthermore is impossible. But, from the beginning, the universe was
so created that certain results would be preceded by certain signs, which
are given sometimes by entrails and by birds, sometimes by lightning, by
portents and by stars, sometimes by dreams, and sometimes by utterances
of persons in a frenzy (Cicero *Div.* I 118).[55]

This attitude explains why the Stoics did not conceive of divination as some kind of irrational religious hocus-pocus, nor as a form
of theurgy, but as a science.[56]

---

[54] For the Platonic and Aristotelian background of the problem, see Mansfeld (1979).
See also Long (1985) and Algra (1995) 301–302.
[55] See also Seneca *NQ* II 32.3–4.
[56] Cf. Chrysippus' definition as recorded by Sextus *M* IX 132 (Latin version in Cicero

The identification of god with fate also raised the question whether there was any sense in which humans could meaningfully address such a god in prayers. For how could god's will (theistically speaking) or the structure of what he brings about (pantheistically speaking) ever be changed?[57] Seneca (*NQ* II 35) gives what for a Stoic would seem to be the most strict and rigid answer to this question:

What use are expiations and precautions if the fates are immutable? Allow me to support that rigid sect of philosophers who accept such practices with a smile and consider them only a solace for a troubled mind. The fates perform their function in another way and they are not moved by any prayer.

Yet, in general, a more liberal attitude toward prayer appears to have been acceptable as well. Cleanthes' famous *Hymn to Zeus* (SVF 1.537) is a prayer, or at least ends as a prayer. And we may also point to the prayer by Cleanthes, which is quoted at the end of Epictetus' *Manual*:[58]

Lead me, O Zeus, and you, Destiny,
to wherever you have assigned me to go.
I will not falter, and follow; and should I be unwilling,
and be bad, I shall follow even so.

The first thing to note, however, is that neither this short text nor the more monumental *Hymn* offers the kind of traditional prayers that ask for ordinary and particular favours. The small prayer simply asks Zeus to lead Cleanthes wherever he has ordained him to go, and where he would lead him anyway. Cleanthes does not ask god to change his mind. The *Hymn* offers a slightly different case. To be sure, it does address Zeus with the traditional epithet 'bountiful' (*pandôros*, line 28), but the bounties he is asked to confer are of a moral, intellectual, or even 'spiritual' nature. What the *Hymn* (29–34) prays for appears to be virtue:

Protect mankind from its pitiful incompetence. Scatter this from our soul, father. Let us achieve the power of judgment by trusting in which you steer

---

Div. II 130): 'the science which contemplates and interprets the signs which are given to human beings by the gods'.

[57] Related problems involved in the acceptance of the feasibility of prayer are the following. Why would god need to be asked to grant benefits? What would it mean for god to be 'moved' by prayer? Shouldn't god, who is perfectly virtuous, also be unaffected by anything (*apathês*)?

[58] Epictetus *Ench.* 53 (rough Latin version in Seneca in *Ep.* 107.10).

all things with justice, so that by winning honour we may repay you with honour, forever singing of your works, as it benefits mortals to do.

We are dealing, in other words, with a prayer for rationality.[59] That this is what prayers should really be like is also suggested by Marcus Aurelius (IX 40). To someone who wonders to what extent prayers can be useful, he replies as follows:

Who has told you that the gods are not also helping us with regard to that which is in our power? So begin to pray for these things and you will see what happens. The man over there prays 'how can I manage to sleep with her?' – you pray: 'how can I stop wanting to sleep with her?' [...] Put your prayers, quite generally, in this form, and see what happens.

Yet to the extent that this passage from Marcus and Cleanthes' *Hymn* might be taken to suggest that god can at any moment bestow or withhold rationality as it pleases him, and can also be moved by prayer to do so, we are again facing the problem of how god is able (and why he would be willing) to change the course of his action. Perhaps we should simply conclude that in formulating such prayers, Stoics like Cleanthes were simply giving in to tradition, or allowed themselves to be carried away by the theistic elements of their theology at the expense of its overall philosophical coherence. There seems to be a way out, however, which the Stoics might have taken, although our sources offer no unambiguous evidence that they actually did. The short prayer at the end of Epictetus' *Manual*, though professing to address Zeus (and fate), may in fact be regarded as a form of self-address. It represents a form of meditation, of telling one's rational self that Zeus will lead, and that one will have to follow the decrees of fate anyway. This, obviously, is why Epictetus introduces it by telling us that he wants us 'to have these thoughts at our command upon every occasion'.

Similarly, the prayer for rationality at the end of the *Hymn* need not be conceived as urging god to *do* anything, but as a request simply to reveal himself to human reason (which after all is said to be able to 'acquire the power of judgment' by which Zeus steers all things). That, in its turn, could be explained as an 'indirect' way (i.e., couched in traditional and theistic form) of trying to perfect one's own reason;

---

[59] The injunction that one should only pray for what is good, virtue or rationality, is a familiar one in the context of ancient philosophical theologies; see, e.g., Xenophanes fr. B 1, 15–16; Xenophon *Mem.* I, 3, 2; Plato *Leg.* 687 e.

in other words, as equally a form of self-address: a reminder that one should have one's own internal daimon in tune with the cosmic reason (DL VII, 88). One might even go one step further and speak of a *direct* self-address in this case. After all, our 'rational self' is, in Stoic terms, a part (an *apospasma*, DL VII, 143) of the cosmic god, so that the prayer could be conceived as directed toward this inner *apospasma* (i.e., toward what Seneca would later describe as 'the god in us').[60] The divine help 'with regard to that which is in our power' of which Marcus speaks could equally be conceived not as help from an external god but as help from the god within us.

Conceived as a kind of self-address (whether direct or indirect) of reason, Cleanthes' prayers would to some extent be comparable with his famous internal dialogue between reason (*logismos*) and passion (or anger, *thumos*) quoted by Galen (*PHP* V 6, p. 332 De Lacy = SVF 1.570).[61] In general, moreover, such a revisionary conception of prayer – in which the relation between god and man is no longer one between man and an external 'giver of gifts', but has rather been internalized – would not be at odds with what the Stoics otherwise thought about providence and determinism, for it is precisely the assent or non-assent of this rational self to whatever presents itself to it which constitutes the only thing which is 'up to us' and hence in a sense free from the inexorable laws of fate.[62]

Such a revisionary conception of prayer would also fit in well with some other examples of the Stoics re-interpreting the relation between god(s) and men as traditionally conceived. In this connection, one may point to the way in which the early Stoics apparently redefined the concept of being a 'friend' or 'enemy' of god or the gods, viz. as referring to one's being (or not being) one in mind with god.[63] And later, in Seneca, we find the claim that when talking about the

---

[60] See Seneca *Ep.* 41, 1: 'You are doing a very good thing [. . .] if you are persisting in your effort to attain sound understanding (*bonam mentem*). It is foolish to pray for this if you can acquire it from yourself. We do not need to lift our hands up towards heaven, or beg the keeper of a temple to let us approach the ear of the idol [. . .] God is near you, he is with you, he is within you (*prope est a te deus, tecum est, intus est*)'.

[61] As an example of inner dialogue in later Stoicism, one might adduce the self-scrutiny advocated in Seneca *De ira* III 36.

[62] Cf. Seneca, *Ep.* 10.5, who claims that if we pray primarily for a *bona mens*, we do not pray for something alien (*nihil eum de alieno rogaturus es*).

[63] Stobaeus *Ecl.* II 7 106; SVF 3.661). Here also one may point to parallels in other philosophers offering a rationalized theology; see, e.g., Plato *Leg.* 716 c–d.

relation between man and god, the traditional notion of beneficence (*beneficium*) should be re-interpreted: We do not honour the gods by bloody offerings, but by our right and virtuous intention (*Ben*. I, 6, 3). God seeks no servants, and the proper cult of god is to know him, and to imitate him (*Ep*. 95, 47, and 50).[64]

Just as Stoic theology rejected some elements of the traditional stories about the gods (anthropomorphism), Stoics also rejected some elements of traditional cult. Thus, Zeno's *Republic* advocated the abolition of temples and cult statues as being unworthy of the real god.[65] And just as the Stoics could re-interpret certain elements of traditional myth (i.e., the cosmic gods in Hesiod), they could re-interpret the meaning of certain elements of traditional cult (e.g., divination, prayer). Although this means that strictly speaking they could only accept a philosophically 'enlightened' version of traditional Greco-Roman religion, they did not in practice adopt a radical attitude toward the religious tradition. Plutarch reproaches them for sacrificing at altars and temples which they professedly believe should not exist at all (*St. rep.* 1034 C). Indeed, Epictetus admits that a Stoic should in practice respect the religious conventions of his country (*Ench.* 31, 5). The Stoics were by no means alone in advocating this basically conservative approach. It is ascribed to Socrates by Xenophon (*Mem.* I, 3, 1 and IV, 3, 16), it can be found in the Platonic (or pseudo-Platonic) *Epinomis* (985c–d), and it is presented as something enjoined by Apollo in a Theophrastean fragment (fr. 584D FHS& G). Interestingly enough, it is also a view to which both Academic (Cicero *ND* III, 5–6; 44–45) and Pyrrhonian (Sextus *M* IX 49) sceptics subscribed. However, whereas the sceptics severed the link between the tradition, which they thought should be kept for practical reasons, and the truth, which they thought could not be established with any certainty, the Stoics took a different view. As we have seen, they believed the truth about gods and religion was in principle accessible and that traditional forms of cult and belief could at least be seen as approximations – however primitive and partial – of that truth. That being so, they presumably believed that

---

[64] What we get in return are the benefits of virtue; this is arguably the point in Seneca *Ep.* 41.2.

[65] See the texts printed as SVF 1.264; here the influence of the Cynics (in particular Diogenes) may have played its role, on which see Goulet-Cazé (1996). See also Seneca *Ben.* VII 7, 4.

one should not too easily dispose of traditional religion, where the majority of mankind will probably never be able work itself up to accepting the right philosophical attitude (compare the claim, quoted at the beginning of this chapter, that 'it is quite a struggle to hear the right things about the gods and to get hold of them'), whereas a religious tradition that encompasses at least *some* elements of the right preconception of the gods could be thought to be better than nothing.

7   Stoic Determinism

I. BACKGROUND

Stoicism is a philosophy of moral rigor. This rigor has given rise to two stereotypes. First, a Stoic either has no feelings or successfully suppresses them. Second, the Stoics' belief in an all-encompassing fate only leaves humans with the option of readily complying with its predetermined order. If compliance with fate is the bottom line of Stoic philosophy, what could be more reasonable than an unemotional resignation to its ineluctable decrees? Though in antiquity both friends and foes had a much more complex view of Stoic philosophy, its particular version of determinism was the target of attacks by members of rival schools from early on. What could be the point of moral reflections and an active engagement in life's concerns if everything is fated to happen anyway? The debate on the question of the compatibility of fate with human responsibility therefore never ceased during the five hundred years of that school's existence. Though the long and intensive intellectual life of the school makes it unlikely that its entire philosophy was based on inherently contradictory principles, the continued attacks and counterattacks at least suggest some *tension* in the type of determinism fostered by the Stoics. What then, is the gist of Stoic determinism and in what way is it compatible with their insistence on an active life in compliance with carefully worked-out moral principles? Since pioneers like Pohlenz, Sambursky, Long, Rist, and Sandbach have drawn attention to the intricacies of Stoic philosophy, the debate on Stoic compatibilism in secondary literature has steadily increased, and to this very day the question has not been settled to everyone's satisfaction. In view of the complexity of the present discussion, this chapter will provide no more than an overview of the main principles of Stoic determinism. In the interest of 'streamlining', the discussion may neglect developments within the Stoic school and the changing attitude of the Stoics' adversaries. Instead, it aims to construct as coherent a picture as our sources permit.[1]

Like most 'isms', determinism is a latecomer.[2] But determinist thought in some form or other has occupied philosophers and scientists since early antiquity. The most prominent versions are nowadays summed up under the titles of 'physical determinism', 'logical determinism', 'ethical determinism', and 'teleological determinism'. The first type deals with the connection between cause(s) and effect, the second with reasons and conclusions, the third with the preconditions of human decisions, the fourth with the determination by an overall purpose or end. All four types are already present in Aristotle's physical, logical, and ethical works. Not only that, Aristotle recognizes their interconnections and also employs suitable vocabulary to mark off the difference between what is determined in some way (hôrismenon) and what lacks determination (ahoriston).[3] But despite this recognition, the issue of a universal determination of all that happens in nature and in human life does not seem to have preoccupied him much. This may seem surprising, given his well worked-out set of four causes, his concern with the factors that determine human action, and his insistence on necessity as a prerequisite for science proper.

A brief review of the Aristotelian conception of causality will set in relief the Stoics' quite different presuppositions, which made them protagonists in the debate on determinism throughout later

---

[1] Bobzien's (1998) monograph on *Determinism and Freedom in Stoic Philosophy* is a 'must' for anyone interested in this topic. It gives a comprehensive picture of the history and the difficulties of the problematic as well as of the reasons for disagreement in the secondary literature. For a shorter and less detailed discussion, cf. Hankinson in Algra et al. (1999), Chs. 14 and 15.

[2] The article 'Determinismus/Indeterminismus' in (ed.) J. Ritter *Historisches Wörterbuch der Philosophie*, Vol. 2 1972, 150–5, traces back the use in German to the second half of the eighteenth century. The *OED* (second edition 1989) *sv.* 'determinism' refers to Sir W. Hamilton, *Reid's Works* 1846, note 87: 'There are two schemes of Necessity – the Necessitation by efficient – the Necessitation by final causes. The first is brutal as blind Fate; the latter rational Determinism.'

[3] Cf. *Phys.* 196b28. Since Aristotle is not our topic here, readers are referred to Bonitz's *Index Aristotelicus, s.v. horizein* and *ahoristos* or *apeiros*. The Latin cognates, *determinatio* and *indeterminatio*, became standard in later antiquity.

antiquity. Admittedly, Aristotle was not the first philosopher to reflect on the question that is central to the problem of determinism: whether there are certain 'laws' that govern nature, including human nature, to the extent that all or certain events necessarily occur. In fact, Cicero claims an old pedigree for necessitarianism.[4] Even if one may doubt the correctness of his list, it is clear that the question of necessity was debated from early on. Nor is that surprising. In addition to the long-standing Greek concern with divinely grounded inevitability (moira), the Presocratic project of offering large-scale rational explanations invited the philosophical worry. Once Parmenides had challenged the very possibility of generation and change on the grounds that nothing can come from nothing and that nothing can turn into nothing, philosophers were aware of the need to give proper accounts for all that happens in nature. The so-called Parmenidean challenge was met by his successors in various ways, and the most comprehensive accounts of nature inevitably seemed to necessitate as well as to explain.

If Aristotle, rather than Plato, is presented as the antagonist of the Stoics here, it is because he shares with them certain important presuppositions on the basic nature of the universe. Since many readers are more familiar with Aristotelianism than with Stoicism, a comparison will be helpful. First, the points of agreement. (1) Both Aristotle and the Stoics regard the universe as finite, with earth in its centre. (2) The Stoics shared the Aristotelian conviction that physical nature is based on a continuum of matter, space, and time; they also rejected the notion of a void within the universe. (3) Like Aristotle, the Stoics supported 'two-sided possibility' or 'contingency' in the sense that certain states are neither necessary nor impossible. And (4) like Aristotle, the Stoics upheld the principle that there is no motion without cause and that, given the same circumstances, there will always be the same outcome.

Whether Aristotle himself is really an adherent of the last tenet has often been questioned. It is worth reviewing the extent to which he can be called a causal determinist because this will bring out

---

[4] Cicero, Fat. 39: '[...] there is the opinion of those who held that everything takes place by fate in the sense that this fate exercises the force of necessity – the opinion to which Democritus, Heraclitus, Empedocles and Aristotle adhered [...].' For a brief overview of the history of determinist thought, cf. Bobzien (1998), 2–6. On the question of fatalism in earlier Greek thought, cf. D. Frede (1992), 195–9.

the main points of divergence between him and the Stoics. There are four types of causes in Aristotle: matter, form, the moving or efficient cause, and the final cause or *telos*. This explanatory schema is applied by Aristotle to account for the nature of all things, in physics as well as in ethics and in his metaphysics.[5] If Aristotle – despite this comprehensive causal scheme – is not usually regarded as a determinist, this is primarily because of four reasons:

- since substances and the conditions of substantiality stand in the centre of his metaphysics, as well as of his natural philosophy, his explanatory scheme does not focus on the causes of events and their interconnections, but rather on the explanation of what is typical of substances, their properties, and specific activities;
- Aristotle's causal scheme is just what its name suggests: it is a mere schema – there is no common nature but only an analogy between the matter, form, efficient cause, and *telos* of different things or events;[6]
- for Aristotle, every process finds its natural conclusion with the attainment of its particular *telos*; though he does not exclude the possibility that this result may be a factor in some further causal nexus, the notion of endless causal chains is not a concern of his; and
- the distinction between what does and does not belong in a given teleological context allows Aristotle to distinguish between regular and irregular results. The criteria for what is irregular are quite clear cut; chance (*apo tuchês*) or accidental (*apo t'automatou*) results are due to an overlapping of different trains of events with separate ends or purposes. Only what happens necessarily or 'for the most part' is the

---

[5] We leave aside here the problem of 'logical determinism', especially the question in what sense the truth of propositions about the future 'necessitates' the outcome. This problem may have originated with the dialecticians of the Megarian school. It vexed not only Aristotle, as witnessed in his famous Ch. 9 of *De interpretatione*, but also played an important role in the Stoic theory (cf. Bobzien [1998], 59–86 and D. Frede [1992]).

[6] On the question in what sense Aristotelian causes deserve their name cf. Sorabji (1980), Chs. 2 and 3. On the role of the Stoic conception of causality in the development of the conception of an 'efficient cause', M. Frede (1980).

subject of science. There is no need to account for accidental overlapping.[7]

This list should suffice to show that despite certain common features, the Aristotelian and the Stoic conception of nature and causality are far apart:

- Stoic philosophy does not focus on substances, their properties, and activities, but on the physical constitution of bodies and their interactions.
- Instead of an analogous causal scheme, there are two all-pervasive principles in nature. There is in each case one active, rational force that permeates its passive counterpart, determining the form and consistency of all objects in the universe.[8] This divine spirit works as form, *telos*, material, and efficient cause all at once. In compliance with traditional religion, the Stoics identify the active element with Zeus, the passive element with Hera – as the indispensable consort of the active element.[9] Both elements are physical bodies; the active rational principle is a mixture of air and fire that is called *pneuma*. The passive principle has no positive attributes but is associated with the traditionally inert elements of water and earth.
- Given the inner unity of these two principles, teleological explanations are not confined to the aims or ends of specific processes. Everything is part of an all-encompassing causal network.
- Since there are no uncoordinated trains of events in the universe, there are no irregular occurrences that do not 'belong' in a given context. Though the Stoics do not deny the difference between what happens regularly and rare occurrences, the latter are as much part of nature as the regular events. Chance and luck are therefore merely a matter of human

---

[7] Cf. D. Frede (1992).

[8] Cf. Alexander of Aphrodisias, *Fat.* 191, 32–192, 5. 'They say that this universe, which is one and contains in itself all that exists, and is organised by a nature which is alive, rational and intelligent, administers what is eternally in accordance with a sequence and progressing order...'

[9] On this issue, see also Ch. 5, White, this volume.

ignorance: what seem to us like freak accidents are part of the overall order of nature.

2. UNITY AND PLURALITY IN THE STOIC UNIVERSE

The uniform nature of the active and passive powers within the cosmic order also explains why there is, in contradistinction to Plato and Aristotle, no separation in Stoicism of the super- and the sub-lunary world. The heavenly motions are ruled by the same principles that operate on earth: All of nature is administered by the supreme divine reason, and hence there is a global teleological determinism that the Stoics identified with *fate*.[10] The omnipotence of the active principle explains the Stoic conception of an overall *sumpatheia* within nature, an inner connection between seemingly quite disparate events. Divination, the study of divine signs and portents, is therefore treated as a science in Stoicism rather than as superstition. Careful observation leads to the discovery of certain *signs* of those interconnections, even if human knowledge does not fully comprehend the rationale behind the observable order of all things. This explains why the Stoics not only supported the traditional practices of divination, but also helped establish astrology as a respectable science in the Greek and Roman world.[11]

This overview suggests that the main difference between the Stoics and Aristotle lies in the scope of their teleology. For the Stoics there is one all-embracing world order and universal coordination. In Aristotle, all causes, including the *telos*, are confined to their 'local' context. There is no necessary interconnection or coordination between all that happens in the universe. Before we settle for this picture of Aristotelian 'localism' versus Stoic 'globalism' and accept the latter as the basis of the tensions within their system, we should take a closer look at their attempt to introduce finer distinctions that do not readily agree with the undifferentiated 'globalism' attributed

[10] On the all-encompassing power of fate, its identity with reason and god, cf. Alexander of Aphrodisias, *Fat.* 192, 25–28: 'Fate itself, nature, and reason according to which the whole is administered they say is god...' – No distinction between fatalism and causal determinism will be made here, in view of the fact that the Stoics etymologically derived *heimarmenê*, their standard term designating fate, from *eirô* = 'to string together'. Cf. also Bobzien (1998), 45–50.
[11] On the Stoic attitude to astrology, cf. Long (1982). For a general overview of ancient astrology, cf. Barton (1994).

to them so far. In fact, their faith in an overall unity within nature does not prevent them from analysing individual connections among events and from studying the nature and conditions of particular beings and occurrences. Contrary to what one might expect, the Stoic ideal of 'living in accordance with nature'[12] – is not based on a romantic pantheistic conviction that 'All is one and all is well.' They did not regard it as a sufficient precondition for the proper conduct of life that human beings should be familiar with the broad features of reality and learn to play by the rules they seem to set. Instead, they recommended a careful study of the nature of all things, including human nature, in order to learn how to comply with what happens naturally in the appropriate way. Since human beings are endowed with reason, they have to work out an adequate understanding of the order of things – both at the cosmic and at the individual level.[13] These considerations explain why the Stoics – despite their unitarian cosmology – also adopt finer distinctions within their causal analysis. Although every individual and every particular event is part of the divine order, different entities play different roles in that causal web. The need for a proper understanding of those connections is all the more pressing, since human beings are not omniscient and possess at best a partial understanding of the divine order.

That there is plurality in the overall cosmic unity explains, then, why the Stoics worked out distinctions among the causal factors that determine the state of different kinds of entities and insisted on a certain amount of autonomy for individual beings. The Stoics were pantheists in the sense that for them the entire world is permeated by the divine *pneuma*. But this type of pantheism is not to be confused with panpsychism: the divine *pneuma* is not present everywhere in the same form and does not give consciousness and reason to all things. There is a *scala naturae* in Stoicism. In lifeless entities like stones or water, the divine *pneuma* constitutes their inner coherence and physical properties (*hexis*), including their changes. The *pneuma* allows plants to sustain themselves (*phusis*); it gives animals perception and mobility (*psuchê*). Human beings not only share the kind of *pneuma* that constitutes life, but are also ruled by a portion of the *pneuma* in its purest form, namely reason (*dianoia*).

---

[12] Cf. DL VII 87–88. The precise meaning of this maxim is very much a matter of debate; cf. Inwood (1985), 105 f.

[13] Cf. Cicero, *Fin.* II 34; III 73.

As their leading principle (*hêgemonikon*), the rational *pneuma* determines all their actions.[14] In complex organisms there is, then, a highly diverse set of 'pneumatic' forces at work that keeps them alive and functioning at the physiological as well as mental levels. Due to the relative stability of the inner 'pneumatic' state, the individual forms a microcosm within the macrocosmic network of causal factors. Therefore, individual entities have a certain autonomy. It is the inner makeup of human reason that determines the way in which a person interacts with his or her environment. There are, then, good reasons for the Stoics to distinguish between inner and outer circumstances in an individual's life, despite the all-pervasive cosmological forces that constitute and maintain the nature of all things. As these considerations indicate, there is room for overall unity as well as plurality within the Stoic system. How this inner autonomy of the individual agrees with the Stoic conception of overall determinism remains to be seen.

We should note that the fact that the Stoics attribute a certain degree of independence and autonomy to individual beings also explains the Stoics' interest in the question of the nature of surfaces and boundaries. The boundary of every individual entity is a function of the equilibrium of its inner *pneuma* that keeps it together and separates it from its environment. It seems a mistake, therefore, to deny surfaces the status of real beings and to treat them as mere constructs of the human mind.[15] It is in order to avoid paradoxes of a Zenonian type that the boundaries are not classified as bodies, but as their properties.

3. THE STOIC NOTION OF CAUSALITY – PRELIMINARY CLARIFICATION

The need to combine unity at the cosmic level with plurality in their inner-cosmic depiction of nature and especially in human life accounts for the differentiation between the causal factors on which the Stoics based their defense of the compatibility of determinism with individual human freedom. Before we can turn to the arguments themselves, a brief elucidation of the Stoic notion of causation is nec-

---

[14] Cf. Philo *Leg. Alleg.* II Section 22 1, 95,8 (SVF II, 458). On the details of this theory, cf. Ch. 6, Algra, this volume.
[15] Contra White's contention in Ch. 5 and Long and Sedley (1987), 301. The status of lines and surfaces in mathematics is quite another question.

essary. This is a particularly difficult task since the accounts in our sources disagree in important ways. Some sources treat the Stoics as causal unitarians. Witness, for instance, Seneca's insistence on the simplicity of the Stoic conception of cause, *Ep.* 65, 11: 'When we look for the cause, we mean the reason that produces it, and that is god.'[16] Whereas some sources concentrate on the *one* active force, others speak of a 'swarm of causes', insinuating that the Stoics tried to obfuscate the embarrassing consequence of their determinist principles by a set of bewildering distinctions.[17] It is therefore necessary to sort out the different kinds of causal factors recognized by the Stoics and to explain their interconnections. The Stoic distinctions of causes and causal factors are indeed difficult to comprehend, unless one keeps separate the different levels and aspects of their accounts. At the cosmic level, there is indeed only one cause, the active divine spirit or *pneuma*. At the intra-cosmic level, the Stoics assign different functions to the different kinds of conditions within a given causal network. Attempts at reconstruction are complicated by the fact that our sources come from different times and sometimes address different versions of the Stoic theory.[18]

Despite diversity in details, there emerges the following rough dichotomy. As the metaphor of a 'chain' or 'web' of fate suggests, the Stoics distinguished between the main 'links' within the causal connections and the factors that fit them together. Such a dichotomy of main causes and antecedent causes is in fact attributed to Chrysippus in Cicero's treatise *De fato*, our earliest extant source.

Among the causes some are complete and principal, others auxiliary and proximate. For this reason when we say that everything happens by fate through antecedent causes, we do not want this to be understood as if it were through complete (*perfectae*) and principal (*principales*) causes, but through auxiliary (*adiuvantes*) and proximate (*proximae*) ones. (*Fat.* 41; cf. Chapter 11, Hankinson, this volume.)

---

[16] Cf. also Aetius, *Placita* I 11,5: 'The Stoics hold that all causes are corporeal; for they are *pneumata*.'

[17] Alexander of Aphrodisias, *Fat.* 192, 18: 'They enumerate a swarm (*smênos*) of causes, namely the preceding causes (*prokatarktika*), the co-causes (*sunaitia*), 'hectic' (*hektika*), 'sunhectic' (*sunhektika*), and some others.' Alexander sees no need to work this out in more detail because the main difficulty remains that under the same circumstances the same result happens of necessity. His catalogue therefore aims neither at completeness nor at accuracy.

[18] Cf. M. Frede (1980), Bobzien (1998), Hankinson (1999), Ch. 14. See also Ch. 11, Hankinson, this volume.

There are some disturbing features about that allegedly neat dichotomy, however. First of all, it is unclear whether the combination of the epithets 'complete' and 'principal' on the one hand and 'auxiliary' and 'proximate' on the other is to be understood epexegetically or whether their conjunction indicates further subdivisions. Furthermore, since we cannot be sure what Greek terms Cicero rendered by his Latin expressions, we also cannot be sure whether antecedent causes are confined to the role of auxiliary causes. Cicero's own text gives reason for doubt in that respect, for earlier in the *De fato* he attributes to the antecedent causes a much more dominant role than in his final 'mediation' among the warring parties over the notion of fate. Initially, Cicero accuses Chrysippus of holding that antecedent causes are responsible for the general principle of *sumpatheia* in nature. As such, they allegedly predetermine people's moral personalities to the extent that they necessitate their actions (Sections 7–9). Cicero objects strongly to such preconditioning: 'If there are natural antecedent causes (*causae naturales et antecedentes*) why different people have different propensities, this does not mean that there are therefore also natural antecedent causes for our will and desires [...]. For though intelligent as well as stupid people are born that way from antecedent causes [...] nevertheless, it does not follow that it is also determined and settled by principal causes that they should sit or walk or do whatever' (*Fat.* 9). A similarly powerful role is assigned to the antecedent causes in Cicero's mock-defense of the Epicureans against Stoic determinism in *De fato* 23, and in his report of Carneades' criticism in *De fato* 31.

The uncertainties about the Stoic conception of causes and their respective power are also reflected in the report of Clement of Alexandria: 'Some of the causes are antecedent (*prokatarktika*), some are containing (*sunhektika*), some are contributing (*sunerga*), some are necessary conditions (*hôn ouk aneu*)'.[19] It is not immediately obvious how Clement's distinction of causes matches the Ciceronian division in *De fato* 41, nor how the antecedent causes are related to the 'contributing' causes and the 'necessary conditions'. Nor is it clear whether for Clement the antecedent or the mysterious 'sunhectic cause' plays the role of the 'principal' cause.

---

[19] *Strom.* VIII 9.25.1 ff. = SVF 2.346.

Some order can be established by recognising the most important restricting clause in Stoic theory that distinguishes proper causes and mere contributing factors. As Seneca succinctly puts it (*Ep.* 65, 4): 'The Stoics posit as one cause that which acts (*id quod facit*).' At the same time he accuses Aristotle and Plato of introducing a crowd of causes (*turba causarum*), since they acknowledge not only remote causes, but also necessary conditions like time and place. This remark contains an important clue that agrees with other reports on the Stoic notion of cause. The term 'cause' applies only to a body that is actively engaged in some process or responsible for some state. This restriction also explains a feature in the Stoic theory that is at first hard to comprehend, namely their peculiar distinction between cause (*aition*) and effect (*apotelesma*). Although this distinction seems to us like a natural part of every language, it was not only the invention of the Stoics, a relatively late sect of philosophers in the Hellenistic Age, it also had a special meaning for them.[20] Contrary to what one might assume, the effect is not the affected body itself, but merely some change or difference of state in that body. Effects are therefore classified as incorporeal states of affairs. As Sextus Empiricus explains (*M* IX 211): 'A body, like a knife, becomes the cause to a body, the flesh, of an incorporeal predicate (*katêgorêma*), namely being cut. Or again, a body, fire becomes the cause to another body, wood, of the predicate, being burned.' Leaving aside the question of why the Stoics associate changes or effects with predicates, it is clear that such incorporeal effects themselves cannot in turn act as causes of change in other bodies.[21] Fate, the eternal overall causal development in the universe, is therefore not spelled out by the Stoics in terms of a concatenation of causes and effects. Instead, it is defined as a concatenation of causes only, that is, of bodies that interact with each other. This explains why the word 'effect' does not turn up in the Stoic definition of fate. Fate is always defined in terms of a series of causes: there is an eternal causal nexus, where cause gives rise to cause. Given the overall coherence between all things in the universe, fate is best understood not as a linear sequence but as a network of interacting causes.

[20] For the history of the terminology and its rationale, cf. M. Frede (1980).
[21] On this point, cf. Long and Sedley (1987), Vol. 1, 340. Since the effect can consist either in a process or in a static quality-change, Bobzien (1998) introduces the term 'occurrent' to cover both kinds of effects, 26–7.

This distinction between corporeal cause and incorporeal effect and the limitation of causes to bodies is noteworthy because it speaks for the subtlety of the Stoic theory of causality. It also explains why mere contributing factors or necessary conditions are not treated as causes if they are not actively contributing bodies, a distinction that was disregarded once Stoic terminology had become common usage, as witnessed by Clement's and Alexander's reports.[22] But in what way do these differentiations enlighten us about the function of the different causal factors and the uncertainties about the 'distribution of power' mentioned previously?

Some order within Alexander's alleged 'swarm of causes' is established if we realize that the 'co-causes' (*sunaitia*) form a special subclass of 'principal causes': in some cases one body is not sufficient to produce the change in question, as when several oxen are needed to pull a cart. Hence none of them individually is *the* 'principal' or complete cause of the event. Further reduction of the swarm of causes is achieved if we recall the special nature of certain causes. As the name *'sunhektikê aitia'* = 'containing' or 'sustaining cause' suggests, it refers to the inner pneumatic structure of the acting body: it acts the way it does on account of the inner tension of its *pneuma*.[23] In the case of co-causes, there is of course no unified inner tension; hence, they do not function on the basis of a joint 'containing' power.[24]

These considerations, then, also shed some light on Cicero's distinction (that is mirrored in other sources) between 'perfect' and 'principal' causes: the distinction makes sense if perfect causes are only those that require no factors for their activities – as in the case of the sun's emission of heat – while principal causes presuppose certain contributing factors.[25] There may be a similarly harmless

---

[22] Clement of Alexandria's report in *Strom.* VIII 9.98.7 ff. is a good example of this type of terminological mixup: the Stoics themselves would not have recognized as causes mere contributing factors or necessary conditions, such as time and place.

[23] On this issue, cf. M. Frede (1980), 244.

[24] Whether the Stoics also distinguished between 'hectic' and 'sunhectic' causes as Alexander suggests is unclear. The former term does not occur in any other source and may well be Alexander's addition to illustrate the nitpickiness of the Stoic distinctions.

[25] Bobzien (1999) denies that Chrysippus had worked out a systematic taxonomy of causes and argues that the distinction between the auxiliary and principal function concerns the antecedent causes only, but her reasons for rejecting the 'received view' are too complex to be evaluated here. If the received view may overburden Chrysippus, Bobzien may sometimes be overly scrupulous. What did he write in the many volumes attributed to him?

explanation for the distinction between 'proximate' and 'auxiliary causes'. The condition of proximity would exclude remote or ancestral causality, like that which Seneca criticizes in rival theories. Not everything that precedes is an antecedent cause. Nor is everything that precedes a mere 'auxiliary' or 'initiating' cause, as we shall see later. Hence, there seem to be good reasons for the differentiation in Cicero that is quite in agreement with the rough dichotomy between antecedent and principal causes. We can therefore return to our main question: in what way this distinction supports the Stoic claim that their universal causal determinism is compatible with contingency and human autonomy. None of the distinctions mentioned so far seem to offer any help in solving the central difficulty. Despite the somewhat ethereal conception of 'incorporeal effects', the underlying causal determinism looks as crude as it looked before. If the outcome of every development is ineluctably settled by its causes and circumstances, the future for the Stoics is linear; it is not like a tree with potentially infinite branches.

To see what leeway there may be despite a tight causal web, we have to take a closer look at how the fabric of causes is woven together in Stoic theory. We should therefore return to the disagreement within Cicero's *De fato* about the power that is assigned to the antecedent and principal cause. This question is all the more pertinent since the same uncertainty is mirrored to some degree in later sources. Closer scrutiny of the interaction between these two kinds of causes is necessary in order to find out in what way their difference in function leaves room for human autonomy. Once again the problem is aggravated by terminological difficulties in our sources. Some of them call the antecedent causes '*prokatarktika*' – a name that seems to limit it to the 'initiation' of a process of change.[26] Other sources instead employ the term '*prohêgoumenon*' = 'leading', a choice that suggests that the antecedent cause is the decisive factor in the causal interaction. Thus, the question arises what difference, if any, there is between the antecedent and the principal cause.[27]

Whether there is merely a terminological confusion or a conscious distortion at work in some of our sources, this much seems clear; the

---

[26] Cf. Gellius' use of '*initium*'.

[27] That the *prokatarktikon* is designed to act as an incentive but not as a principal cause is attested by Plutarch (*St. rep.* 1056b–d: *prokatarktikon aition asthenesteron esti tou autotelous*). Plutarch attacks this Chrysippean move as an inconsistency because it limits the power of fate.

Stoics relied on a distinction between the antecedent or external and the principal or 'inner' cause to explain how human beings are part of the web of causal interconnections in such a way that there is room for personal responsibility. The Stoic justification consists in making the internal but not the external causes the principal causes of human actions. Though the environment acts on us in a way that is not subject to our control, our reactions are 'up to us' since they depend on our inner state. Clement explains this interaction as follows. The sight of beauty provokes love in an uncontrolled man (akolastos). The beautiful sight is the antecedent cause. The person's reaction is, nevertheless, 'up to him' because his amorous attitude toward physical beauty is, after all, part of his internal makeup and not caused by the external impression. This distinction between inner and outer causes is the crucial point in the debate about the coherence of the Stoic theory. We shall now try to see, as far as our sources permit, what justifies the Stoics' claim that despite an all-embracing 'fatal ordinance', which also includes human personalities, we are responsible for our own actions.

4. CAUSALITY, COMPATIBILITY, AND WHAT IS 'UP TO US'

Neither their friends nor their adversaries ever tried to deny that the Stoics were compatibilists in the sense that they tried to prove the compatibility of human responsibility with a general physical and teleological determinism. Their critics, however, contested the defensibility of their solution to this problem, given their adherence to the principle that everything is preordained by fate. This point is indeed a major obstacle to our understanding of Stoicism to this very day.[28] What, precisely, is the solution that the Stoics advocated? It is clear that they did not try to exempt human actions from general causal determination: human beings are as much part of the causal network as is all else. But what precisely does that mean? As indicated previously, human beings are conditioned internally by the particular consistency of their inner *pneuma* that constitutes their reason, including their character. In addition, humans are conditioned externally by the impressions they receive from outside and

---

[28] Cf. Salles (2001).

by the impact these have on their inner state. Given that there are no motions without causes, the Stoics hold that in each case, if the internal as well as the external conditions are the same, the person will invariably act in the same way. If the outcome is different in seemingly identical circumstances, there must be some hidden difference either in the external conditions or in the person's inner makeup.

This invariability represented a major weakness in the eyes of the Stoics' opponents. Again and again, they raised the objection that given the fixity of the inner condition at every moment, the external impressions trigger a kind of mechanism so that the person cannot help reacting like an automaton. Is this critique justified? As Cicero indicates, the Stoic counterargument was designed to limit the role of the antecedent cause in that mechanism. They insisted that although antecedent causes initiate every process, they are not involved in the ensuing activity itself. This is, of course, not an implausible move to make, given that our inner *pneuma* is indeed independent of the external circumstances and constitutes our personality. As their general argument for the external causes' limited power indicates, the Stoics did not confine their model to human beings. Their explanation even extends to lifeless objects, as witnessed by the example of the rolling cylinder or cone in both Cicero's and Gellius' reports. Cicero (*Fat.* 42) says: 'But then he resorts to his cylinder and his spinning top: these cannot start moving without an impulse; but once this has been received, he holds, for the rest it is through their own nature (*suapte natura*) that the cylinder rolls and the top spins around.'[29]

Although both Cicero and Gellius treated the theory and its exemplification with considerable sympathy, most of the critics of Stoicism regarded this attempt to justify a compatibilist position as a failure.[30] Especially Alexander of Aphrodisias in his treatise *De fato* spent quite some time and effort to prove its incoherence. Although he says little about the example of the cylinder itself,[31] to him the very fact that the model applies to nonrational and rational beings alike represents its major flaw. Nor is his lack of sympathy surprising. From our modern perspective, the comparison with

[29] Cf. Gellius, *NA* VII 2.1–15; XIX 1.15–20.
[30] The attempt to limit the power of antecedent causes is criticised by Plutarch, *St. rep.* Ch. 47.
[31] *Fat.* 179, 12–17.

a rolling cylinder would appear quite unsuitable to demonstrate the independence of the object's behaviour from the antecedent cause. It seems to confirm rather than to deny the view that the Stoics treat human beings like pieces on a divine chessboard that have no choice over the roles assigned to them. Is not the external push the decisive factor in the ensuing process? Once set in motion, it is not 'up to the cylinder' to roll or not to roll. Transferring the example to human beings seems to make the deficiency of the model even more prominent. If I give someone a push so that he falls over and breaks his leg, no law court will accept the excuse that my action was merely the antecedent or proximate cause of the accident. Not even the best advocate will get me off the hook by pleading that the main cause of the damage was really the victim's form and inner state. There may be some legal quibble about whether my push was really a push and not just a nudge, whether the victim's bones were unusually brittle, and so forth. But none of these possible legal loopholes alters the fact that given the antecedent action, none of the consequences were really 'up to the victim'. It is therefore *prima facie* quite perplexing that the Stoics did not alter their strategy in the century-long debate, but held on to their model. If they did not just stick to their explanation out of foolhardy stubbornness, they must have assumed that the comparison, properly understood, suffices to show how human behaviour is 'up to us', despite the fact that it is determined by inner and outer circumstances. But what more favourable interpretation can we give to the stereotypical example to make the Stoic position intelligible?

Once we overcome our reluctance to see ourselves compared to rolling cylinders and spinning tops, we can see that the crucial point of the model is not the inevitability of the interaction between the two causal factors, but rather the moving object's *inner nature*. This fact is not captured by the example of the push, because it treats the victim as a mere physical object rather than as a human being. In the case of humans, their inner nature does not consist in their 'pushability' but in their particular state of mind and character. We therefore have to modify the example to see in what sense the analogy with the cylinder applies to human beings. If I offer someone a bribe, do I thereby compel the person to act in a certain way? Except in pathological cases, we would deny that there is any compulsion. It is up to the person whether to take a bribe and to comply with its conditions. This is true even in cases where the person is well known to be open to bribery, to the extent that 'he can't resist a bribe'. Despite such predictability, persons are not automata. However weak their character may be, they do make up their minds and in so doing act in accordance with their inner nature. Of course, in this particular case, had no bribe been offered, the person would not have acted the way she or he did. Nevertheless, my offering the bribe is merely the initiating and not the principal cause of the act itself.

That this is indeed the point that Chrysippus was trying to make is confirmed by the subsequent explanation in Cicero (*Fat.* 43):[32] 'Just as he who pushes the cylinder initiates its motion but does not give it the ability to roll, so the impression, once it has occurred will leave its imprint and, as it were, stamp its image on the soul. But the assent (*adsensio*) itself will be in our power. Having been prompted from outside, it will be kept in motion for the rest of the time by its own proper power and nature (*suapte vi et natura*), just as was said of the cylinder.' Cicero does not here dwell on the inner mechanism of the human soul that enables it to withhold assent. But we know from other sources that this is a crucial point in Stoic psychology. They took great pains to explain the psychological mechanisms that enable rational beings to withhold assent and not simply to give in to the impressions from outside.[33] This is not the occasion for a protracted discussion of Stoic psychology and its physical underpinnings. Suffice it to say that the external impressions on the human mind can be quite complex: in practical matters they consist in a depiction of the individual's situation, as well as in the impressions of the appropriate action. It is up to the individual's judgment whether to give or to withhold assent to this impression. Once the assent is given, the impulse to act will follow. It is easy to see why despite the complexity of the inner processes that lead to human action, the Stoics upheld the tenet that persons always act in the same way under the same circumstances. Given the same impressions and the same inner dispositions, the individual will always consent to those impressions.

These considerations show that the Stoic position was not as simplistic as the model of the rolling cylinder suggests at first sight. Their insistence that human beings – just like everything else in the universe – must always act in the same way in the same

---

[32] Discussed also in Ch. 11, Hankinson, this volume.
[33] Cf. Epictetus, *Diss.* I 1.7–12. For an extensive discussion of Stoic psychology and its interconnection with the principles of their ethical convictions, cf. Inwood (1985) and Long Ch. 17 in Algra et al. (1999).

circumstances does not rule out that decisions are up to them. Nor does that tenet contradict our own presuppositions concerning human dependability and consistency of behaviour. This is confirmed by the fact that we often attribute deviations in our behaviour to sudden mood swings or to a change in the state of our health. Such excuses are not supposed to deny our responsibility for our actions. They merely intend to show that our 'inner nature' is not normally the way that our eccentric behaviour may suggest. Thus, responsibility does not depend on the condition that we are always capable of acting otherwise; responsibility depends on the condition that human beings have it 'in them' to make up their own minds on how to act. That there is a regular pattern of behaviour does not diminish our responsibility; it just brings out a fact that we have to come to terms with anyway: that we are preconditioned by our personality. This does not rule out the possibility of improvement. Experience can affect the inner conditions of an individual in such a way that he or she learns to avoid hastiness in his or her reactions to immediate impressions. Therefore, society's reprimands and rewards are not futile: there may be a lasting effect on a person's inner nature.

Have these ruminations not taken us all too far away from the Stoic position? I do not think so. There are in fact good reasons for thinking that they shared especially our concern with the inner moral conditioning in the case of human beings. How this works is one of the main topics in Stoic ethics and psychology. They were concerned with the question of how to attain the right inner makeup that enables a person to comprehend the decrees of reason and to follow them in the right way. Therefore, the Stoics paid attention not only to the right kind of moral and intellectual education once the stage of reason has been attained, but also to the conditions of the development of individuals from the cradle on.[34] Once the inner conditions of a person are settled, it is difficult to change the individual's personality. This kind of 'ethical determinism' has important consequences. Judgment of moral conduct will focus less on what a certain person does in a specific situation than on the inner condition that is responsible for the act.

According to the Stoic conception, human beings are then, in principle, predictable – at least for an omniscient being who knows all the

[34] Cf. Inwood (1985), Ch. 6 'Moral Evolution'; and Brunschwig (1986).

wrinkles of a person's reasoning and character. As we have seen, this does not rule out a certain amount of autonomy and responsibility in the full sense. Is the polemic against this type of compatibilism by the Stoics' adversaries due to a mere misunderstanding of the rationale of their defence? If so, is that misunderstanding due to the simplistic model of the cylinder, which stood in the way of a better understanding? I do not think there is a simple misunderstanding and that other examples would have served the Stoic cause any better. Even those of their critics who were aware of the complexity of the psychological mechanism to which the Stoics subscribed would not have accepted the fact that the outcome is in each case rigidly predetermined by the cooperation of the external and internal causes.

Nor did the Stoics deny that tenet. They saw no reason to dissociate themselves from its determinist consequences. But their allegiance to the model of the cylinder also reflects a crucial concern: that it is the inner nature of the agent that is responsible for the act itself. Is this not so in all possible cases? It takes little reflection to show that this is far from self-evident. In many cases the antecedent cause may in fact be the principal cause. Take the case of the cylinder: If someone did not merely give it a push but deformed its shape, then it could no longer roll. Instead, it would receive a different shape and a different nature. The same impact by an antecedent cause could also be exerted on a human being: an impression from outside may be so strong as to alter a person's inner conditions. The possibility of rigidly determining antecedent causes probably explains why Cicero, in the case of the cylinder and human actions, treats what precedes as the 'proximate' and 'auxiliary' cause, while the thing's own nature acts as the principal cause. The qualification suggests that this condition is not automatically fulfilled in all causal connections, but may vary from case to case. Nor does the qualification 'auxiliary' show that Cicero confuses the role of the antecedent cause with a mere 'helping condition' (*sunergon*). In the case of the push of the cylinder and the impression in the human soul, the initiating factor does act as a proper cause, though its influence on the act itself is like that of a *sunergon*.[35]

---

[35] The limited power of the antecedent cause in the case of human actions may explain why Cicero (and probably his source) in *Fat.* 41–42 uses various synonyms at this point: preposited (*praepositae*) or ante-posited (*antepositae*) cause. Long and Sedley (1987), Vol. 1, 343, therefore regard 'antecedent cause' as a generic name only.

Cicero's brief summary of the Chrysippean position may be too compressed to do full justice to the presuppositions of the latter's original theory, but even Cicero makes clear that the kind of 'fatal' necessity Chrysippus wanted to liberate humans from is only the external compelling force that would leave nothing to the individual. That is why he denies that (*Fat.* 41), 'everything happens by complete and principal causes in such a way that since these causes are not in our power, neither is the impulse itself in our power.' There may, then, not have been a clear dichotomy: in some cases the antecedent cause worked as the principal cause, in others it functioned as the initiating factor.[36] In addition, the role of the antecedent cause may differ depending on the level of discussion: at the cosmic level, the antecedent cause stands for fate's overall order, whereas at the level of individual processes, its scope is determined by the special circumstances. The hypothesis that the power of the antecedent cause is not uniform in the Stoic system would explain, then, why Cicero in the main part of the text identifies the 'antecedent cause' with the power of fate *tout court*. As we have seen earlier, Cicero at first attacks the notion of a causal interconnection (*sumpatheia*) in nature on the grounds that 'antecedent causes' are all-embracing necessitating powers that leave no room for individual autonomy. They supposedly not only determine different human personalities and propensities (*Fat.* 9), but also act as 'principal' causes of individual human actions. To such causal predetermination Cicero objects: 'It nevertheless does not follow that it is also determined and settled by principal causes that they should sit or walk or do whatever.'[37] Given the difference between the levels of discussion, the seeming vagaries in Cicero's attribution of power to the antecedent causes may not be due to overhasty compilation of arguments on his side, nor due to the fact that he is following different Stoic sources in the different parts

---

[36] This far I agree with Bobzien's (1999) contention that not all antecedent causes have the same power. Galen in his work *On Sustaining Causes* makes a clear distinction between antecedent and preliminary causes. Unfortunately, this work is preserved only in Arabic, so we cannot be sure about the terminology, and it is unclear in how far the later medical schools understood the Stoic conception, as witnessed in Galen's complaints about his colleagues' lack of understanding of the original Stoic distinction of causes (*Synopsis of the Books on Pulses*, 9.458, 8–14).

[37] In what way external factors act as principal causes is discussed in Sedley (1993).

of his treatise.[38] Instead, there is a distinction between the amount of power attributed to different antecedent causes depending on the perspective. When Chrysippus is concerned with the general picture, he emphasizes that nothing happens outside the all-encompassing ordinance of the causal order of fate so that nothing can turn out other than in accordance with that ineluctable order (*Fat.* 19). He then uses 'antecedent cause' as a term to cover all that happens in the natural order of things, so that there are no fortuitous events in nature. When it comes to the explanation of individual events, the perspective changes, and it turns out that 'fate' is not a uniform concatenation of necessitating antecedent causes, but rather a web that contains quite different elements with different functions and powers.

That such a differentiation is called for is indirectly confirmed by Alexander of Aphrodisias' protracted discussion of the power of antecedent causes in his treatise *De fato*. For he insists at great length and with a good deal of repetitiveness that the Stoic concept of antecedent cause is incompatible with contingency and human responsibility. For Alexander's construction of a Peripatetic conception of fate, this is the crucial point, because it separates his position from that of the Stoics (cf. *De fato* Chapters 2–6, especially 168, 24–169, 20). Hence, he is particularly concerned with the difference between necessitating and non-necessitating antecedent causes. For this reason he denies that everything that happens comes from antecedent in the sense of primary causes.[39] Alexander is much less conciliatory to the Stoic point of view than is Cicero: he treats the antecedent cause as 'dominant' throughout[40] and denies that the Stoics could hold the position that there can be anything that is 'up to us'. Unless Alexander's rigidity is due to the fact that he is responding to a Stoic position that was less flexible than Chrysippus',[41] it is unclear whether he is always arguing *bona fide* against the Stoics. Like

---

[38] The seeming clash in perspective may be due to Cicero's initial plan to treat separately the arguments for and against Stoicism, an arrangement he gave up in favour of a unitary disputation, once he had decided to dedicate the work to Hirtius. This may explain the fact that most of the time Cicero treats Chrysippus like an unmitigated necessitarian (esp. Sections 7–11; Sections 20–22; 28; 34–37), but in his final evaluation attributes a middle position to him (Section 39: 'he leans towards those who want the motions of our soul free from necessity').

[39] Cf. *Fat.* 173, 14–21.

[40] Cf. Alexander's combination of *prohêgoumenon* and *kuriôs* at 174, 28.

[41] Cf. Sharples (1983), 142–146.

Cicero, he uses a host of different terms to designate preceding causes that may allow for greater differentiation than he is ready to admit.[42] Alexander also plays with the different tenses of *prohêgoumenon* in such a way that indicates a distinction between 'leading' and merely temporally 'preceding' causes: '[...] those who maintain that everything that is or comes to be does so of necessity by certain antecedent (*prohêgesamenois*) and principal (*prohêgoumenois*) causes, each of the things that come to be having some cause laid down beforehand (*prokatabeblêmenon*), on account of which it is or happens of necessity'. In addition, in one of his *reductio ad absurdum* arguments he suddenly treats all temporally preceding states as antecendent cause (*prohêgoumenê*) (Chapter 25). Alexander makes short shrift of the example of a rolling cylinder (179, 17; 185, 18) and treats as pointless the argument for the sovereignty of the inner nature of different things (*De fato* Chapters 13–15). He denies that the need for assent makes any difference in the case of human beings. The Stoics cannot claim rational assent as a special condition in the case of human beings since fate presupposes that humans, like all other beings, must yield (*eikein*) to their impressions, if the outcome is fated anyway.

So far, I have concentrated on the Stoic defence of responsibility and on the concept that there is something 'up to us'. The word 'freedom' has largely been avoided. This is not only because, as Bobzien has shown, *eleutheria* originally had political connotations and was not used in the debate of fate until fairly late.[43] It is also because 'freedom' is a term that would need to be carefully defined, if it does not just mean freedom from external constraint or force. In moral discourse, 'freedom' cannot mean the absence of any kind of influence from outside since no such vacuum exists. Nor can freedom mean the absence of any inner conditioning. There are no persons without character, without opinions and purposes of their own that condition their decisions. Given these uncertainties with the word 'freedom', perhaps the Greeks were wise to give preference to the term 'what is up to us' in the debate of moral responsibility.

---

[42] Besides *prohêgoumenon* we find *prokatabeblêmenas* [*aitias*] (169, 16; 178, 8; 179, 13 et pass.), and *prohuparchousais* [*aitiais*] (178, 9) *exôthen hêmas peristâsin aitiois* (180, 5–6). Alexander does not employ the term *prokatarktikê* – except in his enumeration of the allegedly needlessly complicated Stoic causes (192, 18–21). On the distinction, cf. Sharples (1983), 132–133, and Zierl (1995), 164–166.

[43] Bobzien (1998), 276–290, 338–341, and Bobzien (1998a), 164–173.

5. INDIVIDUAL RESPONSIBILITY VERSUS
FATAL RESIGNATION?

If the Stoics tried to maintain a theory of human responsibility that at least the 'causalists' among us will find sympathetic, what then was so objectionable in their theory that kept the polemics against them alive for centuries? Aristotle, after all, was likewise convinced that their acquired inner dispositions determine people's actions in such a way that it is next to impossible to act out of character. Was it, then, really only their 'fatal' terminology and the misleading example of the rolling cylinder that provoked such resistance against their theory? There is an additional difficulty for the Stoics, which neither the Aristotelian nor the modern determinist has to face. That problem consists in the fact that according to Stoic theory, not only do people act the same way in the same situation and do so necessarily, but that this causal sequence is also supposed to be preordained teleologically. If everything in the universe not only follows causal laws that have been fixed for eternity, but all events and beings are also somehow *meant* to come out the way they do by divine reason, then the attempt to keep human responsibility intact by an appeal to the independence of the person's inner nature seems futile. For global teleology has the consequence that it is not 'up to us' who we are. If someone turns out to be a ne'er-do-well and acts accordingly in whatever situation, is he really to blame for that, given the fact that divine reason assigned to him that kind of personality? The question is, then, how the Stoics can maintain personal responsibility in view of an ineluctably settled world order. Even if most of us are causal determinists in the sense that they regard it as likely that human beings always act in the same way under the same conditions, they do not hold that these mechanisms are necessarily a good thing, let alone that they are due to a benign rational world order.

To tackle this problem, it is necessary to recall once again how the Stoics understood the working of divine reason. Although they identify the omnipresent rational principle with Zeus and elevate it by a host of high-sounding epithets, their divine active power is not a transcendent omniscient being. It is not a deity that stands above or outside nature, supervising its creation according to a pre-established plan. The divine element is immersed in nature itself. Hence, the ne'er-do-well cannot claim that his role had been assigned to him in the script of destiny since eternity. There is no pre-existing divine plan or secret decree of fate that gives each being its place and role. Instead, in every object in the world, there is some portion of the divine element that accounts for its behaviour. This portion of the inner *pneuma* does not represent a foreign element. The active element in us *is* our personality, just as the shape of the notorious cylinder is its nature that accounts for its 'rollability'. In the case of human beings, the divine element is responsible for everything that they do, on both the physiological as well as the psychological levels. If humans are privileged over other parts of the universe, it is because they possess the divine element in its purest, rational form. It is up to us to strive for the perfection of our reason by living a life that comes as close as possible to that of a Stoic sage. In short, every one of us is just as 'divine' as our behaviour and way of life proves us to be.

If we set aside the strangeness of the idea that divinity is at work in all of us, the fact that there is quite a lot in us that is simply a given, whereas other factors depend on our own efforts, is common knowledge. Our talents are certainly not 'up to us', though the use we make of them is. We may be envious if someone turns out to be a genius and has the ability to create unusual works of art or to work out solutions for problems that others have tried to solve in vain. But if would-be geniuses do not make the best of the abilities they possess, we usually blame them for their negligence. That they are simply not 'the persons to exert themselves' may be true in some sense, but such explanations are nevertheless treated as bad excuses. We seem to go on the assumption that a potential for active engagement is there in all normal cases and that it is therefore up to us to put it to good use. Our failures and successes, insofar as they depend on us and are not impeded or forced on us from outside, are the manifestation of our inner nature.

The identification of the divine *pneuma* with human talent and moral dispositions also explains why the so-called 'lazy argument', the *argos logos*, is not a valid objection to Stoic fatalism.[44] We do not know for sure who its originator was. It may have been put forward by one of the paradoxologists from the Megarian School, and the Stoics

---

[44] In contradistinction to Cicero and Origen (*Contra Celsum* II 20, 342.62–71), who regard the lazy argument as a sophism, Alexander treats it as a valid objection against determinism (186, 31–187, 8; 191, 13–26).

may not have been its original target. Whatever its early history, the Stoics were soon confronted with the objection that if determinism is true, then there is no reason for humans to exert themselves. The argument runs as follows: If it is fated that someone recover from an illness, then he will recover whether or not he consults a doctor. So what is the point of consulting a doctor, if he either recovers or does not recover in any case?[45] The Stoics countered this claim with the contention that most cases depend on the fulfillment of certain causal conditions so that the outcome is 'co-fated' in the divine order. If we strip this justification of its unusual terminology, the explanation at first sounds quite trivial. For it amounts to no more than the claim that there are necessary and sufficient conditions for all causal connections. In that case the Stoic theory of 'fate' would seem to reduce to the belief in universal causality: everything that happens in a given context is 'fated' in the sense that all conditions will be fulfilled. Everything that does not happen is equally fated not to happen because the respective conditions are not going to be fulfilled. What separates the Stoics from modern determinists or causalists would then be only their peculiar habit of calling the causal factors 'fate' and to attribute a 'divine' nature to it.

Although this deflated picture of Stoic fatalism as universal causal determinism may recommend it to sober modern philosophers, clearly this attempt to diffuse the Stoic theory by such a reduction with the 'divine active principle' as a kind of honorific title omits a central feature of their theory. It does not seem to take sufficient notice of the cosmic teleological principle, which accounts for the coordination between all events in the world. What this principle adds to the picture needs further elucidation.

In our initial confrontation of the Stoic and the Aristotelian model, we noted that for the Stoics the future is linear because there are no real alternatives to what will actually happen. Such alternatives are ruled out because there are no isolated causal developments in the universe that could interfere *impromptu* with unrelated trains of events. This teleological connection between all things has been largely neglected in this chapter's account of human responsibility in Stoic philosophy. Their explanation of how antecedent and principal

---

[45] Cicero, *Fat.* 28–30. The notion of what is co-fated (*confatalis*) is not to be confused with the causes that are efficient only in conjunction (*sunaitia*).

causes interact treated the individuals as autonomous entities. But such relative isolation of an individual by an appeal to 'its own nature' is actually an artifice in Stoicism. Just as every cylinder, so every individual human being is part of the overall cosmic divine organisation. Whether a cylinder will roll or whether and to what extent people will make use of their talents has been predetermined since eternity, given that the same causes always have the same consequences.[46] Moreover, even if someone works as hard as possible to attain a certain desirable end, the outcome could not have been otherwise than it turns out to be. The factors that are co-responsible for his or her success or lack of success are equally part of the overall causal network. The question is, then, what justifies the artificial causal isolation in the defence of human responsibility? Is this just a trick, as many of the Stoics' adversaries claim? I believe there is more to it than that.

The need to treat human beings as autonomous beings is due to human ignorance of the world order at large. It is precisely because we do not know what is at stake in the future that we have to do the best we can. In each case what we do may or may not be the decisive condition.[47] Given our present state of knowledge, we have to act in the way that seems best even though we do not know for sure whether our actions will lead to the desired result. Nor is the ignorance in question a condition that could be surmounted. In order to know whether a particular action will succeed, nothing short of the knowledge of the entire world order would suffice.[48] Only if we possessed that kind of omniscience could we predict whether a certain action is ultimately 'fated' to be successful or not. As has repeatedly been pointed out, the Stoics neither assumed that human beings are capable of such knowledge nor that there is a transcendent divine mind that takes care of everything. The world's wisdom is immanent in the world itself.

[46] The fact that there is a fixed order is the reason why in the polemic against the Stoics the claim of a natural concatenation of causes and a preestablished order of things recurs, even if the opponents concede the Stoic differentiation between immediate efficient causes and mere necessary conditions (cf. Cicero, *Fat.* 32–7).

[47] Alexander treats the argument from ignorance as a bad excuse (cf. 193, 25–30).

[48] Because of the complexity of the causal web, Bobzien refuses to speak of 'causal laws' in the sense of fixed general patterns of sequences (1998), 173, 224. This may be an overly purist use of language, given that Stoic rationalism does demand the study of general 'theorems' and an appropriate adjustment.

If the Stoics, nevertheless, believe in divine providence, then it is the consequence of their cosmic optimism in the overall causal order, where everything is rational and therefore works for the best. For them the causal network is rational in the sense that there can be no better overall order. For this reason, they believe in the eternal identical recurrence of all things and events in every world cycle. The complicated causal network will always follow the same pattern, not because there is a divine plan laid out in heaven, but because it is the only rational development that things can take. Within this general order, many events may occur that thwart an individual's purposes. Many human beings may lead lives that seem short, sad, and brutish. Although the Stoics were quite aware of that fact, it did not alter their faith that the overall cosmic economy works to the best for all inhabitants. If humans knew more than they do about the causal network of which they are a part, they would understand the rationale for seemingly senseless personal tragedies. Such cosmic optimism may not be to everyone's taste. But this is what made the Stoic doctrine attractive to generations of adherents who regarded the faith in an overall divine order as the most plausible explanation of how the world works. They clearly saw it as a more plausible theory than the purely mechanistic view offered by the atomists or than the 'partial teleology' of the Peripatetics – not to speak of the quietism recommended by the sceptics who desisted from any attempt to make sense of the world.

To what degree, then, is the contemporary stereotype justified that sees Stoic moral rigor and suppression of all emotions as the consequence of a 'fateful' resignation? It was the aim of this chapter to show that the Stoics were not only far from such resignation, but that they also had good reasons for recommending an active involvement in the world's concerns. If they treated human passions as an impediment, it is not because they advocated acquiescence to fate's ordinance. Rather, they believed that passions interfere with our ability to deal as reasonably as possible with the existing conditions and to follow our view of what is the best, most rational course to take – even if there is no guarantee of success. Stoic determinism, therefore, does not lead to resignation, but to a careful study of our capabilities and limitations.

8   Stoic Metaphysics*

I. INTRODUCTION

Is there a Stoic metaphysics? The answer obviously depends on what we mean by 'metaphysics', a word which no classical philosopher would have understood, despite its two Greek components and its familiarity as the title of the most famous of Aristotle's works. No matter what we might mean by 'meta-', in more than one sense the Stoics have no metaphysics: for them, no science comes 'after' physics (again, in whatever sense of 'after' you like); neither is there any science studying entities which, in some sense, are 'over and above' physics or 'beyond' physics – that is, 'metaphysical' (literally, 'super-natural') entities. For them, 'nature' (*phusis*) encompasses everything, including things, phenomena, and events which in other worldviews might seem to be 'super-natural' in some way. They had a firm conception of how philosophy (more exactly, its discursive exposition or *logos*) is and should be divided; and their primary division (into logic, ethics, physics) did not provide any place for anything like 'metaphysics'.

In another sense, however, one might suggest that the Stoics had not only one but two 'metaphysics'. One is merely a *part* of physics; the other is a study over and above their standard tripartition of philosophy.

Let us introduce the first. According to Diogenes Laertius (DL VII 132), the Stoics offered two divisions of their physics, the first one called 'specific', the other 'generic'.[1] According to the 'specific'

---

* I would like to thank Victor Caston for a very friendly and helpful discussion.
[1] The Greek text labels these divisions with adverbs: the first one is made 'specifically' or 'from a specific point of view' (*eidikôs*), the second one 'generically' or 'from a

division, the Stoics distinguished five topics: (1) bodies; (2) principles; (3) elements; (4) gods; and (5) limits, place, and void.² According to the 'generic' division, they distinguished three topics: (1) the world (*kosmos*), (2) the elements, and (3) the search for causes (*aitiologikos topos*). These labels are probably the result of the fact that some topics belonging to the 'generic' division are common to physics and various specialized disciplines, like mathematics and medicine (cf. VII 132–133);³ the topics listed in the 'specific' division must, by contrast, strictly belong to physics proper.

It is fairly obvious, however, that the 'generic' topics are paradoxically situated at a relatively more concrete level than the 'specific' ones: they take the *kosmos* – that is, the organized 'whole' (*holon*) – with its present cosmic organization (*diakosmêsis*) as their primary object, and inquire not only about its elementary furniture, but also about its causal workings; in this sense, they look, at least vaguely, like what we would mean by 'physics'.

By contrast, the 'specific' way of dividing physics is situated at a more abstract and theoretical level. The mention of 'void' in it (and only in it) is already significant: the Stoics used to distinguish the 'whole' (*holon*) from the 'all' (*pan*), the 'all' being the sum of the 'whole' (i.e., the *kosmos*) and the infinite void that surrounds it. Given their belief in the unity, continuity, and cohesion of the *kosmos*,⁴ they denied the existence of any void within it; but they posited an extra-cosmic infinite void, in order to make room for its cyclical expansions and contractions. The simple mention of void in the 'specific' division thus shows that the main object of physics, 'specifically' understood, is the 'all' together with its basic

generic point of view' (*genikôs*); these words seem to support the interpretation I suggest later. For brevity's sake, however, I call them the 'specific' and the 'generic' division.
² Although the Greek text is not compelling on this point, limits, place, and void probably form together one single topic in the division (cf. however Ch. 5, White, this volume).
³ Posidonius, the most scientifically minded of the Stoics, was known for (i) having expressed views about the relationships between philosophy and specialized sciences, and (ii) having devoted much time and energy to inquiries into causes: he probably offered or influenced the 'generic' division. In later doxographical traditions, however, this division was clearly not considered as rival, but as complementary to the 'specific' one.
⁴ Their main 'prior commitment' in physics; cf. Ch. 5, White, this volume.

constituents. Similarly, the best explanation for the presence of the 'elements' (i.e., earth, water, air, and fire) in *both* divisions is probably that, in the 'generic' perspective, they are directly subordinated to the *kosmos*, of which they appear as the first and most basic but still observable constituents; by contrast, in the 'specific' perspective, they are mentioned only after the 'principles' (i.e., matter and god), which are more fundamental entities, but inaccessible to empirical investigation.

The inclusion of 'gods' in the 'specific' division should also be stressed: theology, according to the Stoics, is just a part of physics. True, Cleanthes precociously reshaped the standard tripartition by dividing each of its members to yield a six-part division: dialectic, rhetoric, ethics, politics, physics, and theology. The most religious of the early Stoics, he was probably anxious to separate the parts of wisdom concerned with our everyday world and with the divine. But this remoulding was not adopted by later Stoics. The teaching method used by Chrysippus still gave pride of place to theology, but he firmly reanchored it within physics, saying: 'what should come last in the physical tenets is theology; hence the transmission of theology has been called "completion"'.[5]

Generally speaking, the topics in the 'specific' division clearly share a common feature: all of them are in some sense primary. Bodies, we shall see, are the only genuinely existent beings; principles (as indicated by their traditional name, *archai*, both 'beginnings' and 'governing powers') are the primary factors of reality as a whole; elements are the first and simplest cosmic products of their interplay; gods are the most perfect beings; and limits, place, and void are the primary conditions without which the existence and interaction of bodies would be neither possible nor intelligible. Officially, all these topics strictly ('specifically') belong to the domain of physics; nevertheless, in view of the focus on primary entities, many modern commentators understandably suggest that they belong rather to the province of 'metaphysics'. One may well agree, if one means by 'metaphysics' something like what Aristotle called 'the science of first principles and first causes', and also 'first philosophy', which

---

[5] Plutarch, *St. rep.* 1035a-b. The Greek word translated 'completion', *teletai*, designates the last step in the initiation to the Mysteries.

either includes theology or coincides with it. Later on in the tradition, this science of certain particular objects, privileged by virtue of their eminent ontological position or perfection, will be called *metaphysica specialis*. In a way, the Stoic 'specific' notion of physics might thus be seen as an ancestor to *metaphysica specialis*.

On the other hand, it seems possible to connect a number of Stoic concerns and theories with another type of metaphysics which is related upward with what Aristotle called 'the science of being *qua* being' and downward with what will be later on called *metaphysica generalis*, or 'ontology'. Here, as is clearly shown by the Aristotelian phrase, the purpose is not to study some privileged objects but rather to study any and every object from a certain point of view ('*qua* being', and also *qua* such and such type of being). The Stoics cared much about characterizing, defining, and classifying the ontological status of the items which had any role to play within their philosophy, so that the modern commentators who speak of their 'ontology' are certainly correct to do so. However, it is important to point out that the Stoics raised such questions not only about physical items such as bodies, but also about ethical items like virtues and the good and logical items like predicates and propositions. Their thoughts about logical and ethical problems, no less than physical ones, have connections with many of their 'ontological' concepts and theories. It is clear that this 'ontology' cuts across a number of divisions or boundaries, and includes not just a 'meta-physics', but also a 'meta-ethics' and a 'meta-logic' as well. This might explain the fact that we do not find it summarized in the ancient doxographical accounts of Stoicism, which are limited by the standard tripartition. To reconstitute it, we have to pick out pieces of evidence from various sources and bring them together as well as we can. But this should not lead us either to doubt its existence or to underestimate its importance and philosophical interest.

If this distinction is granted between, say, a metaphysics which is a part of the physics and another which is not, one will see that the first one is adequately covered elsewhere in this volume.[6] This chapter, accordingly, will be mainly devoted to the Stoic general 'ontology'.

---

[6] See especially Ch. 6, Algra, and Ch. 5, White, in this volume.

2. BODIES

The most prominent feature of the Stoic 'onto-logy' is that, *stricto sensu*, it is limited to bodies: it recognizes only bodies (*sômata*) as genuinely existent beings (*onta*). This was nothing new: in the famous 'Battle of Giants' in the *Sophist*, Plato had described one of the parties to the battle, the 'Sons of the Earth', as people who 'strenuously affirm that only that *exists* which can be handled and offers resistance to the touch, defining existence (*ousia*) as the same thing as body'.[7] The main reason for the Stoics' firmness on this point stems not from their definition of body, a definition which is not specific to their school ('what has threefold extension together with resistance'[8]), but rather from the combination of this type of definition with a superior principle, which takes as a criterion of existence the capacity (*dunamis*) of acting or being acted upon. This essentially 'dynamic' criterion was already offered by Plato to the corporealists, in order to force them to admit that some incorporeal entities at least, like the soul and moral virtues, should be recognized as real beings, given that they possess a power either to act on something else or to be acted upon. As we shall see (later in this chapter), this approach to existence left the way open for the Stoics to subvert Plato's own anti-corporealist intentions.

It is important to point out that the Stoic formula (like Plato's own) is 'acting *or* being acted upon'. This disjunction leaves open the possibility, for some bodies at least, of being either only active or only passive. Such is the case for the two ultimate principles, namely, matter (merely passive) and God or the *logos* (merely active)[9]: despite some variant readings in the textual evidence (DL VII 134), the Stoic view about them must be that both of them are bodies. Otherwise, one could not understand how they might play their respectively active and passive roles – even if it is also difficult to understand

---

[7] *Sophist* 246a–b. This passage describes the Stoic position so well that, quoted by Clement of Alexandria, it has found its way into von Arnim (1903–1924) *SVF* (2.359). I have tried elsewhere (Brunschwig [1988]) to show how carefully and consistently the Stoics read the *Sophist*, taking up all the challenges sent by Plato to the Sons of the Earth, and rejecting all the concessions which he believes he can extort from them.

[8] Sometimes 'together with resistance' (*antitupia*) is omitted; I shall try to see why (see n. 10).

[9] More on the principles later in this chapter.

how the matter, defined as 'unqualified being' (*apoios ousia*), could be a body if 'resistance', which looks like a tangible quality, were implied by the very notion of a body.[10]

However, these difficulties only affect the principles, which are theoretical borderline entities, never open to any direct cognitive access. Ordinary bodies, by contrast, are able both to act and to be acted upon, and the world is the grand theater of their unceasing and admirable interaction: unceasing, because the active principle, the ultimate source of every activity, essentially and totally active, is permanently and everlastingly so; admirable, because this principle is God and he puts his rational and providential mark on everything he creates and does. Far from being an impediment to his cosmic omnipresence, his bodily character allows him to permeate the physical reality down to the smallest detail. This already deepens the difference between the specifically Stoic version of 'materialism', a vitalist-teleological one, and a mechanistic-antiteleological one like the Epicurean version.

The dynamic approach of the Stoics to the notions of existence and body does not merely result in giving the stamp of full existence to entities commonly recognized as bodies. It also helps them to justify the claim of corporeality for entities which are not *obviously* corporeal. In this respect, they differ from the 'Sons of the Earth': far from *reducing* the class of genuinely existent beings to ordinary bodies like tables or trees, they use the action-passion criterion so as to *enlarge* the class of corporeal existent beings to imperceptible entities. Taking up Plato's counter-examples, and turning against him his own weapons, they claim that soul, the moral virtues, and more generally the qualities are bodies since they satisfy the action-passion criterion. Soul, for example, is perceptibly acting on the body ('when it feels shame and fear, the body turns red and pale respectively'[11]) and acted upon by it (feeling pain when it is sick or wounded[12]). Virtues, and qualities in general, are causes – through their presence – of the animated body being qualified in a certain way; since they are acting on it, they must also count as bodies.

---

[10] This difficulty could perhaps account for the fact that 'resistance', although essential to ordinary bodies, is not always mentioned in the Stoic definitions of body.

[11] Cleanthes ap. Nemesius Ch. 2, 78–79 (p. 21 ed. Morani) = SVF 1.518.

[12] *Ibid.*

Within this general strategy, aiming at often paradoxical corpo-realizations, however, the use of the action-passion criterion is not the only Stoic tactic. They also make use of the following one: If some entity can be described as a certain body disposed in a certain way, this entity can be categorized as being itself a body. Consider the fist, a typical example for the Stoics.[13] What is a fist? Neither exactly the same thing as a hand, which is a body, nor a completely different thing, but a hand disposed in a certain way; hence, a body itself (if one grants that a body disposed in a certain way *is* a body[14]). The same tactic is also employed, together with an explicit com-parison with the fist example, to prove that truth (in contrast with 'the true') is a body: it is 'scientific knowledge capable of stating everything true'; hence, it is 'the commanding-faculty[15] disposed in a certain way'. This tactic is also unobtrusively present in a num-ber of Stoic definitions or descriptions that put first the name of a body and second the mention of the way it is affected or disposed. For instance, vocal sound (*phônê*) is described as a body, not only because it is acting upon the hearers,[16] but also because it is defin-able as 'air [i.e., a body] struck' in a certain way:[17] an interesting for-mula, because it seems to be a self-conscious inversion of Plato's and Aristotle's descriptions of vocal sound as 'a blow of/on the air' (*Tim.* 67b, *De anima* 420b29).[18]

3. INCORPOREALS

The Stoics, however, did not try to force everything they recognized as real into the category of fully existent bodies. Paradoxically, their

---

[13] Cf. the famous gestural similes used by Zeno for illustrating the various steps between impression and science (Cicero *Acad.* II 145) and the difference between dialectic and rhetoric (S. E., *M* II 7).

[14] A principle disputed by Alexander of Aphrodisias in Aristotelian terms (*In Ar. Top.* 360, 12–13): 'the fist is not a hand, but it is in the hand as in its subject'.

[15] I.e., the *hêgemonikon*, the commanding-part of the soul, itself a body.

[16] DL VII 55–56.

[17] *Ibid.*

[18] Elsewhere, Plato had used descriptions of the 'Stoic' type (snow = frozen water, *Tim.* 59e; mud = earth mixed with moisture, *Tht.* 147c), descriptions interestingly criticized by Aristotle (*Top.* 127a3–19), roughly because snow is not water in the first place, nor mud earth. The debate was thus already in the air in the fourth century: far from being merely verbal, it had ontological implications which were clearly recognized.

'ontology' allows for a number of items which are not *onta* but which are not nothing either: although incorporeal, they are 'something'. It goes without saying that existing bodies also are 'something';[19] hence the Stoic claim that the supreme genus, encompassing all that is 'real' in some sense is not 'being' (*to on*) but 'something' (*to ti*).

The standard list of Stoic incorporeals counts four items: place, void, time, and the 'sayables' or 'things said' (*lekta*). Since this list apparently is not homogeneous (the first three items, roughly, are conditions for physical processes, whereas the fourth one seems rather to be connected to the philosophy of language), and there are reasons for believing that they were not recognized as incorporeal realities for exactly the same motives and at the same time, it will be clearer to deal with each of them before discussing their genus, the 'something'. Why did the Stoics resist the double and symmetrical temptation to make them 'nothing at all' and to make them full 'existents', that is, bodies?

The void is probably the simplest case, and the most obviously incorporeal of the four; the question it raises is not primarily what its ontological status is but rather whether it has to be admitted in the 'ontology' in the first place.[20] Once the 'subsistence' (*hupostasis*) of an (extra-cosmic) void is admitted, for the cosmological reasons already mentioned, it goes without saying that the void is incorporeal, and even the incorporeal *par excellence*: capable of being occupied by body, but ceasing to be void when it is actually occupied (hence destroyed as such, not just acted upon and altered by the entering body), it is definitionally 'deprived of body'.[21]

---

[19] The distinction between 'somethings' which are 'existents' and 'somethings' which are not was paralleled by the verbs and nouns the Stoics used for designating their respective ontological status. In contrast with *einai* and *ousia*, *huphistanai* and *hupostasis* were usually reserved for non-existent (i.e., merely 'subsistent') 'somethings'.

[20] Recall that the early Atomists called it the 'nothing' or 'non-existent' (*to ouden, to mê on*), by contrast with *to den*, the 'full' or the 'existent' (*to plêres, to on*), while awkwardly adding that 'what exists by no means exists any more than what does not exist' (Aristotle, *Meta.* A, 985b8).

[21] 'Its notion is extremely simple: it is incorporeal and intangible, it has no form and cannot receive one, it is neither acted upon nor does it act, it is purely and simply capable of receiving a body' (Cleomedes, *Cael.* 8.11–14). The notion of void seems to tally so well with the notion of incorporeal that a sentence in DL VII 140, which aims at justifying the incorporeal status of the void, has been wrongly read as an 'absurd' definition of the incorporeal itself (SVF I 95 and II 543, app. crit.).

With place (strictly conceived as the portion of space exactly occupied by a given body at a given time[22]), the problem seems to
be inverted: the Stoics do not go against the general opinion that
'existing things are somewhere',[23] especially since for them 'existing things' are bodies. Moreover, place is certainly 'something' else
than the occupying body, since the body can move to another place
without ceasing to be what it is, and the place can be occupied by
another body without ceasing to be what it is. But it is not obvious
whether this 'something' is corporeal or not. The Stoics might have
been tempted to make it a body, by arguing either that bodies do act
upon their place through actually occupying or coming to occupy it
(causing thereby a portion of space to get a definite shape and definite limits), or again that the place of a body is nothing other than
that body placed somewhere, that is, 'disposed in a certain way' (say,
relative to other bodies, e.g., the containing body). If they did not do
so, it might be because when a body is expelled from its place by
another one, the former offers some resistance to the latter, whereas
its place does nothing of the kind.

The case of time, the next incorporeal in the Stoic list, is both
complicated in the extreme and so central to the Stoic doctrine that
an important book-length study has been devoted to it: *Le système
stoïcien et l'idée de temps*.[24] To make a long story short, we might
first point out that, although time shares with the void a number of
important features (e.g., continuity, infinity, infinite divisibility), it
is unlike it in that its parts do not seem to have the same ontological
status as its whole, nor as each other. For instance, unlike time as a
whole, past and future are unlimited 'on one side only', their other
side being limited by the present; it seems obvious that they have a
much weaker 'degree' of reality than the present since the past is no
longer and the future is not yet.

---

[22] Chrysippus defined place (*topos*) as '(i) what is entirely occupied by an existent
[i.e., a body] and (ii) what is able to be occupied by an existent and is entirely
occupied either by some ⟨existent⟩ or by some ⟨existents⟩' (Stobaeus I 161.8–19).
The second definition seems to be designed to solve, not the problem of ordinary
bodies (generally speaking, two distinct bodies can occupy, not the same 'place',
but the same 'room' (*chôra*), larger than the sum of their particular 'places'), but
the specific problem of the place of the 'total mixture' of two bodies completely
permeating each other. Such a mixture occupies a single place, because this place
could be occupied by a single body, although it actually is occupied by two bodies.

[23] Plato, *Tim.* 52b; Aristotle, *Phys.* IV, 208a29.

[24] Goldschmidt (1953).

However, there is a nest of difficulties on this last point, because if the present is strictly conceived as the durationless limit joining past and future, *its* ontological status turns out to be precarious in the extreme: 'no time is exactly present (*enistatai*)'.[25] The Stoics boldly solved this problem by introducing a broader way of conceiving the present, namely 'as extended' (*kata platos*), that is, as containing a part of itself already past and another one still to come. In this sense, the present has a higher degree of reality than the past and the future: Chrysippus said that only the present 'is the case' (*huparchein*),[26] whereas the past and the future 'subsist (*huphestanai*), but in no way are the case'. He also compared this broad present with a predicate like 'walking', which 'is the case for me when I am walking, but not when I am lying down': a comparison which suggests that what gives the broad present its special status is the actual motion of which it is the 'interval' or 'dimension' (*diastêma*). The same analysis is probably applicable to what we might call the 'cosmic' parts of time, namely, the ones determined by the circular motions of the sun and the moon, like the day, the month, the year: if we can correctly say 'the present day', 'the present month', and so on, it is because these periods of time are in some way actualized by the motions of the celestial bodies that achieve their cyclical revolutions through them.[27]

Here again, one might wonder whether the Stoics did not take this 'actualization' to be a form of 'corporealization'.[28] As a matter of fact, according to many modern scholars, they did so, at least in respect to 'cosmic' periods of time. A soritical ('little by little') argument worked out by Chrysippus[29] inferred from the premiss

---

[25] Stobaeus, I 106.

[26] Stobaeus, *ibid*. This third ontological verb seems not to coincide either with *einai* or with *huphistanai*. Usually, as here, it expresses a comparatively higher ontological status than *huphistanai*; but it still seems to be distinct from *einai*, in the sense that it is apposite to use it when speaking not of objects (bodies), but rather of *actual* states of affairs, or of predicates assertible of their subjects in a true proposition.

[27] Even the whole of time, according to the Stoic Apollodoros, 'is present' and can be said 'to be the case' (Stobaeus, I 105). This assertion seems to be authorized by the double definition of time as 'the dimension of any motion whatsoever' and as 'the dimension of the world's motion', respectively attributed to Zeno and Chrysippus (Simplicius *in Ar. Cat.* 350, 14–16).

[28] The statement quoted previously, that 'only the present is the case, whereas the past and the future subsist, but in no way are the case', might suggest that only the past and the future are incorporeals; but see n. 26.

[29] Chrysippus' argument is reported by Plutarch (*Comm. not.* 1084d = SVF 2.665).

that night and day are bodies that such must be the case for evening, dawn, each day of the month, the seasons, the year. The standard interpretation of this argument reads it as a *modus ponens*: the initial premiss is supposed to be accepted by Chrysippus, so that he should endorse the conclusions as well. But nothing prevents taking the argument in the reverse way, that is, as a *modus tollens*: if the conclusions are supposed to be absurd, the initial premiss should be rejected. The second reading might be supported by a distinction, attributed to Chrysippus, between the month (*mên*) and the monthly phase (*meis*): he defined the former, a temporal measure, in a neatly 'decorporealizing' manner ('the period of the course of the moon') and the latter, a physical state of affairs, in corporealizing manner ('the moon having one part visible relatively to us').[30]

All in all, the fundamental claim seems to be that time, the whole of it as well as its various parts (including the present), is incorporeal. Their reasons for that, one might suggest, are structurally akin to their arguments about place, and based on differences of speed (a definition of time attributed to Chrysippus, says that it is 'the dimension of motion according to which the measure of speed and slowness is spoken of'[31]): the time taken by the motion of a body cannot be identified with this motion itself (neither, therefore, with this moving body) because a given motion (defined by its spatial limits) may take different times, and a given time may be taken by different motions. The motion of a body during a certain time does not make this time a body any more than the occupation of a place by a body makes this place a body.

At first sight, one could believe that the birthplace of the *lekton*, the fourth official Stoic incorporeal, is totally different from that of the three other ones: no more the inquiry about the spatio-temporal conditions of bodies and bodily motions, but the theory of language.[32]

---

[30] Cleomedes (*Cael.* 202, 11–23) distinguishes no less than four meanings of 'month' (not necessarily all of Stoic origin), adding that two of them make the month a body (they primarily refer to the moon or to the air), the other two making it incorporeal 'since time itself is incorporeal' (they primarily refer to time). The most Stoic-sounding of the four is probably the third one: 'the temporal interval (*chronikon diastêma*) between two new moons'.

[31] Stobaeus, I 106.

[32] This special status of the *lekton*, compared with the other incorporeals, might be supported by its conspicuous but understandable absence in the following testimony: 'Chrysippus said that bodies are divided to infinity, and likewise things

However, even in a rough and provisional approach to this difficult matter, one can see that it is in terms of bodies and incorporeals that the analysis of language led the Stoics toward both positing the reality of something called *lekton* and giving it the ontological status of an incorporeal.[33] As we already pointed out, the 'vocal sound' is a body, 'air struck in a certain way'. According to a famous and much discussed passage in Sextus Empiricus,[34] usually taken as the fundamental document about this topic, the Stoics distinguished three items 'linked together': (1) the vocal sound, which is 'the thing signifying' (*sêmainon*), and a body; (2) the external object, again a body, which is the thing designated by the vocal sound; and (3) the actual thing 'made manifest' by the vocal sound, which is 'the thing signified' (*sêmainomenon*). Of this last item (which we can at least provisionally identify with a *lekton*, as the transmitted text seems to allow), Sextus says that it is incorporeal and that 'we grasp it in exchange [for the sound?] as subsisting along with our thought, whereas the barbarians [i.e., non-Greek speakers] do not understand it, although hearing the sound'. This seems to be a reasonable argument in favour of the incorporeality of the *lekton*.[35]

But this is not the whole story. By itself, this passage prompts us to inquire about the relationships between the notion of a *lekton* and two connected notions: 'thing signified' (*sêmainomenon*) and thought (*dianoia*). As for the 'signified' of a linguistic expression, a complete identification between it and the *lekton* seems to be already forbidden by the very names of these two items: if we pay attention to the ending of the word, a *sêmainomenon* must be the actual passive correlate of an actual utterance-token (*sêmainon*); on

comparable (*proseoikota*) to bodies, such as surface, line, place, void and time' (Stobaeus, I 142).

[33] For this section about *lekta*, I am much indebted to Frede (1994a).

[34] *M* VIII 11–12. We cannot here go into the exegetical and (perhaps) textual difficulties raised by this controversial passage.

[35] Reasonable and nothing more, because (i) if the Greek and the barbarian, hearing the same sequence of vocal sounds, differ in that the former understands and the latter does not, there must be something different also in the psychophysical apparatus of their commanding-faculty; and (ii) understanding or not an information, an order, a prayer, etc. (all of which are kinds of *lekta*), can make a big difference in the beliefs and/or behaviour of the hearer. On the problem how a demonstration (i.e., an incorporeal item) can in some sense impress the commanding faculty, S. E. (*M* VIII 406–409) set out a Stoic answer, which one may find either fairly clever or somewhat laborious and unconvincing.

the other hand, a *lekton* (which is nowhere called a *legomenon*, 'what is said') is not (or at least: not only) what is said, but (or: but also) what *can* be said; that is, we might suggest, a certain *type* of *sêmainomenon* that is available to any speaker, and which is still what it is even if nobody actually makes use of it in order to signify any token of that type.

A parallel conclusion might be drawn from what seems to be said by Sextus about the *lekton* 'subsisting along with our thought'. True, a standard formula defines it as 'what subsists in conformity with a rational impression';[36] that is, with an impression such as those of rational beings, by nature fitted to express their impressions discursively. But that does not necessarily mean that the *lekton* is a mind-dependent item: notice that the only 'thought' mentioned in the Sextus passage is the hearer's. Of course, that was the best way to show the difference between the vocal sound being heard and the message being understood (or not): no such difference could be easily brought out on the side of the speaker, who normally understands what he is saying. Nevertheless, if a *lekton* is something that can be received by some addressee, it is also something that can be sent by some addresser; this might be a reason why it is conceived as ontologically independent from the actual thought of either of them, although being able to 'subsist along with' the thought of each of them (together, no doubt, with other, idiosyncratic thoughts). Intersubjectivity is at least a step toward objectivity.

There is no room here for a proper development of these suggestions. However, in order to show that the notion of a *lekton* is not only and perhaps not primarily linked to linguistic and psychological considerations, it is apposite to point out that the earliest mention of it is attributed to Cleanthes, within the framework of a theory according to which that of which the causes are causes (i.e., the effects) are predicates (*katêgorêmata*), or *lekta*, 'since Cleanthes called the predicates *lekta*'.[37] As a doctrine concerning predicates, the theory is justified as follows: 'every cause is a body which becomes the cause to a body of something incorporeal: for instance, the scalpel, a body, becomes the cause to the flesh, a body, of the incorporeal predicate "being cut"'.[38] As a doctrine concerning *lekta*, the theory is

[36] S. E., *M* VIII 70.
[37] Clement of Alexandria, *Strom.* VIII 9.26.
[38] S. E., *M* IX 211.

somewhat perplexing because, in other testimonies, predicates will be called 'incomplete *lekta*', and contrasted with 'complete *lekta*' (e.g., *axiômata*; roughly: propositions – cf. Chapters 4 and 12). These phrases tend to suggest that the notion of a *lekton* had been first elaborated in reference to complete *lekta*, and then only modified so as to allow for incomplete ones. But perhaps, on the contrary, we can imagine that the notion of a *lekton* was initially coined in order to support the following ontological and aetiological consideration: each time we look at some object having some quality or property, we have to say that the quality, as such, is the cause of something other than itself; namely, the *fact* of the object having this quality. For example, if we want to account for the fact that Socrates is wise, we have to consider not only Socrates, who is a body, and wisdom, which (as a cause making him wise) is also a body, but also a third item, roughly expressed by 'being wise' or ' ... is wise', which is not a body. Unlike an object, which is nameable, ' ... is wise' is something predicable of an object, sayable about it (whether truly or falsely). It was only at a later stage and for different purposes that the notion of a *lekton* would have been enlarged, so as to cover both the new 'complete *lekta*' and the original *lekta*, now retroactively labeled as 'incomplete'.[39] Viewed in this way, the *lekta* are, after all, quite like void, place, and time: they can be listed among the incorporeal although 'objective' conditions, without which the interaction of bodies in the world would neither be analysable nor fully intelligible.

A last question about the Stoic incorporeals: Is their canonical list of four exhaustive? Although the effects, 'that of which causes are causes', are said to be incorporeal, as we just saw, it would be a mistake to add them to the list since they are adequately covered by the label '*lekta*'. The only serious supplementary candidates (on both textual and conceptual bases) are the geometrical limits: surfaces, lines, and points. One might hesitate between adding them to the canonical list, or putting them under one of the Big Four (e.g., place), or else saying that they are, in some way, neither corporeal nor incorporeal. Their ontological status is aptly discussed in Chapter 5,[40] so I leave them aside and turn to some of the more general questions that they indirectly raise.

[39] On this hypothesis, see Hülser (1987) (= FDS), p. 832.
[40] See Ch. 5, White, this volume.

4. SOMETHING, NOT-SOMETHING, NOTHING

In such an ontology as this, which admits not only 'existent beings' (i.e., bodies) but also incorporeals, which are neither existent beings nor nothing at all, the supreme genus can no longer be 'being'. Hence,[41] the Stoics offered the 'something' (*to ti*) as the supreme genus in their 'ontology': being something is the only common feature of bodies and incorporeals. To be something is to be *some* thing; that is, some *particular* thing: this seems to be confirmed by the fact that, according to the Stoics (at least in the traditional interpretation), the only or principal items left outside the supreme genus are *universals*, whether misconceived as Platonic Forms or legitimately described as 'concepts' (*ennoêmata*).

This doctrine (let us call it D°), paradoxical in many respects and subjected to criticisms from various sides, apparently underwent various modifications and reshapings. Seneca's *Letter to Lucilius* 58 is here an important but controversial piece of evidence. Seneca (himself a Stoic, of course, but a quite free-minded one) presents there, in connection with an account of 'Platonic' ontology,[42] but with several marks of personal assent, a division (D¹) in which the supreme genus is 'being' (*quod est*), and the first two species are corporeal and incorporeal things; the latter are exemplified by two of the Stoic incorporeals: void and time. Their inclusion under *quod est* (a name which is, Seneca admits, 'not very appropriate') seems to be somehow justified because they are 'quasi-beings' (*quae quasi sunt*). Seneca also says that the Stoics want to posit 'another genus, more primary', above 'being'; but when he details their view, far from describing D°, he attributes to 'some Stoics' a nonstandard division (D²), in which the supreme genus is indeed the 'something' (*quid*), but the 'things which are not' and which nevertheless are included 'in the nature of things' are no longer the four canonical incorporeals, but rather fictional entities like Centaurs and Giants. Such items 'present themselves to the mind, having issued from false thinking and

---

[41] And perhaps on the basis of a critical reading of Plato's *Sophist*: cf. Aubenque (1991a), 370–5, who judiciously completes Brunschwig (1988) on an important point.

[42] And with one passing reference to Aristotle, but not very significant (*homo species est, ut Aristoteles ait*).

taken on some imagistic consistency, despite having no existence (*substantia*)'.

I have elsewhere[43] tried to show that (D¹) was a remodeling of the standard Stoic division (D°), a remodeling which may be attributable to some Stoics (followed by Seneca himself) who were happy to come back to the less paradoxical choice of 'being' as the supreme genus, and found a way of doing so by suggesting that the incorporeals could be described as 'quasi-beings', and thus brought again under 'being'.[44] Then, (D²) could be an attempt by 'some Stoics' to combine the advantages of (D°) and (D¹): like (D°), (D²) takes the supreme genus to be 'something', and thus reverts to the Stoic orthodoxy; like (D¹), it presumably treats the canonical incorporeals as 'quasi-beings' (nothing explicit is said about them but, otherwise, one would not see why the box of 'non-existent somethings' is now filled up with fictional creatures[45]).

This reconstruction has been criticized, and these criticisms should probably be mentioned here if we want to present an up-to-date *status quaestionis*. According to Mansfeld,[46] Seneca's apparent marks of assent to (D¹) are purely didactic and should not be taken at face value; he reads (D¹) as 'a scholastic (Middle) Platonist' doctrine, the disparate elements of which come from Plato, Aristotle, and even the Stoics. 'It is true', he admits, 'that Seneca, before describing [(D²)], says that he will show that the "being" about which he has spoken so far has rightly been considered to be the highest genus, but this need not entail, *pace* Brunschwig, that he believes the Stoic idea that the *ti* is the highest genus is wrong [. . .] but merely that it is correct to say that being is the highest in the context of the Aristotelian division'. In a brilliant recent paper,[47] Caston endorses this objection; he adds that 'nothing prevents [(D²)] from being [not later, as I had argued, but] *earlier* than the orthodox, Chrysippean [(D°)]' (his emphasis), and he actually claims that (D²), 'far from reporting the renegade doctrines of some later and otherwise unknown faction', might

---

[43] Brunschwig (1988); but my account here is not exactly the same.
[44] But is a quasi-X an X? I have quasi-finished writing this page; I have not finished writing it.
[45] In a similar vein, see FDS, p. 852–854.
[46] Mansfeld (1992), 84–85, n. 22; 99–100, n. 48.
[47] Caston (1999), 151, n. 10; 157, n. 24; 175–176.

very well be 'the doctrine of the founders of the school' – namely, Zeno and Cleanthes – 'a doctrine soon abandoned by "Chrysippus, Archedemus, and most of the other Stoics"'.[48]

If I am allowed here to indulge in some self-defence against these objections, I could briefly and partially answer (1) that Seneca's personal approval of (D¹) seems hardly questionable if we consider the whole of Section 13;[49] (2a) that even if Seneca is not a scholar, it would be strange from him or from his sources to designate Zeno and Cleanthes as 'some Stoics'; and (2b) that (D²), as Caston reads it, seems to put too many heterogeneous items in the class of 'non-existent somethings': not only fictional creatures, as attested by Seneca's text, but also concepts, which Caston argues to be 'non-existent somethings' and not 'not-somethings', as commonly believed (more on this later). If so, it would be strange to see only Centaurs and Giants explicitly classed as 'non-existent somethings' and not also concepts.

The 'something' as supreme genus raises at least two other problems. The first one is to determine whether or not its division into bodies and incorporeals is exhaustive. According to one piece of evidence, '"something" is said only of bodies and incorporeals'.[50] Nevertheless, some commentators think that the Stoic division, here as often, was in fact tripartite and made room for items which are indeed 'somethings', but neither corporeal nor incorporeal, in this sense at least that the question whether they are corporeal or incorporeal makes no sense. They tentatively suggest that fictional entities and geometrical limits are of such a kind.[51] But Alexander's testimony cannot be so easily dismissed as 'probably too polemical': the sentence just quoted is a premiss in an argument which is

---

[48] This last phrase comes from Syrianus *In Ar. Met.* 105,25, a fascinating passage where various views about Platonic Forms and the reasons for their introduction are attributed to several Stoic philosophers. I cannot properly discuss here the exciting use Caston makes of this text.

[49] *De quo* (sc. the Stoic supreme genus, higher than being) *statim dicam, si prius illud genus* (sc. being), *de quo locutus sum, merito primum poni docuero, cum sit rerum omnium capax. Merito* is justified by *cum ... capax*, which is offered as a true proposition, not merely as a coherent one with some context (*cum* with subjunctive does not imply any distancing and is as often straightforwardly causal as it is concessive: cf. the common expression *quae cum ita sint*).

[50] Alexander *in Ar. Top.* 359, 12–16. Cf. also, in Seneca's (D¹), '*Quod est in has species divido, ut sint corporalia aut incorporalia: nihil tertium est*'.

[51] Long and Sedley (1987), Vol. 1, 163–165, Vol. 2, 183.

indeed critical, but which is combined with another premiss saying that 'the concept (*ennoêma*) is neither (body nor incorporeal) *according to those who say these things*'. It would be an uncommonly bad strategy to combine a genuinely Stoic premiss with a forged one.

This mention of 'concepts' leads us to a second problem: What is the opposite of 'something'? The obvious answer seems to be: 'nothing at all'. However, the Stoics are standardly credited with entertaining the queer notion of 'not-somethings' (*outina*), supposed to describe the ontological status of universal concepts.[52] On the basis of an admittedly small number of controversial texts, the Stoics are thought to identify Platonic Forms with concepts, while denying that concepts are 'somethings', thus putting them outside their supreme genus, and granting them the status of 'not-somethings'.

The main occurrences of this expression are (1) in Stobaeus (*Ecl.* I 136.21–137.6): '(Zeno's doctrine).[53] They say that concepts are neither somethings nor qualified ⟨somethings⟩ (*mête tina einai mête poia*), but quasi-somethings and quasi-qualified ⟨somethings⟩ (*hôsanei de tina kai hôsanei de poia*), mere phantasms of the soul. These, they say, are what the old ⟨philosophers⟩ called Ideas; for the Ideas are of the things which fall under the concepts, such as men, horses, and in general all the animals and as many other things of which they say that there are Ideas. But the Stoic philosophers say that the latter have no reality (*anhuparktous einai*), and that while we *participate* in concepts, we *bear* those cases which they call appellative ⟨i.e., common nouns⟩'; and (2) in Diogenes Laertius (DL VII 61): 'a concept is a phantasm of the thought, which is neither something nor a qualified ⟨something⟩ (*oute ti on oute poion*), but a quasi-something and a quasi-qualified ⟨something⟩ (*hôsanei de ti on kai hôsanei de poion*), in the way that an image of a horse arises even when none is present'.[54]

It has been noticed only recently[55] that whereas the first of these apparently parallel texts is clear, the second is ambiguous, and that

---

[52] Cf. Sedley (1985).

[53] Diels, followed by von Arnim, adds 'and those of his school'. This addition is perhaps, but not certainly, justified by the plural *phasi* which precedes the account of the doctrine, and by the mention of 'the Stoic philosophers' at the end of it. The *meaning* of this addition might be more acceptable than the addition itself.

[54] Translations mine, but provisional.

[55] Cf. Brunschwig (1988), 79–80 [= (1994a), 127–128] and Caston (1999), 168–169, who suggest opposite conclusions.

the evidential value of the first one depends on the way we dis-ambiguate the second. The passage from Stobaeus clearly says that concepts are (copulative use of 'to be') not somethings; the one from Diogenes could mean either the same or that a concept is not some-thing *existent*[56] (existential use of 'to be'). Then, Stobaeus' copula-tive *einai* could be a mistaken adaptation of the existential *on* of Diogenes (or of some common source); but Diogenes' text has gen-erally been read in the light of Stobaeus'. What is at stake in these seemingly byzantine discussions is crucially important: namely, the Stoic attitude toward Platonic Forms on the one hand, toward uni-versal concepts on the other; in sum, nothing short of their position in the age-old quarrel on universals. If we follow Stobaeus, what is denied to the concepts is being 'somethings'; if we follow the second reading of Diogenes' text, what is denied to them is being '*existent* somethings'; they are still 'somethings', but non-existent ones (just like the four incorporeals in the canonical system).

The main argument in favour of the traditional view is probably that it offers a quite simple way of explaining why concepts are not-somethings: namely, that they are universal. Treating universals as if they were particulars (a reproach already made to Platonic Forms by Aristotle) leads to catastrophic consequences, as the Stoics seem to have especially wanted to show by their analysis of the so-called Not-someone (*Outis*) Argument. Let us start from the perfectly in-nocuous argument: (1) if someone (*tis*) is in Megara, he is not in Athens; but Socrates (a particular man) is in Megara; therefore, he is not in Athens. Now let us try the same with the universal term 'man': (2) if someone is in Megara, he is not in Athens; but man is in Megara (understand: there is at least one man in Megara); therefore, man is not in Athens (i.e., there is no man in Athens). If the conclu-sion of (1) is true, whereas that of (2) is false, it is because 'man is not someone, since the universal ⟨man⟩ is not someone; but we took him as someone in the argument'.[57]

In the magisterial paper already referred to, Caston has launched a powerful attack against the traditional view. His paper is full of exciting philosophical, exegetical, and historical novelties, but es-sentially he argues (1) that the very notion of 'not-somethings' is

[56] Or perhaps: not some existent.
[57] Simplicius *In Ar. Cat.* 105, 8–16.

philosophically misconceived, and (2) that the Stoics do consider Platonic Forms as nothing at all, but concepts, not as 'not-somethings', but as 'non-existent somethings' (following the second reading of the Diogenes Laertius' passage). Let us quote at least some of his arguments in favour of the negative part of (2): (2a) if the Stoics recognized not-somethings, they should have posited a supreme genus beyond 'something', able to encompass both somethings and not-somethings – but there is no trace of any such genus in the preserved texts; (2b) it would be paradoxical in the extreme to say that there is something which is not something: 'everything is something'; (2c) if concepts were not-somethings, the absurd consequence would be that they could not even be thought, since Sextus Empiricus[58] says that 'according to the Stoics, not-somethings are non-subsistent for thought (*anhupostata têi dianoiâi*)'.

This long and thought-provoking paper challenges many accepted views and will certainly generate scholarly debates; I shall just note some of the reasons why one might be shaken but still not convinced by Caston's arguments.

A general objection would be: if the concepts were 'non-existent somethings', that is, if they shared the ontological status of the Big Four, why are they never mentioned in any preserved list of the official incorporeals?

More technically now:

1. The second reading of Diogenes' text raises a problem: what exactly does this text oppose to *ti on* ('something *existent*', in Caston's translation – his emphasis), that is, to what a concept *is not*? What the concept *is*, in the Greek text, is *hôsanei de ti on*, 'as if it were something *existent*' (Caston again). In order to fit Caston's interpretation, *hôsanei* should bear on *on*, so as to get the meaning: a concept is not something existent, but something quasi-existent. I doubt that the Greek phrase, with *hôsanei* at the beginning of it, could convey this meaning;[59] even conceding an existential use here for *on*, we might understand that *hôsanei* bears on the whole of *ti on*; that is, that a concept is not something-existent,

---

59 Perhaps it would need … *ti men, hôsanei de on.*

but quasi-something-existent.[60] Then, to Caston's intimidating challenge ('the only options for the Stoics are something or nothing – *tertium non datur*),[61] we could reply: yes indeed, *tertium datur*; namely, 'quasi-something'. Let us concede that 'ordinary not-somethings', so to speak, which are not even quasi-somethings, are 'nothings' (or, preferably, nothing, since it is absurd to quantify over nothings). But it is of course perfectly all right to quantify over concepts, and such is the case because they are not ordinary not-somethings,[62] but *also* quasi-somethings. A 'not-something-but-quasi-something' is neither something nor nothing at all; it has differentiating features in relation to each of these.

2. It is probably unfair to demand from the Stoics that they introduce some supreme genus other than 'something', which would be common to somethings and not-somethings. If we mean by these latter 'ordinary' not-somethings, which are 'nothing at all', such a genus would have 'nothing' as one of its species, and thus would be simply identical with its other non-empty species. On the other hand, if we mean quasi-somethings, we could still bring them together with the full-fledged somethings under the common heading 'something', but taken in a broad or rather equivocal sense: 'everything is something' indeed,. but sometimes we get the fakes and sometimes the genuine article. However, such a grouping, made of non-synonymous kinds, would not properly constitute a genus. Thus, the Stoics would still be right to treat their 'something', in the strict sense, as 'the most generic of all ⟨genera⟩ (*pantôn genikôtaton*)'.[63]

3. As for Sextus *M* I 17, Caston's 'most decisive objection'[64] against treating concepts as not-somethings, I would not

---

[60] Why then not simply: a concept is not something, but quasi-something? The point of the addition of *on*, in this perspective, would be that a concept (e.g., man) looks much more like existent somethings, i.e., bodies (e.g., men), than like non-existent somethings, i.e., incorporeals.

[61] Caston (1999), 167.

[62] In this respect, a formulation like Simplicius' *outina ta koina par' autois legetai* (*in Ar. Cat.* 105, 11) is perhaps misleadingly shortened.

[63] S. E., *PH* II 86.

[64] Caston (1999), 164.

put so much weight on it. Consider the following argument: (p1) concepts are not-somethings (the usual view); (p2) not-somethings are 'nonsubsistent for thought' – that is, cannot be thought (Sextus); therefore, (q) concepts cannot be thought. The conclusion (q) is 'intolerable' indeed. But perhaps (p2), not (p1), is the premiss to reject or perhaps to emend, so as to get either 'even for thought' or, on the contrary, 'except for thought'?[65] Another solution, which I favour, is to detect a *quaternio terminorum* in the argument: (p1) 'concepts are not-somethings' (yes, but not-somethings which *are* also quasi-somethings); (p2) 'not-somethings are non-subsistent for thought (yes, but *only* not-somethings which *are not* also quasi-somethings); *ergo*, (q) does not follow.[66]

5. 'FIRST GENERA' (THE SO-CALLED STOIC CATEGORIES)

Till now, we have explored the *classificatory* aspects of Stoic ontology: bodies, incorporeals, somethings, and so on are types of entities disposed in a sort of taxonomic tree. We have also to introduce another part of the theory, let us say the *stratificatory* one, which seems to apply to bodies only, or at least basically. It is often called 'the Stoic theory of categories': already in antiquity it was believed to answer the same questions as Plato's theory of 'greatest genera', and above all as Aristotle's theory of categories;[67] modern commentators sometimes carefully avoid this label, but not always.[68] Simplicius uses 'first genera';[69] we don't know what word the Stoics themselves used.

---

[65] In a completely different exegetical context, Goulet has orally suggested the second option, i.e., *anhupostata (ei mê)têi dianoiâi*. Unfortunately, space limits prevent me from reproducing his arguments here.

[66] In this way, Sextus' argument would suffer from the same oversimplification as Simplicius' sentence quoted in n. 62.

[67] Significantly, an exceptionally large portion of the evidence here is provided by the criticisms of Plotinus and Aristotle's neo-Platonist commentators.

[68] Menn (1999), 'The Stoic Theory of Categories' says that he is following the 'scholarly convention', which is 'at least partly justified', although he admits that the Stoic theory of 'categories' is 'a quite un-Aristotelian' one.

[69] *In Ar. Cat.* 66, 32.

In its mature, probably Chrysippean form,[70] the Stoic first genera were four: 'substrates' or 'substances' (*hupokeimena*),[71] 'qualified' (*poia*), and 'disposed in a certain way' (*pôs echonta*), and 'disposed in a certain way in relation to something else' (*pros ti pôs echonta*). From these labels one can see that we do not have here a taxonomic scheme: except for the first, all are adjectives or participles that need a support, so that 'qualified' (not: 'qualities') are qualified substances, 'disposed in a certain way' are qualified substances disposed in a certain way, and so on. The Stoic genera are not only not exclusive, they are actually inclusive: Plutarch says that the Stoics 'make each of us four' (and, similarly, each concrete individual being).[72] I am a certain lump of matter, and thereby a substance, an existent something (and thus far that is all); I am a man, and this individual man that I am, and thereby qualified by a common quality and a peculiar one; I am sitting or standing, disposed in a certain way; I am the father of my children, the fellow citizen of my fellow citizens, disposed in a certain way in relation to something else. The four genera are something like four ontological aspects, more and more concrete, that is complex and complete, under which a given being can be described.

The Stoics found it useful to distinguish them in order to solve many problems and paradoxes, most of them connected with the analysis of change and identity, within the framework of their corporealist ontology. In the already long story of the distinction between substance and quality ('thises' and 'suches'), for example, the Stoics' main innovation is to claim that qualities are bodies, insofar as they are causes; namely, the active causes why (and through the physical presence of which in it) an existent thing is such and such

---

[70] For an attractive and subtle attempt to reconstitute the progressive genesis of the theory, cf. Menn (1999), who not only distinguishes the positions of Zeno, Cleanthes and Chrysippus, but also an early Chrysippus and a later one, both traceable from the preserved titles and the meagre evidence (mainly from Galen) of two distinct treatises, one earlier, *That virtues are poia*, against Aristo; the other one later, *On the Difference of the Virtues*, against Diodorus.

[71] Sometimes the first genus is called *ousia*, i.e., matter. Menn (1999), 215 n. 1 prefers to translate *hupokeimenon* as 'external object', arguing that 'Socrates, who is not matter but a composite, is nonetheless a *hupokeimenon*'. But obviously Socrates is not *only* a *hupokeimenon* in the required sense: 'since he is white he is also a *poion*, although he is not the *poiotês* whiteness' (*ibid.* 217).

[72] *Comm. not.* 1083e. This feature fundamentally differentiates Stoic 'categories' from Aristotle's ones, even if the *Categories* are not strictly taxonomic (see Morrison [1992]).

(i.e., a qualified something). The correlate of this thesis is that what is properly acted upon by such causes is matter, itself corporeal, and defined, as we saw, as 'unqualified being'. A qualified being is thus a mixture of (at least) two bodies.

Any crude version of corporealism is exposed to a famous difficulty, already known for a long time as 'the Growing Argument' (*auxanomenos logos*).[73] It amounts to this: Just as a number to which something is added is no longer the same number which would have grown but just another number, so a man who absorbs his lunch is no longer the same man who would have grown but just another man: no enduring subject is available for the verb ' ... has grown'. Thus, if a man is conceived in purely material terms, as a lump of matter, our everyday intuitions about his identity over time and his capacity to undergo various changes without ceasing to be what he is are dangerously threatened.[74]

The Stoics' answer to the puzzle led them to an important notion. They conceded that the Argument affects not only the man *qua* lump of matter, but also the man *qua* man, since the addition is supposed to generate not only a new piece of matter, but also a new man; therefore, a common quality like humanity (common, in this case, to the man M^1 before the addition and the other man M^2 after it) is not enough to make something a self-identical being over time, and thus immune to the Argument. In order to escape it, one has to introduce another kind of quality, namely the 'peculiar quality' (*idia poiotês*) which causes a thing to be the 'peculiarly qualified thing' (*idiôs poion*) that it is, and that absolutely no other thing is. Then, by definition, a being individualized by its peculiar quality keeps it as long as it exists, whatever changes it could undergo in other respects. Otherwise, the same peculiar quality would pass, for example, from M^1 (before the addition) to M^2 (after the addition), and it would be a common quality after all, not a peculiar one.[75]

---

[73] See the brilliant paper by Sedley (1982), summarized in Long and Sedley (1987), Vol. I, 172–176 and Sedley (1999), 403–406.

[74] Ethical consequences were also drawn, in a semicomical mood: I am not the same man who borrowed money from you yesterday.

[75] 'A bit too easy', no doubt, as Sedley (1982), 265, says. See this paper for further searching analyses of the Stoic argumentation. The fundamental 'Uniqueness Thesis' ('every individual object is qualitatively unique') is somehow connected with various other crucial Stoic tenets: epistemological (two different objects, however alike, are discernible in principle – a claim which is essential to the basic theory

As for the third genus, the *pôs echon* (not further determined as relative, *pros ti*), we have already seen its role in the corporealization of various items not obviously corporeal: if something A is 'a certain thing B disposed in a certain way', and if B is a body, A also is a body. The other side of the coin is that what makes A what it is is *not* a corporeal quality present in it, unlike what is the case with second-genus qualified things. In fact, some Stoics at least,[76] according to Simplicius,[77] explicitly distinguished different sorts of *poia*, some of which *only* are what they are by virtue of a *poiotês*.[78] To take again the handy example of a fist: it would be hard to claim that a hand is a fist if or when or because there is a certain (corporeal) 'fistness' present in it; better to say that a fist is a hand (the parts of which are) disposed in a certain way.

It is not easy to orient oneself in the labyrinthine net of the subtle distinctions the Stoics introduced, here as elsewhere, and to determine the criteria according to which they decided to treat a given being, characterized in some way, either as properly 'qualified' (that is, made such by a genuine 'quality') or as 'qualified' in some relaxed sense or senses, which do not imply the causal intervention of any corporeal quality. Starting from Simplicius' passage, but in a somewhat different vocabulary, and leaving aside some extra niceties, it seems possible to say the following. Strictly speaking, a *poion* is assigned to the second genus if its character is a dispositional state, not necessarily permanent, but highly durable; such features require the presence of a causally active *poiotês* in the subject (for example, prudence in the prudent man). Broader senses of *poion* will allow for temporary and unstable states, as that of a man sticking his fist out, and even for movements or processes, as that of a man running;

of 'cognitive impressions'; cf. Ch. 3, this volume and LS 40 H-J), ethical (from the early masters to Panaetius and Epictetus, the Stoics played an important role in the genesis of the notion of a person), and even semantic-grammatical (a peculiar quality is what is indicated by 'names' – our 'proper names' – whereas a common quality is signified by 'appellatives', *prosêgoriai* – our 'common nouns'). On this last point, see Brunschwig (1984).

[76] Quite probably Antipater.

[77] *In Ar. Cat.* 212, 12–213, 1.

[78] This in straightforward opposition to Aristotle, who defines quality as 'that in virtue of which things are said to be qualified' (*Cat.* 8, 8b25). Not by chance, Simplicius is here our main informant. His comments on *Cat.* 8 are the main thread of Menn (1999), a paper to which I am much indebted for the understanding of this difficult passage.

neither of these characterizations calls for a corporeal cause, and the things so characterized can confidently count for *pôs echonta*, and put into the third genus, provided only that they be *kata diaphoran* (i.e., that it make an *intrinsic* difference in a thing to be or not to be 'qualified' in these broad senses).

This finally leads us to the fourth genus, the *pros ti pôs echonta*. As is clear from their name, those are relative, *pros ti*. But not all relatives are *pros ti pôs echonta*.[79] Those latter are only those which are *not kata diaphoran*; that is, those which can be or not be in some relation to something else without any *intrinsic* change in them (e.g., I can cease to be the man on the right of John, without moving myself at all, if John moves in the appropriate way).[80] The Stoics said, perhaps shockingly for us, that a father ceases to be a father when his child dies, even unknown to him. Other relatives are not so, but second-genus *poia*: as the Sceptics tirelessly repeated, a food that tastes sweet to the healthy man may taste bitter to the sick one, and that makes sweet and bitter relative to tasters. However, according to the Stoics, Simplicius rather obscurely says, 'sweet and bitter could not alter qualitatively if their internal power (*dunamis*) did not change too.' This probably means that a given food would not taste the way it tastes to this or that man (or to the same man at different times) if its internal constitution were not a contributing factor to the result of the tasting.

The attention devoted by the Stoics to *pros ti pôs echonta* is not an idle curiosity about a strange type of change. Chrysippus said that 'the world is a complete body, but that its parts are not complete, because they are disposed in certain ways relative to the whole (*pros to holon pôs echein*) and are not by themselves (*kath' hauta*)'.[81] Obviously, the parts of the world, including us, are causally affected, as bodies, by their physical neighbours; but under another description they are somehow changed, although without internal alteration, by everything that happens anywhere in the world. This has ethical consequences: our various external relatives (family, fellow citizens, gods, the world itself) entail as many 'proper functions' (*kathêkonta*), which we have to fulfill because they are 'the things to do' toward them. An extra neighbour means some extra justice commitments.

---

[79] Cf. Simplicius *in Ar. Cat.* 166, 15–29, and the thorough analyses of Mignucci (1988).
[80] The so-called 'Cambridge change', in modern Anglophone philosophy.
[81] Plutarch, *St. rep.* 1054f.

In this respect, it is probably apposite to recall that the earliest attested mention, perhaps not of the phrase *pros ti pôs echonta*, but at least of the notion, stems from a debate about the age-old problem of the unity of the virtues, famously launched by Plato's *Protagoras*.[82] Aristo, Zeno's independent disciple, substituted for his master's unclear pronouncements on this point a subtle version of the unity thesis: 'he made virtue by essence (*têi men ousiâi*) one thing, which he called (intellectual) "health", and by relativity (*tôi de pros ti*) he made the virtues in a way different and plural, just as if someone wanted to call our vision "whitesight" when it apprehends white things, "blacksight" when it apprehends black things'.[83] Chrysippus criticized Aristo's position, which he quite probably interpreted as locating the virtues in the fourth genus:[84] he argued, in different places, that 'they are *poia*' (the title of his book against Aristo), thus locating them in the second genus, and (in his treatise 'On the difference of the virtues') that they are the commanding faculty (non-relatively) *pôs echon*, thus putting them in the third genus.[85]

These last remarks, brief as they are, might support the suggestion made at the beginning of this chapter. The properly 'ontological' concepts and theories of the Stoics transcend the tripartition logic-ethics-physics: they find their application, possibly their origin sometimes, in each of these fields. It would perhaps not be too bold to describe this ontology as a meta-philosophy.

[82] For an illuminating analysis of the various possible positions on this question, see the classic study by Vlastos (1972).

[83] Plutarch, *Virt. mor.* 440e–f.

[84] DL VII 161 says that Aristo 'did not allow a plurality of virtues, like Zeno, nor one single virtue called by many names, like the Megarians, but (solved the question) by means of "to be disposed in a certain way in relation to something else"'. But this doxographical summary does not prove anything about Aristo's *ipsissima verba*.

[85] For the complexities of these positions, see Menn (1999), 234–241.

9 Stoic Ethics*

I. INTRODUCTION

In one of the talks 'after class' given by the Stoic Epictetus, he is recorded as warning his audience against supposing that they can turn themselves into professional teachers of philosophy overnight, simply by rehearsing the principles they have worked up. His remarks include this intriguing passage (III 21.18–19):

It may be that not even being wise suffices for taking care of young people. There is a need in addition for a certain readiness and fitness for this task, in heaven's name, and a particular physique, and above all it has to be the case that god is advising one to occupy this position, as he advised Socrates to take on the job of cross-examination, Diogenes the job of kingship and castigation, Zeno the job of teaching and formulating doctrine.

Two things are immediately obvious: (1) In talking of Socrates, Zeno, and the Cynic Diogenes in this way, Epictetus is not doing history of philosophy. These great names – of thinkers who lived over four or (in Socrates' case) five hundred years previously – are simply his authorities and paradigms. (2) Epictetus is not thinking of

* A first introduction: Sharples (1996), Chs. 5 and 6. Longer introductory treatments: Long (1974/1986), Sandbach (1975), Inwood and Donini (1999), together with Schofield (1999a). Important essays in Schofield and Striker (1986), Long (1996), Ierodiakonou (1999). See also the general studies of Forschner (1981), Inwood (1985), Striker (1991/1996a), and Annas (1993). This chapter does not attempt to provide a general survey of the topic. What it assumes is a reader who wants to know how we know what we know about Stoic ethics, how the Stoics conceived the project or projects of ethics, and what kinds of argument they had about it among themselves and with philosophers of other persuasions. Most ancient texts cited are reproduced in the SVF and LS collections, and may be tracked in their indexes. References to the modern literature are on any topic restricted to one or two key items.

Socrates, Zeno, and Diogenes as authors or proponents of distinct although no doubt related philosophies, as they would standardly be presented in modern accounts of Greek philosophy. The implication is rather that there is one philosophy – or one thing, philosophy – but that the three of them each adopt a different mode of communicating it to others: a different mode of 'care', or what one might roughly and in generic terms call 'therapy'.

In observing Epictetus thinking about the identity of the tradition of philosophical ethics he works in, we need bifocal if not multifocal lenses. We are looking *at* him, and at why Socrates, Diogenes, and Zeno should look the way they do to him – and so (inevitably) at how his conception of philosophy and the tradition relates to what Stoic ethics has become in his hands. But we will find it hard to avoid also looking *through* him at the pictures he presents of Socrates, Diogenes, and Zeno and of philosophy as they practised it, and wondering whether they would have recognised their own and (in the cases of Diogenes and Zeno) each others' likenesses – in particular, what they would have made of the implication that Cynicism and Stoicism are simply versions of Socratic ethics. Hard not just because of the irresistible pre-post-modernist urge to ask of a portrait whether it was really that way, but also because Socrates wrote nothing, and while Diogenes or Zeno did write, nothing of it has survived intact – so our only access to them is through the eyes of later authors.

Here is an argument for thinking that Epictetus' portraiture is good history as well as a reflection of his own preoccupations. Let us take for granted that for Socrates it was a fundamental truth and the guiding principle of philosophy (1) that the only thing worth caring for is the true self (the soul, as he sometimes puts it), not the body or any of the externals that fortune may or may not send our way; and (2) that the only things which are intrinsically good and bad are conditions of the self: above all virtue and vice. Let us also take for granted that Diogenes and Zeno each concurred in making these propositions the guiding principle of philosophy. Then it is historically plausible that the crucial differences between the three of them are to be found not in *what* they believed, but in how they sought to convert others to acceptance – practical as well as intellectual – of what they were united in seeing as the key to the good life.

Epictetus' identification of the *elenchus* as the characteristically Socratic method for achieving this object of course agrees with much recent discussion of Socrates.[1] As for Diogenes, 'kingship and castigation' need some unpacking, but Epictetus elsewhere (III 22) makes clear his view that what distinguishes the Cynic is a way of life – one open to constant public scrutiny – which gives him a special authority to take other people to task for their failings. The Cynic *shows* us through his own character and behaviour, above all a regal fearlessness and freedom of spirit and of speech, that what he says or implies about good and evil is true. I suggest that this interpretation of Cynicism as paradigmatic offers us something modern scholars have not by and large succeeded in producing: an account which makes sense of Diogenes' philosophical project as philosophy, and which deserves serious consideration as a historically viable account of what he saw himself as doing.

The account of Zeno's historical significance that one might speculatively extract from III 21.19 also has considerable attractions. For what Epictetus says there chimes well with the picture of Zeno as a Socratic which recent scholarship has painted,[2] as well as with evidence that his first teacher was Diogenes' pupil Crates (DL VI 105, VII 1–4). And in characterising his work as didactic and focused on the formulation of doctrine, it suggests the way Zeno himself may have conceived his own philosophical project in relation to the projects of Socrates and Diogenes. In one way or another, Socrates and Diogenes devoted their energies to challenging the assumptions being made by everyone around them, with their own moral and intellectual commitments generally emerging by contrast and unsystematically. Zeno may have seen a compensating need for a direct and explicit articulation of the Socratic vision (glimpsed in part through Cynic spectacles) to be built upon the definitions later Stoics so prized, to be rooted in a theoretical account of nature, and to recapitulate all that was most valuable in previous thought, whether from Heraclitus or Plato's later dialogues. On that hypothesis, he will not have perceived himself as presenting a philosophy of human life different from Socrates' or Diogenes' (hence the difficulty we have in finding any palpable divergences between Zeno and the early Cynics where their views on the same topics are recorded), but as communicating that very same philosophy in a new form: the form of a system.

---

[1] The classic modern treatment is Vlastos (1983).
[2] See especially Long (1988).

2. A SYSTEM OF ETHICS

At the close of the presentation of Stoic ethics in Book III of *De finibus*, Cicero makes its mouthpiece Cato comment on 'the marvellously systematic way in which Stoic philosophy sets out its doctrines' (III 74):[3]

Surely no work of nature (though nothing is more finely arranged than nature) or manufactured product can reveal such organisation, such a firmly welded structure? Conclusion unfailingly follows from premise, later development from initial idea. Can you imagine any other system where the removal of a single letter, like an interlocking piece, would cause the whole edifice to come tumbling down? Not that there is anything here which could possibly be altered.

Cicero's observation no doubt reflects the Stoics' own ambitions, and certainly their practice. We possess three major expositions of early Stoic ethics – in Book VII of Diogenes Laertius (VII 84–131) and in the Byzantine anthologist Stobaeus (*Ecl.* II 57–116, perhaps deriving from the Augustan encyclopedist Arius Didymus), as well as *De finibus* III 16–76.[4] All appear to reflect with variations the same original plan, and from Diogenes Laertius and Stobaeus in particular we can infer a systematic order of topics, each of which is then subjected to an elaborate process of classification and definition. At the end of his account, Stobaeus appeals particularly to the authority of two general works of Chrysippus: *On doctrines* and *Outline of the theory* (*Ecl.* II 116.11–15); it is highly probable that it is Chrysippus who stands behind the plan underlying the three surviving compendia. In the same context Stobaeus refers to Chrysippus' writings on individual topics. He is probably thinking of the many ethical treatises on definitions, divisions, and so forth whose titles are recorded in the Chrysippus catalogue in Diogenes Laertius (VII 199–200). Not that Chrysippus was the only early Stoic to produce writings in this vein: we know of a work by his contemporary Sphaerus entitled *On the arrangement of ethics* (DL VII 178). Sphaerus also appears to have been active in producing ethical definitions – in fact, Cicero tells us that

---

3 I quote from the new translation by Raphael Woolf (Annas 2001): not very literal, but lots of style.

4 Translations of Diogenes Laertius: Hicks (1925), Inwood and Gerson (1997), Goulet-Cazé (1999); Stobaeus: Inwood and Gerson (1997); Cicero: Rackham (1931), Annas (2001).

the Stoics rated him as 'their best framer of definitions' (*Tusculan Disputations* IV 53).[5]

'They[6] divide the ethical part of philosophy', reports Diogenes Laertius (VII 84), 'into [A] the topic of impulse, [B] the topic of goods and bads, [C] the topic of passions, [D] of virtue, [E] of the goal, [F] of primary value and actions, [G] of appropriate functions, [H] of persuasions and dissuasions.' This statement promises to offer a helpful way into the Stoic system of ethics. It is actually problematical.[7] The list does cover in one fashion or another most of the main areas we find treated in the expositions of Cicero, Stobaeus, and Diogenes Laertius himself. But if construed as an *order* of topics (which is what seems to be intended), it looks more like an uneasy attempt to accommodate two *rival* sequences of topics rather than the presentation of a single agreed-upon sequence. What emerges from a brief comparison with our three main systematic accounts of Stoic ethics[8] is that the order of Stobaeus' exposition is much closer to the list at DL VII 84

---

[5] For more on the different versions of the Stoic system, see Long (1983b).

[6] 'They' is Chrysippus and a list of Stoic philosophers of the second-century B.C.

[7] Two problems internal to it: (a) One would have expected 'indifferents' to be included (i.e., things neither good nor bad which contribute nothing to happiness or misery) – but any discussion of 'value' (cf. [F]) would have to locate that concept within the conceptual matrix governed by the notion of the indifferent. (b) '... and actions' (*kai tôn praxeôn*) is not usually treated as a topic coordinate with, for example, [D], [E], and [G]. I am inclined to guess that the words have become slightly misplaced: if we suppose they originally followed *tôn kathêkontôn* ('appropriate actions'), [H] would then read: 'of persuasions and dissuasions to actions' (cf. Eudorus' discussion of discourse focused on action: Stob. *Ecl.* II 44.7–9).

[8] Cicero and Diogenes Laertius begin with [A], very much en route to [E], which is followed in Diogenes Laertius by [D] and only then [B]. Cicero is much more discursive, and does not discuss [D] as a discrete topic at all; he does eventually reach [B] – quite where he does so might be disputed: it is not until *Fin.* III 55 that he very briefly takes up the kinds of distinctions which Diogenes Laertius explores at VII 94–9. In Diogenes Laertius [F] (or rather 'indifferents') and [G] follow [B], and subsequently – without any obvious rationale – [C]. Cicero treats [F] 'value' at III 41–50, 'indifferents' at III 50–4, [G] 'appropriate functions' at III 58–61. By contrast, Stobaeus' plan of campaign is a lot clearer. He begins with [B], construed as a general heading covering all of [D] to [G]: which he then discusses in that order. Only after that does *he* reach [A] and [C]. This positioning of [A] with its annex [C] immediately after [G] is well-motivated, since Stobaeus launches his treatment of impulse with the remark (*Ecl.* II 86.17–18): 'What activates impulse... is precisely an impression capable of directly impelling an appropriate function'. All the expositions end with material relating to the good or wise person's activity as a social and political animal, which was doubtless a principal subject of [H], 'persuasions and dissuasions' – that is, discourse focused on the practical application of philosophy.

than are the sequences in Diogenes Laertius' and Cicero's versions, except that [A] impulse is their starting point, not his (he starts with [B] goods and bads). It is tempting to conjecture that (1) in its original form the list followed precisely the *same* order as in Stobaeus, but (2) Diogenes Laertius himself promoted the topic of impulse to first place on the list – so as to achieve a degree of harmonisation between its ordering and his decision to begin his own exposition of Stoic ethics with an account of the natural impulse which leads a rational being to the goal of living in accordance with virtue.[9] If the conjecture is correct, it is likely that Chrysippus – as the principal authority cited at the end both of Stobaeus' exposition and of Diogenes Laertius' list – advocated the order of exposition: (1) [B] goods and bads, taken as including *inter alia* [D] virtue, [E] the goal, [F] indifferents, primary value, [G] appropriate functions; (2) [A] impulse, including [C] passions; and (3) [H] persuasions and dissuasions.[10]

The suggestion of two rival sequences of topics needs some nuancing. The situation is perhaps rather that Diogenes Laertius' list, like his own exposition of Stoic ethics, reflects two distinct *projects*. One (Type 1) is the project of working through the key concepts of Stoic ethics in logical order, and making definitions, divisions, and subdivisions which capture appropriately the use of the concepts in discursive ethical discourse.[11] What Stobaeus offers us is a more or

---

9 Two subsidiary hypotheses: (iii) In general, Diogenes Laertius will not, however, have bothered to alter the order of subsequent items on the list, even though it does not marry well with his own exposition: doubtless because he thought it was at the *beginning* of the list that a discrepancy would be too noticeable for comfort. (iv) However, because in Stoicism passions are a species of impulse (thus [A] and [C] belong closely together), an effect of promoting impulse to the head of the list is to make the position of the passions particularly unstable. I guess Diogenes felt he had no option but to promote it higher too. Placing it as [C] after [B], good and bad things, seems arbitrary, just as does Cicero's inclusion of his one paragraph on the passions within his continuing treatment of the goal as *summum bonum* at *Fin.* III 35.

10 I am supposing that the list had an overarching tripartite structure, with [B], [A], and [H] designating the three relevant main headings. On this view, we find a close reflection of the Chrysippan scheme in the scheme attributed by Stobaeus to the Academic Eudorus of Alexandria (first-century B.C.): *Ecl.* II 42.7–45.6 (NB, e.g., 42.13–23). For discussion of Stoic theorising on [A] impulse and [C] the passions, see Brennan (Ch. 10, this volume), and of Stoic presentation of [H] 'persuasions and dissuasions' Gill, Ch. 2, this volume.

11 Stobaeus interestingly states that Zeno's definition of happiness as the 'smooth current of life' (Stob. *Ecl.* II 77.20–1) was used by Cleanthes in his own writings, and by Chrysippus, and by everyone after them (*ibid.* II 77.21–3).

less undiluted exercise of this kind, and I take it that the original list of topics Diogenes Laertius decided to rearrange was designed as a contents list for just such a project. The other kind of project (Type 2) is rather different: it consists principally in an attempt to explain and argue discursively for the distinctive Stoic view on some key subject in ethics – whether the goal, or the good, or appropriate function. This is mostly the sort of enterprise undertaken in Book III of *De finibus*. In a highly condensed form, it is what Diogenes Laertius engages in in the first paragraphs of his account of Stoic ethics (VII 85–9), before he shifts for much of the rest of it into Stobaean mode. It is also what we see Hierocles doing in the surviving papyrus columns of his *Elements of Ethics* (*Elementa Moralia*); and no doubt Chrysippus' *On goals* (cited at DL VII 85 and 87) was a project of this second kind too. All four of the works mentioned under this head were either designed to introduce the reader to Stoic ethics in general or evidently could be read as dealing with its key concepts in an introductory way. No surprise, then, if projects of Type 2 drew on those of Type 1 as well as vice versa, or if hybrids of the two types were produced – or, if as suggested previously, the list of topics for a project of Type 1 used by Diogenes Laertius (VII 84) was adapted by him to reflect the Stoic practice of beginning their discursive treatments of ethics with considerations about natural impulses, a practice followed in all four works of Type 2 just cited, as also by Cicero in *De officiis*, echoing Panaetius's *On appropriate function* (*Peri kathêkontos*).

3. FOLLOWING NATURE

Here is how Stobaeus launches his Type 1 account of 'the principal points of the necessary doctrines' (*Ecl.* II 57.18–58.4):

Zeno says that those things exist which participate in being. And of the things which exist some are good, some bad, some indifferent. Good are the following sorts of item: wisdom, moderation, justice, courage, and all that is virtue or participates in virtue. Bad are the following sorts of item: folly, intemperance, injustice, cowardice, and all that is vice or participates in vice. Indifferent are the following sorts of item: life death, reputation illrepute, pleasure exertion, wealth poverty, health sickness, and things like these.

We cannot always trust ancient ascriptions of Stoic material to Zeno: sometimes his name functions simply as a symbolically authoritative place-holder for the school in general. But we have no reason to query this particular attribution. Indeed, it is easier to explain Chrysippus' huge commitment to definition and classification if Zeno – as suggested in interpreting Epictetus' remark about his special role as a philosopher – had already made them salient elements in Stoic philosophising. Diogenes Laertius suggests that Zeno and Cleanthes did not construct the detailed systems of ethics characteristic of Type 1 projects (VII 84), but the way Zeno handled the topic of goods and bads makes it sound as though he approached it from a systematic perspective and conceived it as fundamental to the subject.

Compared with the baroque proliferation of forms of virtue and the further divisions of goods and bads Stobaeus goes on to present, Zeno's classification is simple. Two aspects of it are particularly worth noting. First, it is couched in ontological terms. Zeno evidently wanted to make it clear that ethics is concerned in its own way with what there is. What he proposes is a division of things that participate in being. For a Stoic, that means they are conceived of as bodies or physical qualities of bodies; and doubtless one reason why virtues and vices take pride of place in this list of goods and bads is that, according to the Stoics, as stable characteristics of individual persons they are qualities of bodies. Second, the thesis Zeno propounds is thoroughly Socratic: not so much in his adoption of the quartet of cardinal virtues which the Socrates of, for example, Plato's *Republic* treats as canonical, but because he counts things which would conventionally be regarded as goods and bads, such as health and sickness, as neither good nor bad in themselves – a position he likely thought he found attributed to Socrates in Plato's *Apology* and *Euthydemus*.[12] Other texts tell us how Zeno defined these virtues. Here the intellectualism of his Socratic outlook becomes apparent. He specified each of the other three in terms of *phronêsis*, practical wisdom (thus exhibiting a unity in plurality that Chrysippus would turn into a particularly subtle form of inseparability): justice as wisdom in matters of distribution, moderation in matters requiring choice, courage in matters requiring endurance.[13]

---

[12] See Long (1988).
[13] Plutarch *Virt. mor.* 440e–441d, *St. rep.* 1034c–e.

Zeno's classification of goods and definitions of the virtues were presumably presented in the treatise on *Ethics* which is listed in the catalogue of his writings in Diogenes Laertius (VII 4). Probably[14] this is where Zeno also articulated the famous Stoic distinctions between those indifferents that are in accordance with nature and have 'value' (*axia*), those that are contrary to nature and have 'disvalue' (*apaxia*), and those that are neither; and – some vocabulary particularly associated with Zeno (*Ecl.* II 84.18–85.11) – between particularly valuable indifferents which are 'preferred' and particularly disvalued ones that are 'dispreferred'. Diogenes Laertius tells us that life and health, for example, are 'not goods but indifferents of the species "preferred"' (DL VII 102): critics of the Stoics ancient and modern have found this way of talking and thinking problematical, and we shall need to return to the issue.

It seems likely, too, that the *Ethics* was where Zeno spelled out the general definition of virtue attributed by Plutarch to him, Chrysippus, and Ariston of Chios: 'reason consistent and firm and unchangeable' (*Virt. mor.* 441C), and where he presented his definitions of the goal as 'living consistently' (*Ecl.* II 75.11–12)[15] and of happiness as the 'smooth current of life' (*Ecl.* II 77.20–1). It is worth dwelling a moment on 'living consistently'. As Long and Sedley point out, this 'has the ring of Zeno's etymologies'.[16] With a little ingenuity, the Greek expression 'consistently' (*homologoumenôs*) can be dismantled into a telegrammatic version of 'in accordance with one concordant reason' – which is what Stobaeus says was meant, 'since those who live in conflict are unhappy'. As we proceed we shall get more of a sense of why the Stoics thought that a rationality in behaviour that exhibits admirable and attractive harmony, ingenuity, wisdom, resourcefulness, and art trumps all other candidates for the goal.[17] For the moment, let us just catch the Heraclitean echo in *homologoumenôs* and in the etymologising analysis Stobaeus

---

[14] Diogenes Laertius presents his version (VII 101–2) of the division of goods we have quoted from Stobaeus as the preface to his account of the theory of indifferents (VII 102–7).
[15] Connected by Diogenes Laertius to the definition of virtue: 'Happiness consists in virtue, since virtue is soul which has been fashioned to achieve consistency in life as a whole' (VII 89).
[16] Long and Sedley (1987), Vol. II, 390.
[17] See especially M. Frede (1999), whose formulation I echo.

attaches to it[18] – perhaps designed to suggest a holistic metaphysical underpinning for the Stoic vision of the good life.

Elsewhere Zeno is recorded as having made the goal something a little different: 'living consistently with nature' (DL VII 87), although Stobaeus (to the general disbelief of scholars) says this was an innovation of Cleanthes – taking Zeno's formula to be incompletely expressed (*Ecl.* II 76.1–6). I suggest that Zeno employed both formulae: the shorter one in the *Ethics*, in the context of a Type 1 project; the longer one in *On human nature*, as Diogenes Laertius explicitly attests (*ibid.*), in the context of what was likely a Type 2 project. They do not say the same thing, as Striker points out:[19] 'It is evident neither that following nature will lead to a harmonious life nor that consistency and harmony could be achieved only by following nature'. In line with the way we have been envisaging projects of Types 1 and 2, we might take 'living consistently' to characterise the behaviour which satisfies the conditions that are implicit in the *concept* of goal, but 'living consistently with nature' to be an attempt at something rather different: an indication of how from the point of view of a student of nature such consistent behaviour relates to the natural order – indeed, a pointer to the *explanation* of how it is that someone could achieve consistency in living. On this view of the matter, there is something like a nonaccidental pun on 'consistently', and the two formulae do in a sense come to the same thing: we shall live consistently (i.e., each with his or her own self) if and only if we live consistently with nature.

After introducing the second formula, Diogenes Laertius amplifies it briefly. 'Living consistently with nature is living in accordance with virtue, since nature leads us to virtue' (VII 87). The idea is that we all have as our natural endowment (*euphuïa*) certain inclinations which are 'starting points for virtue' (Cleanthes)[20] or the 'foundation of appropriate behaviour and matter for virtue' (Chrysippus).[21] In fact, Zeno etymologised the key notion of *kathêkon*, appropriate

---

[18] Cf. Heraclitus Fr. 50 in particular; among surviving texts deliberate Stoic reminiscence of Heraclitus is most pronounced in Cleanthes' *Hymn to Zeus* (Stob. *Ecl.* I 25.3–27.4). See further Long (1975/6), Schofield (1991/1999), Ch. 3.

[19] Striker (1991), 4.

[20] Stob. *Ecl* II 65.8–9; Cleanthes probably developed the theory in his book *On excellence of natural endowment* (DL VII 175) – although this is not the only title Diogenes Laertius lists that could have accommodated it.

[21] Plutarch, *Comm. not.* 1069e.

behaviour, as what 'proceeds in accordance with' the nature of humans or animals or plants or whatever (DL VII 108).[22] To spell out the theory: the Stoics proposed that humans are naturally programmed by what they called *oikeiôsis*, 'affinity',

1. both for behaving in ways that promote, for example, their own health, wealth, or reputation,[23] and for acquiring the qualities required to do that appropriately – notably moderation (the virtue concerned with the stable condition of their impulses) and courage (the virtue concerned with acts of endurance);[24]

2. for identifying with the interests of, for example, one's parents, friends, and country, and so for justice (the virtue concerned with weighing up varying interests as they deserve); and so in general

3. for 'discovering what is appropriate' – the job of *phronêsis*, wisdom or understanding.[25]

But we are also naturally programmed to become rational creatures – and so to acquire a disposition such that 'reason supervenes as craftsman of impulse' (DL VII 86), with the result that we perform

---

[22] *kata tinas hêkein*. The phrase is translated variously. LS 59C have 'to have arrived in accordance with certain persons'; IG II-94.108 have 'extending [or applying] to certain people'; Hicks, in the Loeb translation, has 'reaching as far as, being up to, or incumbent on so and so'.

[23] Values such as these are accordingly classified as 'in accordance with nature' (Stob. *Ecl.* II 82.20–83.7); a subset – e.g., life, health, and the proper functioning of the sense organs – are so fundamentally related to basic human design that that they are identified as 'the primary things in accordance with nature' (*ibid.* 79.18–80.13, 82.11–19), and may themselves be described as 'starting-points' (*initia, principia*) for virtue (cf. Cic. *Fin.* III 20–2).

[24] Little evidence survives of how the early Stoics explained why and how these virtues are the ones we need for coping with our natural attraction to health, wealth, reputation, and so on. But from Book I of Cicero's *Off.* we get some impression of how Panaetius tackled the issue – although how much of the material is Panaetian, how much Ciceronian we will probably never know. Further discussion is in Section 4 of Striker (1991).

[25] Stob. *Ecl.* II 62.9–12; Stobaeus adds (*ibid.* 12–14): 'Each virtue, by harmoniously performing its own function, ensures that a human being lives in accordance with nature.' At *Ecl.* II 59.4–7 (cf. 75.7–8) he indicates that according to the Stoics, the cardinal virtues are specifically the excellences of a rational animal that is naturally social or political: presumably it is because they are social and political animals that humans have the particular natural tendencies they do.

whatever is appropriate with unfailing consistency – which is the disposition of virtue itself. This evidence confirms that when the Stoics say the goal is 'living consistently with nature', they intend their formula not as a prescription for action so much as a specification of what human nature programmes us for.

'Nature' here seems then to be 'human nature', as Zeno's book title implies.[26] But it is not *just* human nature. Diogenes Laertius goes on to report as follows (VII 87): 'Further, living in accordance with virtue is equivalent to living in accordance with experience of the natural course of events, as Chrysippus says in *On goals* Book I.' He adds the explanation: 'For our own natures are parts of the nature of the whole.' And he sums up like this (VII 88): 'Therefore, the end turns out to be living in agreement with nature, taken as living in accordance both with one's own nature and with the nature of the whole.' Can we work out what led Chrysippus to complicate the story in this way? I think we can see two intimately related points – one more negative, the other positive – which he wanted to make.

The negative and narrower point is that to articulate adequately the idea of the appropriate behaviour characteristic of virtue, it will not do simply to refer to human nature, or at any rate to human nature understood in too limited a fashion. For although ordinarily the appropriate thing will be to look after one's health and one's possessions and so on, in some circumstances it will not be. If the alternative to military service with a tyrant in an unjust cause is self-mutilation, or if the alternative to letting the boat capsize is throwing the cargo overboard, in these cases reason will enjoin self-mutilation and the jettisoning of one's possessions as the appropriate behaviour (DL VII 109; cf. S. E. *M* XI 64–7).[27] What prompts these actions is not natural human impulse at all but 'experience of the course of natural events'; that is, of nature at large, as we might say.[28] In these cases,

---

[26] Later Stoics such as Panaetius and 'some of the younger Stoics' evidently agreed: Clem. *Strom.* II 21.129.4–5.

[27] The Stoics standardly defined the appropriate and inappropriate as what reason enjoins or forbids/doesn't enjoin (e.g., DL VII 108–9). In developing his point here, Diogenes Laertius makes use of this same vocabulary: VII 88.

[28] That Chrysippus' invocation of experience had as its context discussion of whether concern for what is in accordance with nature (e.g., health, wealth) is invariably appropriate appears to be confirmed by Posidonius: he took Chrysippus to be rejecting thereby the idea that the goal consists in 'striving meanspiritedly to obtain the indifferents' (Galen *PHP* V 6.12).

reasonable people act contrary to natural impulse on the experiential knowledge that waterlogged vessels overburdened with cargo usually capsize, and that persons with mutilated limbs are mostly unfit for military service.[29]

I take it that Chrysippus will have introduced his reflections about 'experience of the course of natural events' not as his own positive interpretation of the consistency with nature formula,[30] but to show that an account of 'nature' in the formula which restricts its reference solely to human nature understood in too limited a way will yield an inadequate treatment of what it is to live in accordance with virtue. The broader underlying point – which *does* get reflected in Chrysippus' reading of the consistency formula itself – is indicated in the supporting remark: 'for our own natures are parts of the nature of the whole.' On his view it is not merely that we have to respond to the way things happen in nature at large if we are to act rationally and do the right thing. Stoicism offers a deep explanation for why this should be so; we achieve our true identity only when we function as parts of a whole – that is, of the providentially ordered universe. And that is what – on Chrysippus' interpretation – the consistency formula must be construed as implying. We are programmed to live consistently with the nature of the universe, not just with human nature.[31] Or rather, in understanding what it is to live consistently with human nature, we have to bear in mind that rationality is the crowning human attribute, but as such an attribute we share with and derive from the universe itself. In other words, our notion of human nature cannot be confined to reflection on the impulse to concern ourselves with health, possessions, and the like: to what we might call the merely human.

---

[29] There are few clues as to what Chrysippus meant by 'experience of the course of natural events'. Long and Sedley (1987), Vol. I, 400, suspecting an implicit reference to fate and to 'the "right reason" of what actually happens', say: 'Such experience could be taken to comprise awareness of, say, the normal preferability of health to sickness, and the recognition that everyone can expect to be ill some of the time.'

[30] Which is how Stobaeus interprets him: *Ecl.* II 76.1–8. But we have already noted the unreliability of one other aspect of Stobaeus's account in this passage. It is clear enough from Diogenes Laertius (VII 88–9) that Chrysippus cashed out the formula in terms of the conjunction 'both human nature and the nature of the whole'.

[31] We may infer that Cleanthes gave particular emphasis to this point from Diogenes Laertius' report that unlike Chrysippus he took the formula as referring *only* to 'the common nature' (VII 89). This would certainly be consistent with the general thrust of the *Hymn to Zeus* (Stob. *Ecl.* I 25.3–27.4).

Diogenes Laertius goes on to explain what this conception of how we are programmed adds up to (VII 88). In obeying the injunctions of right reason,[32] we are obeying the divine reason which presides over the administration of reality. If we obey them consistently, we will have achieved virtue and the 'smooth current of life' because all our actions will then be in accordance with harmony between the divine in us and the will of the administrator of the whole. So to return to self-mutilation, although we have no natural human impulse to engage in such a thing, when it dictates it right reason is at one with nature – in the more profound sense of embracing what is fated by the providential design of the universe. Once again, following nature turns out not to be the prescription for how the human ethical project is to be undertaken, but rather a description of how it is possible for us to succeed in that project. 'The "theocratic" principle', suggested Gregory Vlastos, 'changes one's conception of the relation of virtue to the universal order (it tells me that if I am virtuous my way of life is congruous with the order of the universe), but *does not change* either the *content of virtue* ... or the *conception of happiness* (virtue remains the necessary and sufficient condition of happiness ...).'[33] It changes one's outlook in another way also. When I ask myself who I am, I have to remember that I am a citizen of the universe and a part of it, and in exercising my reason, treat nothing as merely a matter of private advantage nor deliberate as though I were detached from the whole.[34]

4. CONTROVERSIES

Is there evidence that in developing their system the Stoics locked horns with the Epicureans? The one point at which the presentation of Stoicism is clearly designed to counter Epicureanism is – perhaps not surprisingly – the starting point of the entire Type 2 account of ethics we have been recovering from Diogenes Laertius. Epicurus claimed that there was no need even to argue or discuss why pleasure should be pursued and pain avoided; it is sufficient just to point it

---

[32] I.e., in performing appropriate actions: see n. 27.

[33] Letter reproduced in Long (1989), 86–7.

[34] Epictetus II 10.3–4: who – contra Annas (1993), Ch. 5 – is here as elsewhere simply following Chrysippus' lead in developing this train of thought (cf. Long [1989], 96 n. 21).

out. But the claim itself he *did* argue: from the observation that all animals as soon as they are born – before nature can be corrupted – seek pleasure and enjoy it as their greatest good and shun pain as the greatest bad that can happen to them. Cicero represents this as Epicurus' opening gambit in his treatment of the goal of life (*Fin.* I 29–30). Chrysippus evidently saw it as imperative to undermine the Epicurean strategy. It is an attractive conjecture that this is why he made consideration of impulse the first topic to be treated in a Type 2 account of ethics such as his own *On goals* presumably was. According to Diogenes Laertius (VII 85–6), he argued in Book I of the treatise that animals' first impulses are focused *not* on pleasure but on self-preservation: in the first instance, they identify with their own constitution and with consciousness of it. That is why they reject what is harmful to them and accept what they have an affinity with. What babies sense is the need for nourishment – that is why they want their mother's breast, not because they enjoy feeding and the full stomach they get afterwards. Pleasure is merely a by-product which *may* occur when what is suitable for the animal's constitution is attained – but it doesn't always do so. Seneca draws attention to toddlers who insist on standing upright and trying to walk, even though it is a painful business that makes them cry – they are always falling over (*Ep.* 121.8).[35]

Flat rejection of the tenets of the Epicurean system is one thing; vigorous debate over key issues in ethics is another – and something for which we have rather more evidence. It was conducted for the most part not with the Epicureans, but sometimes within the Stoic school, sometimes against Academic opponents, sometimes both together. The fiercest early controversy we hear of does not quite fall under any of these heads. It involved one of Zeno's pupils, Aristo of Chios, who appears to have found Zeno's Socraticism insufficiently Socratic. Like Herillus, another pupil of Zeno, he ruled out any distinctions within the category of indifferent things: to call, for example, health 'preferred' was in his view equivalent to judging it a good. The point evidently assumed the importance it did for him in part because he identified the goal as living in a state of indifference to

---

[35] Epicurean and Stoic 'cradle' arguments are subjected to searching examination in Brunschwig (1986).

everything which lies between virtue and vice.[36] He likewise disagreed with Zeno over the question of the unity of virtue. Zeno, like Socrates, made virtue unitary (he talked of it in terms of practical understanding, *phronêsis*). Aristo followed suit – but he thought one should not then go on to recognise a plurality of virtues, as Zeno had appeared to do. Instead, courage should be treated simply as virtue exercised in one sphere, justice in another, and so on – or, as Chrysippus characterised his view, virtue is single, the rest its relative states.[37] Nothing in all this about consistency with nature – a silence which makes it unsurprising news that Aristo had no truck with physics or logic: physics as being beyond our reach, logic as not addressed to our concerns (DL VII 160).

There is more at stake here than the truth about virtue and happiness. Aristo is challenging the very idea that Socratism ought to be cast in a Zenonian mold. He is a minimalist, against elaborateness in any form – and no doubt the aversion extended to the notion of philosophy as a system. However, Zenonianism was to prevail, and it became the template for the ethics developed by Zeno's most influential immediate successors, above all Chrysippus.[38] At least some of the development was worked out in response to Aristo's minimalism. It was in a book against Aristo entitled 'On the Fact that Virtues Are Qualities' that Chrysippus presented his complicated theory of the mutual implication of the virtues, defending Zeno's common-sense belief in a plurality of virtues in such a way as to exhibit its compatibility with the Zenonian thesis that virtue is knowledge or understanding.[39]

I have taken it that Aristo was *rejecting* Zeno's treatment of virtue. Sometimes scholars have seen him rather differently: as *interpreting* Zeno's perhaps not wholly determinate position on the unity or plurality of virtues. But this is to turn Aristo into something more like a Stoic proper than, on the evidence, he was. From it we can infer that for Aristo, *Socrates* was the authority, and right philosophising a matter of getting Socrates right. It was only among more wholehearted Zenonians, especially as and after Zenonianism

[36] DL VII 160, 165; S. E. *M* XI 63; discussion in Long (1988).
[37] DL VII 161, Plu. *Virt. mor.* 440e–441d, *St. rep.* 1034c–e. Discussion in Schofield (1984).
[38] Cf. Sedley Ch. 1, Section 4, this volume.
[39] DL VII 202; Galen *PHP* VII 2. Discussion in Schofield (1984).

achieved some durability and eminence among Hellenistic versions of Socratism, that Zeno's *ipsissima verba* became the authoritative focus of Stoic exegesis and controversy.[40] A good example – at least if we may believe Sextus Empiricus (*M* VII 227–41) – is an early disagreement over Zeno's use of the word *tupôsis*, 'printing', in his definition of *phantasia*, 'impression'.[41] Cleanthes took the word literally: the physical effect of an impression on the soul was like the imprint of a signet ring on wax. 'Chrysippus', says Sextus, 'regarded such a thing as absurd'. He thought what Zeno must have meant by *tupôsis* – given the large number of impressions we are simultaneously bombarded with – was the kind of alteration the air undergoes when several people speak at once. But the debate did not stop there. Sextus devotes ten more paragraphs to reporting ever more ingenious and complex exegeses of Zeno's *tupôsis* – and the objections (he does not say from what quarter) that each of them then prompted.

We do not possess any comparably full, lucid, and explicit accounts of the no doubt comparable diachronic debates over Zenonian definitions in ethics which must have been conducted by successive generations of Stoics and in some cases fought out between Stoics and Academics. For example, we have from Diogenes Laertius the summary report (VII 127): 'Chrysippus holds that virtue can be lost, on account of intoxication or depression, but Cleanthes takes it to be irremovable owing to secure cognitions'. Was Cleanthes drawing an inference from a Zenonian definition of virtue? And was Chrysippus pointing out that the inference was invalid? For another example (where the evidence is richer), consider Chrysippus' treatment of the passions as judgments. Posidonius represented this as a divergence from Zeno's position, which he thought made passions irrational contractions, swellings, and so on *resulting* from judgments. But Chrysippus' theory was probably a reasonable explication of Zeno's account of passions as excessive impulses, and intended as such. What is worth noting here is Posidonius' use or abuse of Zeno's authority (which, by a further twist, he does not himself acknowledge as final on this subject) to bolster his attack on the Chrysippean position.[42]

[40] Cf. Sedley Ch. 1, Section 5 this volume.
[41] Cf. Hankinson, Ch. 3, this volume.
[42] Galen *PHP* IV 3.2–5, IV 4.38, V 1.4–5, V 6.33. Discussion in Cooper (1998). See also Brennan, Ch. 10, this volume.

There is abundant information about the various definitions of the goal proposed by a whole sequence of leading Stoics in the second-century B.C. All of them are couched in terms which suggest they were conceived as explications of Zeno's formula 'living consistently with nature'. Some sound as though they are designed to improve on other versions too. Thus, Antipater's 'continually and undeviatingly doing everything in one's power toward obtaining the most important of the things which accord with nature' (call this A) may well be in some dialectical relationship with Diogenes of Babylon's 'reasoning well in the selection and disselection of things in accordance with nature' (call this D) – although it is not clear which of these may be responding to what difficulties in the other. According to Plutarch, the view was held by some that Antipater resorted to D (apparently regarded as his own invention, however) 'under pressure from Carneades', who was indeed probably the author of a critique of A.[43]

We have some idea of the way Carneades developed his line of attack. A key point he seems to have made is that in A the notion of *goal* ends up disjoined from one of the formulae the Stoics used in defining it: 'that to which everything in life should be referred' (*Ecl.* II 46.5–10; let us call this the *reference point*).[44] For A makes 'obtaining the most important of the things which accord with

---

[43] But modern scholars have thought the move Antipater made went in the opposite direction: from D to A. Discussion in Long (1967), Striker (1986).

[44] This is explained by Plutarch (*Comm. not.* 1071a–b) as follows, in a passage scholars have subjected to much emendation, in my view wrongly at some crucial junctures. I take him to be offering merely a demonstration of the claim that a proposition such as A makes goal and reference point embarrassingly different, not yet an attempt to extract further absurdities from it. I translate as follows, indicating points at which the MS text should be retained: 'For if it is not the primary things conforming with nature themselves that are good, but the rational selection and taking of them [cf. D] and doing everything in one's power for the sake of getting the primary things conforming with nature [cf. A], then all actions must have this as their reference point, viz. getting the primary things conforming with nature. [And this reference point R can't then be the goal G], for since [*eiper gar*] they think that it isn't by aiming at or desiring *getting these things* that we locate the end, the purpose for which the selection of them must be referred [i.e., the goal G in *its* role as reference point] is something different [sc. different – *allo* MS, not *ep' allo* – from the reference point R] and not them [*tauta*, i.e., *getting them*]. For the goal is selecting and taking them wisely, whereas they and getting them are not the goal but the underlying matter, as it were, having "selective value".' As Cherniss (1976), 751, says in his note d, in the second sentence the emphasis is on the phrase 'getting these things' – the point is that *that*'s not where we locate the end.

nature' the reference point, but 'doing everything in one's power' to secure them the goal. There is then an obvious problem: the reference point turns out 'to be simultaneously the goal (by definition) and not the goal (by hypothesis)'.[45] One way in which the difficulty was driven home was simply by rewriting A with its description of the goal substituted for its account of the reference point to which – on Stoic theory – it should be definitionally equivalent. A was then reduced to an absurdity like that of saying: 'an archer in shooting does everything in his power not for the purpose of hitting the mark but for the purpose of doing everything in his power' (Plutarch, Comm. not. 1071c). D fared no better at the hands of the critics. Its subordination of outcomes to the actions taken to secure them was represented as a topsy-turvy way of looking at things ('against the common conception', as Plutarch complains), like making the selection of drugs more important than health (so Plutarch, ibid., 1071C–E), while at the same time actually rendering selection pointless – 'if getting the things selected is indifferent and does not contribute to the end' (Alexander of Aphrodisias, De anima II 164.8–9).

Quite how to untangle the strands of this controversy – and there is much more than there is space for here – will probably always itself remain controversial. A clearer though still conjectural story can be told about the dialectical triangle formed by the arguments of Carneades, Diogenes, and Antipater on justice.[46] Justice was the topic on which Carneades gave his famous pair of contradictory lectures on the occasion of the Athenian embassy to Rome in 155 B.C.; and no doubt he deployed similar lines of thought on many occasions. A key difficulty he raised occurs in different guises in different texts. Cicero (as reported in Lactantius Div. inst. V 16) presents it as an attempt to drive a wedge between wisdom and justice. There was an explicit political point:[47] Rome won its empire by pursuing its advantage regardless of the injustice involved. And there were some memorable examples:

If a good man has a runaway slave or a house that is insanitary and disease-ridden, and if on this account he announces that he is selling: should he

---

[45] So Striker (1986), 191.
[46] This and the following two paragraphs reproduce material from Schofield (1999a), 764–5.
[47] Perhaps to be related to the object of the Athenian embassy, which was to overturn a fine imposed for aggression against Oropus.

confess that the slave he is selling is a runaway or the house disease-ridden, or should he conceal this from the buyer? If he confesses, he is certainly a good man, because he is not practising deceit; but he will nonetheless be judged a fool, because he will sell either at a low price or not at all. If he conceals, he will certainly be wise, because he looks after his interests; but the same person will be wicked, because he is practising deceit.

Other examples also are introduced to make the same point, notably the instance of the shipwrecked traveler in the water who gets the opportunity to dislodge someone else from a plank that floats past: if he pushes him off, he behaves unjustly (committing an act of violence against another); if he does not, he is a fool (sparing another's life at the expense of his own). The anonymous commentary on the *Theaetetus* (col. 5.18–6.31) alludes to this same example in an argument ascribed to 'the Academics'. Here it figures as one limb of a dilemma for *oikeiôsis* theory. Either *oikeiôsis* relative to others is of the same intensity as *oikeiôsis* to oneself: in which case justice is preserved, but at the cost of psychological implausibility. Or it is weaker: in which case the shipwreck example supplies an instance where, if *oikeiôsis* is the mainspring of a person's behaviour, identification with self will conflict with identification with others and win out over it. On this alternative, all that identifying with others can generate is *philanthrôpia*, kindly feeling toward other people, nothing as strong as a source of real commitments, which is what justice is.[48]

The Stoics disagreed among themselves about how best to meet such difficulties. Cicero records what he presents as a debate between Diogenes of Babylon and Antipater on the subject (*Off.* III 51–7). Both apparently aimed to remove the grounds for alleging a conflict between justice and the pursuit of one's interest. In the case of the sale of goods, Diogenes held that it would not be unjust of the vendor to remain silent about the defects of the house or the slave, and so to pursue self-interest. He argued that it is one thing to conceal, another to be silent. Silence would be tantamount to concealment only if it was the vendor's responsibility to ensure that the buyer knew everything it might be in his interest to know. But the buyer is a free agent, and the responsibility is primarily his. Justice conceived as looking

[48] A text and translation of the relevant passage from the *Theaetetus* commentary is conveniently available in Long and Sedley (1987), Volume 1, 350 and 2, 348–349.

after another's interest seems to reduce here to refraining from deliberately harming his interest. To Antipater's way of thinking, justice
imposed greater demands than this, and in the example given would
require the seller to confess. But he seems to have suggested that,
properly understood, the common interest coincides with one's own
advantage or should be made to coincide with it. How he argued for
the suggestion is not disclosed. It would presumably imply that for
a quite different reason there is no real conflict between justice and
self-interest. The problem of how to deal with such a conflict or apparent conflict continued to exercise the school. Panaetius made it
the subject of the third and final division of discussion of appropriate
action, but notoriously never wrote the treatise he promised about it
(Cic. Off. I 9, III 7). Among his pupils, Posidonius claimed it was the
most important topic in all philosophy, but had little to say about
it (Off. III 8); on the other hand, Hecato's On appropriate actions
tackled all the puzzle cases in its sixth book, and appears to have
defended a subtle form of utilitarianism (Off. III 89–90).[49]

5. PRACTICAL ETHICS

Stoic ethics was meant above all to be lived, not just systematised
and elaborated to meet criticism and challenge. The most important
division of the subject was the last – the part focused on practice:
'persuasions and dissuasions of actions'. 'The philosopher's lecture
room', says Epictetus (III 24.30), 'is a hospital: you ought not to walk
out of it in a state of pleasure, but in pain – for you are not in good
condition when you arrive!' The Stoics wrote a great deal in 'therapeutic' mode and, in fact, much of the surviving material actually
by Stoics is what might be called practical ethics, not articulation
of doctrine – for which we have to turn to doxographers, anthol-
ogists, encyclopedists, and sometimes to hostile or unsympathetic
witnesses like Plutarch and Alexander of Aphrodisias.

So, for example, in the three major collections of Stoic literature
we still possess, we can listen to Marcus Aurelius admonishing himself, Seneca in his letters advising a friend, and Epictetus berating his
pupils. Its general purpose was doubtless (as Epictetus puts it with
respect to the Cynic agenda) 'to show people that where what is

---

[49] For fuller discussion of the Diogenes-Antipater debate, see Schofield (1999b).

good and bad are concerned, they have gone astray: they look for the essence of good and bad where it is not; where it *is* never enters their minds' (III 22.23). But Stoic practical ethics – as was true for other ancient philosophical schools – came in a variety of genres. Much of Epictetus is aptly described as protreptic, summoning his audience as it does to the radical reorientation of their priorities which philosophy entails. As well as the letters, Seneca's oeuvre, by contrast, includes for instance 'consolations' (one to Marcia, daughter of one Cremutius Cordus, who was grieving for the loss of a son more than two years previously; another to Claudius' freedman Polybius, on the death of his brother; and a third to his own mother, urging her not to mourn his exile); *On anger*, which represents itself as an answer to a request for advice on how to restrain the passion; and *On clemency*, one of the few substantial extant specimens of the extensive 'mirror of princes' literature generated in Greco-Roman antiquity, published soon after the young Nero's accession to power.

There were a number of standard topics in practical ethics. For example, we know of numerous Stoic treatises entitled *On appropriate action*, although the only survivor is Cicero's transmutation, expansion, and far-reaching Romanisation of Panaetius' version in his *On duties*. Another subject treated by more than one Stoic was *On acts of benefaction*: again, we possess only a Latin version, a massive work by Seneca in seven books devoted to the casuistry of a practice which was a major ingredient in the moral and social glue of Roman society. *On marriage* seems to have been a particularly popular topic, best represented in an extensive anthology of extracts from various writers preserved in Stobaeus (*Ecl.* IV 494–568) – including, for example, the Stoics Antipater, Hierocles, and Musonius Rufus. Finally, I should mention *On lives*, on which Chrysippus wrote a work in four books as a contribution to the ancient philosophical debate about the choice between the philosophical and the political life. From surviving fragments and reports that appear to relate to it, we can infer that this was at least one place where Chrysippus discussed at length the implications of the Stoic appropriation of the Aristotelian idea that humans are by nature social and political animals.[50]

[50] Many (although not all) of the texts collected in SVF III 685–704 bear out this point.

It is in Stoic writings on practical ethics, which are still available to us, that we get perhaps our keenest sense of what it was like for ancient thinkers not just to subscribe to Stoicism as a philosophy, but also to move about in it as their intellectual home and as the air they breathed. Nowhere does that come across more vividly than when a Seneca or an Epictetus draws on its resources and its radical perspectives on life to think through questions of how we should behave toward others and how we should face threats to health and happiness. Sometimes we think of Stoicism as an emotional desert – and passages like the following, wintry in more ways than one, are common enough in Epictetus (III 24.84–7):

> Whenever you are getting attached to someone, don't let it be as though they're something undetachable – but more as if you had a jar or a crystal goblet, so that when it breaks, you'll remember that it's that sort of thing and not be upset... In the same way, remind yourself that the person you love is mortal, not one of your own possessions, something given to you for the present, not undetachably nor for ever, like a fig or a cluster of grapes, in the due season of the year – and if you hanker for that in winter, you're a fool. If you long for your son or your friend like this, at a time when that has not been given to you, rest assured: you are hankering for a fig in winter.[51]

But Stoicism did not have to be always like that. Listen, for example, to Seneca on the transformation effected by Stoicism in the ancient Mediterranean ethics of reciprocity: in the system whereby acts of assistance were swapped as need arose by neighbours or the favours of the great offered in return for services rendered by the small man would generate the expectation of further assistance in the future – one good turn deserving and often getting another.[52] He says (*Ben.* II 31.1–2):

> This is in my opinion the least surprising or least incredible of the paradoxes of the Stoic school: that the person who receives a benefaction gladly has already returned it... When a person gives a benefaction what does he aim at? To be the cause of profit and pleasure to the person to whom he gives. If he accomplishes what he wished, and his intention is conveyed to me, and affects me with a reciprocating joy, he gets what he aimed at. He didn't

---

[51] Annas aptly entitles this the 'alienation' strategy, and suspects that it is particularly characteristic of Marcus Aurelius, citing VI 13: Annas (1993), 176.

[52] Discussion in Inwood (1995).

want me to give anything in exchange. Otherwise it would have been not a benefaction, but a business transaction.

And here is some remarkable advice from the same book of *On acts of benefaction* on *how* to perform them (*ibid.* II 17.3–4):

I wish to make use of an illustration that our Chrysippus drew from playing catch. If the ball falls to the ground, it is undoubtedly the fault either of the thrower or the catcher. It maintains its course only so long as it is kept in play between the hands of the two players throwing and catching it just right ... If we are dealing with a practised and educated partner, we should be bolder in our throwing of the ball. No matter how it comes, his ready, nimble fingers will whip it back. But if we are playing with an uneducated novice, we shall not throw it so hard or with such force, but lob it more gently – in fact we shall move towards him in a relaxed manner and guide the ball right into his hand.

And the moral? Seneca goes on (*ibid.*):

The same strategy should be adopted in helping people. There are some people we have to teach how to receive help. And we should judge it sufficient if they try, if they dare, if they are willing.

Perhaps it is not surprising that a book about generosity should itself be so generous.[53]

---

[53] For further discussion of Stoic practical ethics and with fuller bibliographical information, see Ch. 2, Gill.

10   Stoic Moral Psychology[1]

I. INTRODUCTION: THE SCOPE OF MORAL PSYCHOLOGY, ANCIENT AND MODERN

Moral psychology addresses itself to the interface between ethics and psychology. One of the basic principles of moral psychology is the apparently trivial one, that all ethically correct actions are, to begin with, actions: inasmuch as they are the deliberate or at least intentional actions of human beings, ethical actions will share features with the class to which they belong, and fall under whatever constraints belong to the larger kind.

This of course raises an immediate question about the coherence of the topic so described. Psychology is clearly a descriptive field, and ethics is the normative field *par excellence*; the one tells us how the human mind *does* function, the other tells us how human agents *ought* to act. Given this fundamental difference, we may not assume, without further argument, that the first discussion can place any constraints whatsoever on the second. The mere fact that psychology places limits on what is humanly possible does not show, without further argument, that ethics must keep its demands within those limits.

[1] The greater part of this chapter is a distillation of views expressed in Inwood (1985); all work on the Stoic philosophy of action since then has consisted in footnotes to that path-breaking volume. I have ventured to disagree on a few points, to elaborate others, and to simplify and streamline for the purposes of this volume, but the broad lines of my position are indebted to that work, and the student who wishes to pursue any topic in this chapter should make it their first point of reference. In addition, I am grateful to Richard Sorabji for having nurtured my interest in this topic, and to Charles Brittain and Rachel Barney for discussions. And as always, my deepest thanks go to Liz Karns.

The further argument tends to come, nowadays, in terms of a sort of mixing axiom of morality and modality, that the agent cannot be obligated to do anything it is not possible for the agent to do. This is usually abbreviated to the slogan that 'ought' implies 'can', though its teeth are more often bared in the contrapositive formulation, that 'not possible' implies 'not obligatory'.[2]

In practice, however, the limitation of ethics by psychology can be adroitly resisted by the skillful use of such clauses and provisos as *'pro tanto'* and 'to the extent possible'. Ethics cedes a great deal of territory when it accepts the 'ought-can' rule, but immediately starts a revanchist campaign to recapture it via the 'regulative ideal'. When that ideal has its origins elsewhere than in the human psyche, facts about our psyches enter at a later stage, importing limits and imperfections to which ethics never fully reconciles itself.

This gives to many recent discussions of moral psychology the flavor of a catch-up game or a damage-control operation; an attempt to show how our psychology is roughly adequate to the tasks set for it by our ethics or how we can cordon off its failures. I have in mind especially two types of discussions: those which start from a view about the centrality of altruism to ethical behavior, and then attempt to make it possible for our psychology to accommodate altruism; and those that start from a view about the importance of autonomy and freedom, and then try to show that our psychology allows us to be free in the requisite ways.[3]

In antiquity, the bridge between ethics and psychology is constructed on a different plan. Because they all embrace some type of naturalism in their ethical foundations, ancient theories tend to begin their ethical theorizing along with their psychology, not prior to it. They are thus more sanguine about the innate coherence of moral psychology, and less likely to see psychology as an *ex post facto* constraint on ethical ideals drawn from distant sources.

---

[2] Indeed, one very seldom finds arguments from 'ought' to 'can'. Even those who claim the most confident access to the realm of ethics seldom seem so confident as to infer new psychological powers from the new obligations they discover. If *a priori* ethical certainties contradict the findings of psychology, it is more often the 'ought-can' rule which is made to bend, even by its partisans.

[3] For contemporary manifestations in typical, handbook presentations of the topic, see, e.g., Slote (1999) and Thomas (2000).

The symmetry of the situation is mirrored in what might be termed the analogous ancient mixing axiom of moral psychology: the perfectly representative human psyche belongs to the perfectly ethical human agent. Violations of ethical standards always reflect lapses in psychological hygiene, and our obligations are set for us by the actual practice of psychologically perfect agents – even if the scarcity of such agents reduces the 'actual' to a rather notional status. There is never an initial stage in which ethics sets up an ideal that is distinct from or in any conflict with the true nature of human psychology; rather, the two disciplines study the same object from different vantage points. This is why their results are guaranteed to agree, and this is why the discipline of moral psychology is coherent from the start. Or so the ancient view would have it.

From the contemporary standpoint, it must look as though ethics and psychology are being adjusted to one another in a deeply suspect manner, like a jigsaw puzzle being assembled with a penknife. In particular, it seems that any threat that psychology might pose to the autonomy of ethics is being avoided by the extreme idealization of psychology itself. No longer the empirical, descriptive discipline we thought it to be, psychology turns out to be the study of an ideal just as much as ethics is, and the actual creatures that jostle against us are now declared imperfect specimens, poor guides to the true nature of the beast.

I note these differences neither to praise ancient ethics for its naturalism nor to condemn ancient psychology for its reliance on the armchair, but in order to give context and background to what follows. Ancient moral psychology shares the bulk of its problems and concerns with its modern descendants, and familiar questions will be addressed, including questions related to altruism and autonomy. But some larger doubts and deeper difficulties are never broached. The assumption is that the project can work, not that the project's very working needs to be justified.

In moral psychology, as in most areas of Stoicism, the agenda is set and the terms largely dictated by the Socrates of Plato's early dialogues, especially the *Protagoras*.[4] Rejecting the model of psychic complexity embraced by Plato in later works and by Aristotle, with

---

[4] *Protagoras* 358d.

its interplay and conflict of rational and irrational psychic forces, the Stoics retained Socrates' insistence that all motivations be analyzed as forms of belief. The characteristic intellectualist stance, that all rationality is theoretical rationality, is felt most explicitly in the demand that practical irrationality be analyzed as a form of theoretical irrationality, and that errant motivations be reduced to erroneous beliefs. The Stoic theory proceeds along lines that will allow it to provide these analyses.[5]

PART I: THE MAIN LINES OF THE THEORY

I.1. ITS BACKGROUND IN EPISTEMOLOGY AND ETHICS

A theory of human action must draw upon terms and concepts more properly belonging to epistemology, on the one side, and to axiology, on the other; for detailed discussions, the reader is referred to Chapters 3 and 9. For this chapter, a brief review will suffice.

In Stoic epistemology, everything starts from the doctrine of impressions.[6] An impression is an alteration of the soul, commonly though not necessarily brought about by a sensible object in the agent's environment, which presents itself as providing information about how things are. Although non-rational animals also receive impressions, it is only adult human beings whose impressions are rational,[7] in the sense that they are each correlated with a unique proposition-like item, the *axiôma*, which is partly constitutive of the identity of the impression (i.e., two visual impressions may be completely alike so far as their visual content goes, and yet be distinct

---

[5] On the lines of influence, see Price (1994).
[6] This was the Stoics' own view of the matter; cf. DL VII 49 (SVF 2.52 = LS 39A). For impressions in general, see SVF 2.52–70, LS 39.
[7] The term 'rational' (*logikos*) does at least double duty in Stoic epistemology. In its more inclusive sense, impressions are rational if they are correlated with propositions, and animals are rational if their impressions are rational. By this criterion, all and only gods and adult human beings are rational, and all of their impressions are rational, as are any beliefs or impulses constituted by their assent to these impressions. All non-human, non-divine animals are irrational, as are children, and all of the impressions of non-rational animals are non-rational impressions. In a stricter sense, impressions (and the beliefs and impulses consequent on assenting to them) are rational only if they are in accord with the perfected reason of the Stoic Sage or God. By this standard, all of the beliefs and impulses of all of the actual adult human beings we encounter (given the current shortage of Sages) are irrational.

impressions even at the level of type because of the distinctness of their accompanying *axiômata*).[8]

---

[8] The Stoic assumption that every impression is correlated with only one *axiôma* is thus not the naïve assumption that each photograph has only one possible caption, but rather a matter of how the impression is defined to begin with. The comparison to a photograph already errs by supposing that the content of the impression is exhausted by its sensory, e.g., visual, content; instead, a rational sensory impression combines some sensory content with some further non-sensory content, i.e., some aspect of the alteration of the soul in virtue of which this impression is correlated with the *axiôma* 'there's a mirror in front of me' rather than 'there's a man in front of me'. This further, non-sensory content is not the *axiôma* itself (since every part of the impression is corporeal, i.e., the psychic *pneuma* in a certain state), rather it is the part of the impression, distinct from the merely sensory content, that points to or signifies that *axiôma*. Thus if the same visual content were accompanied by different *axiômata*, the Stoics would not say that it was still the same impression, correlated with different *axiômata*, but that there were different impressions, the difference consisting in a physical difference in the alteration of the soul. Since we are stipulating identity of narrowly perceptual content, the difference will not be found in the portion of the pneuma that encodes that content, but rather in the portion that encodes the pointer to the *axiôma*.

There are thus four things to be distinguished, taking a visual impression as an example: (1) there is the visual appearance of things to be acquired from a particular location; (2) there is the configuration of one's soul that records the uninterpreted appearance of that scene; (3) there is an *axiôma* which is an incorporeal proposition and has no location; and (4) there is the configuration of one's soul that is correlated with that *axiôma*. The first is something like the photographic image, or Epicurean *eidôlon* that would strike anyone's eye, were there such things as *eidôla*. But this is no part of the impression, which is an entirely internal, psychic entity, a disposition or *hexis* of the individual's *pneuma*. In animals, this disposition is exhausted by its sensory content, (2); in adult human beings we can discern a second part (4), which arises from the impact of the sensory object on the framework of concepts that the individual has. This second part is also pneumatic, a portion of *pneuma* or air under tension that has been struck in a certain way, and has a semantic content inasmuch as it is correlated with an *axiôma*. Thus, as a bit of struck air which signifies something (sc. the signified *axiôma*), it fulfills the definition of *logos* (i.e., the kind of *phônê* or struck air that is articulated and significant). But this *logos* is a relatively persistent state of the soul, persisting as long as the impression does, and it is not uttered through the mouth. Thus it is internal *logos* (i.e., *logos endiathetos*), and it is in virtue of the fact that rational impressions are partly composed of some semantic struck air that they are called rational (i.e., *logikai phantasiai*).

The only text (S. E. *M* VII 246 = SVF 2.65 = LS 30F) that seems to offer evidence that individual impressions might be correlated with multiple *axiômata* is actually a reference to type-impressions (e.g., the impression that it is day), tokens of which are had by many individuals at many times, with differing truth-values. Even in this text, the different tokens of the type-impression are not accompanied by different *axiômata*, but by the same *axiôma* whose truth-value varies. This text has worked an astounding amount of mischief in recent years, persuading some critics that the Stoics countenanced impressions whose content was sub-propositional (e.g., impressions of concepts) (M. Frede [1983]), others that one and the same impression

Where animals and children respond directly to the impression by taking some action suggested by its apparent content (e.g., fleeing from the impression of danger), adult human beings first respond to the status of the impression as a whole, by adopting an attitude toward the relation between its content and the state of affairs it pretends to represent. One possible attitude takes the content of the impression to be an accurate representation, saying, as it were, 'yes, things really are as this impression shows them to be'; this is called assent (*sunkatathesis*). Only then does the content of the impression move the agent in further determinate ways; it is only if one assents to the impression that some danger is imminent that one flees or prepares defenses. Otherwise, one can withhold or suspend one's assent, taking the impression to be a 'mere' impression, not an adequate representation of the world.[9]

It is tempting to imagine this process as a quasi-deliberative or discursive process, like the investigation of a witness's bona fides before their testimony is admitted as evidence; and some texts encourage this impression.[10] But I take it that such sub-vocalized scrutiny is extremely rare, and can only occur in the first place if the agent has already suspended judgment, at least temporarily. (There is no more elevated vantage point from which one can decide whether to assent or suspend; the very fact of scrutiny entails that one has suspended judgment, at least temporarily.) Whether one will initially suspend or assent straightaway is a matter completely antecedent to and thus immune from such conscious or deliberate methods, and I take it that it is also a fact fully determined by the nature of the impression and the state of the agent's soul at the time of receiving it.[11]

could have contradictory *axiômata* correlated with it (Joyce [1995]). Shields (1993) sees some of the difficulties, but not the solution. Its latest victim is Caston (1999), who bases part of his excellent article on Stoic universals on a misreading of this passage. For the beginnings of the proper view, see Heintz (1933) *ad loc*, though he damages his case by framing it in terms of an unnecessary textual emendation.

[9] Some texts (e.g., *Diss*. III 3.2) seem to offer a third option, namely rejecting the impression (*ananeuein*, a sort of no-saying, on the model of assent as a yes-saying), but I suspect that this should be analyzed in some cases as a mere suspension without commitment to the contrary of the impression, and at other times as an initial suspension to the initial impression, followed by a distinct assent to a distinct impression which is the contrary of the first (I don't believe the oar is bent, and indeed, I believe it is straight).

[10] The classic texts for this view are Epictetus *Ench*. 1 and *Diss*. III 12.15.

[11] I mean this not only in the sense in which every occurrence, for the Stoics, is determined to occur from all eternity – though that this applies to assents and other

If one does assent to the impression, one thereby has a belief; the belief is the same event as the assenting.[12] From the standpoint of epistemology, the most important sub-types of belief are mere opinions (*doxai*) on the one hand, whether false, true, or cataleptic; and knowledge on the other hand, which involves strong assent to cataleptic impressions, and occurs only in the Sage. What makes an impression cataleptic is discussed in depth in Chapter 3; here we may say that it is a feature of the impression as a whole – both its content and its causal history – that guarantees its truth.

Next, we should review a few points from the Stoic theory of values. Only virtue, along with whatever shares in it, is good; only vice and its participants are bad. All else is indifferent, where this means that it is neither beneficial nor harmful, or equivalently that it has no effect on one's happiness or misery. However, indifferent things like health and disease do have a sort of value called 'selective value' (*axia eklektikê*); we might instead translate it 'planning value' in order to bring out the fact that it is only relevant to future-oriented impulses.[13] When we are already in possession of an indifferent, its 'planning value' falls out of consideration and the object is purely indifferent; thus, we should react with equal equanimity to

mental events as well as to external events is a fact of some significance, which will be discussed later. Rather, what I have in mind is that we should not suppose that the rare cases of conscious scrutiny give us a guide to the normal cases or show us a slowed-down version of a process that occurs in every instance. In these rare cases we at least seem to experience some phenomenological indeterminacy about whether we will assent or not, and so it may be tempting to suppose that every instance of assent occurs after a process of scrutiny, perhaps a rash or hasty one, that at least in principle could have turned out otherwise. Quite the opposite; the normal case is the one in which an impression produces an automatic response of assent, or an automatic response of suspension. The scrutiny cases merely show us the sequelae of one sort of automatic suspension; i.e., what occurs when automatic suspension in response to an impression is followed by automatic suspension in response to its contrary – and yet the agent for whatever reason feels some desire to arrive at a determinate opinion on the matter; this is when one gets into a position to ask the impression for its 'tokens from nature'. (And this, in turn, will generally not involve actual intensified scrutiny of the *same* impression, but rather the deliberate acquisition of a distinct impression; i.e., taking another look). It is actually the fast cases that show us more accurately what occurs in the slow cases, because they more clearly bring out the fact that the assent, when it occurs, is completely determined to occur by the impression and the state of the agent's soul.

[12] For example S. E. *M* VII 151.

[13] Stobaeus II 83 (SVF 3.124 = LS 58D). The term is attributed to Antipater, but I take it to represent Chrysippean doctrine.

our possession of health or disease considered as a *fait accompli*. But when surveying the future, the fact that health has greater 'planning value' than disease (indeed, disease has selective 'disvalue') gives us rational grounds for pursuing health and avoiding disease – though in concrete cases these considerations may be overridden by others, leading us to pursue disease rather than health. Types of indifferent things that have considerable selective value, or its contrary disvalue, may be called 'preferred' and 'dispreferred' indifferents, respectively.[14]

The general run of mankind is not especially misinformed, on the Stoic view, in its beliefs about ordinary matters of fact – our senses inform us about the world in a fairly reliable fashion, and most of our beliefs about medium-size objects are true (though failing, for other reasons, to amount to knowledge). However, the Stoics postulate pandemic error when it comes to matters of evaluation: all of the individuals around us, as well as our cultures, laws, and institutions, are wildly misguided in our assessments of what is good and bad. We routinely and habitually judge that indifferent things such as health, life, money, affection, honor, and comfort are good, and their opposites bad, and all such judgments are false. It is true that we also on occasion do make the correct judgments that virtue is good and vice is bad, and on occasion we can correctly see the indifference of some indifferent things. But the average ethical agent (as opposed to the normal agent – see the previous discussion) spends his or her life pursuing health, wealth, and comfort with the false belief that they are good, and avoiding and fearing disease, poverty, and pain from the false belief that they are bad. These false beliefs – which are also the operative psychological motivations for the agent's intentional actions – are known to the Stoics as *pathê*, or emotions, one species of impulses. Although they are anomalous and flawed as examples of human motivation, they are also the most familiar form of impulse, and – by some sort of irony – we have significantly more evidence from Stoicism about these vicious motivations than we do for any of the virtuous motivations that the Stoics espoused.

---

[14] These are conventional translations for *proêgmena* and *apoproêgmena*, but in the Greek terms there is no connection with any underlying theory of the preferences that agents do have or tend to have or should have. The Stoics' own comments on the terms suggest that more accurate translations might be; e.g., 'promoted' and 'demoted' or 'advanced' and 'relegated'; see Stobaeus II 84–II 85 (SVF 3.128 = LS 58E).

We will examine the evidence about particular kinds of impulses, especially the copious evidence about emotions, that we can use to fill out our picture of the other kinds. But before we begin that investigation, we should first consider the evidence we have about the general structure of all impulses, considered as a class.

I.2. IMPULSES

The notion of impulse, or *hormê*, is at the core of Stoic moral psychology. Or rather – since animals too act on impulses, though not rational ones – the rational impulse (i.e., the propositionally articulated impulse of an adult rational agent) is the central notion in Stoic moral psychology. Whatever the Stoics have to say about human motivations, desires, inclinations virtuous or vicious will all be spelled out in terms of impulse.

Impulse is a necessary condition for action; a series of texts tells us that unless the agent has an impulse, no action will result, and this claim was central to the long-running debate between the Stoics and the Academics about the possibility of living without assent.[15] But impulse is also a sufficient condition for action; when an agent has an impulse to do something, the agent thereupon and forthwith does it.[16]

Each impulse is an assent, and thus a motion of the soul.[17] In saying that an impulse is a motion of the soul or mind toward some action, the Stoics are following a model familiar from the *Republic*;

---

[15] Plutarch *St. rep.* 1057A (SVF 3.177 = LS53S); Stobaeus II 86–87 (SVF 3.169 = LS 53Q); I also take Plutarch *Col.* 1122A–F (LS 69A) as indirect evidence.

[16] *appetitus impellit ad agendum;* Cicero *Off.* I 132 (LS 53J).

[17] *phoran psuchês epi ti;* expanded, in the case of rational animals, to *phoran dianoias epi ti tôn en tôi prattein* Stobaeus II 86–87 (SVF 3.169 = LS 53Q). See also the definition of emotion, a species of impulse, as an irrational movement of the soul (*kinêsis tês psuchês* in, e.g., Stobaeus II 88 = SVF 3.378 = LS 65A). Plutarch is mistaken in saying that the Stoics make assent a body (*Comm. not.* 1084B); one can see how he arrived at the erroneous conclusion that the Stoics make activities into bodies by contrasting Aëtius IV 21 with Seneca *Ep.* 113.23 (both included in SVF 2.836 = LS 53H, LS 53L). Seneca's *ambulatio* (walking, i.e., *peripatêsis;* cf. Plutarch's *orkhêsis*) is ambiguous between an action-word and a capacity-word, just as *horasis* (sight), *geusis* (taste), and so on are. (Walking was a typical example as far back as the *Gorgias* 468 cf.; it occurs often in Aristotle's discussions of action; e.g., *De Motu* 701a). But in Aëtius, these latter words clearly refer not to episodes of seeing or tasting, but to the faculties of sight, taste, and so on, as faculties of the soul. The passage that Seneca translates, and that Plutarch misrepresents, was likewise talking about *peripatêsis* as an ambulatory faculty or capacity, not about the activity of taking a walk. Seneca contrasts two views on whether the body

Socrates describes desires and aversions as psychic pushes and pulls.[18] Like other assents, impulses constitute beliefs; depending on the kind of assent and the kind of impression to which it is given, the belief will fall into one of the types canvassed previously.[19] From the standpoint of moral psychology, the most important division of impressions cuts across the distinction between the false, true, and cataleptic mentioned previously, and characterizes the content of the impression as either practical or theoretical. Practical impressions – or 'impulsive' impressions as the Stoics call them (*phantasiai hormêtikai*) – are those whose content involves some evaluative predication; some attribution of goodness, badness, or other value to a state of affairs; and, in particular, to a description of an action that the agent might take.[20]

The words 'impulse' and 'impulsive' have misleading connotations of whimsy or obsession, which form no part of the Stoic picture – this clearly follows from the very fact that every human action, no matter how deliberate and fancy-free, is analyzed in terms of 'impulsive' impressions. But the translation redeems itself by emphasizing the strong connection with action; impulses on the Stoic view are psychological events that eventuate in action (provided that externals cooperate).

It is important to keep this in mind as we delve more deeply into the sub-types of impulse (e.g., the one called desire). In the normal acceptation of that word, it is certainly possible to have and not act

which is my dispositional capacity to walk is the same as my *hêgemonikon* or an extension of it; the passage does not show that an action like my walking could be a body like the *hêgemonikon*.

[18] *Republic* 437b–c; and for more on Platonic precedents, see Brunschwig 1994b.

[19] Stobaeus II 88 (SVF 3.171 = LS 33I) says that every impulse is an assent, and this settles the question. Doubts have arisen because the next sentence seems to say that assents and impulses have distinct objects; but it does not. All assents are assents to propositions (this relation specified by the dative *axiômasi*); those assents that are also impulses are also directed toward predicates (this relation specified by '*epi*' with the accusative – cf. '*phora epi ti*' in the generic definition of *hormê*). If impulses were not bona fide assents, it would make no sense to say that the emotion of fear or desire is a *doxa*, or to describe emotions in general as *kriseis*.

[20] Stobaeus II 86–87 (SVF 3.169 = LS 53Q). For discussion of this all-important passage, see Inwood (1985), pp. 224–242. Long and Sedley's translation, is incorrect; for a demonstration that Inwood has the correct translation, see Brennan (2003). In Brennan (1998), I consider and reject the interesting proposal of M. Frede (1986) that what makes impressions impulsive might not be a matter of the content that they represent, but rather of the way or manner in which they represent that content.

on desires of many kinds; on a standard two-factor theory of action, no desire can produce an action unless combined with a belief of the right sort (e.g., one stating that means to the satisfaction of the desire are ready at hand). Stoic impulses, and thus the Stoic term translated by 'desire', are unlike this in both respects. One cannot have an impulse without acting on it – the very having of it (i.e., the assent to the impulsive impression) is the initiation of the action envisaged in the impression.[21] And the impulse contains in itself everything requisite to action: not only a general evaluative pro or con attitude, but also a specification of the action in terms of ulti- mate particulars, sufficient to the task envisaged. In this respect, a Stoic impulse is not like the major premiss of an Aristotelian prac- tical syllogism, but rather like the psychological synthesis of both premisses together.[22] It is a mental event that synthesizes a descrip- tion of a particular, determinate state of affairs with an evaluative attitude toward that state of affairs and leads to immediate action. It is the causally sufficient, immediately antecedent, psychological motivation of an intentional action.[23]

[21] I ignore the con-cases involved in fear and the like (e.g., those in which I have a sudden and horrifying thought of jumping from the high balcony, think 'that would be a terrible thing to do!' or 'mustn't do that!' and back away quickly). The story is roughly the same for them, even though the action that immediately eventuates is the contrary of the action depicted in the impression (i.e., the emotion is an impulse away from the action, or a flight from the impending evil – an 'endeavour fromward' the action, as Hobbes says of aversion, Leviathan i.vi.23). See Clement's report of a definition of *hormê* as a 'motion towards or away from something' (*phora epi ti ê apo tou*) *Strom.* II 460 (SVF 3.377).

[22] Aristotle notoriously denies that the conclusion of such a syllogism is a further psychological entity – perhaps to avoid a regress or an unbridgeable explanatory gap, he says only that what follows is an action (*Nicomachean Ethics* 1147a25 et seq.). But even Aristotle must say that, in addition to seeing the premisses independently, one must see them fitting together into a unified whole, *as* the premisses of a syllogism rather than as unrelated observations, and to the extent that this is a psychological event over and above the grasping of each separate premiss he should not hesitate to countenance it, while still insisting that what results from this synthesizing grasp is the action itself.

[23] The Stoics recognize a secondary sense of 'impulse' in which it means a disposition to have impulses of the canonical kind; and the ambiguity between event-term and disposition-term runs throughout much of the vocabulary. For example, there is a distinction in the official terminology between emotions *per se*, which are punctual and event-like motions of the soul toward something, and state-like dispositions of the soul to have particular emotions, which are called 'diseases' or 'proclivities' (see SVF 3.421–3.430, LS 65S, 65L, though note that the phrase 'the passions' is mistakenly added into the first sentence of 65L). Thus my burst of anger on Tuesday

The evidence for the generic content of impulses is contained in a remark that is as close as we have to a definition of an impulsive impression: 'they say that what moves impulse is nothing other than an impulsive impression of what is *kathêkon, ipso facto*'. I follow Inwood in taking this to mean that every impulsive impression is, in the first instance, an impression to the effect that something is *kathêkon*. Or, to put this in terms of the *axiôma* that accompanies the impression, every impulsive *axiôma* is governed by a sort of impulse-operator at its highest node, which reads 'it is *kathêkon* that p' where p gives the rest of the content of the impulsive *axiôma*, by spelling out some candidate action that the agent might take.

That this is right is strongly suggested by the doctrine of Epictetus, whose orthodoxy on this point we have no reason to question:

... for all human beings there is one and the same origin [of action]. Just as for assent the origin is the feeling that the thing is the case, and for rejection the origin is the feeling that it is not the case ... so too for impulse toward something the origin is the feeling that it is advantageous (*sumpheron*) to me. It is impossible to judge that one thing is advantageous but to desire something else, or to judge that one thing is *kathêkon*, but have an impulse toward something else. (*Diss.* I 18.1)

Whenever someone treats you badly, or speaks badly of you, remember that he did or said it because he believed this was the *kathêkon* thing for him. It isn't possible for him to follow how things appear to you, only how they appear to him. (*Ench.* 42)

Both of these quotations claim that every action is motivated by the thought that something is *kathêkon*. It also seems from Epictetus' usage that there is nothing magical about the term '*kathêkon*'; he is happy to replace it with any one of a short list of predicates – 'appropriate', 'reasonable', 'advantageous' – all of them playing a structurally similar role.[24] It seems we are being told that

the 23rd is an emotion; my perpetual irascibility is not an emotion, but rather a proclivity. See Brennan (1998) for extended discussion. (However, we also find 'emotion' used catachrestically of dispositions – see, e.g., SVF 3.456, and Galen's explicit notice of the point in SVF 3.429.) This puts the Stoic theory of emotions at a fundamental distance from those theories (e.g., Wollheim [1999] following Sartre [1933]) that take the central case of emotions to be dispositional in nature (e.g., syndromes and patterns of feeling-response, strategies for relating to the world, or stances one adopts toward it).

[24] *oikeion, eulogon, sumpheron*, etc.: see *Diss.* I 11.28–32; III 22.43; I 28.5–6; I 19.8–15; I 2.3–4. See also Plutarch *Col.* 1122A–F (LS 69A) – since I hold that Arcesilaus'

there is one conception of things that is *per se* motivating, though this conception lines up with several linguistic expressions. The ethical significance of the uniformity of content in the generic impulse is discussed in Section II.4, as well as the significance of the fact that the conception that motivates is not the conception that our object is good.

I.3. EMOTIONS, EUPATHEIAI, AND SELECTIONS

Surviving discussions of Stoic impulses are overwhelmingly concerned with one species, the emotion or passion (*pathos*).[25] This slant in the evidence reflects both the fact that most of the motivations of actual persons (i.e., non-Sages) consist in emotions, and the fact that the analysis of emotions became the focus for the debate between Stoics and the other schools over the structure of the soul and the question of its irrationality.

What distinguishes emotions from other impulses is the fact that they include a characterization of their objects as good or bad, and that they are constituted by beliefs that fall short of knowledge. Typically what makes them fall short of knowledge is the fact that they are false; in most of the examples, an agent picks out an indifferent object, such as money or pleasure or death, and falsely predicates goodness or badness of it. The four main species of emotion are produced by distinguishing attributions of goodness and badness directed toward present and future things; desire involves the attribution of goodness to some future state, fear is an apprehension of a future evil; pleasure is an attribution of goodness to a present state, pain an attribution of evil to a present state. In the fullest and most explicit definitions we are given of these mental events, they are defined as follows:[26]

comments about practical agency here are part of an *ad hominem* reply to Stoic theory, I take this passage as strong evidence of the Stoic stance – see Brennan (1996) and (2000b). The claim there that action requires only two things, namely a '*phantasia* of what is appropriate' (*phantasia oikeiou*) and a *hormê* toward the apparent appropriate thing (*pros to phanen oikeion hormê*) offers a striking confirmation of Inwood's translation of the crucial phrase in Stobaeus II 86 (i.e., *phantasia tou kathêkontos*) as well as further evidence that '*kathêkon*' could be replaced by other roughly equivalent terms such as *oikeion*.

[25] SVF 3.377–420; LS 65.

[26] See SVF 3.391, 393, 394.

> *Desire* is an opinion that some future thing is a good of such
> a sort that we should reach out for it.
> *Fear* is an opinion that some future thing is an evil of such a
> sort that we should avoid it.
> *Pleasure* is an opinion that some present thing is a good of
> such a sort that we should be elated about it.
> *Pain* is an opinion that some present thing is a bad of such a
> sort that we should be downcast about it.

Other emotions are defined as sub-species of these four; for example, jealousy, regret, and mourning are all species of pain.[27] In each of these definitions there is some mention of the value of goodness or badness, but there is also a reference to the thought that we *should* be moved in a certain way; that phrase translates a version of the word *kathêkon* again (i.e., the indispensable content of the impulsive impression). Every impulse involves thinking that this determinate action is the thing to do; when one has an emotion, this thought is consequent on the initial thought that there is something good or bad at stake in the matter.

To think that an indifferent thing is good or bad is obviously false; thus, Sages will never have emotions. However, they are said to have *eupatheiai* ('good emotions' etymologically), impulses which consist in episodes of knowledge. Instead of predicating goodness or badness of such indifferents as money or health, the Sages attribute goodness to virtue and badness to vice. The impulse that relates them to the virtue that they currently have is not pleasure but joy (*chara*); what they feel toward their future virtue is not the emotion of desire, but willing or volition (*boulêsis*). Their skillful avoidance of future vice is called (not fear but) caution (*eulabeia*). Naturally, there is no fourth *eupatheia* analogous to pain because the Sage does not have any vice present to himself at all, and so *a fortiori* none at which he might feel downcast. Thus, there are four emotions but only three *eupatheiai*.[28]

---

[27] SVF 3.414.

[28] This point, first raised by Inwood (1985), pp. 173–175, shows that *eupatheiai* cannot be directed toward indifferents as is sometimes thought (in Brennan [1998] I added a few more arguments to the same end). The simple view, in which the Sage's attitude toward avoiding disease is *eulabeia*, seems to me sufficiently disposed of, but there is a more complicated version in which every attitude toward an indifferent is paired up with an *eupatheia* toward the virtuous or vicious action

The third class of impulses contains only two items: selection and disselection. If we may take the definitions of the emotions as paradigmatic, these impulses will consist in the veridical attribution of planning value or disvalue to items that have it. For example, when I take a clear-eyed view of my next meal, I think of it as an indifferent thing but nevertheless one that it is reasonable to pursue because of its positive planning value.[29] An impulse of this sort is a selection; that is, I think of the food as a preferred indifferent of such a sort that it is *kathêkon* that I should pursue it, or I think of my falling from a cliff as a dispreferred indifferent of such a sort that I should avoid it, thus having the impulse of disselection. It is because this class of impulses relates to planning value and so is essentially future-oriented that it has only the two future-tensed members; the veridical assessment that some indifferent thing is already present to you leads to no impulse at all. If you really see that it is indifferent, then you will feel indifference toward it – and this is not a recommendation of psychological hygiene, but rather a general law of psychology.

Only non-Sages have emotions, but not all of their impulses are emotions; only Sages have *eupatheiai*, but not all of their impulses are *eupatheiai*. Selections are the common property of both camps, in this respect bearing an important structural resemblance both to *katalêpsis* and to the *kathêkon* itself, all of them shared by Sages and non-Sages alike, with the Sage's version differing only in its greater fixity and immunity from error. Among the utterly wicked (i.e., probably all human beings currently alive), most impulses are emotional – people act with the sincere though misguided thought that life, health, and money are good things, and they fear death, disease, and poverty as bad things. But even those among us with the most thoroughly corrupted values are familiar with what it means to treat something as a matter of indifference (e.g., one paper cup among an abundance of them). We can see that our happiness and misery are completely unconnected to the fate of this paper cup and that nevertheless there may be perfectly good reasons to use this cup to drink

that would be constituted by pursuing or avoiding that indifferent. This will be considered later.

[29] Recall that 'planning value' translates *axia eklektikê*; i.e., value relevant to selection, *eklogê*.

from, or to forgo using it, or to give it to someone else without feeling the least emotional attachment to it.

The ancient equivalents of papers cups were ceramic pots, which is why Epictetus tells us to start from our experience of what it is like to treat something the way we treat a little pot (i.e., a familiar object of indifference).[30] Using this model, we can come in time to see even life as an indifferent thing, and the most important component of our ethical progress comes in the replacement of emotions by selections (i.e., the correction of our false beliefs about values). But because selections are still impulses (i.e., productive of action), it is possible for us to abandon the false belief that our health is a good, without losing all motivation to maintain our health. I used to feel an emotional attachment to my health because I thought it was a good thing, and my impulses to preserve it were emotions. Now I understand (at least for the most part, since I'm not yet a Sage) that it is not a good thing, and I have impulses toward its preservation based on an accurate assessment of its status as a preferred indifferent. But my active involvement in life is nowhere threatened by this evaluative revolution, because of the fact that selection is an independent kind of impulse, on all fours with emotions; thus I do not need to worry that my increasing indifference toward what I used to take to be good and bad things will lead to idleness.

In distinguishing the sub-categories of impulse, it is worth pausing over the Stoic theory of reservation (*hupexairesis*, or *exceptio*).[31] Epictetus tells us that the future-oriented emotions of desire and fear bring in their wake certain expectations of success: the promise of desire, he says, is that one will actually obtain what one desires, and the promise of aversion is that one will actually avoid that to which one is averse.[32] These entrenched expectations redouble the damage done by having the emotion in the first place; not only do you mistakenly think it would be good to win the lottery, you also daydream about all of the desirable things you will do with the money – and come to think that it is practically yours, thus ensuring

---

[30] *Ench.* 3.
[31] *Ench.* 2, Marcus Aurelius IV 1, V 20, VI 50, XI 37; Seneca *Ben.* IV 34 (SVF 3.565); Stobaeus II 115 (SVF 3.564). These paragraphs summarize the main findings of Brennan (2000a), and also reflect some later thoughts in light of the comments of Brunschwig (forthcoming).
[32] *Ench.* 1.

an even greater upset when the future turns out contrary to your wishes.

To combat the emotions, we should employ mere selections instead (or 'impulses', as Epictetus calls selections, using the generic for the particular).[33] To combat the expectations, we should have our impulses 'with reservation', where what this means is that we should abstain from promising ourselves that we will get what we want and remain aware that there is some chance that we will not get it.[34] We should keep in mind, in particular, that various contingencies can easily prevent our getting what we want, so that instead of confidently predicting 'I will have dinner tonight', we should instead merely say, 'I will have dinner tonight, unless something intervenes to prevent me from having dinner tonight.'

When we have an impulse with reservation, we do not alter the content of the impulse itself, we simply alter the beliefs about our future success that typically accompany impulses, especially emotional ones. Impulses with reservation do not constitute a distinct class of impulses, and the addition of a reservation to an emotion does not render it any less an emotion. Reservation is a useful technique

---

[33] For a demonstration that 'impulse' in Epictetus means what 'selection' had meant in earlier Stoicism, see Inwood (1985) pp. 115–119.

[34] Here I record a development of the view published in Brennan (2000a). Brunschwig has persuaded me that an objection I had fashioned against other positions applies equally to my own; even when reservation is merely a matter of cognitive belief rather than an internal feature of the impulse, there is still a problem about its tautological form. It is not clear how adding the belief 'p unless not p' to our beliefs can change them in any way, much less any beneficial way, since it is consistent with any set of beliefs we may previously have had. I accept this concern, and think that it reflects a failure of expression on the part of the Stoics. They formulated their position in terms of conditionals, but what they really had in mind is more accurately put in terms of subjective probabilities or degrees of credence. When they ask us to believe 'I will eat dinner unless I do not eat dinner', the intention is to reduce my confidence and complacency in the promise that desire makes, i.e., the promise 'and I will eat dinner'. But of course, the conditional cannot produce that affect. Because I accept all tautologies, I accept 'two plus two will make four unless two plus two does not make four'; but accepting that one does not reduce my absolute conviction that two plus two makes four. So really what they want to achieve is for me to change from believing 'I will eat dinner' to believing 'there is some chance that I'll eat dinner, but also some non-zero chance that I will not eat dinner'. Their failure to express the point in these terms is unsurprising, given the utter absence of explicit probabilistic reasoning in antiquity, and the 'unless' formulation is a natural attempt to suggest the assignment of non-zero probabilities to each contradictory.

for Epictetus' beginning students, and it is also a feature of all of the Sage's impulses.[35] In neither case does it guarantee that what we want will come to pass, but it does prevent us non-Sages from being surprised by the failure of our fondest hopes. And it fits naturally into the Sage's normal avoidance of opinion, since there is no way to be sure of the truth of a future contingent such as 'I will eat dinner tonight.'

It is now possible to dispose of the question of weakness of will fairly easily in these terms. Every action reflects an underlying impulse; had I not assented to the thought that eating the cake is the thing to do, I would not have eaten the cake. But each belief, and so each impulse, maximally occupies the mind; one can only fit a single belief into one's 'belief box'.[36] The phenomena that have misled other theorists into positing conflict between multiple occurrent beliefs are instead explained as a vacillation in thought, which is so rapid that it escapes our notice (thus, also revealing some limitations on introspective access to our thoughts).[37] I first believe that I ought not to do X, but then this thought is driven out by the contrary thought, during which phase I actually do X, only to be overwhelmed by regret on the return of the belief that X was not the thing to do. Here my beliefs about what I should do are revealed as uncertain, unstable, and shifting; I have various opinions, but none of them amount to knowledge. I neither see clearly what I should do nor assent to it strongly. It is the Sages' knowledge that guarantees that they will never suffer from weakness of will because, for any given pattern of values present to them in the world, they have a stable and unshakeable knowledge of what they should do.[38]

---

[35] *Ench.* 1; Stobaeus II 115 (SVF 3.564). The quote from Stobaeus does not tell us whether the Sage uses reservations with his or her *eupatheiai*, or only with their selections; it mentions *orexis*, *hormê*, and *epibolê*, but none of these is clearly the name of an *eupatheia*.

[36] The term is common in contemporary discussions of philosophy of mind, but I have searched in vain for its originator.

[37] Plutarch *Virt. mor.* 446F (SVF 3.459 = LS 65G).

[38] It is one of the consequences of the perversely anachronistic Joyce (1995) that even Sages can be of two minds at once. Joyce rejects the evidence from Plutarch about vacillation, and then misreads S. E. *M* VII 246 as evidence that we can entertain contradictory thoughts simultaneously. But in trying to make it possible for the vicious to suffer conflict, he deprives the Stoics of part of the structure that prevents the Sage from suffering conflict. Knowledge loses its sovereign force over behavior if the knowledge that I should pursue X does not exclude the belief that I should not.

PART II: CONTROVERSY AND SPECULATION

II.1. THE SIGNIFICANCE OF STOIC COGNITIVISM AND
THE PHYSIOLOGY OF EMOTIONS

Chrysippus' claim that emotions are beliefs occasioned considerable controversy in antiquity; the revival of interest in his views has revived the controversy. The first question is whether Chrysippus really intended to identify emotions with certain beliefs, instead of saying something saner and more modest, such as that emotions arise from or incorporate or are correlated with certain beliefs. Despite Galen's best attempts to muddy the waters, I think the interpretive picture is clear: Chrysippus really meant the stronger claim, that each emotion simply is a belief.[39] This leaves three further questions: How might Chrysippus have defended this extreme cognitivism, with its attendant disregard for the affective and physiological phenomena that we sometimes associate with emotions?, What did Chrysippus have to say about these other phenomena, given that he had expelled them from the realm of emotions proper?, and What is at stake in saying that an analysis of emotions is or is not cognitive?

It is the second question that has garnered the bulk of recent attention; critics whose interests are primarily psychological (in the contemporary sense) have made much of the scant discussions of tickles, twinges, and prickles handed down to us from Chrysippus.[40]

In particular, the Stoics at some point began discussing a class of physiological reactions that are, at least in some cases, the precursors to genuine emotions. Called *propatheiai* (i.e., 'pre-emotions'), these reactions, such as turning pale or blushing, were very clearly distinguished from genuine emotions by the fact that they did not involve any assent on the agent's part, and so can neither constitute any genuine belief nor lead to any intentional action.[41] Related to this discussion is a doctrine in Posidonius of certain predisposing conditions, called 'emotive tugs'.[42]

---

[39] On Galen's mischief, see Tieleman (1996), passim, and Cooper (1998).

[40] See, e.g., Nussbaum (1993), Nussbaum (1994), Sorabji (2001).

[41] Graver (2000) is a brilliant piece of philological detective work, which also shows a very controlled understanding of the significance of *propatheiai* for the larger theory of emotions.

[42] Cooper (1998).

Interesting as they may be, such discussions cannot be of any direct relevance to the topic of this chapter. In the context of moral psychology, what matters about emotions is how they are sensitive to one's beliefs and how they function in the production of action. How they feel, whether as a matter of physiology or mood, is neither here nor there. Indeed, I am inclined to think that the perspective of moral psychology is not just one among several perspectives on Stoic emotions: I think it is *the* characteristically Stoic perspective on Stoic emotions. The object of their theory is not the range of psychological data we associate with emotions; what they care about is human action and its sources, especially as those different sources may be correlated with different ethical properties of the action. Emotions are of interest as the typical motivations for vicious action, and what is of interest about them is the way that they both encode conceptual errors about the value of items in the world and then in turn produce flawed actions. In this light, we should not be surprised that the Stoic theory of emotions is so unforthcoming about what interests modern students of the emotions.

But at some point this line of thought should provoke a question about why the Stoics employed the vocabulary of emotions at all, if they had so little interest in the phenomenology of emotions – and this was the first of our three questions. Why use the word '*pathos*' to begin with, and why use dozens of other words that can only be translated 'jealousy', 'longing', 'cheerfulness', 'rage', and so on if the qualitative phenomena are of no interest?[43] After all, the inclination to associate emotions with characteristic patterns of introspectible qualia is not merely a modern preoccupation; it is already a thought in Homer that wrath is sweeter than dripping honey.[44] What justifies the Stoics in identifying wrath with a characteristic belief rather than with a characteristic drippy sweetness?

Here it may help to keep in mind a general Stoic view that identifies reality with causal efficacy.[45] Only things that can act or be acted upon can be truly said to be or exist; and although the primary consequence of this view is a restriction of 'being' to bodies, I am inclined to think that the view plays a role in this context as well.

---

[43] For lists of such terms, see Andronicus *peri Pathôn* 2–5, excerpted at SVF 3.397, 3.401, 3.409, and 3.414.

[44] *Iliad* XVIII 108–109.

[45] For example, DL VII 134 (SVF 2.300 = LS 44B).

Alongside the causal criterion for existence, which states that only causal agents really exist, we may posit a predicative version of the principle, that only the causally F agent is really F (i.e., that what is really F is whatever plays the role that F plays when F is invoked in causal contexts). On the Stoic view, the proper signification of the term 'winter', for instance, turns out to be not a period or length of time but a causal agent: winter is the air above the earth, cooled because of the distancing of the sun.[46] This is to award proper ownership of the term to the entity that explains the causal claims we make in using the term. When we say 'it's winter now', no causal claim is made; but when we say, 'the winter has killed my fruit trees', it is very plausible to claim that it is the chilled air to which we are referring.

In the case of the emotions, then, the Stoics would have felt justified in saying that 'wrath' properly denominates a certain belief rather than a certain feeling-tone, because it is the belief that is the explanans for claims like 'his wrath led him to strike his friend'. By contrast, the sweet or drippy kind of wrath and the way that emotions feel in general would be seen as epiphenomenal, as causal dead ends, and so not deserving of the names. This view can also be seen in the Stoic view that the proper signification of 'pleasure' is a certain belief; it is the belief that motivates and causes. The Stoics need not deny that pleasure typically feels like something; they simply claim that the feeling-tone doesn't do any work and so does not deserve the name. In commenting on the Epicurean's theory of pleasure (which is clearly not a cognitivist one), the Stoics say 'this pleasure – if it *is* pleasure – is an epiphenomenon (*epigennêma*) which arises when a nature seeks what is fitting to its own constitution and succeeds in acquiring it'.[47] All the explaining to be done in this context is done by invoking nature, constitutions, conceptions of what is fitting, and

---

[46] DL VII 151 (SVF 2.693). I borrow the translation, and the line of thought (though not the application to emotions), from LS Vol. 1, 177. See Ch. 8, Brunschwig, this volume.

[47] DL VII 85–86. To this catachrestic usage of 'pleasure' should also be relegated the claim that 'the *pathos* of pleasure is an aftereffect (*epakolouthêma*)' at Clement *Strom.* II 491 (SVF 3.405), as well as references to the 'pleasure concerning the body' which is an indifferent at Stobaeus II 80 (SVF 3.136). Pleasure properly so-called (i.e., the opinion) cannot be an indifferent, since it is a vicious action (*hamartêma*) and a bad thing (*kakon*); see Plutarch 449D (SVF 3.468), Galen *de animi pecc.* I 5.58K (SVF 3.172), Stobaeus II 96 (SVF 3.501), Stobaeus II 77 (SVF 3.113).

so on – no work is left over for 'pleasure' in its noncognitive, feeling-tone sense. And when something needs to be explained by invoking pleasure *per se*, what explains is a belief or pattern of beliefs, not a feeling-tone. Thus the Stoics have a principled way to respond to the charge that their cognitive analysis of emotions either grossly over-looks the phenomenology or flagrantly abuses our ordinary linguistic practice.

The last question about cognitive analyses arises when we are faced with Stoic strategies for the alteration or elimination of emotions. One might suppose that part of the point of making emotions beliefs, and locating them in a unified reasoning soul, is to take a stance on their responsiveness to reasoned argumentation and change of view. Theorists who view emotions as essentially irrational products of the sub-rational soul will naturally think of them as relatively unresponsive to the ministrations of reason; the Black Horse of the *Phaedrus* needs the whip and goad.[48] Beliefs, by contrast, should be open (at least in principle) to modification by reasoned argumentation – that need not be the *only* way of changing beliefs and it need not be the *fastest* or most efficient method. But one would hope that for any false belief, there is a way of bringing its owner over to the truth by purely rational methods (e.g., considerations of evidence, argument, thought-experiment, and so on). Thus, it is quite striking how much of the Stoic therapeutic practice involves methods that seem, at least *prima facie*, to be directed to the non-cognitive modification of non-cognitive entities. It is perhaps not too shocking that Epictetus tells us to recite the same piece of school doctrine over to ourselves repeatedly – although hearing p for the fifteenth time is not being given a further reason to believe p, we must also acknowledge that we use repetition to memorize our multiplication tables, too, without this impugning the rationality of mathematics.[49] On the other hand, some of the methods envisioned

---

[48] *Phaedrus* 253e. But it is a mistake to think that the irrational parts of the soul, even in the *Phaedrus* or *Timaeus*, are not also capable of responding to reason in some way. The picture in all three dialogues is that irrational parts can be trained, over time, to an ultimate state in which they are directly responsive to the guidance of reason, but that the process of their domestication will involve the complete and forcible elimination of some kinds of desires, and the taming of the rest by non-rational means. There is an initial period when the whip is necessary; later the Black Horse feels fear on its own and awaits the word of reason.

[49] 'Say this over to yourself' (*epilegein*) or 'have the following thought ready to hand' (*procheiron*) or 'remember' (*memnêso*) or combinations of these injunctions appear

by Epictetan *askêsis* should prompt us to ask the general question: Can cognitive theorists help themselves to just any possible means of behavior modification, while still claiming that what they are attempting to do is to reshape beliefs? What if they claim that our actions are the result of a belief that we do not avow and are unaware of having, and further claim that we cannot rid ourselves of this putative belief, even in principle, except by the use of electric shocks? What sort of a belief is this, when it can only be altered this way? We should at least be disappointed when the bright Socratic hope of rationally arguing our way to virtue is replaced by the grim Epictetan tedium of catechetical pushups; in time, I think we should also be deeply skeptical of the theoretical coherence of the underlying conceptions of psychology and rationality. It is a plausible rule of thumb that what can only be altered by non-rational means is a non-rational state; even if we reject it as too simplistic, we must still ask what in detail separates cognitivism of the Stoic sort from a full Platonic acceptance of irrational parts of the soul, when our means of altering the dispositions for behavior amount to the same thing in each case.

II.2. DELIBERATION

A theory of ethics should tell us how to make our deliberations responsive to the right considerations so as to ensure that we will arrive at ethically correct decisions. A theory of practical rationality should tell us about the form of deliberation, in particular about how it manages to transmit normative or justificatory force from ends to means. A theory of moral psychology should at the very least tell us what types of mental operations are involved in deliberation and how they differ from other kinds of mental operations, including theoretical and non-practical thoughts on the one side, and completely specified motivating intentions on the other. In the case of Stoicism, it is quite striking how little we can achieve of any of these desiderata. My aim in this section is merely to advertise a problem, offer some speculation, and indicate why I think the point worthy of attention.[50]

---

in six of the first ten sections of the *Enchiridion* (*Ench.* 1.5, 2, 3, 4, 9, 10), and recur throughout the remainder at a lower rate.

[50] I was helped to see how little we yet know about Stoic deliberation by Rachel Barney's comments on Brennan (2003), originally delivered to the *Boston Area*

There are several closely related philosophical puzzles here. One is that we do not know what types of mental acts lead up to the formulation of an impulse, in the sense of occurring temporally prior to it. On the one hand, it seems implausible that they can all of them be mere theoretical assents, without evaluative content – deliberation surely differs from theoretical contemplation in virtue of its subject matter; that is, it is an examination of what should be done or where the good lies. On the other hand, I have suggested that impulses, which certainly do have evaluative content, are *per se* practical, and sufficiently so; that is, that they do not need any further item in order to produce action. But then it is not clear how the Stoics can make room for evaluative thoughts formulated in the course of a deliberation that will be properly tentative and not lead headlong to action at a premature stage. The problem, then, is how to characterize such a thought as 'I should do something about that cut on my foot' in order to give it both its practical content and yet distinguish it from a full-blown impulse. This problem is the converse of a problem that Aristotle faces about practical thoughts. For the Stoics, some intrinsic motivational force seems to be built into the very having of evaluative thoughts, and this makes it hard to accommodate deliberation; Aristotle has an easier time schematizing deliberation, but then has difficulty explaining why the last thought in a deliberation makes us act when the prior ones had not. One theory is in danger of going off half-cocked; the other seems to hang fire.

There is a different puzzle about which factors the Sage considers in arriving at a decision. I argued previously that the Sage's impulses toward the indifferents surrounding them will be selections; for example, when the Sage decides to eat some food, it will be with the thought, 'this food is an indifferent which has positive planning value of such a sort that it is *kathêkon* (or reasonable or appropriate) for me to pursue it'. But we should recall that nearly all of the Sage's practical dealings in the world will involve indifferents in this way – whether it is a matter of feeding himself or rescuing others from starvation, returning deposits or executing criminals, the material for his actions are all such indifferent things as food, money, and

Colloquium on Ancient Philosophy in 1999. She is developing her comments for publication as Barney (forthcoming).

human life.[51] We may stipulate that all of the Sage's actions are virtuous actions, but it also seems that every virtuous action consists
in a virtuous way of responding to indifferents. In any situation, the
Sage will have an infallible grasp of which indifferents require attention, what their respective planning values are, and which actions
are likely to result in the production of which further indifferents
with which further values. But how does that knowledge function
in the Sage's deliberations?

One popular model goes back to a comment by Cicero: our end
is 'to conform to virtue always, and so far as the other things go
which are in accordance with nature, to select them if they do not
conflict with virtue'.[52] So on this view, the Sage's deliberations look
something like maximizing with side constraints: one pursues what
is in accordance with nature (i.e., has positive planning value), but
always within the bounds set by the demands of virtue. Borrowing
a phrase of Bonhöffer's, we may call this the *salva virtute* model of
deliberation.[53]

In contrast to this is what we might call the 'indifferents-only'
model,[54] according to which the Sage's actions are fully determined
by their consideration of indifferents (although this consideration
need not take the form of maximizing). Having identified a course of
action on this basis, the Sage can then recognize that it is the virtuous
thing to do (inasmuch as it is endorsed by a Sage), and then be motivated to do it both by thoughts about planning value and by thoughts
about virtue. Although it may be surprising that no thoughts about
virtue feature in the stage of deliberation during which the action
is identified, this reflects two general points about Stoicism. First is

[51] Chrysippus wrote that natural things (i.e., preferred indifferents) are the 'material
of virtue'; see Plutarch *Comm. not.* 1069E (SVF 3.491 = LS 59A). Clement tells
us that virtuous actions and vicious actions cannot be constituted without the
indifferents, 'which have the status of material'; see *Strom.* IV 6 p. 581 Pott (SVF
3.114).

[52] *Cum virtute congruere semper, cetera autem, quae secundum naturam essent, ita
legere, si ea virtuti non repugnarent, Off.* III 11. Cicero tells us that this is his own
formula, which he proposes as a way of reconciling the *honestum* with the *utile*,
which his Stoic source had thought needed no reconciliation. I think this passage
should not be given any weight as evidence for an authentic Stoic view.

[53] Bonhöffer (1894, repr. 1968), p. 195.

[54] Rachel Barney used this phrase to characterize my view in her comments on
Brennan (2003). My view there was inspired by Cooper's account of deliberation
about suicide in Cooper (1989).

the fact that there are no rules of virtue that could play an action-guiding role at the first round of action-identifying deliberation.[55] Stoicism simply does not espouse any rules of the 'thou shalt not kill' sort; instead, the question whether one should kill or not is always dependent on the question whether this act of killing is a fitting or appropriate one in the circumstances, and this in turn is not susceptible of determination by any more abstract but contentful rules. That is not the type of system that the Stoics espoused. Second, there are a number of Stoic texts that spell out in a fairly straightforward way the claim that the Sage deliberates only about indifferents. For instance, Cicero tells us:

> But since these intermediate things [i.e., indifferents] form the basis of all *kathêkonta*, there is good ground for saying that it is to these things that all of our deliberations are referred; and among these deliberations are those concerning departure from life or remaining alive... When one's circumstances contain a preponderance of things in accordance with nature, it is *kathêkon* to remain alive; when one possesses or sees in prospect a majority of the contrary things, it is *kathêkon* to depart from life.[56]

The claim made here, that 'all of our deliberations are referred' to indifferents, goes well with the evidence that the Stoics had no rules of virtue that could enter into deliberations; both together constitute strong evidence against the *salva virtute* model of deliberation. But many options remain: Is the Sage's consideration of planning value a maximizing one or not? Does he attempt to maximize or otherwise distribute planning value only for himself or for other agents as well? Perhaps the algorithmic model is wholly inappropriate, and they were intuitionists of some form?[57] These are central questions

---

[55] In an extensive and searching debate in the critical literature, advocates of a rule-following model of Stoicism have repeatedly failed to provide any evidence of such rules, and critics of the model have provided compelling arguments from psychology and ethics which show why the Stoics would not have formulated them. The most recent round in the debate, with references to previous discussions, can be found in Inwood (1999) and Mitsis (1999).

[56] *Fin.* III 59–60. Cooper (1989) drew my attention to the significance of this passage. See also Plutarch *St. rep.* 1042D (SVF 3.759) and [Alexander] *Mantissa*, e.g., 160.29.

[57] It should be noted that they defined the *kathêkon* as 'that which when once done receives a reasonable defence' Stobaeus II 85 (SVF 3.494 = LS 59B). Thus they were presumably not intuitionists of the sort that deny that there can be reasoned justifications for ethical actions, at least of a retrospective sort (note 'once done', translating the aorist participle '*prachthen*'). However, Aristotle is often thought to have combined an acceptance of retrospective justifiability with something like an

in moral psychology; our current inability to answer them points to important avenues for research on the Stoics.[58]

II.3. MOTIVATION SUB SPECIE BONI

There are two broad approaches to studying the moral psychology of the Stoics, which we may characterize as 'top-down' and 'bottom-up' approaches. The first starts from some general considerations about the kind of philosophers the Stoics were – rationalists, theists, teleologists, psychic monists, and so on – and works its way down to psychological details from that basis. The other begins with the evidence for the content of individual psychological events and episodes, and by paying close attention to their logical form it tries to expand the meager evidence into a whole picture of moral psychology. The best exemplar of the first route is Michael Frede; the best exemplar of the second is Brad Inwood. Here and elsewhere, I have followed in the methodological footsteps of Inwood's work, starting from the bottom-level details of individual psychological episodes and trying to work up from there. But I also feel a great deal of sympathy for the type of picture that Frede produced by following the contrary course.[59] In this section I want to highlight some of the differences that arise between the views so developed, as well

intuitionism about prospective deliberation, and perhaps the Stoics had something like this view.

[58] I should note in passing that no progress can be made so long as we confuse species of impulse with stretches of deliberation. Annas (1996) p. 241 claims to 'establish that the Stoics mark a sharp distinction in practical reasoning between the moral and the non-moral' by pointing to the Stoic distinction between choice (*hairesis*) and selection (*eklogê*). She is right to say that the first kind of impulse has as its objects only genuine goods, and thus only the virtues themselves (plus virtuous actions, the virtuous friend, and the like), while the second has as its objects only the preferred indifferents. But this is a difference between kinds of completed impulse, not a difference of kinds of reasoning or deliberation (and that Annas is confusing deliberations with impulses is clear from her comments that she will use 'deliberation' to refer to a genus whose species are choice and selection). Choice, as a subspecies of volition (*boulêsis* – see SVF 3.173), is an *eupatheia* that can only occur in a Sage; only Sages can choose things, and no vicious person, including those making ethical progress, ever can (SVF 3.483). So if the word 'choice' meant, as Annas thinks, 'practical reasoning that involves moral considerations', then the Stoic view would hold that considerations of morality only arise in Sages; i.e., only those who are already perfect in their moral development can even entertain moral considerations, much less act on them. That would be absurd.

[59] See M. Frede (1999).

as the issues that I think will be involved in any resolution of the disagreement.

If we are impressed by the fact that the Stoics were rationalists, eudaimonists, and psychic monists, then it will be natural to suppose that all human action, on the Stoic view, is motivated by the agent's conception of the good, as confused or faulty as this conception may happen to be: whatever agents pursue, they pursue *sub specie boni*.[60] This will seem all the more natural when we reflect that the Stoics frequently modeled their views on the Socrates of Plato's dialogues, who expresses views very like the *sub specie boni* rule at several places (e.g., *Protagoras* 358c); and that Socrates' espousal of it is closely linked to his rejection of the possibility of *akrasia*, which the Stoics also reject.

However, we have seen a number of texts that suggest that the core content of an impulsive impression – the thing about it that produces an action, instead of a mere belief, when you assent to it – is that you envisage an action you could undertake, and entertain the thought that it is *kathêkon*; that is, the thing to do, or the thing you should do. And the assent itself – that is, that mental motion which is the impulse – is directed toward the action you have in mind, saying, 'Yes, that's the thing for me to do.' Here the psychological trigger to action is just as unitary as under the *sub specie boni* rule, but the unitary trigger is a different one; namely, the thought that something is *kathêkon*.

Sometimes, the thought that the action is *kathêkon* seems to accompany a thought that the action is good or bad; in the case of the emotional desire for food, for instance, I have the thought that my eating would be a good thing, of such a sort that it is *kathêkon* that I should pursue it. The *eupatheiai* probably follow this model as well; as a Sage, my *boulêsis* consists in the thought that my virtue is a good thing of such a sort that it is *kathêkon* for me to pursue it (i.e., preserve it in the future). But neither of these cases shows clear support for the *sub specie boni* view; in both of them, thoughts about goodness seem to be merely the ground or basis for the thought that something is *kathêkon*. It is this further thought that is the intrinsically motivating one, as the definition of impulse in general would lead us

[60] By 'human' action, I mean the actions of adult human beings; the child's soul is like that of an animal.

to expect: 'what moves impulse is nothing other than an impulsive impression of what is *kathêkon, ipso facto'*. So when thoughts about the good enter into an agent's motivation, they do not directly and immediately provide the motivating conception; rather, they provide one type of grounding for the genuinely motivating thought, which is phrased in terms of the *kathêkon*.

Furthermore, selections are a class of impulses in which, I have argued, thoughts about the good are wholly absent; one thinks only about planning value (or equivalently about what is preferred or what is natural). Judgments of planning value and the like play a role analogous to the role played by judgments of goodness or badness in emotions; they ground the further thought that the action is *kathêkon*, but they do not directly motivate the action itself: I think of the food as a preferred indifferent of such a sort that it is *kathêkon*, or reasonable, or natural, and so on for me to pursue it. If it is possible to be motivated to act by the thought that preserving my health, for example, is a preferred indifferent, where thoughts about goodness do not figure in any explicit or covert way, then the Stoics did not embrace a *sub specie boni* view of moral psychology.

We can observe another difficulty for the *sub specie boni* view if we think about how such a view must describe the impulses of an advanced student who is not yet a Sage. It's not difficult to see how the ordinary vicious person can be motivated to eat dinner, given their false belief that doing so is a good thing – that's the familiar case of emotion, which fits easily into the *sub specie boni* account. Nor is it difficult, on this account, to see how the Sage can be motivated to eat dinner, once she has identified eating dinner as the rational thing to do for whatever reasons, and so the virtuous thing to do. What motivates her is not some conception that the food is good or that eating it is good *qua* pleasurable or even *qua* nutritious. Rather, what motivates the Sage, on this account, is her perception that this instance of eating (unlike the vicious person's instance of eating) constitutes a *virtuous* action, and thus a good thing; she has a eupathic desire for it *qua* good. So each of these agents' actions can be easily explained by the *sub specie boni* rule.

The puzzle is how we can provide some motivation to the student who has made significant moral progress, but is not yet virtuous. We may assume that this student has largely eradicated any inclination to think of the food as a *good* thing, and has a relatively reliable grasp on its genuine indifference. On the other hand, the student must also be fully aware that his eating dinner that evening cannot be a good thing, either, since as a non-Sage he is not in a position to perform a virtuous action. Thus, neither of the two options canvassed in the last paragraph is open to the student making progress.

Progressors pose a serious problem because there is a deep sense in which doing something good in the near future is simply not a possibility for them – and they are sufficiently aware of their state to realize that. They can neither enjoy the true belief that their eating is good nor the false belief that it is good. In fact, eating in general is indifferent, and any act of eating that they can perform will be not indifferent but positively bad and vicious (since all of the actions of non-Sages are *hamartêmata*, errors and wrongdoings).[61] They know this, yet they still must be motivated to eat. The theory of selections, understood as *per se* pursuits of indifferents, easily allows for this; the progressor can be motivated by the thought that eating is the thing to do. Their eating is still a *kathêkon*, even if it cannot be a *katorthôma*, and viewing it in this light is sufficient to trigger action. But if they can only be motivated to act by the thought that their action is somehow good, then they will not be able to find any motivation whatsoever.

Connected to this is a puzzle about the moment of one's beatification. I have argued that even Sages think very little about virtue: when a Sage deliberates about whether or not to eat some food, this deliberation occurs entirely in terms of indifferents, and terminates in the formation of a selection; that is, an impulse toward the food considered not as a good but as something with some planning value that makes it *kathêkon* to pursue. On my picture, the structure of this deliberation and the ensuing impulse are exactly parallel in the advanced progressor and in the Sage; this is important since it makes it possible for the progressor to become a Sage without being aware of it, as the Stoics claimed was possible.[62] This will be much harder to do on a *sub specie boni* view. At the moment an individual becomes a Sage, a whole new world of goods opens up to the individual; suddenly, their every movement, their mere bending of a finger is a good of the highest order. In their final impulse before becoming

---

[61] Stobaeus II 7.105 (SVF 3.661).
[62] Plutarch *Comm. not.* 1062b (LS 61U), and see SVF 3.539–541.

a Sage, they would be moved to eat their food by the thought that it was good. Then in their first virtuous impulse, they would take the next mouthful of food motivated by the thought that virtue is good – and never notice the reversal in perspective.

These are the sorts of difficulties, as it seems to me, that face the proponent of the view that every action of an adult human being is motivated by some impulse toward the good. But since the *sub specie boni* view derives its strength from high-level, 'top-down' considerations of Stoic views on the nature of the good and the cosmos, perhaps it will also be useful to show how the 'bottom-up' approach delivers results that make sense when viewed from the more Olympian perspective. The key thought to keep in mind is that the Stoic theory of indifferents entails the view that the Sage must navigate through a world of indifferent affairs, and select among objects and actions that are *per se* indifferent; yet it makes all the difference in the world which objects and actions the Sage selects. The Sage must never have the false belief that any of the things around him are good; yet he must be endlessly, exquisitely sensitive to the respective values of the things around him. And he must act from that sensitivity; his virtue actually consists in his knowledge of indifferents and his expert handling of them. But it is not only the Sage who must be sensitive to indifferents: anyone who wants to make progress must also come to see the world as a place in which the various distributions and dispositions of indifferent matters around them provide reasons to act in one way rather than another. No psychology that was only motivated by explicitly good-directed impulses could give a clear-eyed agent sufficient reason to act in a world of indifferents (and once again, the advancing non-Sage is the best example of this, since not even their own actions count as good things). It was for reasons of this sort, I think, that the Stoics felt the need to make this fundamental modification in the Socratic psychological model.[63]

---

[63] Charles Brittain reminds me that this picture must be kept consistent with the picture of God's providential activity, and I think it is consistent. God's action in the world is a matter of selecting certain distributions of indifferents, and he too attends only to indifferents *qua* indifferents. It is tempting to think that, as teleologists, the Stoics must have thought that this world is *better* than the other worlds that God could have brought about, but I think the evidence suggests a different view, according to which God's providence is exactly like a Sage's virtuous activities. When the Sage rescues a child from drowning, it is not because the Sage falsely supposes that a world with a living child and rejoicing parents is any *better* than a

A defender of the *sub specie boni* view may reply to this string of objections by proposing a modification of their view that preserves its essential motivation. They can agree that agents do sometimes exercise selection; that is, they are sometimes moved to pursue indifferents in light of their planning value on the basis of an impulse that does not contain any explicit reference to goodness. But this responsiveness to indifference will not be independent of an overarching belief about the good, which will act as a type of major premiss in their practical syllogism: they will pursue indifferents with the belief in mind that pursuing indifferents will be good for them, at some future time. So, for instance, the advanced student may have an impulse to perform this indifferent action of eating dinner this evening, with the thought in mind that doing so is part of a long-term pattern of solidifying the state of character that will one day turn into his virtue.[64] So it is still his desire for a good (sc. his virtue in the distant future) that motivates him to eat dinner this evening because he can see how the eating, though itself indifferent, will be

world with a dead child and despairing parents; the two worlds are of exactly equal value in respect to considerations of the goodness and badness of those outcomes. Nevertheless, there are considerations of planning value and indifference that may make it rational on a particular occasion for the Sage to step in to bring about a world with an undrowned child, not because that outcome is better, but because he judges it to have the right pattern of indifferents. (At least on this occasion; when the indifferents are distributed in some other way he may drown children like unwanted puppies, and do so virtuously, too). And when the Sage acts in this way, the world so produced does, indirectly, wind up being the better one, because of the presence in it of the Sage's rational activity and virtue. So too with God in his organization of the world. *Ench.* 31, for instance, does not say that God does everything for the best, but that he does it with the best judgment. And when Cicero in *ND* II 38 seems to be about to declare that this world is the best, he does not: he declares this world complete and perfect (*perfectus*) inasmuch as it *contains* the thing which is best (*optimum*); namely, rationality and virtue. What we can say about the furniture of this world is that it is appropriate, fitting, well adapted for use, and beautiful in the way a house might be (where clearly no Stoic would say that a house, however beautiful, was *kalon* in the sense of genuinely good). All of these descriptions tell us that the world has the right patterns of indifference of the preferred sort, not that it is good, much less that it is better or best. The good resides in the world only through God's rational and virtuous selection of this appropriate, fitting, and so on distribution of indifferents. Accordingly, God's own actions in constituting the world are themselves the result of deliberations (or something analogous to deliberations) about indifferents, not about goods.

[64] We need not attribute any great confidence to the student; it is sufficient for the *sub specie boni* view that the progressor believe that the slim possibility of their becoming virtuous is made more probable by the pursuit of the right indifferents.

instrumentally productive of a genuine good. This analysis would seem to allow us to reinstate the *sub specie boni* rule, even for those making progress. This version recognizes selections as a dependent and subsidiary form of impulse, which only functions when supplemented by a sort of hovering major premiss about the good. So the clear-eyed pursuit of indifferents by the person making progress requires two impulses; (1) the selection, which tracks the indifferents but is not intrinsically motivating; and (2) the thoughts about virtue, which provide the motivational efficacy and relate to indifferents only indirectly, as the agent's pursuit of the indifferents may further their eventual acquisition of what is really good.

However, this falls afoul of the most straightforward way to read a series of texts that ascribe a *per se* motivating force to *preferred* indifferents and the planning value that they possess.[65] 'Preferred indifferents are of such a sort as to arouse impulse, and it is in virtue of this that we select them' – there is no mention of the good in this. Of course, sometimes vicious people desire a preferred indifferent like some food based on the error of thinking that it is a good; and sometimes virtuous people choose to eat some food because the food indirectly constitutes part of a virtuous action and thus a good. But these quotations seem to envisage a third kind of case, in which an indifferent is selected without error or indirection, simply in virtue of the value that it has as a preferred indifferent, and not because of any thoughts about the good.

The top-down option faces a further difficulty, when we attempt to characterize the impulse that this student is experiencing for his possible future virtue. From the 'bottom-up' perspective, we shall want to know which of the kinds of impulse discussed above this student's overarching pursuit of the good could be. We certainly cannot class it as an *eupatheia*, despite the fact that its object is the

---

[65] DL VII 104 (SVF 3.119 = LS 58B); Stobaeus II 82 (SVF 3.121 = LS 58C); Stobaeus II 84 (SVF 3.128 = LS 58E). The claim in the last text that we choose preferred indifferents *kata prohêgoumenon logon* means that we choose them for a *per se* reason; the adverb *prohêgoumenôs* is already contrasted with *kata sumbebêkos* in Theophrastus, and forms of this adjective and adverb frequently mean 'per se' or 'intrinsic' in later texts. Epictetus *Diss.* II 6.9 (SVF 3.191 = LS 58J) attributes to Chrysippus the claim that I have impulses toward preferred indifferents because God has made me selective of them – again, the selection and the impulse seem to arise from a clear-eyed view of the items' selective (planning) value, not from any further thoughts about goods.

genuine good of virtue, because only Sages can have *eupatheiai*. But
we should hesitate to classify it as an emotion since it is a very
different sort of motivation from the mistaken belief that an indifferent item like food is really a good thing. We might say that it is an
emotion, but an emotion directed toward a genuine good, which we
might call a 'veridical emotion'.[66] It is an anomaly not sufficiently
remarked upon that the Stoic definition of the emotions clearly does
not require them to be false; yet the vast majority of textual evidence
focuses on cases of falsity, and the vast majority of critics write as
though this is essential to emotions.[67] The one salient exception is
the discussion of progress in Cicero's *Tusculan Disputations* III 77,
where he is discussing Alcibiades' attitude toward his own current
vice and the prospect of his future virtue. If the progressor thinks of
his future virtue as a good of such a sort that he should pursue it,
then he will be having an emotion – there is no way to avoid that
verdict – but it is an emotion that could in time be transmuted into
the *eupatheia* of *boulêsis* without any further revisions than the normal process of solidification and stabilization that transform the rest
of the progressor's true beliefs into knowledge. Defenders of the *sub
specie boni* view might be able to develop the notion of 'veridical
emotions' into a new argument for the claim that thoughts about
the good always feature in the background of the agent's mind.[68]

II.4. THE CONSEQUENCES FOR ETHICS

In two passages quoted previously, Epictetus comes close to drawing
one lesson that clearly follows from the ubiquity of the *kathêkon*-
operator: any predicate that applies equally to all human motivations, both vicious and virtuous, cannot be translated by terms like
'duty' or even 'proper function', the preferred translation in Long and
Sedley (1987). When the villain thinks of his villainy as *kathêkon*,

---

[66] I discussed the possibility of veridical emotions in Brennan (1998).

[67] I myself write that way on occasion for the sake of vividness or clarity, and it is
clear that the case of false belief was in some sense the paradigmatic case for the
Stoics.

[68] Against this, however, it seems to me that *Ench.* 2 also presents obstacles to this
view, inasmuch as it tells the student to employ only impulse and counter-impulse
(= selection and disselection) and to do away with all desire, even for 'the things
that are up to us which it is noble to desire'. This looks like a prohibition against
desire of all types, even for one's own future virtue.

he is not having an inaccurate or perverse thought about his proper functions, much less his duty. Rather, he contemplates an upcoming act of brigandage and takes it in some loose sense to be 'the thing to do' or 'what I should do', where the 'should' there bears its slimmest and most neutral gerundive force.[69] In the parallel theoretical case, one contemplates an impression and thinks, in some inarticulate way, 'yes, that's how things are', this being one's assent. Here, one has a comparably broad and vague sense not of 'how things are' but of 'what I should do', so that assenting to the practical impression is a matter of assenting to the impression that *this* is the thing to do.[70]

It is in this neighborhood that we must look for a Stoic answer to the question mentioned previously as typical of investigations into moral psychology: Does this psychology make it possible for people to act in ways that are moral, unselfish, or altruistic? Part of the answer is clear: There is no room in Stoic moral psychology for the thought that there are two types of motivation that would line up in the right way with the modern moralizer's distinctions of selfish and unselfish ones, or duties and inclinations, or anything of that sort. The difference between the vicious person's emotional desire for food and the Sage's eupathic *boulêsis* for virtue consists primarily in the fact that the Sage is pursuing what is *really* good for her, where the non-Sage pursues something which is only *apparently* good for him, and that is nothing like a difference between moral and non-moral considerations. Nor is there any difference in the Sage's motives when he eats some food and when he rescues a drowning child; in each case, he selects something that is indifferent, while clearly seeing that it is indifferent. And there is no aspect of the saving that qualifies it as a virtuous act more than the eating was; they are both equally virtuous, and equally virtuous in regard to their motivations. To that extent, the charge that the Stoics advocate a scheme of enlightened self-interest is perfectly apt, and more historically faithful

---

[69] I believe I acquired this philosophical usage of the phrase 'the thing to do' from John Cooper.

[70] Note that there is no conflict between having the notion of the *kathêkon* play this relatively neutral motivational role in psychology, while also playing its more familiar role as a central notion in substantive normative ethics (as, e.g., the explicit topic of books on how one should live). This is no more problematic than in the non-practical case, in which people's assents consist in the endorsement of some conception – generally inaccurate – of the way things are, while theorists write scientific treatises claiming to tell us the way things really are.

than the claim that they build their ethics around any distinction between moral and non-moral considerations.

So: if altruism or morality or selflessness requires that there be a fundamental difference at the level of motivation between altruistic (and so forth) actions and other actions, then Stoic moral psychology does not make it possible. But the fact that Stoicism was able to advocate an ethical system of nearly unmatched stringency, scope, and demandingness should make us question whether the details of moral psychology place genuine limits on ethics, or whether this line of inquiry is simply founded on presuppositions about morality and psychology that are fundamentally at odds with Stoicism, and open to question in their own right.

II.5. COMPATIBILISM AND ASSENT

The full account of the Stoic theory of determinism and of their attempt to defend a compatibilist position on moral responsibility is presented in Chapter 7 of this volume. Here we should consider only the question of how their compatibilism relates to the details of their moral psychology. As mentioned at the outset, many contemporary discussions of moral psychology are directed toward showing how our actions can be free, and so it is worth assessing to what extent Stoic moral psychology was invoked in their account of moral responsibility.

At first sight, certain famous Stoic texts seem to give a ringing endorsement of our freedom, and to base it on the freedom of our assent:

Man, you have a *prohairesis* that is by nature incapable of being hindered or compelled . . . I will show you this first from considerations of assent [i.e., to non-impulsive, theoretical impressions]. Is anyone able to hinder you from consenting to what is true? Not a one. Is anyone able to compel you to accept what is false? Not a one. Do you see that in this area you have a *prohairesis* that is unhindered, uncompelled, and unimpeded? Now consider desire and impulse, and it is no different.[71]

[71] *Diss.* I 17.21–24. I leave untranslated the crucial term *prohairesis*. I believe that this means 'one's soul or *hêgemonikon*, considered as the totality of one's dispositions to assent'. So at the level of metaphysics, the *prohairesis* is the same quantity of *pneuma* as one's soul, just as the virtue of the Sage is also the same quantity of *pneuma* as their soul (see Plutarch *Virt. mor.* 441C = SVF I.202 = LS 61B9; Stobaeus

There is a sense in which this kind of Stoic invocation of assent in defense of their compatibilism is a pattern and precedent for later attempts to base the freedom of the will on moral psychology.[72] But there are fundamental differences.

To begin with, it should be noted that in Stoicism there is no causal firewall between an external physical world in which all events are fated and an internal mental world of unfated assents and impulses.[73] Given that our souls are part of the corporeal world, it is difficult to see how the Stoics could have justified such a claim – and there is no evidence that they wished to try. Quite the opposite – what makes them compatibilists is their claim that our assents are just as much the result of fate as any external action is, but that we are responsible for our actions nonetheless. True, there is something about the way that our souls bring about actions that makes each of us responsible for exactly those actions that we perform from an inward impulse, without external hindrance or compulsion. But on the Stoic picture there is no claim that our actions, or the assents on which they are based, are in any way less fully determined, less fully fated, or less fully caused than the motions of inanimate bodies.

Indeed, further passages from Epictetus show us that the sense in which our assent is 'unhindered, uncompelled, and unimpeded' is that when we assent to an impression, there was no possibility that an external force could prevent us from assenting to that impression.[74] However, given that impression and given our psychological makeup, there was also no possibility that we could do anything other than assent to it as we did.[75] Instead of introducing

---

II 64 = SVF 3.305; Stobaeus II 65 = SVF 3.306). But *prohairesis* is the more general term; one's *prohairesis* may be either one's virtue or one's vice, depending on how one is disposed to assent to impressions. This is why Epictetus can advise us to wish to have our *prohairesis* in a natural state, without contradicting his prohibition on our wishing to be virtuous in *Ench.* 2. For more on *prohairesis* in Epictetus, see Long (2002).

[72] On the complicated lines of intellectual parentage, see Bobzien (1998a).

[73] See Sharples (1986), now demonstrated exhaustively by Bobzien (1998). The text that has most strongly suggested a firewall picture, in which an external world of fated events is contrasted with an internal world of complete mental freedom, is Hippolytus *Haer.* I 21.2 (SVF 2.975 = LS 62A). Both Bobzien (1998), pp. 345–357, and Hankinson in Algra et al. (1999), pp. 540–541, argue that this text is unrepresentative of the orthodox Stoic picture.

[74] For example, *Diss.* I 28.1–7; III 7.15.

[75] I agree with Bobzien when she writes '... the moral character, as it were, of a person consists in the individual 'profile' of the individual nature of their mind by which

new possibilities into an otherwise deterministic causal pathway, our assent to impressions simply is the deterministic causal pathway through which characteristically human actions are determined. The philosophical disputes will then center on whether our intuitions about moral responsibility are adequately preserved by the fact that the causal pathway runs through our own preferences, habits, and dispositions. Some will feel that this fact is sufficient to make my actions genuinely mine in a rich sense, whereas others will find small cause for proprietary feeling in the fact that Fate's steamroller drives its inexorable pathway right through our innermost psyches.

For our purposes, what is worthy of note is how little this debate turns on any of the details of the psychology that the Stoics embrace. In order to make their point that we are responsible for actions that arise from our character, a psychology of impressions and assents will do, but no better than a psychology of drives and urges, or passions and instrumental beliefs, or strings and wires – provided that the wires can take some bent, and that this bent reflects differences between persons.

The Stoic strategy for preserving responsibility, then, in once sense lies squarely within the terms of their moral psychology; we are responsible for our actions because they spring from our impulses (that is, our assents), and these are determined by our character (that is, our disposition to assent). But those terms are largely dispensable to the debate. Unlike those theories that exalt rational agency above the empirical causal order or grant some other special status to agent causation, the Stoics leave impulses and actions squarely within the causal nexus.

it is determined to which impressions they give assent' (Bobzien [1998], p. 289). But see my caveats in Brennan (2001) about unintentional confusion arising from her references to an 'ability to interrupt the causal chain'.

11 Stoicism and Medicine

The histories of philosophy and medicine in the ancient world are deeply intertwined. Some individuals we think of as philosophers had serious medical interests (Empedocles and Sextus Empiricus, for instance); rather more doctors exhibited a more than merely avocational interest in philosophy (Alcmaeon, Diocles of Carystus, Herophilus, Erasistratus, Asclepiades, Menodotus, and preeminently Galen). The treatises of the Hippocratic corpus are full of philosophy; and both Plato and Aristotle paid due attention to medicine.

Perhaps the most important single instance of the cross-fertilization of ideas between physician and philosopher consists in the great debate about the nature of science and the limits of epistemology conducted with equal vigour between the sceptical schools and their medical colleagues the Empiricists (and later the Methodists) on the one hand, and the various Dogmatic sects of both philosophy and medicine on the other. Indeed, even the terminology is revealing: anti-theoreticians in both the medical and the philosophical camps standardly refer to their opponents as Dogmatists.[1]

THE SOUL

One obvious area of shared interest between doctors and philosophers concerned the nature, location, function, and mechanisms of

---

[1] The vocabulary in medical contexts is richer, however: Galen indifferently lumps together doctors of a theoretical cast of mind as *dogmatikoi* and *logikoi*, Rationalists, the latter so called by contrast with the sceptically minded Empiricists.

the soul. Plato had argued for its immortality and non-corporeality. Aristotle had rather considered it to be a set of functions of the living creature, hierarchically ordered from the lowest and most general (e.g., reproduction and nutrition) via the animal intermediaries of perception and self-movement, up to the specifically human capacity for discursive, rational thought.

Plato is clear that the soul is a non-physical substance. Aristotle's position on the issue of materialism is less clear-cut; but in *Phys.* VII 2, he insists that all motion-causing is by contact, and consists in 'pushing, pulling, carrying, or spinning' – and it is hard to square that, along with the view that the soul is responsible (among other things) for movement, with any very robust non-physicalism.

From the medical side, the author of the Hippocratic *On Regimen* (which has been classified both as a philosophical and a medical treatise, which rather suggests that such rigid classifications are mistaken) treats fire and water as the fundamental elements of the body, and ascribes intelligence to fire and retentiveness to water (*Regimen* I 35–6).

Equally, both philosophers and doctors argued over the location of the psychic functions. Plato situated his three distinct psychological faculties (reason, emotion, and appetite) in the brain, heart, and liver, respectively (*Timaeus* 69c–72d), and was followed in this by a respectable medical tradition, whose most exalted representative was Galen. Aristotle, on the other hand, identified the seat of sensation and thought with the heart.

This disagreement too mirrored earlier and contemporary medical disputes. Alcmaeon of Croton (*fl.* c. 480 B.C.) identified reason with the brain, on the grounds that the ports of perception led into it; fifty years or so later, the Hippocratic writer of *On the Sacred Disease* (Chapter 17) opted unequivocally for the brain as the centre not only of reason, but of pleasure and emotion, as well. But that no more settled the matter for medicine than it did for philosophy. A much later text, *On the Heart* (usually dated to the mid-third century B.C., and thus contemporary with the greatest period of the Stoa), supports a cardiac location for the intelligence, a view that is evidently the product of extensive anatomical investigation (it is the first text we possess that mentions the cardiac valves). Indeed, following the observation that the left ventricle is 'engineered more precisely', the author remarks:

this is to be expected: for human intelligence, the principle which rules over the rest of the soul, is situated in the left ventricle. (1: *On the Heart* 10)

On the Heart is a short and in many ways maverick treatise. It appears to show the influence of Plato (within its brief compass are references to craftsmanship and to 'an excellent craftsman', although the latter may be no more than a personified Aristotelian nature), although its psychology is clearly not Platonic. Text 1 perhaps suggests a division of the soul, contrary to Stoic theory – but it does not entail it, and it is at least conceivable that its author drew some of his theoretical inspiration from the Stoics, committed as they were to a relatively strong form of teleology, and in view of the fact that Galen credits Chrysippus with the supposition that the left ventricle was the seat of the psychic *pneuma* (discussed later in this chapter).

Passage 1 also shows, what one might anyway have expected, that gross anatomy, no matter how skilled, is unlikely on its own to yield firm conclusions about the location of the intelligence. Praxagoras of Cos, however, a prominent physician of the late fourth century, considered the heart to be the seat of cognition as well as the origin of the vital functions, a conclusion that was probably based in part on his anatomical investigations (his older contemporary Diocles also adopted the cardiocentric view, but apparently also allowed the brain some role: Frs. 72, 78, 80, 101 vdE).[2] Praxagoras differentiated the veins from the arteries, but did not sufficiently distinguish the nerves, supposing them to be the thinned-out ends of the arteries – a fact relevant to his choice of the heart as the seat of intelligence (see Galen, *PHP* V 188–9 Kühn).[3]

For by this stage, dissection was becoming well established as a method for discovering the structure and function of the internal organs and their interrelationships. Herophilus and Erasistratus, doctors active in the first half of the third century B.C. in Alexandria, are even said to have been provided with live prisoners for

[2] vdE refers to van der Eijk (2000).
[3] *PHP* is best consulted in the excellent recent edition of De Lacy (1978–80); however, for ease of reference I continue to use the old Kühn volume and page numbers (reproduced in the margin of De Lacy).

vivisection;[4] whatever the truth of that, both of them (and in particular Herophilus) made great strides in understanding the internal workings of the body. Herophilus was the first properly to distinguish the nerves from other structures (neuron in earlier Greek meant, indifferently, 'nerve', 'sinew', and 'tendon'), and furthermore differentiated the motor from the sensory nerves (T 80–5 vS).[5] He also demonstrated that the nerves coalesce in the brain (T 77 vS), and deduced from this that it was indeed the brain, rather than the heart, which was the seat of intelligence, sensation, and volition (T 79, 143 vS).

Herophilus was a pupil of Praxagoras; and Chrysippus apparently quoted Praxagoras with approval, as maintaining that the nerves originate in the heart, not the head (PHP V 189). But Chrysippus apparently either did not know of or did not care about Herophilus' discoveries; according to Galen, he confessed himself unversed in anatomy (PHP V 187). In Galen's view, this is an egregious omission, not because anatomy in and of itself solves problems in the philosophy of mind, but rather because it provides a framework against which the adequacy of any such theory must be judged. In Galen's view, to maintain the cardiac location of the commanding part of the soul was simply untenable after the isolation of the nerves, the discovery of their location in the brain and spinal column, and the experimental determination (by ligation and section) of their function as the mediators of perception and motor power, all of which are reasonably attributable to Herophilus.

PNEUMA

The Stoics held that the world was permeated by a dynamic substance responsible at the lowest level for the cohesion of material objects; at the next level up for the organisation of a functioning metabolizing and self-reproducing organism; then for animal perception

---

4 The evidence is derived from the first-century historian of medicine Celsus (On Medicine Proem 23–6, = T 63a vS ['vS' refers to von Staden, 1989]) and later sources that may or may not be dependent upon him (T 63–6 vS). Its veracity has often been questioned, but on inadequate grounds; some of the later writers who report and condemn the practice (in particular the Christian Tertullian: de Anima 10.4) are hostile, but Celsus is not; see G. E. R Lloyd (1975a); von Staden (1989), 139–53; Hankinson (1990).
5 See Solmsen (1961); von Staden (1989), 155–61, 247–59.

and voluntary power; and, finally, in humans, for cognition and understanding (*SVF* 2.716). This stuff, light and volatile yet endowed with the ability to generate and maintain structure, they called *pneuma*, and described it variously as a mixture of fire and air, or air endowed with fiery properties, or a dynamic combination of the hot and the cold (*SVF* 1.127, 135; 2.389, 786, 841, etc.).[6]

The term *pneuma* was not, however, proprietory to them. Originally meaning 'wind', it had had a long and confusing philosophical and scientific history. The Hippocratic *On Breaths* 3–4 distinguishes internal *pneuma* ('breath') from external *pneuma* ('air'), and makes it responsible for vitality and health. Here *pneuma* seems to be nothing more than air in motion, and the author has clearly noted the necessity of inhaling air for life (something not all ancient theorists accepted).

In Aristotle's biology, *pneuma* is pressed into service in a variety of ways. Described as 'hot air' (*Gen. an.* II 2, 736a1; cf. II 5, 736b34ff.), it is responsible for the ejaculation of semen 'for nothing is cast to a distance without *pneuma*' (*Hist. an.* VII 7, 586a15–17; cf. X 2, 634b34ff.; *Gen. an.* I 6, 718a2ff.) – here what is at issue are the simple dynamic effects of air in motion. However, *pneuma* is also the cause of the differentiation of parts in the embryo (*Gen. an.* II 6, 741b37ff.): it is the bearer of the animal form carried in the semen, which is water imbued with *pneuma*. Moreover, the active is identified with the hot, and the passive with the liquid (742a15), in a partial anticipation of Stoic theory.

But *pneuma*'s function is not limited to conception and generation. Animals are endowed with an internal *pneuma*, replenished by but not identical with inhaled air, which is responsible for the vital functions; it is also the bearer of voluntary motion from the soul to the muscles, and the cause of their operation (*Mot. an.* 10). The mechanical details of the picture are, unsurprisingly, obscure and unsatisfactory; but the role of *pneuma* as an analogue to the function of the motor nervous system is clear.

---

[6] Aristotle supposed that the elements were associated with pairs of qualities (fire is hot and dry, air hot and wet, earth cold and dry, water cold and wet: *Gen. corr.* 2.3); the Stoics, however, assigned a single quality to each element (fire/hot, air/cold, water/wet, earth/dry: SVF 2.580): it is worth noting that this assignment is attributed to the fourth-century physician Philistion (Anon. Lond. 20.25–30). See Ch. 5, White, this volume.

Diocles' physiology involved *pneuma* too (Frs. 32–4, etc., vdE); and he distinguishes its psychic from its other forms (Frs. 78, 80, 95, vdE). *Pneuma* also plays a role in the physiology of Herophilus, even though he had discovered the function of the nerves. He ascribes vision to the operation of 'sensory *pneuma*' through the optic nerve (T 140 vS); yet, if Galen is to be trusted, he apparently thought that the motor nerves were themselves the organs of voluntary motion, without the need for them to be filled with *pneuma* (T 141 vS; cf. 143).[7]

Erasistratus also theorized about *pneuma* – and he apparently distinguished, as did the Stoics (SVF 2.716), between vital and psychic *pneuma* (*PHP* V 184–5); but against Chrysippus (and the author of Text 1), he held that the left ventricle of the heart contained only the former. In Erasistratus' system, the arteries function (under normal circumstances) solely as conduits for *pneuma*, but not the *pneuma* of intelligence; any irruption of blood into the arteries is pathological (Fr. 109 Garofalo), a view that Galen showed by experiment to be false. But whereas the idea that the conduits from the heart contain *pneuma* would, in its general outlines, no doubt be congenial to the Stoics in view of their cardiocentric theory of the rational soul, the details of the two theories are evidently quite different, and there is no need to posit any cross-fertilization of doctrine between them.

But all of this is of only limited relevance to the Stoics' *pneuma*. Some physicians may have made use of the Stoic idea of a volatile stuff in dynamic oscillating tension in order to sketch an account of the phenomena we associate with neural transmission – but there is little evidence in favour of this, and maybe with good reason. Galen makes the point (*PHP* V 791–5) that there are numerous questions which, while interesting in themselves, are of no relevance to medicine and cannot be settled by any empirical test. Such questions include that of the eternity of the world, the existence of an extramundane void (771), and more importantly for our purposes, the nature of the soul and whether it is immortal (763, 766; cf. *On the Formation of the Foetus* IV 700–2 Kühn). The physician *qua* physician has no need to inquire into the substance of the soul and the question of its possible survival; the limit of his non-philosophical interest is

---

[7] Galen's veracity is contested here as elsewhere; e.g., by Solmsen (1961), 186; but see von Staden (1989), 252–9, for a judicious assessment of the issue here.

determined by clinical exigencies. Thus, it is of vital importance to know that the nerves are the vehicles of sensory and motor functions, since it follows that damage to them will affect, perhaps destroy, those functions. But whether they work by the transmission of *pneuma*, and if so what precisely *pneuma* might be, is of less import. Although he allows that *pneuma* is the means by which the soul communicates its power, he denies that the soul is identical with it (*PHP* V 606, 609). *Pneuma* really functions for him as a place-holder for whatever it is that is in fact responsible for such causal transmission. Galen is enough of an empiricist to allow that there may be modes of such transmission which do not involve an intermediate fluid (an example he cites is that of the electric shock delivered by a torpedo-fish through a fisherman's trident: *On Affected Parts* VII 421–2 Kühn).

So, in sum, while the Stoics take over and develop the concept of *pneuma*, a notion with a long philosophical and medical history, they do so for their own purposes, purposes largely independent of medical concerns.

CAUSES

One unique function the Stoics accord their *pneuma* is that of holding things together: this is the third type of *pneuma*, in addition to the vital and the psychic, which the sources credit only to them ([Galen] *Introduction* XIV 726 Kühn = SVF 2.716), and they described it as a 'containing cause'[8] (*aition sunhektikon*) of things. Galen indeed takes them to task for this: Why posit something to prevent solid things from falling apart? And in any case, how could something as volatile as *pneuma* do the trick (*Caus. cont.* 6.1–3)?

But, as Galen also notes, the terminology of containing causes came to be applied not merely to the necessary and sufficient conditions for object persistence, but also to the necessary and sufficient conditions of events and processes (*Against Julian* XVIIIA 278–9 Kühn), and although this usage was taken up in the medical schools – and Galen for one insists that this is not the original Stoic understanding of the concept – it seems nonetheless to have been embraced

---

[8] Or 'cohesive cause' or 'sustaining cause' – no translation quite does justice to all the nuances of the term.

by the Stoics relatively early on. Chrysippus, in order to elaborate his doctrine of a compatibilist determinism, distinguished between the containing causes of events, which determine their effects, are coeval with them, and whose variations in intensity cause concomitant variations in their effects (cf. S. E., *PH* III 15; Clement, *Strom.* VIII 9.33 = SVF 2.352), with those events' antecedent causes.[9] Antecedent causes (*aitia prokatarktika*)[10] are not sufficient for their effects (in some treatments they turn out not strictly to be necessary for them either); rather, they are the initial impulses which set some train of events in motion. In medical usage, they correspond to the Hippocratic *prophaseis*, the evident, external events which causally precede some pathological process; indeed, they serve to reveal the internal weakness of the patient in this particular case. This connects with the fact that they are not sufficient for their effects.[11]

Galen wrote a short treatise on the subject, primarily designed to rehabilitate their genuine causal status, and hence their importance in diagnosis and prognosis, against the attacks of Erasistratus and his followers, who insist that all causes must be invariably correlated with their effects (Galen, *On Antecedent Causes* [ed. Hankinson, 1998b], esp. i.6–ii.11; viii.96–xiii.172). Of all the people in the theatre on a hot summer's day, Galen says, only four may suffer from the heat and of these only one actually fall seriously ill – but this does not show that the heat wasn't causally implicated; rather, the fact that only one succumbs to its influence is to be explained in terms of that individual's particular susceptibility to heat-stroke. All of the others would have suffered eventually, if they had been exposed longer, or had the heat been more fierce. The antecedent cause (cf. S. E., *PH* III 16), then, sets in motion a primed mechanism within the bodies of susceptible patients; at a certain point, when the onset of the illness is inevitable, that process becomes the *aition sunhektikon* of the illness.

9   For technical reasons, it may be preferable to talk of processes rather than events or states of affairs: see Hankinson (1996). For much of what follows, compare Ch. 7, Frede, this volume.

10   There is no generally accepted orthodoxy of translation here either: Long and Sedley (1987) use 'preliminary causes', reserving 'antecedent cause' as the translation for *aition prohêgoumenon*, which I term 'preceding cause'; other renderings of *aition prokatarktikon* include 'initial cause' and 'salient cause'.

11   On these issues, see Hankinson (1987a).

The connection between this piece of medical doctrine and Stoic theory is explicitly made by Galen, who also adds a further complexity:

Athenaeus of Attaleia...founded the medical school known as the Pneumatists. It suits his doctrine to speak of a containing cause in illness since he bases himself upon the Stoics and he was a pupil and disciple of Posidonius.... Athenaeus' three types are as follows: the first consists of containing causes, the second of preceding causes, and the third of the matter of antecedent causes: for this is what they call everything external to the body which harms it and produces disease in it. If what is produced in the body belongs to the class of what causes disease, then, while it has not actually brought the disease about, it is called the preceding cause. Alterations are produced in the natural *pneuma* by these [i.e., preceding] causes together with those which are external [i.e., antecedent causes], and with the body moistened or desiccated, chilled or heated, these are said to be the containing causes of diseases. (2: Galen, *On Sustaining Causes* 2.1–4)

This confirms our earlier sketch of the role and status of the antecedent cause, but adds a new item to the causal taxonomy, the preceding cause (*aition prohêgoumenon*). Galen explicitly attributes its authorship to Athenaeus, the first-century B.C. founder of the influential Pneumatist school of medicine (the author of the pseudo-Galenic *Introduction*, referred to previously as a source for the classification of types of *pneuma*, was a Pneumatist); Galen himself broadly adopts this classification (cf. *On the Causes of Pulses* IX 2–3 Kühn).[12]

But there is some evidence to suggest that something like this distinction may already have been in play in Chrysippus' theorizing. He distinguished antecedent from containing causes as a central component to his defence of a compatibilist account of fate and human freedom. Anti-Stoic philosophers like Alexander of Aphrodisias (*On Fate*) argued that if the universe is thoroughly determinist in character, as the Stoics insist (SVF 2.917, 2.921, 2.945, 2.975, 2.979, 2.982, 2.1000, 2.1002, 2.1003, etc.), and if everything that happens in it, including our own volitions and actions, are the ineluctable results of causal necessity, then how can we be responsible for what we do? Are we not merely cogs in the machine?

---

[12] For Galen's causal theory, see Hankinson (1998b), Intr. II–III, and commentary, *passim*; (1998a), Ch. XI; and (1994).

304 R. J. HANKINSON

Chrysippus' reply was that fate was a necessary sequence of *antecedent* causes:

'some causes', he says, 'are perfect (*perfectae*) and principal (*principales*), others are auxiliary (*adiuvantes*) and proximate (*proximae*). Hence when we say that everything takes place by fate from antecedent causes, we should not be taken to mean by perfect and principal causes, but by auxiliary and proximate causes'. Accordingly he counters the argument which I have just set out as follows: 'if all things come about by fate it does follow that all things come about from prior (*antepositae*) causes, but not from principal and perfect but from auxiliary and proximate causes'. (3: Cicero, *Fat.* 41, =SVF 2.974 [part], =62C LS [part])

Elsewhere in the medical tradition, we find mention of auxiliary causes, *aitia sunerga*: they are standardly defined as contributing to the intensity of the effect, although not being on their own sufficient for it. 'Proximate causes', *causae proximae* in Cicero's Latin, must – in view of the evidence elsewhere (e.g., SVF 2.997) – answer to *aitia prokatarktika*, although the most likely Greek original here is *aitia proseché*, even if in other contexts (notably Erasistratus' causal theory: Galen *On Antecedent Causes* XIV 173–82) an *aition proseches* appears to be sufficient for its effects. (Erasistratus refused to countenance anything as a cause unless it was so sufficient: his *aition proseches* of inflammation and fever is the transfusion of blood into the arteries, compressing and disrupting the activity of the vital *pneuma*.)

But what Cicero calls 'perfect causes' (presumably *aitia autotelé*: cf. Clement, *Strom.* VIII 9.33 = SVF 2.351) are evidently *aitia sunhektika*. So fate, properly so-called, is not to be identified with the whole causal structure of everything, but rather only with the initiating causes of processes or actions, the external stimuli which set them going. This view aroused Plutarch's (and indirectly Alexander's) scorn: but it is not in fact negligible. Chrysippus' idea is that the real active cause of a particular process is what is actually currently sufficient for it – and antecedent causes by definition are not that. To take a particular example of the sort relevant to the discussion of freedom and responsibility, the stimulus to my seeking food may be a sense impression of something edible; but my merely seeing it is not enough to make me eat – a whole internal structure of beliefs, desires, and volitions is called into play as well.

More importantly, the same stimulus may affect different people differently: oysters move me to gluttonous excess while leaving you cold. The proper explanation of this discrepancy (which closely mirrors the medical case of the single sunstroke victim) is to be found in the differences in our internal dispositions. I am responsible for what I do, even though it is caused, because it is my dispositions and beliefs that are doing the crucial work in producing the outcome. Neither the fact that they would not have done so without the stimulus, nor the fact that, given the stimulus, they cannot (other things being equal) fail to produce the outcome, are relevant.

A few paragraphs later, Cicero reports Chrysippus' famous example of the cylinder: this will not begin to roll without an external push (the antecedent cause), but once rolling, it continues 'because of its own force and nature' (*Fat.* 43 = SVF 2.974 = 62C LS). The antecedent cause serves to set an already primed mechanism in motion – once it has done so, it is the mechanism itself which is responsible.

The question remains: are the pairs of causes of Text 3 meant merely to be synonyms, or does a perfect differ from a principal cause and an auxiliary from a proximate? The issue is not easy to disentangle.[13] But although they are both types of external influence, *aitia prokatarktika* and *aitia sunerga* can hardly be equivalent (*aitia prokatarktika* are not intensifiers of already existing effects), which suggests that perhaps '*causa principalis*' is not simply another way of referring to *aitia autotelê* (i.e., *sunhektika*); but it is perfectly possible that it translates *prohêgoumenon*, which would indicate that, *pace* Galen's claims in Text 2, the term originated with the Stoics and not Athenaeus. Aulus Gellius, in a parallel passage (*NA* VII 2.6–13 = SVF 2.1000 = 62D LS), refers to the cylinder's continuing to roll 'because it has within itself such a form and rollability of shape'. Thus Chrysippus may have thought of the internal form of the cylinder as being the *aition prohêgoumenon* of its rolling, and that form roused into actuality by the external stimulus as its *aition sunhektikon*.[14]

But even if this is right, it is clear that this (rather Aristotelian) distinction does not precisely conform to the medical model of

---

[13] For rather different views, compare Hankinson (1987a) with Hankinson (1999); see also M. Frede (1980).

[14] For a fuller development of this line of speculation, see Hankinson (1999), Sections III–VI.

Athenaeus, where the preceding causes are identified not with standing conditions prior to the impact of the antecedent cause, but rather
with internal features of the process as it unfolds. And the tenta-
tiveness of these conclusions ought to show how difficult it is to
determine with any degree of precision the direction and nature of
the influences involved.

SIGNS

Antecedent causes, in the medical tradition, also serve a semiotic
function, and in more than one way. First, the impact of the cause
is at any rate a defeasible indication that some pathological event
might follow (and if one knows in advance of a particular patient's
susceptibilities, may provide a firmer indication than that of trouble
ahead); but second, in the cases in which harmful results follow, it
serves to bring to light the existence of the patient's susceptibility.

The Stoics and their opponents (in particular, the Epicureans and
the Pyrrhonian sceptics) also concerned themselves with signs; the
topic of sign inference in general and of the nature of particular signs
also greatly exercised the medical schools. Sextus says that there
are, broadly speaking, two sorts of signs, which he calls indicative
and commemorative respectively: the former, which are anathema
to the sceptic, are supposed to be evident signs of hidden conditions; whereas the latter (which Sextus allows) simply serve to show
the presence of something temporarily nonevident. Thus smoke is a
commemorative sign of fire since fire is not intrinsically imperceptible; but sweating is supposed to be an indicative sign of the existence
of imperceptible pores in the skin (PH II 97–102). The latter is a Stoic
example; they define an indicative sign as 'an antecedent in a sound
conditional which is revelatory of the consequent' (II 101, 104). Signs,
then, are supposed to take us from evident facts to the hidden heart
of things, a view which has obvious medical resonances; indeed, it
has Hippocratic (as well as pre-Socratic) antecedents.

Sceptics like Sextus argue that there are, as a matter of fact, no
such evident signs. To take the phenomenon of sweating as conclusive proof of the existence of pores is to rely on the (certainly Stoic
but perhaps less certainly unexceptionable) thesis that nothing can
pass through a perfectly solid body (PH II 142), as well as to assume
that the moisture does indeed come from within.

The Stoics certainly did think of their signs as showing with logical certainty what they signify. The Epicurean Philodemus speaks of their employing the 'eliminative method' to ground their sign inferences, which essentially amounts to testing the soundness of the conditional ('if there is sweating, there are pores') by contraposition: how could there possibly be sweating if there were no pores (Philodemus, *Sign*. 11.32–12.31 De Lacy = 18F LS)? The Epicureans rather contend that the source of the validity of sign inference is the 'method of similarity': induction. The reason why we expect fire when we see smoke (it is significant that Philodemus employs an example of what Sextus would call a commemorative sign) is that 'smoke has been seen in all cases to be a secretion of fire' (24.29–36.17 = 18G LS). The Epicureans allow that such connections may have a sort of conceptual necessity – we cannot think of a human being as being other than mortal – but that is not equivalent to logical necessity.

Sextus calls the type of sign he is prepared to allow 'commemorative'. He does not explain the origin of the term, but it is significant that the medical sect known as the Empiricists made much of memory in their epistemology.[15] Indeed, they defined the 'experience' from which they took their name as 'the memory of what one has seen to happen often and in the same way' (Galen, *Outline of Empiricism* 4).[16] Moreover, they too distinguished between two sorts of inference – one acceptable, the other not – which they called *epilogismos* and *analogismos*, respectively. *Epilogismos* roughly corresponds to the commemorative sign and Epicurean induction (the term itself is used by Philodemus to mean something like 'empirical inference'); *analogismos*, which they attribute to the Dogmatists, to the indicative sign.

Medical Empiricism began in Alexandria at the end of the third-century B.C.; it was inaugurated by Serapion, a pupil of Herophilus. Empiricists had no time for physiological or pathological theory: they thought that knowledge of the deep structure of the human body and of the fine-grained causal facts of its working was unobtainable. But fortunately, or so they thought, it wasn't necessary to effective therapy either. The Empiricist doctor simply observed collections of

---

[15] For which see M. Frede (1990): he even calls the epistemology 'memorism'.

[16] *Outline of Empiricism* is one of our major sources for the school's doctrines; the others, Galen's *On Sects* and *On Medical Experience*. All three are translated in M. Frede (1985), with a useful introduction.

signs and symptoms, what was correlated with what, both prognostically (what illness tends to follow what symptoms and which antecendent occasions) and therapeutically (what treatments have been effective in similar cases); this is *epilogismos* (see Galen, *Outline of Empiricism* 4 and 6).[17] Everything else – grand theories of the humours or of *pneuma*, complicated accounts of the internal workings of the body – is irrelevant.

Again the precise lines of influence are hard to determine, but at the very least, it is clear that the Empiricists rejected the sort of inference that the Stoics considered central to their method of discovery, and in so doing contributed in their turn to the debate about signs that dominated later Greek philosophical and scientific methodology. By contrast, the Empiricists' Dogmatist opponents relied on something they called 'indication' (*endeixis*: an obviously close relation of the indicative sign):

Logical (i.e., Dogmatic) transition[18] based on the nature of things lays hold of knowledge by means of indication (*endeixis*). But the Empirical variety relies on what is discovered by experience, not because it is persuasive or plausible that the similar should be productive of something similar, or require similar things, or undergo similar things; it is not on the basis of this, or anything else of this sort, that they think it justifiable to make the transition, but on the basis of the fact that they have discovered by experience that things behave this way. (4: Galen, *Outline of Empiricism* 9)

Text 4 clearly evinces the Empiricists' determination to have nothing to do with any speculative metaphysics. In line with this, they allow that they make use of antecedent causes, but even those they accept only as signs: as good sceptics, they have no theory of causal interaction.[19]

That there was a good deal of theoretical borrowing and lending between the various competing schools of medicine and their

---

[17] Galen attributes the introduction of *epilogismos* to Menodotus, a moderate Empiricist of the first-century A.D.; if this is right, the term had already had a long Epicurean history before being taken up by the doctors (*Outline of Empiricism* 12, = Fr. 10b 87–8 Dr); but Galen may only mean that Menodotus explicitly allowed it *as a method of inference*.

[18] 'Transition' is simply any inferential move designed to get you from one fact to another, and does not here specifically refer to the Empiricist technical term 'transition to the similar', a form of analogical reasoning allowed by some (but not all) Empiricists (see Hankinson [1987b]; and Frede [1990]).

[19] See Hankinson (1987b).

equally contentious philosophical cousins, including the Stoics, in the Hellenistic period is clear. Quite how these exchanges worked and in which direction is altogether less clear, not surprisingly perhaps in view of the fragmentary nature of our evidence for the period. It is also evident that both doctors and philosophers learned from each other; indeed, Galen went so far as to assert that no one could be a good doctor unless they were also a philosopher, and he prided himself, with justification, on his own philosophical ability. But it is equally clear that some philosophers paid less attention than they usefully might have done to the staggering advances in medical knowledge taking place at the time. And the Stoics stand particularly convicted of such a neglect, under the withering attack of Galen's acid pen; had they only learned a little anatomy, they would never have based an argument for the cardiac location of the soul upon the supposition that the windpipe connected directly with the heart (*PHP* V 240–58; he also accuses them of mistakenly supposing that the organ of causal control of something must be adjacent to what it controls).[20] Galen saw clearly that the results of scientific investigation on their own could not settle philosophical questions about the nature of the soul: but he and other doctors also saw clearly – much more clearly than the Stoics did – that any serious solutions to such questions must at least be sensitive to the framework provided by those results.

[20] On these arguments, see Hankinson (1991).

12 The Stoic Contribution to Traditional Grammar

The phrase 'traditional grammar' refers to the body of knowledge about the correct use of word-forms and syntax transmitted in the West at least since the early Middle Ages for the study of Latin and Greek and whose categories were used as a template for the study of other languages. It has long been recognised that traditional grammar shares numerous terms and concepts with the linguistic studies of the Stoics, and this chapter examines the relations between them.[1]

I. SOURCES

As is so often the case with Hellenistic philosophy, the dearth of reliable, high-quality, first-hand material is a serious obstacle to reconstructing Stoic thought in this area. No Stoic grammatical treatise of any period survives; indeed, only one text with what can be called, broadly, grammatical interests is extant in even something like its original form; in any case this book of Chrysippus' *Logical Questions* (*PHerc* 307) belongs rather in what moderns would call philosophical logic and the philosophy of language – although this overlap is significant in itself (see Section 2.2).

What is known of the general character and organisation of Stoic grammatical work and of its position within Stoic philosophy comes, first, from doxographical sources, the most important being the lengthy report of Stoic dialectic in Diogenes Laertius (DL VII 41–83) and the bibliography of Chrysippus' works on linguistic topics, again in Diogenes (DL VII 190–2). Such sources, typically, can boast only

---

[1] On the development of grammar, see, e.g., Pinborg (1975) and D. J. Taylor (1986).

a limited understanding of the material they are handling, which will itself be of widely variable quality; fortunately, the relevant portion of Diogenes' report seems to go back to Chrysippus' pupil Diogenes of Babylon (second century B.C.). A major source for the Stoic-influenced grammar of Tauriscus, a pupil of Crates of Mallos (mid-second century B.C.), is a Pyrrhonist (sceptical) philosopher, Sextus Empiricus, who probably wrote in the late second century A.D. (M I).[2] Information otherwise emerges indirectly from whatever particular theses survive in or are reported and typically criticised by non-Stoic grammarians and philosophers (see Section 2.2). The details of Stoic grammatical theories have likewise to be extracted from later authors, such as Apollonius Dyscolus (mid-second century A.D.) or the Byzantine commentators on the grammatical *Technê* attributed, almost certainly wrongly, to Dionysius Thrax (*c.* 100 B.C.); these writers are bound by different allegiances and have different aims than those of the theorists whose views they are reporting.

An additional complication is a general lack of information about grammar outside the Stoa in the crucial period: third through the first century B.C. No grammatical text survives complete before the works of Apollonius Dyscolus; the earliest school grammars or grammatical handbooks are Roman. Further, evidence exists to show that the earliest stages of grammar as something like a distinct discipline were marked by deep disagreements about the scope, contents, and internal structure of grammar.[3] The later, extant, texts are marked by comparable, if less violent, variations. Peripatetic texts of the fourth century B.C. and later, such as Theophrastus' *On diction* (or *On style*, *Peri lexeôs*), which may well have influenced grammatical theorising, have likewise disappeared (although of course Aristotle's *Poetics* and *Rhetoric* have survived). The consequence is that distinctions between and comparisons of Stoic and non-Stoic contributions to traditional grammar are at best a hazardous undertaking, whether in terms of organisation and general content (see Section 2.2) or of particular theses (see Section 4).

It cannot even be assumed that classical antiquity produced an independent discipline of 'grammar' akin to modern linguistics. Two important differences between modern and ancient grammatical

---

[2] See the translation and commentary in Blank (1998).
[3] See, e.g., Blank (2000).

studies must be noted. First, studies we would call 'grammatical' were from the start housed within or were seen as contributing to a variety of disciplines, themselves often owing allegiance to philosophy, broadly construed: poetics, rhetoric, stylistics, literary and textual criticism, and dialectic or logic. A broad intra-disciplinary distinction was eventually arrived at in the Hellenistic period (cf. e.g., Varro *On the Latin Language* VIII 6, S. E. *M* I 57f., 91ff., 248ff., DT Sch. 135.7ff.) between 'parts', 'tools', or 'offices' of 'grammar' dealing on a mostly *ad hoc* unsystematic basis with the philological and the exegetical-cum-literary-critical study of texts, on the one hand (say, the authenticity of a text, or the explication of religious practices, or topographical features, mentioned in it), and, on the other, 'technical' grammar, the division or function of grammar which dealt systematically with the elements of spoken and written language and their appropriate combination, and with the formal and syntactic properties of the parts of speech. Second, technical grammar was practiced for various purposes. On the level of research, it was intended to explain various usages as deriving in a codifiable way from original, correct norms, thus justifying the existence of a scientific study of language and establishing a framework for the use of grammar in the study of literature. In the schools, it was not a descriptive discipline, but rather formulated a set of prescriptions for writing and public speaking.

One piece of cargo traditionally carried by the historiography of grammar must quite definitely be jettisoned, however: that a Stoic, philosophical, anomalist grammar, the creation of a Pergamene 'school', waged war on an Alexandrian, philological, analogist grammar. Further, the assumption that Stoic philosophy helped slow the emergence of a 'pure' linguistic grammar from other disciplines represents a profound misunderstanding of the nature of ancient grammatical discourse (see Sections 2.2 and 3).

Finally, on a general note; the notion of 'influence' is notoriously slippery; thus, for example, failure of an accredited Stoic thesis to survive does not show that such a thesis did not have a role in the shaping of the orthodoxy, a role which may be exercised as much by provoking counter-argument and counter-theorising as by earning approval, whether universal or qualified (see Section 4). The following survey, of necessity highly selective, focuses on topics in which more definite influence, positive or negative, can be discerned.

2. DIFFERENT PERSPECTIVES

2.1 Ancient versus Modern

A first crucial distinction to be made in this area is between what was important and influential work in antiquity, and what happened to survive into medieval, early modern, and ultimately 'traditional' grammar. It is through the work of the greatest technical grammarian of the ancient West, the Alexandrian Apollonius Dyscolus – who, despite his implicit or explicit rejection of particular Stoic theses, adapted the Stoic approach to syntax (see Section 4.1) – that Stoic theorising in this area found its way into the medieval tradition. It did so, however, not directly, but in modified form, and at two removes: for Apollonius' treatises were themselves filtered through the work of his Latin acolyte, Priscian (sixth-century A.D.).[4] Another important influence on the development of Latin grammar was the Roman polymath Varro (first century B.C.). Fragments of his work show a decidedly Stoic cast, for example in the division of different types of pronominal expressions by the 'definiteness' of their reference, or in his work on syntax (*On the Latin Language* Books XIV–XXV), the sole fragment of which corresponds to the subject matter of the Stoic 'syntax of sayables' in DL. In contrast, the most copied and (to judge by the number of scholia on it) most used text in technical grammar, the handbook attributed to Dionysius Thrax already mentioned (the authenticity of which was already questioned in later antiquity; e.g., DT Sch. Vat. 160.24ff., and which is in large part almost certainly a product of the period after the second century A.D.) is clearly often incompatible with Stoic theorising. Indeed, that what little is known of Dionysius' own genuine work is strongly marked by Stoic theory is an argument against the authenticity of the *Handbook*.[5] Yet this does not mean that Stoics did not exercise profound influence on technical grammar in its formative period (see Section 4). Less clear is how far elements or fragments of Stoic theorising became known in the most widely diffused manifestations of

---

[4] In the Byzantine East, a similar role was played by Georgios Choiroboskos (ninth century A.D.) and other commentators on the supposititious '*Technê*' of Dionysius Thrax, as well as scholars such as Maximus Planudes (twelfth century A.D.).

[5] On Dionysius Thrax, see Linke (1977); on the (in-)authenticity of the treatise transmitted under his name, see, e.g., Di Benedetto (1958–1959) and Lallot (1997).

'grammar' in antiquity – first, the teaching to the very young of the basic skills of reading and writing (*grammatistikê*) and second, instruction of (élite male) children approximately eight to twelve years old in the more advanced arts of reciting and paraphrasing canonical literary texts, and of basic composition as a preparation for rhetorical performance proper.

2.2 Stoic versus Autonomous Grammar

Not only can nothing like a distinct, autonomous discipline we might call 'Stoic grammar' be securely identified, but also theorising of the kind which would later be called 'grammatical' had its home in at least two, and possibly four, different areas within Stoic philosophy.

First, the 'dialectical' part of Stoic 'logic' analysed and described the properties of *logos* – rationality, ratiocination, rational thought, and discourse – relevant to the philosopher's function as constructer and arbiter of human reasoning activity, the perfecting of which is integral to human happiness. It thus comprises (using the most widely accepted division of 'logic') parts of psychology; epistemology; the theory of the elements of speech and of the parts of the sentence; stylistics, poetics, and music theory; the study of definitions and of ambiguities; semantics and syntax; philosophical and formal logic; and the theory of fallacies. The pioneering work of M. Frede (1987a, b) has shown that whereas the parts of the sentence, usually called the 'parts of speech' (*merê tou logou*), were classified within the subsection of dialectic, which is concerned with 'voice' (*phônê*) or 'signifiers' (*sêmainonta*), syntax was understood primarily as a relation at the level of items 'signified' (*sêmainomena*) by (complexes of) the parts of speech, and hence was the subject of a different subsection of dialectic.[6] Stoic metaphysics insists that sounds and words are material objects (primarily, bits of air shaped by speakers; secondarily, their written representations), whereas significations constitute one of four species of incorporeal: *lekta*, literally 'sayables' (or *pragmata*, 'things (done)', and 'significations', as they are also labeled).[7] *Sayables* are defined as dependent (in a way that,

---

[6] On Stoic syntactic theory, see Egli (1986).
[7] See Ch. 8, Brunschwig, this volume.

it must be admitted, is not entirely clear) on rational thoughts, but seem to be the contents of those thoughts and of the sentences that express them; they are thus shareable and communicable by members of a linguistic community, in a way that private psychological states are not.[8]

Sayables themselves are either complete or incomplete. Of the former, the most important species is that of the prime bearers of truth and falsity, 'propositions' or *axiômata*. Surviving accounts approach syntax by identifying the proposition's two principal constituents: the 'case' or *ptôsis* (e.g., 'man', 'Socrates'), and the 'predicate' or *katêgorêma* (e.g., 'writes', 'sees') which is defined as an incomplete *lekton*. (Syntactic analyses of other complete sayables have not survived.) A 'non-compound', verbal, predicate (e.g., 'walks') or the verbal portion of a 'compound' predicate (e.g., 'hits') is what is signified by a 'verb' (*rhêma*), one of the five Stoic parts of speech. The character and ontological status of the 'case', albeit clearly related in some way to the nominal parts of speech (i.e., the proper name [*onoma*], the appellative [*prosêgoria*], and the pronoun), is far more problematic and is discussed in Section 4.3.

Crucially for Stoic dialectic and philosophy generally, the structure of complete sayables allows the articulating of distinctions – above all that between a physical object and its properties – which have no physical correlate (in that the properties are physical parts of the object or are reducible to it without metaphysical remainder). The forms of words in a sentence will provide information about the contribution of their correlates at the level of the sayables to the meaning(s) of the sentence as a whole. Further, complexes of propositions go to make up arguments, which, when sound, articulate real (e.g., causal) connections obtaining in the physical world; hence, the conjunctions that link propositions must in some way have meanings that can also capture such real-world relations. The non-accidental properties of sayables are presumably immune from change, in a way that words and their properties are not; perfect isomorphism between the two levels is also compromised by solecism, synonymy, and ambiguity. The dialectician's interest in grammar is stimulated by the need to minimise these defects in his own usage,

---

[8] On key concepts of Stoic linguistic theory, see Müller (1947), Long (1971a), M. Frede (1974, 1987a, b, 1994a, b), and Atherton (1993).

and to detect and compensate for them in others'. Correct language embodies as close as possible a match between the constituents and structures of sentences, and those of the sayables which those sentences express, and which constitute the contents of impressions. But since proper control of assent to one's impressions is essential for building up a system of correct beliefs and for governing correct behaviour, sensitivity to linguistic correctness will be a useful – and may be an essential – asset for the Stoic philosopher.

A third home of 'grammatical' theorising within Stoic philosophy may well have been the study, within the topic of 'voice' or linguistic signifiers, of the 'virtues and vices of speech' (*aretai kai kakiai tês lexeôs*).[9] Unusually, this portion of the Stoic theory seems to have been adapted from Theophrastus, with the (characteristic) addition of a virtue of 'conciseness' (*suntomia*) to those of 'purity' (for Greek: *hellênismos*; later, for Latin, *latinitas*), 'clarity' (*saphêneia*), 'appropriateness' (*to prepon*), and 'elegance' (*kataskeuê*). 'Vices' or 'defects' are or include barbarism and solecism. A *solecism* is defined as a word-complex (*logos*) that is 'incongruent' (*akatallêlos*); the key concepts of 'congruence' (*to katallêlon*) and its opposite we will meet again in Section 4.1. Again, we have very little information about which criteria of linguistic purity were endorsed by the Stoa, but the standard association of Stoics with an 'anomalistic' grammar is incorrect (see Section 3). Further, although etymological researches seem to have been of interest to the Stoa as part of a general philosophical account of the origins of language, demonstrating the natural suitability of signifiers to significations (cf. Augustine *de dialectica* Ch. vi), the most that can be said is that this does not preclude the application of these principles in prescriptive grammar, or in a theory of tropes and metaphors as the prerogative of poetic creativity working to extend the boundaries of language (Quintilian I viii 14ff., VIII vi 34ff.; Servius *Comm. in Don.* 447.5ff.).

It has been claimed that Stoic grammatical theorising found its way directly into Roman grammar, bypassing the Greek tradition entirely (Barwick 1922). Not only, however, is the sharp distinction on which this thesis is grounded – between a Stoic text or texts on the virtue of Hellenism and a non-Stoic *Grammatical handbook* (*Têchnê*

---

[9] See Stroux (1912) and Barwick (1957), though the latter attributes too much to the Stoics and too confidently.

grammatikê), as the respective sources for Roman and Greek grammar – in itself deeply implausible given even the little we know of the
fluidity and diversity of the Hellenistic tradition, but there is in fact
no hard-and-fast rule that Roman grammarians do and Greek grammarians do not append a study of the virtues and vices of speech to
the study of correctness. Furthermore, the thesis that this supposed
stylistic portion of Roman grammars replaced a treatment of syntax
(to the detriment of the later history of the subject) is at odds with
the evidence that syntax was indeed dealt with by Stoics, only (as
we have seen) not – or not primarily – in the context of a theory of
Hellenism or of the parts of speech.

Lastly, Stoic rhetorical theory, which constituted the other major subdivision of Stoic 'logic', could have borrowed this stylistic
construct, and in some way adapted it to the demands of insti-
tutionalised, formal discourse. The convention that the stylistic
virtues apart from purity would be dealt with by rhetoricians (cf.
Ad Herennium IV 17; cf. Quintilian *inst. rhet.* I ix 6) could have
been adopted by Stoics.[10]

Early Stoic interest in the criticism of literary texts, at least from
an ethical perspective, can be seen in the titles of some of Zeno's (*On
listening to poetry, Homeric problems*, DL VII 4) and Chrysippus'
works (e.g., *How to listen to poetry*), and Stoics are traditionally
linked to the 'allegorical' interpretation of such texts, although here
again scholars disagree about the extent of their interest.[11] A more
substantial literary grammar was associated with Crates of Mallos,
a pupil of Diogenes of Babylon, who is said to have introduced the
study of grammar (in the sense of textual and literary criticism) to
Rome (Suetonius *On grammarians and rhetoricians* 2). What is striking is that his discipline of 'criticism' (*kritikê*), which includes the
orthodox 'grammarian's' expertise in such matters as accentuation
and the literary lexicon (S. E. *M* I 79), but requires familiarity with
the whole of 'logical knowledge' (*epistêmê logikê*), appears – at least
in theory – to be as dependent on (albeit not as embedded in) Stoic
dialectic as is the theorising on 'grammatical' topics evidenced by

---

[10] On Stoic rhetoric, see Atherton (1988).
[11] An idea of Chrysippus' ethical approach to poetry may be gleaned from Plutarch's
How to listen to poetry; the relation of this approach to grammarians' claims about
the ethical value of poets may be seen in S. E., M I 270 ff. and Blank's commentary
ad loc. On allegory, see Long (1992) and Most (1989).

Diogenes Laertius' report. Crates' pupil Tauriscus divided 'criticism' into 'a rational part concerned with diction and the grammatical figures'; an empirical part 'about the dialects [of Greek] and the different forms or types of style'; and a historical part 'about the preexisting unordered raw material' (S.E. *M* I 248f., tr. Blank). The original contents and form of the (or a) Stoic *Handbook on voice* (*Technê peri phônês*) have been the object of extensive study and considerable scholarly disagreement;[12] the basic text is again the summary of this portion of Stoic dialectic in Diogenes Laertius, but possible indirect clues are also found in the earliest structural divisions of grammar which are reported to us, the 'critical' expertise of Crates of Mallos, and the 'expert part' of the grammar of Asclepiades of Myrlea.[13]

To summarise: it remains unclear, and may perhaps always remain unclear, what precisely found its way from which portion of Stoic philosophy into which treatise or monographs of the Hellenistic Stoic-influenced authors writing on grammatical topics, and unclear too what survived of either of these sources (Stoic or Stoic-influenced) in the handbooks and monographs of professional grammarians. The fact of Stoic influence, however, cannot be doubted.

3. SCHOOLS OF GRAMMAR AND THE ANOMALIST/ANALOGIST CONTROVERSY

An important theoretical distinction to be observed is that between formal and semantic anomaly and analogy. Chrysippus is known to have referred to cases of semantic anomaly; that is, of inconcinnity between form and signification: e.g., the inappropriate privative form of the Greek adjective *athanatos* (deathless, immortal), as if death were something of which the gods were deprived (Simplicius *In Ar. Cat.* 396.3ff.); or the gendered forms of different names for the moon deity, *mên* and *selênê*, when the one immanent deity is in fact genderless (Philodemus *Piet.* 11, = SVF 2.1076). The general albeit sometimes disappointed expectation is thus of similarity of some sort between words and what they name (which supports the Stoic project of semantic etymology). In contrast, the traditional association of the Stoics with something called 'anomalistic grammar' is both unfounded (there being no such thing as 'anomalistic grammar',

---

[12] See Ax (1986) 240–252; Schenkeveld (1990).
[13] On the divisions of grammar by Tauriscus and Asclepiades, see Blank (2000).

only different attitudes to the status of the principle of regularity in language) and deeply misleading.

In the nineteenth century, scholars developed a picture of the early development of grammar, including literary studies, centered on the clash of two schools: the Alexandrian 'grammarians', starting with Zenodotus and Aristophanes of Byzantium in the third century, and reaching a zenith with Aristarchus of Samothrace and his pupils in the second; and the Pergamene 'critics' founded by Crates of Mallos, a contemporary of Aristarchus.[14] This picture was based on the presentation by Varro, in his *On the Latin Language* VIII–X, of sets of arguments for and against resolving questions of grammatical usage (e.g., which of two possible forms of the genitive of a particular noun should be used) by choosing forms that are 'analogous' – that is, 'similar' – to those of words that are themselves arguably 'similar' in relevant ways to words whose forms are agreed upon, as opposed to forms that are 'dissimilar' to such analogous forms ('anomalous'). Varro cites Crates as arguing against Aristarchus and analogy (VIII 63–5, 68–9; IX 2) and as relying on Chrysippus, who (as we saw previously) had spoken of 'anomalies' in the relation between names and what they designate. Further, because Crates[15] is known to have studied with Chrysippus' student Diogenes of Babylon, and because he interpreted the Homeric poems in accordance with Stoic physics, scholars assumed that Crates' school had 'anomalist' doctrines which were derived from the Stoics.

This view cannot be adopted, however. Varro himself had already pointed out (IX 3) that Aristarchus did not want to recommend the use of 'analogical' forms which common usage would abhor. The extreme 'anomalist' position, that there are no regularities in language, would be equally implausible, especially for a Stoic, since that school viewed language as a manifestation of the divine reason. We do not know whether, besides the semantic anomalies noted by Chrysippus, the Stoics actually spoke about formal irregularities as well, but if they did, they can only have pointed to them against the overwhelming background of the logical and regular nature of language. The 'analogy-anomaly controversy' is rather part of a much larger ancient dispute between rationalists and empiricists, in this

---

[14] For details and bibliography, see Fehling (1956–1957) and Blank (1982, 1994).
[15] See the forthcoming edition of the fragments of Crates by M. Broggiato. On his poetic theory, see Janko (2000).

case over the character and use of linguistic rules: should one govern one's usage with reference to rules purporting to derive from an
understanding of the nature of language, or rather by observing the
usage of others in relevant geographical, social, and technical contexts? Sextus Empiricus (*M* I) clearly argues for the latter, and in so
doing summarizes the 'anomalist' case.

As the Stoics and Crates will evidently have been on the rationalist side of this debate, there can be no question of opposing a Stoic or
'philosophical' Pergamene anomalist grammar to a 'technical' grammatical school, perhaps influenced rather by Peripatetics, in Alexandria. Philologists, both Alexandrian and Pergamene, were interested
mostly in literary texts, the establishment of correct texts and their
interpretation. As a preliminary to such work, they had regard to
rules about linguistic usage and these were used, mainly by others,
for instruction in reading, writing, and rhetoric. In their work on
language, grammarians took over what they found useful from the
Peripatetics, and especially from the Stoics, applying it in their own
field and also modifying it as they saw fit. Accordingly, the assumption of a divergence among philologists over the relation of philosophy and grammar must not be allowed to obscure the indebtedness
of Alexandrian grammar and, later, of traditional grammar to Stoic
philosophy.

4. CASE STUDIES

Four particular areas have been selected, on grounds of their centrality to grammatical theory, to illustrate the relation between Stoic
and traditional grammar.

4.1 Syntax

It has already been remarked how Apollonius Dyscolus adopted a version of the Stoic conception of syntax, taking it to hold, not at the
level of words (i.e., word-forms as written or spoken entities), but
rather at the level of the 'intelligibles' (*noêta*) (*Synt.* I ii, p. 2.3ff.).[16]

---

[16] Cf. Baratin and Desbordes (1981) and Blank (1982); on Apollonius, see also Sluiter
(1990) and Ildefonse (1997), along with the new edition, translation, and commentary of Lallot (1997).

These can be identified as what modern linguistics would call the morphosyntactic properties of word-forms (*phônai, lexeis*), such as case, number, gender, voice, and mood, and, where relevant, their semantic and functional properties (e.g., the syntax of adverbs or certain kinds of verbs and pronouns). Further, syntactic relations are, strictly speaking, always correct or 'congruent' (*katallêla*), inconcinnities or solecisms occurring only at the level of expressions or word-forms; what is more, they can be shown to be 'abnormalities' (*pathê*) departing in a rule-governed and rationally explicable way from the correctly formed *logos* isomorphic with the noetic structure.

It is highly plausible that the distinction between imperfect linguistic forms and perfect intelligible structures is again borrowed from Stoic linguistic theory, which assigned such semantic and structural defects of language as ambiguity and solecism to the level of articulate utterance (*lexis*) or discourse (*logos*); in contrast, non-atomic *lekta* such as propositions, questions, or commands are always perfectly formed constructs from the basic building blocks of predicates and cases (and other elements too, such as conjunctions). The Stoic definition of 'solecism' (see Section 2.2) suggests a rational, rule-governed notion of syntax, distinguished by its internal 'congruity', rather than appeal to usage or authority to explain and justify what is taken to be syntactically correct and to outlaw what is not. But it must be admitted that little is known of the general criteria of Hellenism admitted by the Stoa (the grammatical orthodoxy established four or five: analogy, which sometimes includes etymology, history, usage, and authority). Apollonius apparently combined this distinction with the method of 'pathology' (the identification and classification of *pathê*) familiar from the older discipline of orthography to construct his own characteristic procedure for demonstrating the basic rationality of language. Other grammarians tended to take the basic unit of grammatical analysis to be an item on the level of expression, *viz.* the complete *logos* or sentence, consisting of parts of speech (*merê tou logou*) or words (*lexeis*) (e.g., DT Sch. Mel. 57.12ff.), but traces of the Stoic view can perhaps be found (e.g., DT Sch. Vat. 211.27ff., Marc. 354.7f.).

Another, less welcome, legacy of Stoic syntactic theory seems to be the exclusive focus on syntax as grouping (in particular, the grouping of a case and a predicate to form a proposition). The limitations of this conception of syntax can be seen, for example, in the two surviving Stoic classifications of ambiguity types (Galen *De sophismatis* Ch. 4 Kalbfleisch, XIV 591.1ff. Kühn; Theon *Prog.* 81.30ff.). Both contain a category for expressions whose 'significant parts' (roughly, parts of speech: see Section 4.2) can be variously grouped to produce sentences with different meanings, but neither can easily accommodate ambiguities where what is responsible for the multiplicity of possible meanings is the multiplicity of grammatical relations into which two (or more) parts can enter: their entering into some sort of syntactic grouping is not at issue. Thus, in the Greek sentence *touto horâi*, 'this one sees', what is unclear is (using the terminology of traditional grammar) whether *this one* is the subject or the object of the verb. Here a Stoic could identify *this one* either (1) as a nominative case grouped with a 'direct' (*orthê*; roughly, transitive) 'sub-predicate' (literally 'less-than-predicate'; i.e., the verbal portion of the predicate lacking the oblique case required to make a predicate), or (2) as an accusative case grouped with the same sub-predicate to form a predicate, which in turn needs syntactic association with a nominative to make a proposition. But although such analysis is clearly possible in Stoic terms, what is striking is that no room is made for its application in the lists of ambiguity kinds; indeed, the notion of governance, which was to become so central to traditional grammatical analysis, to all appearances has no part in Stoic grammatical theory, although a rough equivalent in logic (e.g., the relation between a negative and a proposition) was well established.

This example does show, however, that the notions of transitivity and intransitivity were, in some form, familiar to Stoic grammatical theorists, who (to simplify the rather difficult sources) appear to have distinguished between 'direct' (*ortha* = transitive), 'reversed' (= passive, *huptia*), and 'neutral' (*oudetera* = intransitive) predicates or sub-predicates, as well as 'reflexive' (*antipeponthota*) ones corresponding to what professional grammarians called 'middle' (*mesa*) verb forms (DL VII 64). The concept of the 'passing over' of the action signified by a verb to another 'person' in a syntactic grouping (or to the same person in 'middle' constructions) was to become a fixture in grammar, such verbs being typically designated 'active' (*energêtika*, *drastika*; e.g., DT Sch. Lond. 548.34ff.), although subject/object syntax was not an ancient 'discovery'. It has been argued that these distinctions among predicates originally reflected the distinctions of Stoic aitiological theory; but evidence for systematic correlation is obscure and controversial – unfortunately so, since clearer understanding of the philosophical underpinnings of Stoic work in the field would greatly assist accurate estimation of what did and did not survive of it into grammar outside Stoicism.

4.2 The Parts of Speech

According to our main sources, Stoics identified at first four, later five, and still later six, parts of speech (*merê tou logou*), as opposed to the later standard eight (e.g., DT 23.1f., DT Sch. 354.4f.). Surviving definitions are strongly semantic and/or functional, but with some formal elements. Of the single original category of noun, two types were distinguished by Chrysippus, each signifying a different type of quality (qualities being corporeals, according to Stoic metaphysics): the proper name (*onoma*), signifying particular qualities, and the appellative (*prosêgoria*), common ones. This distinction was rejected by professional grammarians, who preferred one between the 'general' (*koinon*) and the 'particular' (*idion*) nominal (e.g., DT 23.2f., 24.4f.; DT Sch. Mel. 58. 21ff.). The verb (*rhêma*) was, by some, defined as 'not inflecting for case' (*aptôta*) as well as signifying (parts of) predicates. The conjunction (*sundesmos*) is also uninflected, and serves to combine other parts of speech: a puzzling definition, since known uses of conjunctions are to combine complete *lekta* (e.g., the conjunction *if* combines propositions to form a conditional proposition). Further, it remains unclear whether conjunctions have their own proper significations at the level of the *lekton*; are regarded as significant, not in isolation, but rather because of the contribution they make to the meanings of sentences; or are to be classed as functional, not semantic, parts of speech. The article (*arthron*), which does inflect for case, was subdivided into the 'definite (*hôrismenon*) article' – what came to be called the pronoun (*antônumia*) – and the 'indefinite (*aoriston, aoristôdes*) article', which corresponds to the definite article of traditional grammar (Apollonius *Pr.* 5.13ff., DT Sch. Marc. p. 356. 12f.). The last part of speech, the 'mean' (*mesotês*) may be the adverb (cf. DT 74.3; DT Sch. Heliod. 30.2ff., Vat. 75.5ff.), but other sources report that participles (*metochai*) were classed with nominals or verbs, adverbs (*epirrhêmata*) with verbs, and prepositions as conjunctions.

The puzzle is intensified by the report just alluded to that conjunctions can combine complete *lekta*, as if conjunctions themselves belong to that level, rather than to the level of the signifying *logos*. They are as puzzling in this regard as are cases (see Section 4.3), some of which are 'demonstrative' (*deiktikai*) (e.g., this [male] one [*houtos*]), these apparently being identical with or signified by demonstrative and (some) personal pronouns. The grammarians' pronouns are, roughly speaking, Stoic definite articles. In our principal source here, Diogenes Laertius VII 58, definite articles are characterised in purely formal and functional terms (as distinguishing number and gender of proper names), a definition which, as it stands, is plainly unsatisfactory and, furthermore, is at odds with the Stoics' having labeled the 'definite' article 'indefinite' because of its generalising implication (e.g., 'The walking person moves' is equivalent to 'Whoever walks, moves'; cf. Apollonius *Synt.* I 111, p. 94.11–13. II 32, p. 149.8ff.). Puzzlingly, this is to ignore or overlook the anaphoric use of definite articles perfectly familiar to later grammarians. Apollonius himself favours a semantic definition (a pronoun signifies the being of something, without its qualities), which may have Stoic origins.

A comparable disagreement divides Stoic and non-Stoic grammatical theory over the proper noun (*onoma*) and the common noun or appellative (*prosêgoria*). Chrysippus seems to have been the first to treat these as separate parts of speech (DL VII 57f.), primarily for semantic reasons, although formal considerations were also appealed to (DT Sch. Vat. 214.18ff.); such formal/semantic isomorphism will have characterised language's pristine state. The division was rejected by the grammatical tradition, which did, however, accept the Stoics' inclusion in a single category – that of the 'appellative' – of what traditional grammar would come to call common nouns and adjectives.

4.3 Cases and Morphosyntactic Properties

It is clear that Stoics, as compared with Aristotle (*Poetics* 1457a18ff.; *Rhetoric* 1364b34f., *Topics* 114a34ff.), narrowed considerably the scope of the technical term 'case' (*ptôsis*); as in non-Stoic grammar, it is used only in connection with nominals. But beyond that basic starting point, scholarly disagreement about the Stoic view(s) is rife. An important preliminary is that Stoic metaphysics imposed a sharp distinction between physical objects, which 'exist' (einai) on the one hand, and incorporeals on the other, which merely 'subsist' (huphistanai); that is, depend for their being on corporeal individuals (as lekta 'subsist in accordance with' rational impressions).[17] Accordingly, a sharp cut-off point must hold between those material objects which are words (and their written representations) and the incorporeal meanings of sentences, and of at least some sentence parts. However, and rather oddly, our sources do not always clearly indicate the ontological status of certain key items, such as, and in particular, the 'cases' which go to constitute (certain kinds of) predicates as well as propositions and (presumably) other complete lekta. Scholars are divided as to whether cases are (1) another kind of incomplete lekton complementing the predicate (which is suggested by their figuring in Diogenes Laertius' report of the 'significations' part of Stoic dialectic, and by their combining with predicates [VII 64]); (2) the qualities which are the significations of proper names and appellatives (whether these qualities should be classed as corporeal or incorporeal is the object of a further dispute); and (3) words – that is, words in certain forms: just as, for Stoics, properties of bodies are simply reducible to those bodies in certain states, so cases, being forms and hence properties of words, will be reducible to those words, which are physical objects formally differentiated according as their role in a sentence changes. For the grammarians generally, no such metaphysical constraints operate; and here a gap could well have opened up between them and Stoic grammarians. Thus Apollonius seems to have plumped for something like (3), to judge by his definition of the case, whereas a commentator on Dionysius Thrax states that 'the five cases belong to the meanings, not to the word-forms', citing in support the variety of the latter as opposed to the singleness of the former (DT Sch. Lond. 551.10ff.).

Stoic grammar does not seem to have recognised a 'vocative' (klêtikê) case (cf. DL VII 63 with, e.g., DT 31.5–7, DT Sch. Marc. 384.16ff.), even though Stoic dialectic identified a complete sayable used for 'addressing' (prosagoreutikon) which could comprise cases alone, without a predicate (DL VII 67). Stoic influence can, however, be felt in the general acceptance of the thesis that the nominative

---

[17] DL VII 63. See Ch. 8, Brunschwig, in this volume.

case, called by Stoics the 'direct' (*orthê*, DL VII 64; so also DT 31.5) and by other grammarians also the 'straight' (*eutheia*) or 'nominative' case is itself a case (ct. Aristotle *Int.* 16a31-b5). The motivation reported for the Stoic position is confused and especially hard to interpret (Ammonius *Int.* 42.30ff.; cf. DT Sch. Marc. 383.5ff.), but may reflect what for moderns would be a distinction between the pragmatic and the semantic: although a nominative is formally indistinguishable from its decontextualised nominal, its being used in the context of a sentence by a particular speaker to refer intentionally to an object (to 'the thought of it we have in the soul', Amm. *Int.* 43.10f.) sets it apart from the nominal itself, the enduring semantic properties of which have other origins, perhaps in the larger community of speakers. But this is largely speculative.

Interpretation of this and other Stoic texts is not served by what look to be deficiencies in the Stoic semantic apparatus, which – to judge by available evidence – may well have failed to distinguish systematically among modes of meaning, and in particular to separate (features of) linguistic items having lexical meaning and referring to corporeals or their properties or states on the one hand, from, on the other, ones signifying non-corporeal items (*lekta*) or contributing syntactically (as with conjunctions) or in virtue of their form (e.g., by indicating tense, mood, case) to the semantic content of an entire expression. Most importantly for present purposes, no comprehensive analysis seems to have been developed of the relation between a word(-form), a case (if a case is not a word or word-form), or a predicate, and their morphosyntactic properties (if any). As noted, for the Stoic grammarian syntactic (in)congruity must be at least to some extent a matter of (mis)matches of parts of sayables, but it is unclear if the relevant properties – say, a singular third-person predicate's indicative mood and present tense; perhaps a case's being singular and nominative – are formally distinguished at the level of the *lekton* as they are at the linguistic level and, if not, whether their various contributions to the semantic whole are conceived of differently. Predicate classification certainly requires formal distinctions between cases (DL VII 64: e.g., 'direct' sub-predicates require an oblique case to form a complete predicate; passive predicates are construed with the 'passive particle', i.e., the preposition 'by' [*hupo*] and, presumably, the genitive case).

There is indeed some evidence that the concept of 'implicature' ([*par*] *emphasis*) may have helped to distinguish lexical or referential from other sorts of meaning (as 'signify' [*sêmainein*] and 'denote' [*dêloun*] were used of appellatives and proper nouns, respectively [DL VII 58]). Thus, according to Chrysippus, 'habitual privatives' such as *shoeless* 'signify some implicature' (*paremphasis*) that the thing lacked habitually belongs to the thing which lacks it (Simplicius *In Ar. cat.* 395.12–14). Certain syllables constituting a word can also (fail to) 'implicate' local separation (Galen *PHP* II ii, 15.11ff., especially 16.1). Chrysippus wrote a work *On implicature*, which is classed with works *On the grammatical cases* and *On enunciations definite as regards the subject* (DL VII 192); his *Logical questions* uses *emphainein* for the 'revealing' of a sayable (col. XII 17; that the usage is not exclusively technical is shown by XI 29 [27 Marrone]), and also mentions 'things said implicitly (*paremphatikôs*) in relation to something else' (fr. iii 22f. [21 Marrone]). Definite articles in certain constructions 'implicate' a plurality of persons (Apollonius *Synt.* I 111, p. 94, 11–13, II 32, p. 149.8ff.); the Stoic provenance of the term in this context is highly probable, though not certain, just as it is in a report of the Stoic verbal tense system (DT Sch. Steph. 250.25ff.) which states that someone who uses a present-tense verb 'implicates' (*emphainei*) that his action extends into the past and the future, the same being true, *mutatis mutandis*, of imperfects.

That Apollonius Dyscolus also employs the 'implicature' terminology – and against the background of an apparently vague and unsystematised semantic vocabulary – perhaps argues Stoic influence in this area too. Thus, the distinction between the 'implicature' by possessive pronouns of possessions as well as of possessor(s) (*Synt.* III 112, p. 366.5ff.) may have its origin in the type of problem discussed in *Logical questions* col. VI (Is 'our' [*hêmeteros*] to be classed as singular or as plural?). The labeling of the infinitive as the verb 'lacking implicature' (*aparemphaton*) – that is, of person and mood though not of tense or voice (e.g., *Synt.* III 60, p. 326.1f.) – may perhaps be Stoic in origin (though other sources are against it [cf. Apollonius *Synt.* I 50, p. 44.14ff.; Clement *Strom.* VIII ix 26.4f.). But unfortunately we can only speculate that the Stoics took some word(-forms) to (fail to) 'implicate' gender (e.g., Apollonius Dyscolus *Pr.* 11.23, 28.14, 61.10) or number (*Synt.* II 152, p. 247.6), that the tenses 'implicate' differences of time (Dionysius of Halicarnassus *De compositione uerborum* VI 4), or that some prepositions 'implicate' a spatial relation (A.D. *Adv.* 204.19–23).

13 The Stoics and the Astronomical Sciences

In Stoicism, as in Epicureanism, an understanding of the physical place of humanity in the universe was an integral component of a system of thought underpinning each sect's ethical commitments. At the same time as these schools flourished, non-philosophical disciplines were evolving that laid claim to knowledge of parts of this subject: astronomy, which concerned the composition and regularity of the heavens in their own right; geography, which investigated the form and characteristics of the earth and its inhabited parts; and astrology, which asserted connections between the celestial motions and mundane life. The fundamental assumptions of these scientific disciplines were from the start so completely at odds with Epicurus' atomistic, aleatory cosmology that Epicureanism and the exact sciences were doomed to a relationship of mutual irrelevance so long as they coexisted. Between Stoicism and the sciences the possibilities of interaction were greater; though, as we shall see, there were limits to their readiness to embrace each other's approaches.

ASTRONOMY

The central matter of *astronomia* as it was commonly understood up to the Hellenistic period was the organization of the stars into their constellations and the association of their annual cycle of risings and settings with patterns of weather and human (mostly agricultural) activity.[1] But Eudoxus' astronomical works, which are known to us

---

[1] Goldstein and Bowen (1983). Many presentations of early Greek astronomy give disproportionate emphasis to the antecedents of Ptolemy's celestial mechanics; an exception is Dicks (1970). Fashion may have swung now too far the other way.

only through excerpts and secondhand reports, exemplified and indeed likely pioneered a considerable expansion of the science's scope: in addition to the traditional topics of constellations, weather patterns, and calendrical cycles, he investigated conceptual geometrical models that sought to account for the phenomena of the heavenly bodies and that could be interpreted as reflecting the physical nature of the cosmos.[2]

Eudoxus' modeling, which set the terms for subsequent Greek mathematical astronomy, operated at two levels. First, Eudoxus conceived of the basic frame of reference for the stars as a sphere, the *celestial sphere*, that surrounds and is concentric with a much smaller spherical (and stationary) earth. The celestial sphere revolves at a uniform rate, slightly faster than once in a day and night, on a polar axis. For an observer in the Mediterranean regions, this sphere is tilted so that its north end, the *north celestial pole*, is above the viewer's northern horizon and its south end, the *south celestial pole*, is invisible below the southern horizon (cf. Figure 1). As stars are carried about in the celestial sphere's revolution, they describe circular paths that may be entirely visible above the northern horizon, entirely invisible below the southern horizon, or divided by the horizon into visible and invisible segments – that is, these stars can be seen to rise and set. The points of the horizon due north and south of the observer trace out special circles on the celestial sphere, called the *arctic* and *antarctic circles*, that mark the boundaries separating those stars that rise and set from those that are always above or always below the horizon.[3] Other special circles are traced out by the points due east and west of the observer (the *celestial equator*, which bisects the celestial sphere), and the points of the horizon marking the northernmost and southernmost points of sunrise and sunset (the *northern* and *southern tropic circles*). The *ecliptic*, the annual path of the sun projected on the celestial sphere, is another circle, also bisecting the sphere but tilted with respect to the celestial equator, and tangent to the two tropic circles at opposite points. The properties of these circles and their relations, which determine the order and timings of risings and settings of stars and constellations, constituted

---

[2] Lasserre (1966).

[3] Note that the conventional Greek definition of the arctic and antarctic circles is different from the modern one, and that these circles vary in radius with different terrestrial latitudes of observation.

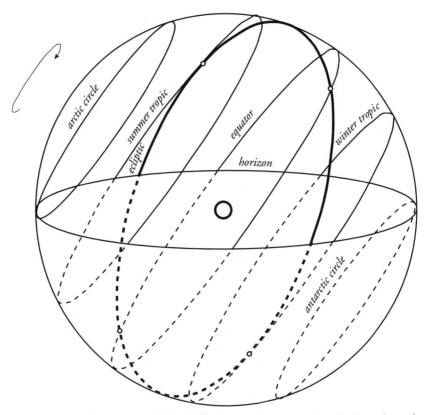

Fig. 1. The two-sphere model with the principal circles of the celestial sphere. The observer defining the horizon is assumed to be at the uppermost point of the terrestrial sphere at the centre of the model, and north is to the left.

a rather abstruse mathematical subfield within Greek astronomy called *spherics*; but the basic facts of the so-called two-sphere model and its principal circles were regarded as elements fundamental for beginners in astronomy and geography.

The second level of Eudoxus' modeling was to account for the phenomena of the sun, the moon, and the five planets visible to the naked eye (Mercury, Venus, Mars, Jupiter, and Saturn), which appear to rise and set with the rotation of the celestial sphere but manifestly have also a slower, independent motion. Eudoxus, according to the reports of Aristotle and Simplicius, explained their apparently complex motions by hypothesizing that each of these bodies was a visible object on the surface of one of a system of several (otherwise invisible) rotating spheres, each with its axis of rotation fixed on two diametrically opposite rotating points of the surface of the next sphere out, with the outermost sphere in each system either being the celestial sphere itself or a sphere having the same diurnal revolution. Although Eudoxus' systems of nested concentric spheres were known by the time of Hipparchus in the second century B.C. to be utterly inadequate to account for the phenomena, the underlying principle of employing combinations of uniform circular motions – though not necessarily concentric ones – became axiomatic in celestial mechanics in the tradition of Hipparchus and Ptolemy.

When Aristotle refers to astronomy (*astronomia* or *astrologia*), he generally has in mind this geometrical aspect of the science. From his allusions we can see that it also encompassed investigations, employing the resources of geometrical optics, of the sizes and shapes of the heavenly bodies – especially the sun and moon – and the causes of eclipses. On the other hand, the astronomy of the end of the fourth century and the beginning of the third has none of the concern with precise prediction of the phenomena (for example, by means of numerical tables) that is so conspicuous by the time of Ptolemy (second-century A.D.). From the beginning of the third-century B.C. we have the first known systematic, dated records of observations of the positions of the moon and planets, although we do not know for which application these observations were intended.

Although the *testimonia* for the earliest Stoics refer to doctrines of Zeno and Cleanthes about the material nature (fiery aether) of the heavens and the composition, sustenance, and intelligence of the heavenly bodies (SVF 1.115–122 and 1.506–513),[4] little of this cosmological speculation is properly astronomical. Diogenes Laertius (VII 145 = SVF 1.119) reports that Zeno, in his *On the Whole*, endorsed the astronomers' explanation of solar eclipses as caused by the moon's passing between us and the sun, and of lunar eclipses as caused by the moon's traversing the earth's shadow. Stobaeus (I 25.3 = SVF 1.120) attributes to him the banal observation that the sun and moon exhibit a second motion together with the diurnal rotation of the cosmos.

---

[4] To this extent their interests are like those of the *phusikoi* whom Aristotle contrasts with mathematical scientists in *Phys.* II 2.

More interesting is the knowledge, from Diogenes again (VII 174 = SVF 1.481), that among Cleanthes' writings was an attack on Aristarchus of Samos (fl. 280 B.C.). The target was presumably not Aristarchus' extant *On the Sizes and Distances of the Sun and Moon*, but rather the 'publications of certain hypotheses' (*hypothesiôn tinôn...graphas*) in which, Archimedes (*Arenarius* 4-6) informs us, 'he hypothesizes that the fixed stars and the sun remain unmoved, while the earth revolves about the sun along the circumference of a circle, [the sun] being situated in the middle of the course [*en mesôi tôi dromôi*], and the sphere of the fixed stars, being situated around the same centre as the sun, is so large that the circle along which the earth is hypothesized as revolving has such a ratio to the distance to the fixed stars as the centre of a sphere has to its surface.' Aristarchus' point, so far as we can infer from the report, was an astronomical application of a commonplace of geometrical optics: that if the eye is in motion, it perceives other objects as having the opposite motion. There is no way to tell whether he insisted on the truth of his heliocentric hypothesis or whether he considered physical aspects of the question; for example, why we do not feel that we are in motion, though it is a corollary of the hypothesis that the earth must spin on an axis daily as well as annually revolving around the sun? Nor do we know in what way Cleanthes approached the refutation of Aristarchus' hypothesis; there is merely Plutarch's anecdote that he 'thought that the Greeks ought to prosecute Aristarchus of Samos for impiety, on the grounds that he was moving the hearth of the cosmos, because the man tried to save the phenomena by hypothesizing that the heavens stand still, while the earth winds about along an inclined circle and at the same time spins on its own axis' (*De facie* 923a = SVF 1.500).

The poem *Phaenomena* by Aratus might seem to testify to the engagement of the early Stoa with technical astronomy. Aratus is said by one of his ancient biographers to have studied under Zeno, and his poem's opening (1-18) reflects the cosmolatry of Cleanthes.[5] But Aratus' scheme allowed him little scope for relating his subject to the physical teachings of his sect. For two thirds of its length, the *Phaenomena* is a versification of Eudoxus' book of the same title, which was a painstaking description of the imagined pictures

---

[5] For this and other Stoicizing elements in the *Phaenomena*, see Kidd (1997), 10-12.

of the constellations, specifying the stars that they comprise and their relative configurations. Although Eudoxus' work is lost, Hipparchus' extant polemical commentary *In Arati et Eudoxi Phaenomena* makes it clear how close the poet cleaved to his source. The final part of the poem, retailing weather signs, is mostly not astronomical and is only tenuously connected to the Eudoxian astronomy. This, in the hands of a later Stoic, could have been rich material for a discourse on causation and *sumpatheia*, but poetic expression furnishes the only substantial difference between Aratus' treatment of the weather signs and Theophrastus' *De signis*. The tale in the ancient biographies of Aratus that he versified the *Phaenomena* at the instigation of Antigonus Gonatas, though perhaps not true history, emblematizes the detachment of the work from Aratus' philosophical allegiance.

A genuinely Stoic presentation of astronomy is to be found in the much later treatise in two books by Cleomedes, traditionally known by the curious title *Kyklikê Theôria Meteôrôn* ('Theory, involving circles, of the things in the heavens'), though its latest editor prefers the terse *Meteôra*.[6] We know practically nothing about Cleomedes, and even his date is controverted. The latest author whom he cites – and he does so extensively – is Posidonius, and he has seen or heard criticisms of Posidonius' ideas; but no ancient author obliges us with a later chronological bound by citing Cleomedes. The best one can say is that his style is Imperial rather than Hellenistic, and that he deprecates the vogue for Epicureanism among 'the men of today, depraved by luxury and softness' (II 1), a complaint that would have lost its force as the sect of Epicurus waned after the end of the second century of our era.[7] At any rate, the close parallels in content and emphasis between Cleomedes and the much terser review of Stoic opinions on astronomy in Diogenes Laertius (VII 140–146) certify him as a good representative of post-Posidonian consensus on the subject.

---

[6] Todd (1985).

[7] Neugebauer (1964), 418 n. 1, and (1975), 2.960, dated Cleomedes to within a half-century of A.D. 370 on the assumption that the positions of the stars Aldebaran and Antares given in 1.11 are tropical longitudes derived from Ptolemy's star catalogue and corrected for precession. Since Cleomedes' philosophical biases argue strongly against such a late date, it would appear that the stellar longitudes are sidereal and useless for purposes of dating. See Neugebauer (1975), 3.960–961, for circumstantial evidence suggesting that Cleomedes lived in the vicinity of the Hellespont.

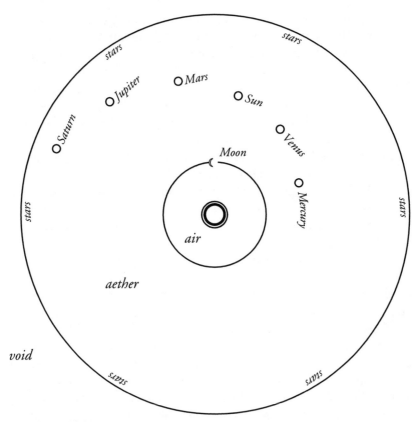

Fig. 2. The cosmology of Cleomedes (not drawn to scale). The innermost spheres are composed of earth and water.

Cleomedes' order of presentation of topics is not always coherent, and there are duplications of material between the two books; gradually, however, the reader assembles a picture of the structure of the cosmos and its relation to the celestial phenomena. The basic cosmology obviously owes much to Aristotle, although the points of divergence are sharply indicated (cf. Figure 2). The material cosmos is a finite spherical plenum within an infinite void (I 1). It is stratified according to its constituent elements: at the centre, a terrestrial globe of earth surrounded by water; surrounding this, a spherical shell of air; and enclosing all, a shell of aether, which is equated with rarefied fire. The shell of aether is the heavens, and it rotates around the earth, providing a concrete instantiation of the celestial sphere. Cleomedes introduces the principal circles of the celestial sphere (I 2), but discusses them chiefly in relation to geographical questions to which we will return in the last part of this chapter.

It is in the treatment of the visible heavenly bodies that the difference between Cleomedes' preoccupations and those of the astronomers is most evident: chiefly, he is vague when it comes to detailed description and mathematical modeling of the phenomena, especially of the planets, whereas he has much to say about the physical constitution of the heavenly bodies. The fixed stars are borne about the earth by the revolution of the aetherial heavens, and are nearest to the periphery of the cosmos. The planets, including the sun and moon, also revolve daily as part of the heavens, but each also has its own motion which is characterized as *prohairetikê*, 'deliberately chosen,' as befits the intellective character attributed to them by the Stoics. The relative distances of the planets can be estimated on the hypothesis that their actual speeds of voluntary motion are equal, so that the periods of their revolutions about the zodiacal belt are proportional to their remoteness from us (II 1). (The same hypothesis, adopted with varying degrees of strictness, was employed by many writers on astronomy from Aristotle, *De caelo* II 10, on.) Hence, one obtains, from outermost to innermost, the sequence Saturn, Jupiter, Mars, sun, moon – Venus and Mercury, having the same average period of revolution as the sun, are placed between it and the moon. The moon is in fact right at the interface between the shells of aether and air, and unlike the other bodies, it is a composite of aether and air, for which reason it perhaps moves slower.

Cleomedes' concern with the distances of the heavenly bodies is motivated by polemic. Epicurus' pronouncement that the sun is only 'as big as it appears' – usually glossed as meaning only a foot in diameter – was the most notorious of his many strange explanations of the phenomena; it is perhaps as a rejoinder to certain of the explanations, and to the antiscientific epistemology that they were meant to exemplify, that we find in reports of the Stoics as far back as Zeno himself expositions of how the circumstances under which eclipses have or have not been observed indicate their true causes. In the opening chapters of Cleomedes' second book, the attack on Epicurus is explicit, descending for long stretches into coarse invective. Nevertheless, he finds room for scientific arguments, due at least in part to Posidonius, leading to values for the actual distances and sizes of the sun, moon, and the other heavenly bodies in terms of the size of the terrestrial globe and in mundane units of distance (stades).

Judged by the standards of contemporary Greek mathematical astronomy, these Posidonian arguments are rather crude. Aristarchus had long before shown in his book *On the Sizes and Distances* how in principle a small number of empirically derived facts about the apparent sizes of the sun and moon and about eclipses could mathematically determine their diameters and distances from the earth; in the third quarter of the second-century B.C., Hipparchus had developed such techniques to the point of measuring the moon's distance by two alternative methods to within 30 and 17 percent of the truth.[8] Ignoring such refinements, Cleomedes simply assumes in the best of his several arguments on this topic (II 1) that the earth's shadow at the distance of the moon is the same in breadth as the earth itself (which amounts to making the sun equal in size to the earth), and that the moon is half the breadth of the shadow. The resulting size and distance of the moon far exceed those found by Hipparchus, but Cleomedes' method can be explained in a few non-technical lines. If he is representative of his sect, it would appear that the Stoics preferred a multiplicity of easily understood arguments,[9] none of which individually might withstand expert scrutiny, to a sustained mathematical deduction the results of which most readers would have to accept on trust.

Cleomedes has next to no interest in celestial mechanics: the only occasion when he indicates the geometrical character of the 'deliberately chosen' motion of the heavenly bodies is when, in I 6, he explains the unequal lengths of the time intervals between the solstices and equinoxes as due to the sun's traveling along a circle that is not concentric with the cosmos. Hipparchus' influence is evident here, but scarcely anywhere else.[10] There may be more to Cleomedes' avoidance of this topic than mere shying away from the mathematics. To the extent that models built on the principle of uniform

[8] Toomer (1975).

[9] Compare Seneca's approach in the *NQ* (Inwood [2002] and Gill, Ch. 2, this volume). Like Cleomedes, Seneca's work engages critically with Posidonius (though also with some of his followers); Seneca's works also contain some characteristically polemical attacks on Epicurean hedonism.

[10] Hipparchus' solar model was designed to fit the lengths of spring and summer cited by Cleomedes, and used interchangeably an eccentric orbit or an epicyclic model; cf. Ptolemy, *Almagest* III 1 and III 4, and Theon of Smyrna ed. Hiller, 151–72.

circular motion successfully accounted for the phenomena, their unchanging radii and periodicities implied an immutability in the matter of the heavens that sat more comfortably with Platonist or Peripatetic cosmology, according to which the material of the heavens behaves utterly unlike that of our terrestrial environment, than with Stoic cosmology with its stars fed by the exhalations of the world's oceans.

A way was open for reconciling the periodicities of the sun, moon, and planets with the universal conflagration, or *ekpurôsis*, that the Stoics believed to mark the end and beginning of the long repetitious cycles of the cosmos' life and death. A few doxographical texts (SVF 2.596, 599, 625) link the *ekpurôsis* to a 'great year,' a tremendously long constant interval supposedly containing exact whole numbers of all the periods of the heavenly bodies, so that each should simultaneously return to its original position at the end of the great year. The pursuit of such a common periodicity would appear to be valueless from a purely astronomical point of view. Yet the concept is attested in an enigmatic astronomical inscription of the first-century B.C. from Keskinto on Rhodes, and its prevalence in Indian astronomy may be attributable to the partial dependence of the Indian tradition on lost Greek sources.[11]

ASTRAL DIVINATION AND ASTROLOGY

It is a commonplace that the Stoics had a great affinity for astrology.[12] The extent to which this is true depends on what one understands 'astrology' to mean. In the broadest sense, the subject can be defined, more or less as Ptolemy defines it in the *Tetrabiblos* (I 1–3), as a science concerned with relations between circumstances in the heavens and circumstances in the terrestrial environment. In historical terms this would cover three divinatory traditions known to the classical world: first, the native Greek tradition of correlating observable periodic phenomena such as the risings and settings of constellations and the moon's phases with weather and agricultural

---

[11] On the Keskinto Inscription and its possible relation to Indian astronomy, see Neugebauer (1975), 3.698–705. Hahm (1977), 185–99, gives a sensible discussion of the connection between the great year and Stoic *ekpurôsis*. Van der Waerden (1952) is highly speculative and should be used with caution.

[12] A well-balanced corrective is Long (1982).

cycles; second, the Near Eastern practice of interpreting supposedly ominous phenomena in the heavens as signs of imminent mundane events; and third, the classical astrology of the late Hellenistic and Roman periods, in which predictions are based on the instantaneous positions of the heavenly bodies in the zodiac and the relative configuration of the zodiac and the horizon at a particular place. Historians of astrology often restrict the term to this last tradition and its medieval and modern continuation.

Unlike the other two varieties of astral divination, the stream concerned with weather and agriculture was traditionally regarded as part of astronomy, and elements of it can be traced as far back as Hesiod's *Works and Days*. In part it was an accumulation of traditional lore – such, presumably, are the various precepts for the appropriate stages of the lunar month in which to carry out specific tasks – but the weather calendars (*parapêgmata*) of the late Hellenistic and Roman periods largely consist of information attributed to specific astronomers, such as Eudoxus and Hipparchus, concerning annual weather patterns and dates of appearance and disappearance of stars. Although it is not known what rationale the practitioners of this tradition had for the validity of what they were doing, it is clear that the observable astronomical phenomena did not merely play a time-keeping role, but were thought to be genuine *signs* of weather changes. As such, they invited Stoic interpretation as a manifest instance of *sumpatheia*; and indeed Sextus Empiricus (*M* IX 79) presents the following as Stoic arguments for the unity of the cosmos as a single body:

For according to the waxings and wanings of the moon many terrestrial and aquatic animals wane and wax, and low and high tides occur about certain parts of the sea; and likewise at certain risings and settings of the stars, changes of the environment and complicated reversals in the air happen, sometimes for the better, sometimes for the worse.

It is surprising that we do not have more allusions in our sources for Stoic physics to the commonly accepted connection between the stars and the weather.

Astral omens were only a part of the vast omen literature of ancient Mesopotamia, according to which the relationship between omen and outcome (*protasis* and *apodosis* in an omen text) had a religious frame of reference: ominous occurrences were signals sent by the gods as a warning of coming circumstances or events.[13] Until well into the first millennium B.C., the apodoses of astral omens were uniformly of national rather than private significance, and the protases were triggered immediately by the sighting of an anomalous phenomenon in the sky. At the end of the fifth century appear the first so-called Babylonian horoscopes (or better, proto-horoscopes), records of astral phenomena falling close in time to the birth of an individual.[14] These documents superficially resemble the horoscopes of later Greco-Roman astrology, but the interpretative framework to which they belonged was still that of the omen texts, with a one-to-one correlation of phenomenon to prediction. However, the pertinent omen texts now refer to the life and character of the individual born at the time of the ominous event.

Cicero cites Eudoxus as having counseled scepticism about the predictions that the 'Chaldeans' made about the lives of individuals from their days of birth (*Div.* II 87), so that it would seem that some knowledge of Mesopotamian birth omens was known in the Greek world already in the fourth-century B.C. Hence it is quite plausible that when Cicero (*Fat.* 12) gives as an instance of a conditional that Chrysippus debated in relation to the certainty of future events the statement, 'If someone is born when Sirius is rising, he will not die at sea,' there is a reflection of Babylonian birth omens such as the attested text, 'The place of Cancer: death in the ocean.'[15] The 'astrology' that – again, according to Cicero (*Div.* II 87–97) – Diogenes of Babylon did not wholly accept and that Panaetius rejected must also have been of this sort, since they lived too early to have known true classical horoscopy. In this passage Cicero remarks that Panaetius was exceptional among the Stoics for his disbelief in the validity of astral birth omens. With Posidonius we seem to return to a less reserved stance with respect to them.[16]

Classical astrology apparently made its first appearance no earlier than the end of the second-century B.C., perhaps in Egypt.[17] Its inventor, whose identity is unknown, combined elements of Mesopotamian divination with a Greek cosmology to obtain a

[13] Rochberg-Halton (1988), 8–17.
[14] Rochberg (1998).
[15] Pingree (1997), 23–24.
[16] Augustine, *De civitate Dei* V 2 and V 5; Cicero, *Fat.* 5–6.
[17] Pingree (1997), 26–29.

system of prediction that was more general in scope, more flexible in application, and vastly more complicated than the birth omens. To the Babylonian idea of interpreting the positions in the zodiac occupied by the heavenly bodies at a particular time (e.g., the moment of conception or birth), classical astrology added the two-sphere model, so that the manner in which the ecliptic circle, treated as a mathematical idealization of the zodiac, is instantaneously divided by the horizon and meridian planes for a particular locality (e.g., the place of conception or birth) came to be of fundamental importance. The very word 'horoscope' refers properly to the hour-indicating point (horoskopos) of the ecliptic that is rising at the eastern horizon at the moment in question, a datum always prominently listed in astrological nativities.

The rationale of this astrology was explicitly physical: in such astrological texts as discuss such matters, the heavenly bodies are regarded as standing in a cause-and-effect relationship with the mundane world. To the extent that one can associate the underlying cosmology with any particular philosophical school, it is Aristotelian, insofar as it presumes that the heavens are absolutely regular, predictable, and uninfluenced by the world below.[18] The mechanism by which the heavenly bodies affect the sublunary world is less clear-cut. The technical term for this influence is aporrhoia, 'flow away,' a term suggestive of a material emanation; but the astrologers write of the aporrhoiai as if they are something qualitative that goes out from heavenly matter into terrestrial matter, thereby altering it.[19] Interestingly, the aporrhoiai are sometimes associated with a Stoicizing appeal to sumpatheia between the heavenly bodies and things on the earth. Thus, Sextus Empiricus (M V 4) asserts as a hypothesis of the 'Chaldeans' (by which he means the casters of horoscopes) that 'the things on the earth have sumpatheia with the things in the heavens and they are continually renewed in accordance with the aporrhoiai from them'. The linkage of aporrhoia with sumpatheia

---

[18] The physical interpretation of astrology appears in its most 'pure' Peripatetic form in Ptolemy's Tetrabiblos; but it needs to be remembered that Ptolemy approached astrology with a sophisticated philosophical grounding (cf. the opening chapters of the Harmonics) such as few actual practitioners of astrology can have possessed.

[19] For example, Vettius Valens IX 8, ed. Pingree 330: 'For nature, by sending the aporrhoiai into us from the immortal elements, works [in us] a cosmic compounding and gently crafts all things without mixture and without complexity....'

may in fact have originated in intellectual circles outside astrology; for Geminus (mid-first-century B.C.), whose familiarity with astrology extended little beyond the Babylonian-style birth omens, argues in a context that has nothing to do with astrology that, whereas the sun and moon manifestly have a power (*dunamis*) that brings about changes in mundane objects that have *sumpatheia* with them, no *sumpatheia* or *aporrhoia* link things on the earth to the fixed stars (*Isagôgê* 17.15–17).[20]

Astrologers were divided on the question of determinism. One school of thought, exemplified by Vettius Valens (late second-century A.D.), held that the lives of individuals are strictly destined by the agency of the heavenly bodies, in such a way that astrological science, when not limited by the imperfections of astronomical theory, can infallibly forecast all details of each life. Ptolemy, on the other hand, maintains that the influence of the heavenly bodies is only one among the powers affecting terrestrial conditions, and that astrology becomes less exact and reliable as the object of interest shifts from entire geographical regions to the individual (*Tetrabiblos* I 2–3). Astrological determinism may have been an offshoot of Stoic thought on the subject – it is not easy to see where else it could have come from – but it was less subtle in that it asserted that the mechanism of fate was a rigid and *knowable* chain of efficient causes, so that the astrologer could read the future with the help of a set of astronomical tables and the enlightenment of an inherited tradition of astrological wisdom. Tacitus reports that the Stoics were aware of this difference, and repudiated astrological determinism (*Annals* VI 22).[21]

The first-century A.D. poem of Manilius presents a surprisingly technical survey of the principles of astrology within an openly Stoic frame, but the union of the two systems of thought does not bear close examination. Manilius evades all serious conflict of ideas by relegating his invocations of Stoic cosmic theology to the prefaces, in passages that scarcely hint at astrology. The long essay on fate that opens the fourth book of the poem, conversely, is free of philosophical content.

[20] The only astrological material in Geminus' *Isagoge* is in the second chapter, where doctrines 'of the Chaldeans' about weather patterns and *sumpatheiai* between people born under the influence of certain pairings of zodiacal signs look like genuine Babylonian concepts under a philosophical veneer. For his date, see Jones (1999).

[21] Long (1982), 171.

Stoic authors of the Imperial period scarcely mention astrology, though it was in the second and third centuries that it reached its peak of popularity. There was seemingly no interest within the school in discussing a form of divination that came with a distinct causal rationale of its own.

GEOGRAPHY

Geography was not an autonomous science with a well-defined subject matter in Greco-Roman antiquity. From the fourth-century B.C., systematic thought about the earth and its inhabited parts radiated from the focal, generally accepted fact that the earth is a sphere, which is of course essential to the two-sphere model. The model predicted that the phenomena of the heavens would vary depending on the observer's location, and it could contribute to physical explanations of the various climatic, environmental, and anthropological conditions encountered or reported in different regions.

What is often characterized as the 'scientific' geographical literature of the Hellenistic and Roman periods was almost wholly concerned with determining positional relationships between places in the interests of cartography. This tradition begins with Eratosthenes in the middle of the third-century B.C., whose treatise on drawing the map of the world is known to us primarily from references in Strabo. Eratosthenes' geography starts off as an offshoot of astronomy, since he knew how to calculate the latitude of a locality from the ratio of an upright stick to its shadow as observed at noon on an equinox or solstice. Famously, he combined this kind of information with a round estimate of the north-south distance between Alexandria and Syene (Aswan) to arrive at a measurement of the circumference of the globe in land units (stades), and this enabled him to merge his measured latitudes with a wide range of other kinds of evidence to establish the outlines of a map of the known world. The lost geographical writings of Hipparchus and Marinus of Tyre and the extant *Geography* of Ptolemy continued this cartographic tradition.

The Stoic geographers *par excellence* are Posidonius[22] and Strabo. Posidonius' interest in geographical matters is attested by several later authors, including Cleomedes, Pliny the Elder, and most

---

[22] The relevant fragments are collected in Edelstein-Kidd (1972, etc.).

valuably Strabo, who gives us a detailed critical summary of parts of Posidonius' treatise *Ōkeanos*.[23] Posidonius began where the mathematical geographers did, with the sphericity of the earth and the astronomical measurement of its size.[24] But his preoccupations thereafter diverge from theirs: where the mathematical geographers investigated climatic and astronomical phenomena as a means to determining geographical positions, Posidonius reversed the priorities by making a special object of study of climatic zones, latitudinal belts inside which the climatic conditions were more or less uniform ('scorched,' 'chilled,' 'temperate') in accordance with their physical situation relative to the sun's revolutions along the ecliptic circle.[25]

Posidonius' earth is above all a physical, not just a geometrical, entity, affected by the heavens as is manifested by the climatic zones, the seasons, and the tides, but also reciprocally affecting the heavens since the abundance of seas in the 'scorched' zone supplies the exhalations that feed the stars and planets.[26] It is dynamic, subject to local upheavals and subsidences over long intervals of time.[27] And it not only provides a habitation for humanity, but through its climatic variations it also physically determines the differences in appearance, character, and even intellectual activity between different peoples.[28]

In contrast to Posidonius, Strabo's Stoicism does not lead him deeply into considerations of the physical basis of the human environment.[29] Although in his two books of general introduction he reviews the fundamentals of the two-sphere model, mathematical geography, and the climatic zones, these concepts are given little

---

[23] Fragment 49 Edelstein-Kidd. The character of Posidonius' geographical writings is discussed in detail by Clarke (1999), 129–192.

[24] Cleomedes I 7 is our principal source for both Eratosthenes' procedure and Posidonius', which was an adaptation of it. Posidonius seems to have wavered on the actual value of the earth's circumference, since the figure in Cleomedes (240,000 stades, close to Eratosthenes' 252,000) is different from that ascribed to him by Strabo at II 2.2 and II 3.6 (180,000 stades).

[25] There are inconsistencies between Strabo's (II 1.2–II 3.3) and Cleomedes' (I 4) reports of the details of Posidonius' zone theory; perhaps he revised his opinions in different works.

[26] Cleomedes I 4.

[27] Strabo II 3.6.

[28] Strabo II 3.7–8.

[29] Dueck (2000), 62–69, discusses Strabo's Stoicism and his conception of geography as philosophy.

play in the regional geography that makes up the bulk of his work. Strabo strikingly remarks at the close of his summary of Posidonius' *Ôkeanos* (II 3.8) that the Stoics (*hoi hêmeteroi*, 'our people') abstain from Posidonius' investigations of causes and 'Aristotelizing' because of the fact that the causes are 'hidden' – though he is not averse to discoursing on how *pronoia*, 'Providence,' arranged the cosmos for the benefit of humanity (e.g., at XVII 1.36). What makes it possible for Strabo to speak of his subject as belonging to philosophy, however, and for us to describe his work as a Stoic geography, is primarily that it is shaped by the ethical motivation he ascribes to the geographer, whose efforts aim at *eudaimonia* by providing information useful in all human undertakings, and not least in those of wise rulers.[30]

[30] Strabo I 1.1 and I 1.16–22.

14 Stoic Naturalism and Its Critics

I.

Three Stoic doctrines have heavily influenced the course of later moral philosophy: (1) Eudaemonism: the ultimate end for rational action is the agent's own happiness. (2) Naturalism: happiness and virtue consist in living in accord with nature. (3) Moralism: moral virtue is to be chosen for its own sake and is to be preferred above any combination of items with non-moral value.[1] These Stoic doctrines provide some later moralists with a starting-point and an outline that they try to develop and amplify. These moralists include supporters of the position that I will call 'Scholastic naturalism'. For other later moralists, Stoicism provides a target; they develop their own positions by explaining why they reject the Stoic position. Still others defend some of these Stoic doctrines and reject others.

For obvious reasons, my account of the influence of these Stoic doctrines will be highly selective. I will simply sketch Scholastic naturalism through a few remarks about Aquinas, Suarez, and Grotius. On the other side, I will examine Pufendorf's reasons for rejecting Scholastic naturalism, and the attempts of Butler and Hutcheson to defend some Stoic doctrines while rejecting others.

My interest in these reactions to Stoicism and Scholastic naturalism is primarily philosophical. I hope to understand how different people argue for or against these doctrines, and to see how reasonable the arguments are. It will be clear that I cannot complete this task

---

[1] The Stoics assert more than this, since they take virtue to be identical to, not simply the dominant element of, happiness. I will not discuss this aspect of their position. For some discussion, see Irwin (1986), (1998); Annas (1993), Ch. 19, Cooper (1996).

in this one chapter; I will simply try to identify the main arguments and to raise some relevant questions about them.

These questions are primarily, but not exclusively, questions in moral philosophy. They go beyond moral philosophy (narrowly conceived) insofar as they involve questions about nature. Stoic ethics takes for granted the conception of nature that belongs to Stoic natural philosophy, including natural theology. We might reasonably expect, therefore, that changing attitudes to the Stoic conception of nature would explain changing attitudes to Stoic ethics.

I believe that this expectation is largely falsified, as far as it concerns the three Stoic doctrines I have mentioned, and the later philosophers who discuss them. That is why I will have rather little to say about the questions in natural philosophy that I would have to discuss if I were seeking to examine later reactions to the Stoic conception of nature more generally. However, I will have something to say about this aspect of Stoic natural philosophy, when I come to examine objections to naturalism in moral philosophy.[2]

2.

The Stoics take these three doctrines to be inseparable. The correct grasp of human happiness shows that it consists in living in accord with nature, which requires living in accordance with virtue in preference to any other aim (Cicero Off. III 21–8).

The connexion between happiness and virtue relies on Stoic claims about nature. Following Aristotle, the Stoics take the human good to consist in the fulfillment of human nature, understood as the nature of a rational agent. When they claim that the human good is living in accordance with nature (Stobaeus Ecl. II 76.16–23; 77.16–19), they refer (among other things) to the rational nature of human beings (DL, VII 89). The things that accord with this rational nature include health, safety, wealth, and the other things that Aristotle calls 'external goods' and the Stoics call 'preferred indifferents'; but they also include the exercise of rational nature in rational efforts to achieve these objects. This exercise of rational nature is virtue (DL VII 88; Stob. Ecl. II 75.11–76.15).

In the course of natural development, we come to recognize a special place for virtue. We begin from self-love, directed to our own

---

[2] See discussion of Pufendorf later in this chapter.

nature and constitution. To secure the goods we seek for our nature and constitution, we begin to exercise practical reason. But in the course of exercising practical reason, we come to prefer 'order and concord' in our actions (Cicero *Fin.* III 21) over the natural goods that we initially seek.[3]

In claiming this priority for the exercise of practical reason over the attainment of the natural goods we try to gain through it, the Stoics point to widespread agreement on the non-instrumental value of virtuous actions.[4] This agreement would be baseless if it did not rest on recognition of non-instrumental value in virtuous action. The Stoics claim to identify this non-instrumental value, in claiming that the virtues prescribe action that awards the appropriate place to the non-instrumental value of practical reason. The virtuous person acts reasonably, and thereby lives in accordance with the nature of a rational agent.[5]

To live in accordance with virtue, therefore, is to live in accordance with human nature, and to live in accordance with the requirements of correct reason.[6] The requirements of correct reason are expressed in a law; since facts about human nature fix the requirements of correct reason, these requirements belong to natural law.[7] Hence, according to the Stoic doctrine of natural law, virtuous people, in following the requirements of correct reason for human nature, fulfill the natural law that applies to all rational agents.[8]

To fulfill the natural law, it is not enough to choose virtuous actions; we must also choose them because they exercise practical reason. To choose them on this basis is to choose them because of what makes them non-instrumentally valuable; their non-instrumental

---

[3] I have discussed this a little further in Irwin (1998), 160–4.

[4] S. E., *M*, XI 99; DL VII 127; Cic. *De legibus*, I 40, 48.

[5] DL VII 85–9; Galen, *PHP*, V 6; Stobaeus. *Ecl.* II 75.11.

[6] When the Stoics speak of living in accordance with nature, they also have in mind cosmic nature, not simply the nature of a human being. I believe the appeal to cosmic nature constitutes an additional argument besides the eudaemonist argument I have just summarized, not a part of that argument. This view is disputed; see, e.g., Striker (1991), 228; Long (1989), 185–9. Cosmic nature is also relevant to the later versions of naturalism that I discuss. I have left it out of this account, since I believe that the issues I discuss are worth discussing independently of it.

[7] Cicero, *De legibus* I 23; Lactantius, *Div. inst.* VI 8.6–9 = Cicero, *De republica* III 33.

[8] In making these claims about the Stoic doctrine of natural law, I pass over several controversies, which may be studied in Striker (1987); DeFilippo and Mitsis (1994); and Vander Waerdt (1994b).

value makes them 'fine' or 'right' (*kalon, honestum*).[9] Some of the relevant features of rightness are these: (1) It rests on some conception of beauty, loveliness, fittingness or appropriateness (*convenientia*), constancy, and order (Cic. *Off.* I 14). Here the Stoics rely on an analogy between rightness and beauty as due proportion (Stob. *Ecl.* II 63.1–5). (2) It involves acting for reasons that are not confined to oneself and one's own benefit; this is why concern for rightness is contrasted with concern for one's own advantage (Cic. *Off.* I 5). (3) It is a proper object of praise, as opposed to liking, pleasure, or admiration, and it makes people praiseworthy (DL VII 100; Cic. *Fin.* III 27). (4) The connexion between these features is explained by the objectivity of the right. It is an object of praise because it deserves praise in its own right, whether or not it is actually praised (Cic. *Off.* I 14). It draws us by its own character, not by its satisfaction of some prior desire of ours (Stob. *Ecl.* II 100.21–2 W).

The Stoics believe that the recognition of virtue and virtuous action as fine is relevant to practice, and not only to theory. For they believe that we cannot have the virtues if we do not both attribute this sort of value to them and see the connexion between fineness and happiness. If we take the final good to be unconnected with virtue, we measure the final good by our own advantage, and not by rightness (*honestas*); in that case, we cannot consistently cultivate friendship, justice, generosity, or bravery (Cic. *Off.* I 5).

Each virtue, according to the Stoics, includes some conviction about the value of the actions it prescribes. The just person, for instance, not only does just actions, but also does them for their own sake, in the conviction that they are worth doing simply because they are just, and not because of some further causal result. Conceptions of the final good that leave out rightness, including Epicurean and Cyrenaic views, demote the virtues to a purely instrumental status that conflicts with the outlook of the virtuous person (Cic. *Fin.* II 35).

This Stoic claim about the connexion between moralism and eudaemonism asserts that we have reason to value virtue and virtuous action as non-instrumentally good if and only if we regard them as a part of happiness. In asserting this, the Stoics dismiss or overlook the view that appropriate regard for virtue and rightness requires us to value them without reference to our happiness, so that we have

---

[9] Aulus Gellius, *NA*, XII 5.7; Seneca, *Ep.*, 76.9.

sufficient reason to pursue them above all other goods or advantages even if they conflict with our happiness or they do not affect it either way. If they are wrong to dismiss this view, they are not entitled to infer that we can value virtue appropriately only if we take it to be a part of happiness.

3.

The three elements of the Stoic position (eudaemonism, moralism, and naturalism) are also elements of some mediaeval ethical theories. The theories of Albert and Aquinas are rightly described as 'Aristotelian', but they incorporate some distinctively Stoic claims about rightness; and so they deserve a prominent place in even a brief description of the influence of Stoic naturalism.

In affirming eudaemonism, Aquinas agrees with the Stoics no less than with Aristotle; but nothing in his account of the ultimate end is distinctively Stoic. Following both Aristotelian and Stoic views, he takes the ultimate good to be composed of goods that are both ends in themselves and worth choosing for the sake of the ultimate good.[10] That is why he believes that we can choose virtue for its own sake as the object of our more immediate aim, even though our ultimate aim is focused on the ultimate good.[11]

His views about moral goodness and moral virtue are not derived immediately from Aristotle.[12] Aquinas relies on the Stoic conception of the *honestum* as the characteristically moral good; he takes virtuous and right action to require the disinterested rational pursuit of a good that is not relative to one's own pleasure or advantage, but involves friendship, the good of others, and a common good for a community. In connecting the *honestum* with these aspects of morality, he captures the Stoic position.

[10] See *Summa Theologiae*, 1–2 q91 a5 ad 1; a6 ad 1, 2; *De malo* 6; *De veritate* q22 a7.
[11] 2-2 q123 a7; *In Decem Libros Ethicorum*, Section 549–50.
[12] The mediaeval Latin translators standardly translate 'kalon' by 'bonum', and never by 'honestum'. See, e.g., 1094b15, 1099a27, 1100b27, 30, 1104b31, 1110b15, 1114b6, 1115a30, b23, 1116a11, b3, 1117a8, 1120a27, 1122b6, 1168a33, 1169a6 ff. Nonetheless, Aquinas often takes Aristotle to be talking about the *honestum* in passages where Aristotle uses 'kalon', but the Latin has 'bonum'. See, e.g., *in EN* Sections 33, 273, 827, 533, 695, 714, 824–5, 1544, 1737, 1848, 1857, 1881, 2051, 2070. The source of Aquinas' claims about the *honestum* is probably Albert's commentary on Aristotle's *Ethics*. See, e.g., Albert, *Opera* XIV 1.48.

Aquinas describes the *honestum* as the non-instrumental good (*Summa Theologiae*, 1–2 q8 a2 ad 2; q8 a3, ad sc) and, specifically, the moral good.[13] *Honestum* action is essentially unselfish.[14] The *honestum* belongs to virtue as a whole (2–2 q145 a1); the virtues are *honestum* because they are ends in themselves though not the ultimate end (q145 a1 ad 1). It is characteristic of the *honestum* to direct all human affairs in accordance with reason; this is what makes it 'fitting' (*decorum*) (q145 a2). *Honestas* is a good discovered by reason, specifying what fits rational nature (q145 a3), and not only good for the individual, but also meritorious because of its contribution to the common good maintained by justice.

This connexion between virtue, rightness, and nature is more fully explained by Suarez. In his view, the right, like the pleasant and the useful, involves some kind of fittingness (*convenientia*). But it cannot be simply the fittingness that belongs to these other goods.[15] Goodness as rightness belongs to the object of a human will, and thereby makes an action morally good.[16] The right is neither the pleasant nor the useful.[17] This moral good that is grasped by correct reason must be appropriate for the nature of human beings as free and rational agents.[18] Appropriateness to one's nature does not imply a reference to one's private advantage; it is to be understood teleologically, by reference to the appropriate ends for a rational agent. Here Suarez captures the Stoic insistence on the unselfish character of rightness, in contrast to the expedient.

He also captures the objectivity of rightness. The right is necessarily connected to correct reason, but it is not relative to correct reason. If it were, things would be right because they are judged to be so; but this would be the wrong direction of explanation.[19] The correctness of correct moral judgment consists in conformity to some feature of the object judged, rather than in the creation of such a feature.[20]

---

[13] See 1–2 q34 a2 ad 1; q39 a2.
[14] 2–2 q26 a12; q110 a2.
[15] Suarez, *De bonitate* (= *Opera* IV) II 1.5.
[16] *De bon.* II 1.3.
[17] *De bon.* II 1.4.
[18] *De bon.* II 2.11.
[19] *De bon.* II 2.3, 11.
[20] *Disputationes Metaphysicae* X 2.12 (= *Opera* XXV). Translated by Gracia and Davis (1989).

Reason or judgment is correct because it conforms to the nature of a rational agent, but the converse is false. For similar reasons, rightness does not consist in conformity to a law, but the correctness of a law presupposes rightness distinct from it.[21]

In these claims about right reason and law, Suarez departs from one aspect of the naturalism of the Stoics and Aquinas. In their view, conformity to natural law follows from and, indeed, is reducible to conformity to right reason. Suarez disagrees, since he believes that the existence of natural law requires divine commands and legislation in addition to natural rightness.[22] But this disagreement about the character of law does not affect Suarez's basic agreement with the Stoics and Aquinas about the existence and nature of natural rightness.[23]

Stoic naturalism about virtue and the *honestum*, therefore, appears to the Scholastics to fit readily into their Aristotelian framework.

4.

This Scholastic naturalism supports Grotius' belief in a natural right (*ius*) that proceeds 'from principles internal to a human being'.[24] By this he means not only that we know them by nature, but also that they are appropriate for rational agents with our nature. To prove *a priori* that something belongs to natural right, we need to show its 'necessary appropriateness or inappropriateness to rational and social nature'.[25]

To this extent, Grotius agrees with the naturalists among the Scholastics. He signals his agreement when he says that his remarks would still have some standing even if we were to grant that God does not exist or that he is not concerned with human affairs.[26] Natural right (*ius*) implies the moral wrongness or moral necessity of

---

[21] *De bon.* II 2.6.
[22] *De bon.* II 6.12.
[23] This claim about the relation of Suarez to Aquinas is controversial, and I hope to defend it elsewhere. Other views may be found in Finnis (1980), 42–8; Darwall (1995), 23–33; Haakonssen (1996), 16–26; Schneewind (1997), 59–66.
[24] Grotius, *JBP*, Prolegomena Section 12.
[25] *JBP* I 1.12.1.
[26] *JBP* Prol. Section 11.

some action, because of its inappropriateness or appropriateness to rational nature.[27]

If some actions are morally right (*honestum*) because they are appropriate for human nature, we have a natural basis for justice, apart from the usefulness of justice in maintaining a society. In Grotius' view, the natural basis of justice is human nature, and especially the human desire and need for society.[28] This 'social' aspect of human nature is, according to Grotius, what the Stoics have in mind in speaking of 'conciliation' (*oikeiôsis*) of each person to himself and of one person to another. He seeks to capture the point that Aristotle makes in calling a human being a 'political' (*politikon*) animal or, as the mediaeval sources render it, a 'social' (*sociale*) animal.[29]

By appealing to the social nature of human beings, Grotius seeks a natural basis for our pursuit of the right (*honestum*) as well as the advantageous (*utile*). Following Stoic sources, he claims that our recognition of the right arises from the growth of reason, as we discover a proper object for 'conciliation'. Our conception of the right is our recognition of what accords with a rational and social nature.[30]

In affirming these claims about sociality and natural right, Grotius follows Aristotle, the Stoics, and Scholastic naturalism in accepting eudaemonism. The social nature of a human being is part of the human nature that has to be fulfilled in human happiness; hence, the claim that a human being ought to take an appropriate role in a society is not at all in conflict with the claim that each human being pursues his own happiness above all. Grotius never challenges the view that the natural desire for society embodies one's desire for one's own good. He does not defend this eudaemonist thesis; nor does he suggest that it needs defence.[31]

5.

Although Aquinas' position strongly influences the later development of Scholastic moral theory, as we can see from Suarez and Grotius, it is not the only Scholastic position. Scotus raises an

[27] *JBP* I 1.10.1.
[28] *JBP* Prol. Section 6.
[29] See Barbeyrac's comment on Prol. Section 6 (in Whewell's edition).
[30] *JBP* I 2.1–3.
[31] Contrast Darwall (1995), 6.

important question about the view common to Aristotle, the Stoics, and Aquinas, since he argues that moralism requires the rejection of both naturalism and eudaemonism. In his view, rational action not aimed at one's own advantage (*commodum*) presupposes an affection for the just, which the virtuous person follows without reference to his own happiness. This affection for justice is an aspect of human freedom, but not a natural desire for some natural end.[32]

These reasons for rejecting eudaemonism and naturalism do not convince Suarez, who argues against Scotus that right action is appropriate for rational nature.[33] But some of Scotus' doubts reappear in later voluntarist criticisms of Scholastic naturalism. Pufendorf's arguments to show that moral properties and facts must be the result of deliberate imposition and legislation by God allow us to examine some reasons for rejecting the Scholastic naturalist position.[34]

It might appear relevant to consider early modern reactions to the Scholastic (and, in the relevant respects, equally Stoic) conception of nature. Scepticism about Aristotelian teleology might be expected to result in scepticism about the Aristotelian conception of nature, which is thoroughly teleological. Such scepticism should apply equally to Stoic claims that rely on an equally teleological conception of nature.[35]

At first sight, Pufendorf provides a good example of the influence of natural philosophy on moral philosophy; we might even take him to demonstrate the untenability of traditional Scholastic naturalism in the face of modern natural science and natural philosophy. He agrees with Boyle in claiming that naturalists believe in some principle independent of and co-eternal with God, and restricting God's freedom, because (in his view) they believe in natural rightness and wrongness that is independent of God's will.[36]

---

[32] Scotus, 3 *Sent.* d26 q1 = Wolter 178; 2 *Sent.* d6 q2 = Wolter 470.

[33] *De bon.* II 2.13.

[34] I am not suggesting that Scotus directly influenced Pufendorf.

[35] Rejection of Aristotelian teleology is not to be identified with complete rejection of teleology. Boyle's objections fasten on the tendency of Peripatetic views of nature to introduce (in his view) additional agents besides God, or to compromise the freedom and transcendence of God; he includes Stoic views in this general objection to 'idolatrous' conceptions of nature. See *Free Inquiry*, Section IV, pp. 48–51. Leibniz answers the attempt to connect a Peripatetic view of nature with idolatry, in 'On nature itself'.

[36] *JNG*, I 2.6.

According to Pufendorf, Scholastic traditional naturalism conflicts with the obvious fact that moral properties cannot belong to
nature itself apart from imposition. This fact is obvious in the light
of modern physical science, which shows that nature itself consists
simply in bodies in motion, and their effects on one another. No
morality can be found simply in movement and application of physical power, since mere physical movements in their own right cannot
be right and wrong. Rightness and wrongness, therefore, must be imposed on nature, and cannot belong to nature in itself.[37]

Pufendorf's contrast between moral and purely natural properties
is instructive, since it relies on a division that has strongly influenced modern meta-ethics.[38] He expresses the widespread view that
a post-Aristotelian scientific view of nature rules out the Aristotelian
conception of normative, and especially moral, properties as parts of
nature in itself. This view may be expressed in the claim that values
are not part of the world.

Why does Pufendorf believe that moral properties must be imposed, and cannot be present without imposition in the natural
world? He might argue in this way: (1) Moral properties are not mentioned in the physicist's description; that is, they are not among the
properties of physical bodies that explain the movements that are
explained by the laws of physics. (2) Every property not mentioned
in the physicist's description is an imposed property. (3) Therefore,
moral properties are imposed.

But though this argument would secure Pufendorf's conclusion
about moral properties, it is open to objection. For the second premiss allows too many properties to be imposed. Biological and medical properties, for instance, are not mentioned in the physicist's description, but it does not follow that drinking sea water is unhealthy
for cattle only because someone has legislated that it is so.

Pufendorf agrees with this objection; for he believes that the properties defining natural benefit and harm to human beings are antecedent to divine legislation (II 3.5). Pufendorf distinguishes natural from moral goodness (following Cumberland),[39] and believes that
natural goodness is not imposed. Certain things are naturally good

---

[37] *JNG* I 2.6. Pufendorf's claims about nature and imposition are emphasized by
Schneewind (1997), 120.

[38] On moral entities, see Schneewind (1997), 120. See also Korsgaard (1996), 21–7.

[39] He refers to Cumberland at II 5.9.

and bad for human beings, but God's goodness causes him to add to the act of creation a further act of legislation, prescribing naturally good actions and prohibiting naturally bad ones. It is this legislative act that adds moral goodness to natural goodness. Hence 'prudential properties' (concerned with benefit and harm to oneself) are part of nature and are not imposed on it. Pufendorf believes these properties are natural; but they are not explicitly recognized in a physicist's description; hence, he cannot appeal to a physicist's description to show that a given property is not natural; hence, his argument against the natural character of moral properties collapses.

We might try to modify our first argument so as to include natural goodness among nonimposed properties. A revised argument would be this: (1a) Moral properties are not constituted by events and properties mentioned in the physicist's description. (2a) Every property not constituted by events and properties mentioned in physicist's description is an imposed property. (3) Therefore, moral properties are imposed. According to this conception of non-imposed properties, the unhealthiness of sea water for cattle is a non-imposed natural property, even though physics does not explicitly mention it as such; for it is constituted by natural properties. Nothing more than the sorts of properties recognized by physics, in the appropriate combination, is needed to ensure the fact that sea water is unhealthy for cattle, even though such facts are not the concern of physics.

We may grant, then, that (2a) provides a reasonable account of non-imposed natural properties, and that it comes closer than (2) comes to capturing Pufendorf's intentions. But if we accept (2a), we must face an objection to (1a), which is far more controversial than (1) was. Why do moral properties not count, by the criterion in (2a), as non-imposed natural properties? At first it seems obvious that the world-view of physical science has no room for rightness and wrongness. But if we allow that it has room for healthiness and unhealthiness, we may also be convinced that moral properties are constituted by facts about what is healthy or unhealthy, or in other ways good and bad, for rational agents. At any rate, the constitutive relation that we must recognize between physical properties and healthiness suggests a way of explaining how rightness and wrongness might belong among natural and non-imposed properties. Pufendorf's argument to show that moral properties must be imposed is worthless, and his appeal to the modern scientific world-view does not help him.

6.

If Pufendorf's appeal to modern science fails to undermine Scholastic naturalism, we must turn to his other attempts to show that morality requires legislation. He agrees with Suarez in taking the existence of law to require some act of legislation, and hence he disagrees with the conception of law underlying the views of the Stoics and Aquinas. But he also rejects the point of agreement between Suarez, the Stoics, and Aquinas, for he denies that nature without an act of legislation includes moral properties. Sometimes he allows that reflexion on our natural good may move us to do the actions required by morality, but he denies that such reflexion constitutes the moral outlook. In his view, actions directed to our natural good rest simply on considerations of advantage (*commodum, utile*) that lack the distinctive rational status of moral principles. This is also one of Scotus's objection against eudaemonist appeals to natural good.

This objection suggests that the eudaemonism of Aquinas and Suarez subordinates everything to one's own advantage. Both Aquinas and Suarez deny this, since they regard the right (*honestum*) as distinct from the advantageous, but regard both as promoting the agent's ultimate good. On this point they follow the Stoics. Grotius follows Scholastic naturalism here. Pufendorf appears to misunderstand this aspect of Scholastic naturalism, since he seems to assume without argument that if we take our own good as our ultimate end, we thereby act simply with a view to our own advantage, and so cannot pursue the morally right for its own sake.

This misunderstanding of the Stoics and of Scholastic naturalism is especially clear in Barbeyrac's defence of Pufendorf against Leibniz's objections.[40] Barbeyrac alleges that Leibniz's eudaemonism overlooks the distinction that 'the wise pagans' have drawn between the right (*l'honnête*) and the useful (*l'utile*) (445); hence, Leibniz's account of motivation reduces all value to the useful. Whether or not this is true of Leibniz, it is clearly false of the traditional eudaemonist position that Leibniz seeks to defend. Like many others, Barbeyrac fails to acknowledge that traditional eudaemonists take themselves

---

[40] Leibniz's objections appear in his 'Opinion on the Principles of Pufendorf'. Barbeyrac's answer appears in Pufendorf (1718), 429–95. The dispute between Leibniz and Pufendorf is discussed in Hochstrasser (2000), Ch. 5. Barbeyrac's defence of Pufendorf is discussed in Schneewind's helpful essay, (1996b).

to be entitled to distinguish the right and the advantageous without abandoning eudaemonism;[41] he is not entitled to assume without argument that they are wrong.

These are not Pufendorf's only objections to Scholastic naturalism, but they are at least as plausible as any of the others. Examination of his objections does not suggest that Scholastic naturalism has a strong case to answer.

7.

Whereas Pufendorf argues that moralism requires the rejection of both eudaemonism and naturalism, Butler tries to defend a position closer to Scholastic naturalism, by defending naturalism and moralism; but he follows Pufendorf in rejecting eudaemonism. He seeks, therefore, to explain how virtue consists in following nature,[42] while denying that we have reason to pursue it ultimately because it promotes our happiness. We have no reason to believe that Butler is specifically concerned with the dispute between Grotius and Pufendorf.[43] Instead, he seeks to answer the objection of rationalist moralists who believe that naturalism encourages the moral position defended by Hobbes on the basis of an account of human nature.

To clarify the conception of nature that is relevant to understanding Stoic naturalism about virtue, Butler tries to distinguish it from conceptions that seem to make the formula totally implausible. We might take 'natural' to mean (1) in accordance with some natural impulse or other, or (2) in accordance with one's strongest natural impulse.[44] But neither of these senses makes the naturalist claim plausible. In the sense that captures the Stoics' intentions, 'natural'

---

[41] I have criticized Reid in similar terms in Irwin (1996), 89–92.

[42] *Sermons*, Preface 13. I cite Butler by sermon and paragraph number, from Bernard's edition. I have discussed Butler more fully in Irwin (forthcoming).

[43] Butler could have known Pufendorf's *JNG*, which was first published in 1672 and translated into English by Basil Kennet in 1703. He could also have known some aspects of Pufendorf's voluntarism from Cumberland's *de Legibus Naturae*, also published in 1672, and discussed by Pufendorf in the second edition of his work (1684). When John Maxwell's translation of Cumberland was published in 1727, 'The Rev. Mr Butler' was one of the subscribers (I have no idea whether this is our Butler).

[44] Butler, *Sermons* II 5–6.

means (3) required by a system as a whole rather than simply by a part or aspect of the system.

Butler implicitly answers the claim that naturalism about virtue and happiness relies on a cosmic teleology that modern natural science has undermined.[45] He relies on a connexion between nature and system. When we study some system or whole, our understanding of it depends on our understanding of its functions, and hence of the point of each part in it. Butler gives the example of a watch (Preface, 14), insisting that we do not understand it unless we grasp 'its conduciveness to this one or more ends', which are the ends of the system as a whole. Similarly, we grasp the system in human nature not by looking at the several passions in themselves, but by considering their relations.

This conception of nature may be called teleological, since it refers to a system in which the working of the parts is regulated by the characteristic functions of the whole. But it does not presuppose cosmic teleology, since it includes no claim about how individual things come to be systems of this type. Nor does it seem especially difficult to understand. If a doctor says 'You need an operation', and explains that we need it in order to remove a cancerous growth, we do not disagree on the ground that the cancerous growth itself does not need to be removed and that it would be better for the growth to be allowed to keep growing instead of being killed. Or if I say 'I need to exercise more', the part of me that enjoys being lazy does not need the exercise, but it is nonetheless true that I need it. In both cases we confirm Butler's suggestion that we recognize some difference between the requirements of the system as a whole and the requirements of particular parts of it. We think of selves as having aims and interests of their own, distinct from a mere collection of the motives, desires, and impulses that constitute us.

Butler tries to clarify natural action by appeal to superior principles. He claims: (1) Superior principles are those that move us by authority, and not simply by strength (II 14). (2) We act according to the requirements of our nature as a whole system in acting on authoritative principles. (3) Therefore, we act naturally by acting on superior principles.

He applies this argument to self-love by insisting that self-love is holistic. When the reflection of rational self-love conflicts with our

---

[45] I do not mean that Butler does not believe in cosmic teleology.

particular passions, it is obvious that reflection should be obeyed; this is obvious 'from the economy and constitution of human nature', irrespective of the comparative strength of the relevant desires. The outlook of self-love results from reflection on the merits of satisfying one or another particular passion, and so it expresses a superior principle. Since self-love takes account of our interests as agents with a future to take care of, it is needed to safeguard the interests of our nature as a whole. And so our nature as a whole requires us to follow rational self-love.

This discussion of natural action and of the natural character of self-love is an accurate and helpful clarification of Stoic and Scholastic claims about appropriateness to nature.

8.

Butler, however, rejects the Stoic position on two points: (1) He endorses one aspect of hedonism, since he takes self-love – my concern for my own interest – to aim exclusively at my own happiness, understood as my own pleasure (XI 5, 7, 9). (2) He rejects eudaemonism, since he recognizes two distinct rational principles – rational self-love and conscience – neither reducible to the other.

Butler agrees with Scotus and Pufendorf in rejecting eudaemonism, but disagrees with them in maintaining naturalism. Both self-love and conscience are natural principles (III 9), but conscience is superior to self-love, and indeed is the supreme principle, because it takes proper account of all the considerations that matter. It does not simply consider my different passions and their effect on my interest; it also considers my interests and legitimate claims in relation to those of other people.

So understood, conscience is easily distinguished from self-love, if we accept Butler's narrow conception of self-love. According to this conception, self-love appraises actions from the restricted point of view of my own pleasure. If this is the only question that rational self-love asks, it clearly fails to cover all the questions that are relevant.

Although Butler takes conscience to be superior to self-love, he also claims that morality and self-love must agree (XI 20). A successful defence of this claim supports the belief that it is natural to follow conscience. We will be more readily disposed to allow that the attitudes connected with morality are central aspects of our nature, if we are not also disposed to believe that they conflict with self-interest. For the thought that we could plan some alternative course of action in our own interest that would dispense with any moral concern tends to support the suspicion that our moral concerns are dispensable, non-essential aspects of ourselves.

Butler, however, makes it difficult to argue for harmony, because of his hedonist conception of self-love. He assumes that when self-love sets out to consider the pros and cons of acting on conscience, it simply considers the possible yield of pleasure, contentment, and so on. This claim about the outlook of self-love rests on the assumption that self-love does not care about actions for their own sake, but only for their causal consequences, insofar as they result in pain or pleasure. But if we accept this view of self-love, it is difficult to agree with Butler's claim about the harmony of self-love and conscience. Different people find different things pleasant and painful, and it is not clear why following conscience should be expected to maximize each person's pleasure.

We may summarize Butler's relation to traditional naturalism and eudaemonism as follows: (1) His claims about nature and the natural character of superior principles accord with traditional naturalism. (2) His hedonist conception of self-love departs from traditional naturalism. (3) His separation of conscience from self-love departs from traditional naturalism. (4) His hedonist conception of self-love supports the separation of conscience from self-love. (5) But this same hedonist conception of self-love also makes it difficult to believe in the harmony of self-love and conscience.

If this is a fair summary, the ways in which Butler departs from traditional naturalism do not leave him with a completely defensible position.

9.

Most of Butler's successors have agreed with his deviations from Stoic and Scholastic naturalism, and have inferred that his mistake lies in his retention of the traditional belief in the harmony of self-love and conscience. According to this view, the claims about harmony are an aspect of traditional naturalism that Butler ought to have dropped.

This revision of Butler is open to objection. If two superior principles – self-love and conscience – were basically antagonistic, it would be difficult to show that either really fulfills the requirements of the system as a whole. If Butler abandons the doctrine of harmony, he seriously weakens his naturalism. This point is already clear in Scotus, whose rejection of eudaemonism I mentioned earlier; for Scotus rejects not only eudaemonism but also naturalism. We might reasonably conclude that Butler has no good reason to maintain naturalism without eudaemonism.

If this would indeed be the result of rejection of the doctrine of harmony, we ought to consider, on Butler's behalf, the possibility of a different revision of his position. We have good reason to reject his first deviation from Scholastic naturalism, his hedonist conception of self-love. If a holist conception is to be preferred, self-love cannot be confined to a desire for my own pleasure; it must also consider my attachment to the good of others, and to the moral virtues, and must count the achievement of these desires as part of my own interest. If it is part of our nature, and hence essential to us as whole selves, to care about moral principles, self-love must take account of our concern with moral principles. If it did not give them the right prominence in its conception of the self, it would be misinformed.

This holist conception of self-love makes it more reasonable for Butler to maintain the harmony of self-love and conscience. If he had stuck to traditional eudaemonism on this point, he could apparently have defended the rest of his naturalist position more convincingly.

If we restore this element of traditional eudaemonism to Butler, what should we say about the rest of his position? If he were to accept a holist conception of self-love, would he have any good reason to maintain the claims about conscience that distinguish his position from traditional naturalism?

A holist conception of self-love seems to be capable of absorbing the demands of morality without recognizing conscience as the supreme principle. It still distinguishes the requirements of morality from those requirements of prudence that do not involve concern for other people; these are the requirements of the *honestum* against those of narrow advantage. But neither of these two sets of requirements lies outside self-love. Butler, therefore, seems to have no reason to insist on the separation of conscience from self-love. The Scholastic naturalist position seems to be both more coherent and more plausible than the one that Butler substitutes for it; indeed, it seems to provide a more plausible defence than Butler himself provides for the natural character of self-love and conscience, and for the harmony of the two principles.

10.

We can illustrate the difficulty of defending naturalism without eudaemonism by comparing Hutcheson's defence with Butler's. Hutcheson's inaugural lecture 'On the natural sociality of human beings' sets out to defend a thesis that he attributes to the ancient moralists. Unlike Butler, he refers explicitly to seventeenth-century discussion of natural law, and claims to defend Grotius against Pufendorf and Hobbes.[46] The favourable references to the Stoics fit Hutcheson's generally sympathetic attitude to them.[47] The inaugural lecture takes up an aspect of Pufendorf's position that Gerschom Carmichael had drawn to Hutcheson's attention.[48]

Several points in Hutcheson's explanation of the naturalist thesis are quite similar to Butler; in particular, he uses some of Butler's claims about superior principles and about the supremacy of conscience (see especially Section 15). In defending natural rightness, he opposes the position of Pufendorf, who restricts the natural to the pleasant and the expedient (Section 22).

His answer to Pufendorf, however, fails to take account of the basic issues about naturalism and moralism, as both Pufendorf and Butler conceive them. Hutcheson takes the issue to turn on whether human beings have natural benevolent desires (Section 24). If they have, then, in his view, morality is in accordance with human nature, and the anti-naturalist position is refuted.

This answer fails to cope even with Hutcheson's own formulation of the initial question. He follows Butler in identifying natural actions and states teleologically and holistically, by reference to the requirements of a human being as a whole (Section 7-9). From this point of view, one might take benevolent desires to be natural, if one

---

[46] The lecture was delivered and published in 1730, four years after the first edition of Butler's *Sermons*. It is translated in *On Human Nature*.

[47] Prevailing attitudes to Stoicism in the Scottish Enlightenment are discussed by Stewart (1991). On Hutcheson and Stoicism, see Scott (1900), 246–54 (which exaggerates Hutcheson's closeness to Stoicism).

[48] Carmichael was Hutcheson's predecessor as Professor of Moral Philosophy in Glasgow. See Moore and Silverthorne (1984).

could show that they contribute to the actions that are required by the needs and nature of human beings; but the mere fact that they arise by nature, and are not derived from the pursuit of the expedient, does not show that they meet Butler's conditions for being natural. Hutcheson's attempt to defend the naturalist thesis shows that he fails to understand it.

The difference between Butler's position and Hutcheson's is clear if we return to Butler's initial formulation of the naturalist position. He recognizes three senses of 'natural', and insists correctly that only the third (referring to the needs of a whole system) captures the naturalist position of the ancient moralists. Hutcheson's attempted defence of naturalism seeks to show that benevolent desires are natural in one of Butler's first two senses (as desires that belong naturally, or as desires that are sometimes strongest). As Butler sees it, this is an inadequate defence of the natural character of morality.[49] Many desires are natural in the first sense, and different people might find that different desires are strongest on different occasions; but does the rational authority of morality depend on such variations between different people?

A way to rebut Butler's objection would be to answer yes to this last question. This is Hume's reply to Butler and to the aspects of Hutcheson that display unjustified – in Hume's view – sympathy with Butler's position. Hume sees that if we accept this reply, we must agree that it is entirely 'unphilosophical' to embrace the traditional view that virtue is natural and vice unnatural.[50] We must also agree that Pufendorf's attempt to accept naturalism about non-moral goodness and to reject it only for moral goodness is an unstable compromise.

It would be rash to conclude from this survey of reactions to Stoic and Scholastic naturalism that any major departure from the naturalist position must force us into a Humean position about nature, reason, and morality. But it is worth considering the difficulties that

[49] Butler implicitly points out Hutcheson's error when he criticises Shaftesbury for failing to grasp the essential features of the authority of conscience (*Sermons*, Preface 26).

[50] *Treatise of Human Nature*, III 1.2 (p. 475 in Selby-Bigge). It would be entirely mistaken to infer from this passage that claims about nature are unimportant in Hume's own moral theory. But I believe that a fuller account of their importance would be consistent with what I have said about his opposition to Stoic naturalism.

Pufendorf, Butler, and Hutcheson all face, for different reasons, once they reject central elements in naturalism. We might decide that, despite these difficulties, they have compelling reasons for rejecting those aspects of naturalism that they reject. But examination of their arguments should persuade us that these reasons are not only not compelling, but also surprisingly weak. If that is so, we should perhaps ask whether the naturalist position is really as implausible as the successors of Grotius took it to be.

15   Stoicism in the Philosophical Tradition: Spinoza, Lipsius, Butler*

I. DIFFUSION AND DIMINUTION

Of all the ancient philosophies, Stoicism has probably had the most diffused but also the least explicit and adequately acknowledged influence on western thought.[1] No secular books were more widely read during the Renaissance than Cicero's *On Duties* (*De officiis*), the *Letters* and *Dialogues* of Seneca, and the *Manual* of Epictetus. Thomas More's Utopians define virtue as 'life in accordance with nature', and this is characteristic of the way slogans and concepts of Stoic ethics were eclectically appropriated from about 1500 to 1750. Neo-Stoicism (capitalized) is a term often used to refer to currents of thought in the seventeenth and eighteenth centuries, and it is

---

* This chapter began its life as a paper for a panel on Legacies of Stoicism, organized by the American Philosophical Association at its December meeting in Atlanta, 1996. I am grateful to Michael Seidler, my respondent on that occasion, for his excellent comments. The paper was given a further airing at a conference on Hellenistic Philosophy and the Early Modern Period, organized by Brad Inwood and Jon Miller of the University of Toronto in September 2000. I thank the participants for their questions and remarks, and especially my commentator, Sarah Marquardt. In revising the section of the paper on Spinoza, I have benefited greatly from written comments by Jon Miller and Stephen Menn, and I am also indebted to discussion with Don Rutherford.

[1] For a brief account, which makes no claim to any original research, see Long (1974 / 1986), 232–47. For Stoicism in Christian Latin thought through the sixth century, see Colish (1985), Vol. II. Traces of Stoic physics are identified by Funkenstein (1986), sv Index, Barker (1985), and Dobbs (1985). General bibliography: Barbour (1998), Morford (1991), Oestreich (1982), and Spanneut (1973). For Kant and Stoicism, see Seidler (1981) and (1983), and Schneewind (1996a). For suggestions that Rousseau and Freud 'each adapted Stoic doctrines for radically different sorts of therapeutic purposes', see Rorty (1996).

quite appropriate to such figures as Lipsius and du Vair.[2] Yet, despite the Stoic traces in Descartes, Spinoza, Leibniz, Rousseau, Grotius, Shaftesbury, Adam Smith, and Kant (traces that modern scholars are increasingly detecting), Neo-Stoicism scarcely had an identifiable life comparable to Medieval Aristotelianism, Renaissance and later Scepticism, seventeenth-century Epicureanism, or Renaissance Platonism and the Cambridge Platonists. It was not determinate enough to mark a whole period or intellectual movement.

In recent decades, ancient Stoicism has become a mainstream scholarly interest.[3] Not coincidentally, this revival is echoed in work by such well-known thinkers as Foucault, MacIntyre, and Taylor; and we now have Becker's intriguing book, *A New Stoicism*, which offers itself as the kind of ethical theory that a modern Stoic could and should defend. But Stoicism as systematic philosophy has hardly been refashioned at any time.[4]

Many explanations for this curiously scattered legacy suggest themselves. Ancient Stoicism is far less accessible in its original and comprehensive form than the philosophies of Plato, Aristotle, Epicurus, and Sextus Empiricus. We have only scraps of the pre-Roman Stoics. A general idea of Stoic physics and logic could be gleaned from the widely read summary compiled by Diogenes Laertius and from Cicero's *De natura deorum*, *Academica*, and *De fato*;

[2] Guillaume du Vair (1556–1621) published three works designed to show the value of Stoicism as a philosophy of life: *La philosophie morale des Stoiques, De la constance et consolation ès calamités publiques*, and *La sainte philosophie*. For Lipsius, see Section III below.

[3] Hegel's rather negative assessment of the Hellenistic philosophers, as expressed in his *Lectures on the History of Philosophy*, tr. E. S. Haldane and F. H. Simson (New Jersey, 1983) Vol. II, esp. 232–6, had an adverse influence on historians of ancient philosophy from which the field is only now recovering. It was noted and politely criticised by Marx in the preface to his doctoral dissertation, *Differenz der demokritischen und epikureischen Naturphilosophie* (Jena, 1841). There Marx announces his (unfulfilled) intention of writing a 'larger work in which I shall expound Epicurean, Stoic, and Sceptic philosophy in connection with Greek speculation as a whole'.

[4] See Foucault (1986), esp. 39–42, 50–68, 183–4; MacIntyre (1981) and (1988) (with criticism of MacIntyre's account of Stoic ethics in Long [1983a]); and Taylor (1989), who has interesting remarks on the Neo-Stoicism he finds in Descartes and Shaftesbury, 147–53, 251–9. Taylor barely mentions Lipsius, omits Butler, and does not connect Spinoza's views with Stoicism. Moore (1903) offers a few remarks on Stoicism, which I discuss in Long (1970/71). For Mill's attack on 'following nature', as an ethical principle, see Long (1983a), 196–7. Becker (1998) is reviewed with a nice blend of appreciation and criticism by Inwood (1998).

but the philosophical significance of these branches of Stoicism has come to light mainly through the scholarly research of the past half century. What was most accessible and influential for the Renaissance and Enlightenment were the treatments of Stoic ethics by Cicero, Seneca, Epictetus, and Marcus Aurelius.

In addition to the fragmentary state of the ancient sources, Stoicism was easily conflated or assimilated, on casual acquaintance, to ideas associated with the much more familiar names of Platonism and Aristotelianism. The conflation is not, of course, wholly mistaken. Outside metaphysics and technical logic, the three philosophies do have much in common, as the Academic Antiochus, Cicero's friend and teacher, recognised. How easily they could be eclectically synthesized is particularly evident in the works of Philo of Alexandria, and even in Plotinus. This assimilation becomes still more complex in the writings of such early Christian thinkers as Origen, Tertullian, Clement of Alexandria, and Calcidius. Some Stoic doctrines, such as the identification of God with fire and the denial of the soul's immortality, were anathema to the early Fathers of the Church – which helps to explain why no complete texts by any early Stoic philosophers have survived. But early Christianity appropriated a great deal of Stoic ethics without acknowledgment.

The results of this complex process of transmission were not conducive to the revival of ancient Stoicism in anything like its classical form. First, much that had been distinctively Stoic in origin was absorbed into the complex amalgam of Judaic and Greek teaching that became Christian theology and ethics. So Stoicism is a part, but a largely unacknowledged part, of the Christian tradition. Second, the assimilation of Christian and Stoic ethics tended to blur the profound differences that really exist between the two belief systems, to the detriment of the Stoics' originality.

There is, however, a third and deeper reason why no fully fledged representation of the ancient Stoa has emerged in Neo-Stoicism. Of all the Greek schools, the Stoa in its Chrysippean phase was the most systematic, holistic, and formal in methodology. It can best be compared in this respect, as we shall see, with Spinoza. Although Stoicism in antiquity was pillaged by eclectics, in the eyes of its greatest exegete Chrysippus, it was an all-or-nothing system. What I mean is not primarily the school's division of the world into fools and the utterly rare sage or its uncompromising insistence on the perfectibility of reason; I mean, rather, the idea, as stated by Cicero on the school's behalf, that Stoic philosophy is coherent through and through – a system such that to remove one letter would be to destroy the whole account.[5] Although Stoicism does not have Spinoza's geometrical rigour, its rationalist ambition was similar to his. No modern philosopher, as far as I know, has ever taken this Stoic claim to complete coherence seriously, but I believe it is the key to the original system and to much of its appeal.

When one reflects on this point, it becomes easier to see why the few creative philosophers with an informed knowledge of the ancient sources would be inhibited from venturing on anything like a comprehensive Neo-Stoicism. We have modern equivalents to Epicurean atomism and hedonism, but there is no modern counterpart to the Stoics' conception of the world as a vitalist and completely rational system, causally determined by a fully immanent and providential God. If, as I think, these concepts are fundamental to the grounding of Stoic ethics, there can be no fully authentic Neo-Stoicism that dispenses with them. From this, it does not follow that we moderns cannot make use of individual Stoic concepts, isolating them from their original cosmological, theological, and epistemic underpinnings. But it does follow, in my opinion, that without those underpinnings the Stoic conditions for happiness and a good life will hardly seem rationally and emotionally compelling.[6]

In the main body of this chapter, I propose to focus upon three thinkers: Baruch Spinoza, Justus Lipsius, and Joseph Butler. My choice is influenced by the wish to exhibit different aspects of the Stoic legacy that have a clear and distinct, though necessarily partial, affinity to the ancient school. In the case of Lipsius, we have the earliest example of a modern writer who seeks to show, by systematic reference to ancient texts, that Stoicism is virtually identical to Christian theology and ethics. Butler's interest in Stoicism is much less direct. In order to refute Hobbes and various contemporaries, Butler invokes the Stoic idea of 'following nature' as part of his effort to ground morality in the psychological constitution of human beings. Much of Butler's reasoning is his own, but his treatment of the two basic instincts, self-love and benevolence, is too similar to

[5] Cicero, *Fin.* III 74. Cf. Long (1970/1971), 90–1.
[6] For a full statement of this judgment, see Long (1989), 97–101.

the Stoic concept of *oikeiôsis* to be adventitious, and the primary role he assigns to conscience has some authentic Stoic antecedents. Spinoza makes only passing reference to the Stoics (see footnote 13), and I know nothing about how much he may have been consciously influenced by them. However, his conception of God's equivalence to Nature and the ethical inferences he draws from his metaphysical propositions make for a fascinating comparison with Stoicism.

2. SPINOZA (1632–1677): A QUASI-STOIC?

Leibniz charged Spinoza and Descartes with being leaders of 'the sect of the new Stoics', but his assessment reveals more about his disquiet with their ethics and theologies than it tells us concerning how either of these philosophers viewed his own relationship to Stoicism.[7] The modern assessment of Spinoza's Stoic affinity is a curious record of extremes. Some authoritative treatments of Spinoza omit mention of Stoicism altogether; others see Spinoza as heavily indebted to Stoicism and concerned to refashion it.[8] For the purpose

---

[7] See G. W. Leibniz, *Philosophical Essays*, ed. and tr. R. Ariew and D. Garber (Indianapolis, 1989), 218–4. I owe this reference to an unpublished paper by Don Rutherford on Leibniz's critique of Stoicism.

[8] As examples of the former, see Hampshire (1951), Garrett (1993), and Lloyd (1994). Of the latter, some, going back at least to Dilthey, have treated Spinoza as a Neo-Stoic through and through: cf. Dilthey (1977), 285: 'Spinoza's entire individual ethics, the aim of his work, is based on the Stoa – in fact in such comprehensiveness and with such agreements in detail that it seems unavoidable to assume his using the most widely read of the reworkings of the ancient tradition by the Dutch humanist Lipsius, his *De constantia*' (my translation of Dilthey's German, as cited by Graeser [1991]). For a study that seeks to show that 'much of the substance and structure of the Ethics...constitute a reworking of Stoicism', see James (1993). James is reacting against the tendency to regard Spinoza as principally influenced by his near contemporaries, above all Descartes. Similarly, Kristeller (1984), who finds Spinoza's determinism 'clearly Stoic', and says Spinoza 'follows the Stoics when he places the doctrine of the passions at the center of his ethics' (5). According to Kristeller (12, n. 23), Spinoza had Seneca and Epictetus in his library. Graeser (1991), 336 n. 5, agrees with Curley (1988), 137, and Bennett (1984), 16, that 'Quellenforschung has not done much to advance understanding of the discussion of systematic problems in Spinoza'. Instead, he focuses on 'the apparent reworking of Stoic thoughts in Spinoza's ontology'. As I do, he calls attention to the affinity between the two primary attributes of Spinoza's single substance, and the two Stoic principles, one 'active' and the other 'passive'. He then engages in a detailed discussion about whether, in Spinoza and the Stoics, these two attributes or principles are to be regarded as objectively distinct, or as merely human ways of experiencing and understanding a monistic reality.

of these remarks, I prefer to view his relation to Stoicism from the perspectives of conceptual similarity and difference, leaving aside the scarcely controllable question of his conscious indebtedness. It may be that he quite deliberately turned to Stoic texts or ideas, or that he was working in a milieu where he could not fail to imbibe them deeply; but even if either of these situations were so, I hesitate to characterise him, as James does (see footnote 8), as 'reworking . . . the ethics and metaphysics of Stoicism', or as having 'a huge intellectual debt' to that philosophy. For, as I shall indicate, Spinoza's striking affinity to Stoicism coexists with striking differences between them. I shall begin by comparing Stoic cosmology with some of Spinoza's principal propositions. Having done that, we shall be in a position to review their main agreements in ethics and also the differences between them in regard to providence and the divine nature.

Here, by way of introduction, is what Alexander of Aphrodisias says about Stoic cosmology, a text that Spinoza is most unlikely to have known (*Fat.* 191, 30 Bruns = SVF 2.945):[9]

They [the Stoics] say that this world is one and contains all beings within itself; it is organized by nature, living, rational and intelligent, and it possesses the organization of beings, an organization that is eternal and progresses according to a certain sequence and order. The things that come to be first are causes of those after them, and in this way all things are bound together with one another. Nothing comes to be in the world in such a way that there is not something else that follows it with no alternative and is attached to it as to a cause; nor, on the other hand, can any of the things that come to be subsequently be disconnected from the things that have come to be previously, so as not to follow some one of them as if bound to it . . . For nothing either is or comes to be in the world without a cause, because there is nothing of the things in it that is separated and disconnected from all the things that have preceded. For the world would be torn apart and divided and not remain one for ever, organized according to one order and organization if any causeless motion were introduced . . . The organization of the universe, which is like this, goes on from infinity to infinity actively and unceasingly . . . Fate itself, nature, and the reason according to which the universe is organized they claim to be God; he is present in all beings and happenings, and in this way uses the individual nature of all beings for the organization of the universe.

The context of this passage is Stoic determinism, and it also includes four other fundamental Stoic doctrines. First, the world is a

---

[9] I adopt, with slight modifications, the translation by Sharples (1983), 70–1.

unitary system that contains all beings; second, the world is infinite in time; third, the world has God or Nature present in it throughout as its organizing principle; and fourth, God or Nature is equivalent to fate or causality, and to reason.

The surface affinities of Alexander's text to Spinoza's metaphysics are obvious. Like the Stoics, Spinoza identifies God and Nature (Pt. 4, Pref.).[10] Like them again, he takes God to be both eternal and the immanent cause of all things (*Ethics* Part I, Propositions 18–19). He insists, as they do, on strict causality: 'Nothing exists from whose nature some effect does not follow' (Pt. I, Prop. 36). And again like them, he makes God the ground of causality (Pt. I, Prop. 29): 'In nature there is nothing contingent, but all things have been determined from the necessity of the divine nature to exist and produce an effect in a certain way'. Spinoza and the Stoics seem to have a strikingly similar view about God's or Nature's causal powers and relation to necessity, the dependence of everything on God or Nature, and God's or Nature's presence throughout reality.

There is, however, one term in Alexander's Stoic report that might suggest that the close resemblances I have adduced are actually superficial. Here and sometimes elsewhere, the Stoics talk about the world in ways that imply it to be conceptually distinct from God or Nature. Spinoza does not do this because he sets out from the position that there is only one substance, namely God, and that 'Whatever is, is in God, and nothing can be or be conceived without God' (Pt. I, Prop. 15). For Spinoza, the world simply is God or Nature. Do the Stoics disagree? The answer to this question is complex.

On the one hand, the foundation of Stoic physics is the postulation of *two* principles: one active = God (*theos*) and the other passive = matter (*hylê*). Stoic matter has three-dimensional extension, but taken by itself it has no other attributes: 'It is without motion from itself and shapeless' (S. E., *M* IX 75 = LS 44C). God, the active principle, is the corporeal cause or reason *in* matter. Because God and matter are constantly conjoined, their conjunction constitutes 'qualified' substance. Accordingly, the Stoics, when characterizing their two principles, reserve the term 'substance' (signifying unqualified substance) for matter, and the term 'cause' for God (DL VII 134 = LS 44A, LS 44C). Strictly, then, the Stoic God is not substance as such but rather the 'qualification' of substance. On the other

---

[10] I cite Spinoza's *Ethics* from the edition by Curley (1985), and I adopt his translations.

hand, because matter (signifying unqualified substance) has no attributes beyond three-dimensional extension, substance is something determinate only by virtue of God's constant causal interaction within it.

In addition, the Stoic principles, notwithstanding their duality, are completely inseparable and correlative; hence, the world that they constitute is unitary rather than dualistic. Its unity is evident in the Stoic claim that, *sub specie aeternitatis*, the world (*kosmos*) is 'God himself, who is the individual quality consisting of all substance' (DL VII 137 = LS 44F). Alternatively, the world may be thought of as the finite system (*diakosmêsis*) that God periodically generates and destroys by his immanent activity. Here we seem to have an anticipation of Spinoza's distinction between *natura naturans* and *natura naturata*, whereby he advises his readers to think of nature, either as active – 'God, insofar as he is considered as a free cause', or as passive – 'Whatever follows from the necessity of God's nature, or from any of God's attributes' (Pt. I, Prop. 29 scholium). This distinction is close to the one the Stoics make between God as universal cause and the organized world that is God's necessary set of effects.

Furthermore, we need to attend to the two propositions Spinoza starts from in Part II of his *Ethics*: (1) 'Thought is an attribute of God, or God is a thinking thing'; and (2) 'Extension is an attribute of God, or God is an extended thing'. Does Stoicism come close to Spinoza's view of the relation between God, thought, and extension?

Here again, the answer must be yes. First, the Stoic divinity is a thinking being. Other names for him are *nous* mind, or *logos* reason (DL VII 135 = SVF 1.102), and these terms signify, as thinking does for Spinoza, an essential attribute of the Stoics' God. Second, the Stoics' God is an extended thing; there is no part of matter in which he is not physically present. Given the complication of the Stoics' dual principles, it is not strictly true for them as it is for Spinoza that, 'The thinking substance and the extended substance are one and the same substance, which is now comprehended under this attribute, now under that' (Pt. II, Prop. 7 schol.). Yet, although in Stoicism God and matter are conceptually distinct, and each of them is an extended thing, their constant conjunction, as we have seen, generates a notion of unitary substance that is quite similar to Spinoza's. In addition, the Stoics would probably endorse his claim that, 'Whether we consider nature under the attribute of Extension, or under the attribute of

Thought, or under any other attribute, we shall find one and the same order, or one and the same connection of causes' (*ibid.*).

Every nameable item in the Stoic world is an effect of God's physical interaction with matter. And because God is all-pervasive mind, God's thought as well as his extension are present everywhere. For Spinoza too, 'particular things are nothing but affections of God's attributes, or modes by which God's attributes are expressed in a certain and determinate way' (Pt. I, Prop. 25 corollary). Precisely how Spinoza construes these affections or modes is a contentious issue I must leave to the experts to debate. What seems to be unquestionably common to him and the Stoics is the idea that ultimately all individual things derive their own mode of existence from the attributes of the single divine substance. In Stoicism, we find this formulation:

> The divine mind or thought pervades every part of the world, just like the soul in us. But it pervades some parts to a greater extent and others to a lesser degree. Through some parts it passes as 'coherence', as through our bones and sinews, and through other parts as 'intellect', as through our mind (DL VII 138–9 = LS 47O).

This text states that the identity of all particular beings, whether animate or inanimate, is ultimately a function of God. God's thought or mind or activity manifests itself in the *coherence* of a stone, the *growth* of a plant, or the *soul* of an animate being. According to this Stoic *scala naturae*, every determinate thing is ultimately, just as Spinoza writes, 'An idea in God, of which God is the cause' (Pt. II, Prop. 13 schol.). The Stoics called these ideas *spermatikoi logoi*, 'seminal formulae', and because God is the *spermatikos logos* of the world, he is the causal principle of everything.

For the Stoic God, then, Spinoza's proposition that: 'The order and connection of ideas is the same as the order and connection of things' (Pt. II, Prop. 7) appears to hold, as does also part of the corollary that he draws: 'From this it follows that God's power of thinking is equal to his actual power of acting'. Unlike Spinoza, however, the Stoics do not speak of God as having *infinite* attributes or *infinite* extension. The Stoic God, though eternal, is finite in spatial extension. Beyond God or the world is infinite void.

Thus far, in the area of metaphysics or cosmology, affinities between Stoicism and Spinoza are unmistakable. It is true, of course,

that Spinoza's manner of deducing his system has little in common
with the Stoics'. They do not begin, as he does, from definitions and
axioms concerning attributes and essences, finitude, *causa sui*, and
so forth. It is also true that Spinoza's God or Nature is far more abstract and remote from empirical reality than the Stoic divinity in
its manifestation as fire or *pneuma*. Nonetheless, the upshot of both
systems is a broadly similar conception of reality – monistic in its
treatment of God as the ultimate cause of everything, dualistic in
its two aspects of thought and extension, hierarchical in the different levels or modes of God's attributes in particular beings, strictly
determinist and physically active through and through.[11]

To test the significance of these connections, I turn now to a comparison of the two ethics. Given Spinoza's analytical rigour and the
Stoics' claims to consistency, my findings thus far may be of more
philosophical interest if we find the similarity continuing in their
detailed ethical theories. Up to a point, the connection continues to
be striking. Here, first, is an indication of this from the Stoic side.[12]

Individual human beings are 'parts of universal nature', which is
to say that they, like everything else, are necessarily connected to the
world system of which God is the cause. God or Nature manifests itself in particular animate natures as an impulse to self-preservation
(see footnote 11). This impulse, which is initially instinctual, becomes rational as human beings mature, and causes them to make
value judgments about what is suitable or unsuitable to their survival. However, the rationality of these judgments is generally imperfect because most human beings fail to understand the organization
of nature and their own individual natures. This imperfection has
effects that show themselves in the passions, which are faulty value

[11] Compare Spinoza's concept of *conatus* (Pt. III, Prop. 7): 'The striving (*conatus*) by
which each thing strives to persist in its own being is nothing but the actual essence
of the thing' with the Stoic concept of *pneuma*. The Stoics explained the persisting
identity of particular beings by reference to the 'sustaining' power of the thing's
internal *pneuma*, which also accounts for each thing's individual substance; cf.
the texts in Long and Sedley (1987): 47 I, J, M, N. What Hampshire (1951), 92, calls
'self-maintenance', in reference to Spinoza, is closely analogous to the Stoic doctrine, and in both philosophers it pertains to animate and inanimate things. Curley
(1988), 112–15, notes the Stoics as antecedents of Spinoza's *conatus* doctrine, but
he misleadingly also associates it with Epicureanism.

[12] For what follows, I draw mainly on DL VII 85–88 = LS 57A and 63C, Stobaeus II
88.8 = LS 65A, Hippolytus, *Refutation of all heresies* I 21 = LS 62A, and Epictetus
I 1.7–12 = LS 62K and II 14.7–13.

judgments.[13] The passions involve treating things that are external to the mind as *per se* good or bad, whereas in fact they are ethically neutral. Happiness and freedom depend entirely on accommodating one's mind and purposes to the necessary causal sequence of nature. One can achieve that accommodation only by understanding that virtue consists in living according to one's nature, which entails consistently following the dictates of correct reasoning and thereby acquiring knowledge of God or Nature. As a consequence of that knowledge, a person sees that his or her momentary situation in the world could not be otherwise than it is. The ideally wise person has a mind-set which, in the coherence of its ideas and their practical implications, mirrors the necessary and rational sequence of natural events.

Spinoza endorses the main thrust of all these propositions. Here is an illustrative selection: 'It is impossible that a man should not be a part of Nature' (Pt. 4, Prop. 4 part). 'Acting absolutely from virtue is nothing else in us but acting, living, and preserving our being . . . by the guidance of reason, from the foundation of seeking one's advantage' (Pt. 4, Prop. 24). 'Knowledge of God is the Mind's greatest good; its greatest virtue is to know God' (Pt. 4, Prop. 27). 'Insofar as a thing agrees with our nature, it is necessarily good' (Pt. 4, Prop. 31). 'Insofar as men are subject to passions they cannot be said to agree in nature' (Pt. 4, Prop. 32). 'A free man thinks of nothing less than of death' (Pt. 4, Prop. 67 part).

Rather than extend the quotations, I quote Hampshire (1951), 121 (who never refers to Stoicism): 'To Spinoza it seemed that men can attain happiness and dignity only by identifying themselves, through their knowledge and understanding, with the whole of nature, and by submerging their individual interests in this understanding'. Numerous Stoic citations of an exactly similar purport could be given.[14]

---

[13] Spinoza misrepresents the Stoics when he writes (Pt. V, Pref.): 'The mind does not have an absolute dominion over [the passions]. Nevertheless, the Stoics thought that they depend entirely on our will, and that we can command them absolutely.' Here, Spinoza seems to confuse the Stoic thesis that passions are judgments or functions of the rational mind with freedom of the will from antecedent causation. Lipsius similarly (*Phys.* I 14).

[14] For instance, Marcus Aurelius IV 40: 'One should continually think of the world as a single living being, with one substance and one soul . . . and how all its actions derive from one impulse'; and Epictetus II 14.7: 'The philosopher should bring his own will into harmony with what happens, so that neither anything that happens

In addition, Spinoza agrees with the Stoics in a number of highly specific ways. In both systems pity, humility, hope, and repentance are rejected as desirable states of mind.[15] The Stoics also agree with Spinoza in extending the value of following virtue from the individual to society, and they do so for similar reasons. In both systems, virtue, construed as rationality and understanding, is treated as a good common to all human beings. Hence, the Stoics argued that all goods are common to the virtuous and that when one wise person acts, all others are benefited (Stobaeus *Ecl.* II 101.21 = LS 60P), and Spinoza writes: 'The good which everyone who seeks virtue wants for himself, he also desires for other men' (Pt. 4, Prop. 37 part).

Spinoza's ethics becomes transparently and profoundly Stoic, when he writes (Pt. 3, Appendix 32):[16]

Human power is very limited and infinitely surpassed by the power of external causes. So we do not have an absolute power to adapt things outside us to our use. Nevertheless, we shall bear calmly those things which happen to us contrary to what the principle of our advantage demands, if we are conscious that we have done our duty, that the power we have could not have extended itself to the point where we could have avoided those things, and that we are a part of the whole of nature, whose order we follow. If we understand this clearly and distinctly, that part of us which is defined by understanding, i.e., the better part of us, will be entirely satisfied with this and will strive to persevere in that satisfaction. For insofar as we understand, we can want nothing except what is necessary, nor absolutely be satisfied with anything except what is true. Hence, insofar as we understand these things rightly, the striving of the better part of us agrees with the order of the whole of nature.

These ethical links between Spinoza and the Stoics, especially when they are related to the ideas about God or Nature in both systems, are hardly coincidental. Yet it would be somewhat crass, in my opinion, to explain them as mainly due to Spinoza's deliberate though unacknowledged appropriation of Stoicism. The Stoic legacy here may have less to do with Spinoza's direct mirroring (possible

happens against our will, nor anything that fails to happen fails to happen when we wish it to happen.'

[15] Pity: SVF 3.452, Spinoza Pt. IV, Prop. 50. Humility: SVF 3.107, Spinoza Pt. IV, Prop. 53. Hope: Seneca, *Ep.* 5.7–8, Spinoza Pt. III, Def. Aff. XII. Repentance: SVF 3.548, Spinoza Pt. IV, Prop. 54.

[16] Aptly quoted as such by D. Rutherford (1999), 457.

though that is) than with intellectual, theological, and methodological affinity.

If you posit strict determinism, the dependence of everything on a single, intelligent causal principle, the physical extension of that principle everywhere, the self-preservative drive of all creatures, the ideal conformity of human nature to rationality and understanding, the incompatibility of happiness with servitude to passions and dependence on worldly contingencies; and if you also believe, as Spinoza and the Stoics did, that a mind perfectly in tune with nature has a logical structure that coheres with the causal sequence of events – if you believe all these things and follow up their implications, the rational constraints on your ethics will lead you to a ground shared by Spinoza and the Stoics – a denial of free will (in the sense of facing an open future), an acceptance of the way things are, and an interest in cultivating the understanding as the only basis for achieving virtue, autonomy, and emotional satisfaction.

To this extent, and it is certainly a very large extent, Spinoza offers us a highly illuminating representation of a Stoic or quasi-Stoic philosophy. However, although I do not think that these findings are remotely superficial, they are certainly incomplete and would be highly misleading if we left matters here. In two related respects that I have so far omitted, Spinoza and the Stoics are poles apart.

The first point has to do with teleology and divine providence. The Stoics take their cosmic divinity to be identical not only to causality or fate but also to providence, and they take the world, as caused and instantiated by God, to be supremely good, beautiful, and designedly conducive to the benefit of its human inhabitants. Spinoza, by contrast, regards it as an egregious error to suppose, as he puts it, 'that God himself directs all things to some certain end... Nature has no aim set before it... This doctrine takes away God's perfection. For if God acts for the sake of an end, he necessarily wants something which he lacks' (Pt. I appendix).[17] Spinoza's target in these remarks was not Stoicism but the Judaeo-Christian tradition and its doctrine of a creator separate from his creation. He does not consider a view like that of the Stoics in which God is both immanent in everything

---

[17] Although James (1993), 306, mentions Spinoza's 'adamant opposition to teleological explanation', she seems to me to overlook the great distance this creates between him and the Stoics' unqualified commitment to providence and God's special concern for human beings.

and at the same time acting with a view to the good of the whole. There can be no doubt, however, that he would reject such a view both for the reasons I quoted and also because it would conflict with his conception of God's infinite nature and non-teleological reasoning.

The second major point of difference is Spinoza's insistence that, while our ideas are also God's ideas (since they are modes of God) and derive such adequacy as they have from God, his intellect must differ completely from ours; for we are only finite modes of God (Pt. I, Prop. 17, coroll. 2 schol.). The Stoics, on the other hand, suppose that though God is not anthropomorphic, the divine mind has the same faculties as human beings have, and that a human being could in theory equal the divine in wisdom and excellence.[18]

If the Stoics had taken Spinoza's route of denying divine providence, they would have avoided a battery of objections brought against them from antiquity onward. As it is, they were faced with having to account for the apparent imperfections of a world whose author was a perfect being in ways we are supposedly equipped to understand and find rationally acceptable. I shall not discuss their responses to this objection here. But their differences from Spinoza over providence and the divine intellect, notwithstanding his doctrine of the 'intellectual love of God', make his system much more remote from theirs in what it implies (if it implies anything) about God's relation to persons.

In treating the divine mind as a perfect paradigm of the human intellect, well intentioned as well as rational, the Stoics wanted to suggest that we can be at home in the universe in ways that are analogous to a citizen living in an excellently administered city. The Stoic God has equipped us to live well as world citizens, who can discover in cosmic order a pattern of rationality we can make our own by cultivating the virtues of justice, moderation, and so forth. Most of us fail to make more than modest progress toward this goal because our dispositions lack the requisite strength and understanding. But the Stoics' God, unlike Spinoza's apparently, does speak to us directly in our own reasoning and appropriate choices, and underwrites the prescriptions of virtuous action. For obvious reasons, these thoughts were more acceptable to Christians and Jews

---

[18] Cf. Cicero, *ND* II 58, and SVF 3.245–52.

than Stoic physical doctrines that so strikingly anticipate Spinoza's metaphysics.

3. LIPSIUS: STOICISM FOR CHRISTIANS

The Flemish scholar Justus Lipsius (1547–1606) was not a philosopher in a deep sense of the word.[19] He was a brilliant classical philologist who also wrote prolifically about ancient history, Christianity, and the political and religious issues of his troubled times. What makes him important, for the purpose of this chapter, is his unprecedented knowledge of many of the ancient sources of Stoicism, and also his cultural influence from about 1600 to 1750. In three treatises, *De constantia*, *Manuductio ad Stoicam philosophiam*, and *Physiologia Stoicorum*, Lipsius produced accounts of Stoicism which are based on a vast selection of Greek and Latin citations.[20] These works, especially the first, were extremely popular in the seventeenth and eighteenth centuries. Lipsius relies heavily on Seneca, his favourite author, but his books include much of the Greek material that any modern scholar of Stoicism must draw on, and he sometimes weighs the value of different testimonies in a manner that anticipates modern scholarship. Anyone seriously interested in Stoicism at the time had to read Lipsius; his accounts of the school were the fullest available.

Unfortunately, Lipsius' works were a disaster for the interpretation of Stoicism as systematic philosophy. This is so for three main reasons. First, despite his extraordinary command of numerous ancient sources, he did not know or did not use the evidence of Galen, Sextus Empiricus, the Aristotelian commentators, or Marcus Aurelius, and even his citations of Cicero are few compared with what he drew from Seneca and Epictetus. Thus he bypasses much of the more technical material on Stoic cosmology. Second, he tends to confirm or correct the sources that he cites by additional reference to

[19] For Lipsius' life and an outline of his works on Stoicism, see Saunders (1955). This is a useful book but rather uncritical in regard to Lipsius, and very out of date in dealing with ancient Stoicism. There is a good study of Lipsius in French by Lagrée (1994).

[20] I cite these works from the following editions, available in the Bancroft Library, University of California at Berkeley: *De constantia* (Leiden, 1584); *Manuductio* and *Physiologia stoicorum* (Antwerp, 1610).

Platonist and Christian writers, so blurring or distorting the original Stoic doctrines. Third, and most damaging, he accepts Christianity as the criterion by which to assess the meaning and propriety of Stoicism.

What Spinoza in the next generation would have found particularly congenial in Stoicism is precisely Lipsius' target – the immanence of God in everything, the unity of God and matter, and universal determinism. Lipsius tries to bring Stoic statements about these issues into line with his understanding of Christian theology. The result is that Stoicism loses its distinctive character and becomes a largely bland anticipation of Christian theism.

Lipsius knows that for Stoicism God or Nature, and matter, are eternal and coextensive principles; that together these principles constitute the living organism which is the universe; and that God or Nature, under the descriptions of fire or fiery breath or reason or mind, functions as the causal agent of everything. Rather than giving the term 'nature' an independent meaning, Lipsius invites his readers to translate it as God: *Naturam dixi, intellego Deum* (*Phys.* I 2). The contrast with Spinoza's reverse usage, *Deus sive Natura*, is striking. Lipsius objects to the ideas that matter is coeval with God and that God could not exist without matter (extension). 'God', he says, 'is contained in things but not infused with them' (*Phys.* I 8): God is truly and primarily mind, and only secondarily the world (ibid.). Lipsius can find some Stoic support for this interpretation, but what he is after, and what he wants to find as the Stoics' intended meaning, shows how far he is from trying to understand them in their own terms.

As the Christian that he is, Lipsius will not tolerate pantheism, materialism, or the suggestion that God could countenance anything bad as humanly construed, or that God could be fully present to the human mind. Wherever he can, then, he tries to shift the Stoics away from a literal endorsement of such claims. He approves of the Stoics for having a vitalist conception of nature as distinct from those (Epicureans?) who make it *bruta et sine sensu* (*Phys.* I 5). However, he shies away from treating God and matter together as nature. We should construe the Stoics' divine fire, he says, as nature *par excellence*, as *above* matter, and we should elucidate it with the help of biblical references to God's manifestation in fire. When the Stoics speak of God as being *in* things, they mean, as Scripture teaches, that 'We have our being in God' (*Phys.* I 9).

With the help of Platonism, as distinct from strict Stoic doctrine, Lipsius confers negative value on matter, and treats it as the source of evil (*Phys.* I 14). This was not orthodox Stoic doctrine, but it enables Lipsius to relieve the Stoics of the problems that their theodicy faced in its attempts to reconcile providence and strict determinism. In a similar vein, he takes Stoic statements about human *voluntas* to imply 'free' will, and thus to be in line with Christianity (*Phys.* I 14).

The points I have just made with great brevity are complex issues. The sources on which Lipsius primarily relied are not free from ambiguity. I do not want to give the impression that he would have had any strong reason, given his time and place, to approach the Stoics more historically and critically. In his most popular work, *De constantia*, he focused not on the basic principles of Stoicism but on the philosophy's utility as a way of strengthening the mind against anxiety and external troubles.

Relying heavily on Seneca, he imagines himself, when fleeing from the troubles of Flanders, confronted by one Longius, who restrains him with the words: 'What we need to flee from, Lipsius, is not our country but our emotions; we need to strengthen our mind to give us tranquillity and peace amidst turmoil and war' (*Const.* 1). Longius proceeds to instruct Lipsius that the chief enemies of mental resolution are 'false goods and evils' (*Const.* 7). In regard to externals, Lipsius should ask himself whether he has really lost something. With references to Stoic providence and determinism, he is told to acknowledge that natural phenomena are controlled by an 'eternal law', which is divine (*Const.* 13–20). The chief thrust of this treatise is the need to cultivate 'voluntary and uncomplaining endurance of all human contingencies' (*Const.* 3). The instrument for this cultivation is 'a good mind' or the rationality that we derive from God.

Lipsius puts numerous objections to his mentor, based on the thesis that the prescriptions he is being offered are not consistent with human nature, and Longius counters them (*Const.* 11). The work includes some original ideas, such as the claim that, of false values, the public ones are more harmful than the private because the mistaken praise attached to patriotism and pity has the bad effect of indoctrinating those who hear it (*Const.* 7). Longius argues persuasively that a high degree of simulation is involved when people grieve over public woes: these do not inflict actual loss on the majority, but they are affected by them because they lack the mental resolution to remain detached.

Lipsius' *De constantia* is a more creative production than his technical writings on Stoicism, which involve only little exegesis. Given his turbulent epoch, fraught with religious disputes and persecutions, the contemporary appeal of the book is fully understandable. It is also, I think, more authentically Stoic than his others, especially in its emphasis on the mind and interiority as the only site of authentic goodness. Yet, in keeping with his heavy reliance on Seneca, the moralising of *De constantia* and its lack of rigorous argument were probably only irritating to philosophers of the calibre of Spinoza or Locke or Hume.[21] Unfortunately, again, the modern world's general image of Stoicism owes a great deal to Lipsius' narrow focus on the uncomplaining endurance of one's fate.

4. BUTLER: THE ETHICS OF FOLLOWING NATURE

I turn now to a philosopher who did appreciate some of the deeper structure of Stoic ethics. Joseph Butler, the Anglican Bishop of Durham in the middle of the eighteenth century, was a devout Christian. But in his *Sermons*, as distinct from his work *The Analogy of Religion, Natural and Revealed, to the Constitution and Course of Nature*, he looks for a grounding of moral philosophy that is to be independent of any appeals to revelation or divine law.[22] Butler's main targets are Hobbes' mechanistic treatment of human nature and the moral sense theory of Shaftesbury who, though 'he has shown beyond all contradiction, that virtue is naturally the interest or happiness and vice the misery, of such a creature as man', yet has no

---

[21] Unlike Dilthey (1977), I find it improbable that Spinoza's affinity to Stoicism was mediated by his reading of Lipsius.

[22] For Butler's works, I refer to the edition by W. E. Gladstone, 2 vols. (Oxford, 1896). *Pref.* = the Preface to the *Fifteen Sermons* (*Serm.*) and *Diss.* = *Dissertation II. Of the Nature of Virtue*. I have read Butler's *Analogy* only cursorily. His purpose there is to find confirmation for the revealed doctrines of Christianity in the providentially generated processes of nature. There may well be affinities with Stoicism in this work, but I have not looked for them. For Butler's ethics I have benefited from reading Penelhum (1985). Penelhum says virtually nothing about the Stoics, and I am solely responsible for the comparisons I make with Butler. For a somewhat fuller discussion of Butler, with emphasis on his relationship to Stoic strands in medieval thought, see Ch. 14, Irwin, this volume.

remedy to answer 'a sceptic not convinced of this happy tendency of virtue, or being of a contrary opinion' (*Pref.* 20).

Butler bases his ethics on an analysis of the human 'constitution' or 'nature'. He starts from the idea that any particular nature consists of a whole of teleologically organized parts. Thus we can only get the idea of a watch, he argues, by considering how all its parts are so related as to serve the purpose of telling the time.[23] For human beings similarly, to get an idea of our constitution we need to view our inward parts ('appetites, passions, affections, and the principle of reflection') not separately, but 'by the relations which these several parts have to each other; the chief of which is the authority of reflection or conscience' (*Pref.* 12).

Butler's main thesis is that, by regarding the human constitution in this teleologically organized way, 'it will as fully appear, that this our nature, i.e., constitution, is adapted to virtue, as from the idea of a watch it appears, that its nature, i.e., constitution or system, is adapted to measure time', with the decisive difference that 'our constitution is put in our own power . . . and therefore accountable for any disorder or violation of it' (*Pref.* 13). He claims that 'the ancient moralists had some inward feeling or other' corresponding to his thesis, which they expressed by saying that 'man is born to virtue, that it consists in following nature, and that vice is more contrary to this nature than tortures or death' (*Pref.* 8). After giving his watch analogy, he writes (*Pref.* 14):

They had a perception that injustice was contrary to their nature, and that pain was so also. They observed these two perceptions totally different, not in degree, but in kind: and the reflecting upon each of them, as they thus stood in their nature, wrought a full intuitive conviction, that more was due and of right belonged to one of these inward perceptions, than to the other; that it demanded in all cases to govern such a creature as man.

Butler's ancient moralists are clearly the Stoics. For his use of the faculty he calls 'conscience, moral reason, moral sense, or divine

---

[23] MacIntyre (1981), 55–6, without mention of Butler, uses the watch example in order to illustrate how an 'evaluative' conclusion, 'This is a bad watch' validly follows from a factual premise such as 'This watch is grossly inaccurate.' MacIntyre's purpose in this context is to defend the Aristotelian idea of man as a functional concept: '"Man" stands to "good man" as "watch" stands to "good watch".' The essentialism that MacIntyre advances is very similar to Butler's teleological view of human nature.

reason', he appeals to the beginning of Epictetus' first discourse (*Diss.* 1), and for taking its object to be acting 'abstracted from all regard to what is, in fact and event, the consequence of it', he refers to Marcus Aurelius IX 6 and Cicero, *De officiis* I 6 (*Diss.* 4).[24]

Butler is aware that 'following nature' is an ambiguous and contested expression. In his analysis of the human constitution, some-one can follow nature in three distinct ways: (1) by acting according to any psychological propensity; (2) by following whatever passion happens to be strongest; and (3) by following the principle of reflection which, in terms of his teleological argument, is superior to all our other faculties. Only in this third sense does Butler recommend following nature as *the* moral principle. What that means, he says, is man's nature as a moral agent, as being a law to himself, as accepting the natural authority of reflection 'to direct and regulate all under principles, passions, and motives of action' (*Serm.* II 19).

Butler takes it that human beings are naturally motivated both by a general desire for their own happiness, which he calls 'self-love', and also by 'a variety of particular affections, passions, and appetites to particular external objects' (*Serm.* XI 3). He holds it to be no less certain 'that we were made for society and to do good to our fellow-creatures' (*Serm.* I 3). For the purpose of analysis, he distinguishes between 'the nature of man as respecting self, and tending to private good, his own preservation and happiness; and the nature of man as having respect to society, and tending to promote public good' (*ibid.*). He grants that these two primary motivations may conflict in individuals, but such conflict, so far from being necessary, is actually a violation of our natural constitution:

These ends do indeed perfectly coincide; and to aim at public and private good are so far from being inconsistent, that they mutually promote each other (*ibid.*).

In regard to self-love and caring for offspring, our natures are broadly similar to those of other animals. What chiefly distinguishes us from them is our unique and governing principle of 'conscience or reflection'.

---

[24] In the passage Butler cites, Marcus Aurelius distinguishes the 'sufficiency' of correct judgment and moral action from everything that happens by external causes. What appealed to Butler in the Cicero passage must have been the claim there that honourableness (*honestas*) is 'to be pursued for its own sake' (*propter se expetenda*). On the Epictetus reference, see the following discussion.

Butler, as we have seen, cites Cicero's *De officiis* in support of his claim that the object of the faculty he calls 'conscience, moral reason, moral sense, or divine reason' is intended action as distinct from any actual consequence. In Sections I 11–15 of Cicero's work, which follow shortly after I 6 (the passage cited by Butler), Cicero gives an account of the Stoic life in accordance with nature that seems much too close to Butler's general thinking to be coincidental.[25] Cicero starts from claims concerning the self-preservative instincts of animals in general, and concludes with the thesis that honourableness (*honestum*) is the goal and fulfillment of a fully mature and rational human being. There is no reference in Cicero's text to God or divine law or a strongly personified cosmic Nature, as is often the case in ancient expositions of Stoic ethics. The exclusion of such ostensibly heteronomous principles could explain why Butler was strongly influenced, as I shall presume that he was, by this further part of the *De officiis*. The key concept throughout Cicero's exposition, as in Butler, is human nature.

All creatures, Cicero tells us, begin their lives by seeking to appropriate those things that are conducive to their survival and natural constitution, and to avoid everything that threatens them. Self-love, according to the Stoics, is the primary motivation, a concept they called *oikeiôsis* to oneself.

Equally innate, but manifesting itself later, is a second or secondary *oikeiôsis* – appropriation to a creature's offspring, which the Stoics took to be the foundation of human sociability.[26] Writing of how this manifests itself in humans, Cicero (*Off.* I 12) says:

Nature, by the power of rationality, connects one human being with another for the purpose of associating in conversation and way of life, and engenders above all a special love for one's offspring. It instills an impulse for men to

[25] Cicero's source, or main source, for this passage was probably Panaetius, on whom he explicitly drew for the Stoic theory he presents in the first two books of *Off.* In earlier versions of this chapter, I proposed that Butler was influenced by Cicero's account of Stoic ethics in *Fin.* III 16–21. That text has much in common with *Off.* I 11–19, and that applies still more to the presentation of Stoic ethics in *Fin.* II 45–7. However, Butler's acquaintance with *Fin.* can be no more than a guess, whereas we know that he read at least parts of the *Off.*; so I now draw only on this latter work for my proposals concerning Butler's use of Cicero.

[26] Michael Seidler has drawn my attention to Grotius' allusion to 'the social tendency the Stoics called sociableness' (*oikeiôsis*) at the beginning of his work *On the Law of War and Peace* (1625).

meet together... and to be zealous in providing life's wherewithal not only for themselves alone but also for their wives, and children, and others whom they hold dear and ought to protect.

The two instinctual motivations Butler makes primary, self-love and benevolence, are exactly prefigured in the self-directed and other-directed objects of Stoic *oikeiôsis*. Like Butler too, the Stoics treated both instincts as equally natural, suitable, and mutually compatible. Thus far, according to Cicero's Stoic account, human beings are broadly similar to other animals in their natural motivations. What distinguishes us from them, as we mature, is the development of our capacity to reason.

In his treatment of human sociability Cicero, as we observe, invokes nature's gift of rationality. What this signifies, however, goes far beyond the instrumental use of reason as a means of managing social life effectively. Rationality endows human beings, he says, with impulses to try to understand the world, and to cultivate truth and justice and propriety. In other words, thanks to rationality we possess a distinctively moral nature, in that (*Off.* I 14):

We are the only animal that has a sense of what order is, what seemliness is, and what good measure is in words and deeds. Therefore, no other animal perceives the beauty and charm and pattern of visible things. Moreover, our nature and rationality transfer these things by analogy to the mind, thinking that beauty, consistency, and order must be preserved in one's decisions and actions.

Taking it, like Butler, that our nature is teleologically constructed so as to promote our human excellence, the Stoics argued that our specific good, as human beings, cannot be identified by reference to things that are merely natural to the constitution we broadly share with other creatures.[27] Our constitution is distinctive in its rationality. Hence, to act in accordance with reason is natural to us in a way that is quite different from the naturalness of trying to stay healthy or looking after our offspring. While in general we have good reason to pursue self-preservation and social solidarity, our instincts to do so must always be submitted to our sovereign capacity to judge

---

[27] See DL VII 87–9 = LS 63C; Seneca, *Ep.* 76.9–10 = LS 63D; Epictetus, *Diss.* I 6.12–21 = LS 63E.

the best action for creatures whose natural goal is virtue: that is, the perfection of reason as applied to human conduct.

Butler and the Stoics, then, agree to the following theses:

1. Nature, with respect to human beings, is a term that has multiple reference. It is natural for us to seek to fulfill those appetites that are conducive to the material well-being of ourselves and our fellow human beings. But 'following nature', as a moral principle, refers to our uniquely human capacity to reflect on our thoughts or possible actions, to approve or disapprove of them as morally appropriate, and to treat conformity to this faculty as our sovereign good and virtue.

2. There is no basis in our given nature for any necessary conflict between self-love and benevolence, or between benevolence and our individual happiness. Butler, in effect, expresses the self-regarding and other-regarding aspects of Stoic *oikeiôsis* when he writes: 'It is as manifest that we were made for society, and to promote the happiness of it, as that we were intended to take care of our own life, and health, and private good' (*Serm.* I 9). He and the Stoics also agree that human beings are just as capable of neglecting their own interests as of neglecting the interests of others.

When I first read Butler, I thought that his description of the reflective faculty as 'conscience' was a Christian intrusion. I now think in the light of his explicit appeal to Epictetus that he took himself to have Stoic support for this term. Glossing conscience as 'this moral approving and disapproving faculty', Butler notes (*Diss.* I): 'This way of speaking is taken from Epictetus, and is made use of as seeming the most full, and least liable to cavil.'[28] It is quite significant that Butler cites Epictetus from the *Discourses* rather than from the much more popular and summary *Manual*. Apart from the passage Butler cites, Epictetus regularly uses the word *aidôs*, literally shame or reverence, and *aidêmôn* (the corresponding adjective), to refer to the internal self-judging faculty which he takes to be natural to (though hardly operative in) every human being.[29] Here are two examples

---

[28] Butler (*ad loc.*) even quotes Epictetus' Greek expression for 'approving and disapproving' (*dokimastikê ê apodokimastikê, Diss.* I 1.1).

[29] For Epictetus' concept of *aidôs* and its role as something like 'conscience', see Kamtekar (1998).

from the *Discourses*:

God has entrusted yourself to you, and says: 'I had no one more trustworthy (*pistoteron*) than you. Keep him for me in his natural state, reverent (*aidêmôn*), trustworthy, high-minded, unperturbed, unimpassioned, undisturbed.' (II 8.23)

How are we endowed by nature? As free, as honourable (*gennaioi*), as reverent (*aidêmones*). For what other animal blushes or has an impression of what is shameful (*aischron*)? (III 7.27)

We cannot know whether Butler was familiar with these passages of Epictetus, but they show that he had good reason to attribute to this Stoic a notion like his own concept of conscience, meaning by this:

a capacity of reflecting upon actions and characters [such that] we naturally and unavoidably approve some actions, under the peculiar view of their being virtuous and of good desert; and disapprove of others, as vicious and of ill desert. (*Diss.* I 1)

In the same context Butler reveals his sympathy for Epictetus by saying, with respect to his observations on conscience: 'This is the meaning of the expression 'reverence yourself''.

Butler, it is clear, has appropriated Stoic ethics to quite a deep extent. Yet I would not call him a Neo-Stoic, for two significant reasons. First, he takes the Stoic ideal of complete freedom from passion to be inappropriate to

mankind... imperfect creatures... Reason alone, whatever any one may wish, is not in reality a sufficient motive of virtue in such a creature as man; but this reason joined with those affections which God has impressed upon his heart: and when these are allowed scope to exercise themselves but under strict government and direction of reason; then it is we act suitably to our nature, and to the circumstances God has placed us in. (*Serm.* V 4)

Butler, unlike Spinoza and the early Stoics, approves of compassion (*ibid.*) and implicitly rejects the Stoics' claim that the passions are errors of judgment. (He probably did not know the ill-attested doctrine of the 'good passions' [*eupatheiai*] that characterize the virtuous in Stoicism.)[30]

Second, and more important, Butler does not identify virtue with happiness. His view is, rather, that God apportions happiness

[30] See Ch. 10, Brennan, this volume.

to virtue in this world notwithstanding apparent evidence to the contrary (*Analogy* I 3.15–20). For Butler, happiness and misery include the material circumstances of persons and are 'in our power' only 'in many respects' (*ibid.* 18). For the Stoics, by contrast, happiness is solely constituted by virtue and is entirely up to us. Butler, then, though he regards the individual's desire for happiness as entirely natural and proper, is not a eudaimonist. His project is not – or not primarily – to establish the necessary and sufficient conditions of happiness, but rather to show, by analysis of human nature, that 'man is thus by his very nature a law to himself' (*Pref.* 24).

Interestingly, the Ciceronian account of Stoic ethics, which I have associated with Butler's principal claims, is virtually silent about happiness. The main argument is devoted to showing that human nature, construed as rationality, provides the seeds of virtue, which is construed as giving ultimate value only to that which is honourable (*honestum*). After this point has been established, we are invited to agree that 'things that are honourable pertain to living well and happily' (*Off.* I 19), but we are given nothing in the way of argument to tie virtue to happiness. That connection is so understated as to seem little more than an afterthought. Cicero is not only reticent about happiness, he also says nothing about Stoic cosmology or theology. If, as I have surmised, Butler closely studied Cicero's text, that would help to explain his selective use of Stoicism in his ethics. Cicero's account depends primarily on claims about the instinctual drives and teleology of human nature, with reason providing an ethical sensibility that is the foundation for an understanding of honourableness and the particular virtues of which it consists. Here, together with Epictetus' concept of an 'approving and disapproving faculty', we have a significant anticipation of Butler's hierarchy of natural faculties and appetites, superintended by reflection. Given his wish to ground moral judgments in human nature rather than divine command or scripture, Cicero's account of Stoic ethics, with its reticence on cosmic nature and divine causality, has an appropriateness Butler could not have found in the doctrines of Stoicism that resonate in Spinoza.

5. THE COMPLEXITY OF THE STOIC LEGACY

Modern scholars are divided in their opinions about what the founding fathers of Stoicism postulated as the foundations of their ethical theory. According to the traditional view, which I have often defended, they started from the teleology and rationality of cosmic nature or God, of which human nature was presumed to be an integral part. A minority of modern scholars has questioned this interpretation, noting the absence of cosmic nature from the seemingly authoritative argument for the evolution of moral awareness in Book III of Cicero's *De finibus*, and urging that, even in evidence where cosmic nature is made prominent, that concept does not make a clear or helpful contribution to the Stoics' principal findings about the human good.[31] I continue to be convinced that the traditional interpretation, grounding ethics in theology and cosmic nature, was the original and essential Stoic position, but I readily grant that this is not emphasized in all of our sources, including Cicero's *De officiis*, with which we have been concerned in the last few pages. How do we explain this discrepancy?

We have to admit that Stoicism, unlike Epicureanism, was never a monolithic church. The differences of emphasis we find in our sources do not simply reflect the idiosyncracies of their authors – the mentality and interests of Cicero as compared with Seneca or Epictetus or Marcus Aurelius; these differences are also due to the fact that Stoic philosophers themselves were creative and critical in the way they presented their system. Chrysippus insisted that 'universal nature and the organization of the universe are the only proper way to approach' ethics (Plutarch, *St. rep.* 1035C = LS 60A), but we hear nothing of this from the later head of the school, Panaetius, who was Cicero's main source for *De officiis*. By focusing on human nature and by understating the early Stoic thesis that 'our natures are parts of cosmic nature', a later leader of the school like Panaetius could present Stoic ethics as a theory that could readily be compared with rival moral philosophies. Debate could centre on questions such as the suffiency of virtue for complete happiness or the role of the emotions in the good life. The stage was set for treating Stoic ethics as an autonomous branch of philosophy, separable from physics and logic.

What I have said about Butler and the Stoics is sufficient to show that the Stoics have left us a significant legacy in ethics as

---

[31] Annas (1993), 159–66, and Engberg-Pedersen (1990), 16–63. I have said why I disagree with these scholars in Long (1996), 152–5. For further treatment of what I take to have been the original Stoic position, see Striker (1991) and Cooper (1996).

so construed; the same point can be made with reference to Kant. The Stoics were the only ancient philosophers who maintained that the 'honourableness' (*to kalon* or *honestum*) of the virtuous life is categorically different from every other positive value. It is therefore tempting to attribute to them a concept of the specifically 'moral' good, anticipating Kant's distinction between actions motivated by ordinary human interests and actions performed purely from duty, irrespective of their material consequences. Yet, despite the Stoics' apparent affinity to Kant on these major points, they hardly foreshadowed the most distinctive principles of Kantian ethics.[32] They did not arrive at their thesis about honourableness by *a priori* reasoning, but by reflection on our empirical capacity to perfect ourselves, as rational beings – by identifying our own *utility* or happiness with virtue and nothing else. In sharp difference from Kant, the Stoics were eudaimonists, determinists, deists, and defenders of the claim that human reason can have incorrigible access to the basic principles of reality. Once we ask why adherence to Stoic ethics coincides with happiness – Why is it rational to identify complete happiness with nothing except virtue? – these non-Kantian claims clamour for attention.

Virtue, the Stoics will say, is necessary and sufficient for happiness because (1) it is the perfection of our rational nature; (2) our happiness is so conditioned by the cosmic Nature of which we are an integral part; and (3) nothing except happiness = moral virtue is a rational object of desire for beings whose nature is autonomous only in respect of their capacity to understand and assent to the causal sequence of events.

This kind of thinking is to be found in the earliest and in the latest Stoicism of antiquity. If we want a general description of the Stoic mentality and its rationale, here, I suggest, is where we best find it. The decisive move is the second proposition of the three I just stated – the conditioning of our happiness as virtue by the cosmic Nature of which we are an integral part. Contrary to what some modern scholars think (and what Butler may have thought), this move does not posit a heteronomous basis for ethics; the Stoics, as I have said earlier, take the voice of cosmic nature to *coincide with* good reasoning by persons. What the move does involve is the

---

[32] See Long (1989) and Schneewind (1996a).

thesis that good reasoning by persons is compliance with the way things are, as determined by God or Nature.

*****

In this chapter I have tried to show that the Jew Spinoza and the Christian Lipsius, albeit in very different ways, echo the deist underpinnings of Stoic ethics. They also help us to see the irreducible tension that exists in Stoicism between its physicalism and determinism, on the one hand (anticipating Spinoza) and, on the other hand, its endorsement of divine providence and qualified human autonomy (anticipating Lipsius).[33] Butler, ignoring these complexities, shows the fertility of some Stoic concepts for developing a naturalistic ethics in which the idea of the specifically moral good is detached from the idea of happiness. The challenge for a new Stoic ethics, as undertaken by Becker, is to find a way of reuniting them without endorsing cosmic teleology.[34]

---

[33] Given the importance Rorty (1996) rightly assigns to providence in her sympathetic account of Stoicism, I am puzzled by her reticence about the obvious difficulties it generates for modern interpreters.

[34] That is precisely what Becker (1998) has bravely tried to do (see n. 4).

BIBLIOGRAPHY

Algra, K. (1995). *Concepts of Space in Greek Thought* (Leiden: Brill).

———— (2001). 'Comments or Commentary? Zeno of Citium and Hesiod's *Theogonia*', *Mnemosyne* 54, 562–81.

———— (forthcoming). 'Zeno of Citium's Contribution to Stoic Cosmology. Some Notes and Two Case Studies' in *Elenchos* 24, 1.

Algra, K., J. Barnes, J. Mansfeld, and M. Schofield (eds.) (1999). *The Cambridge History of Hellenistic Philosophy* (Cambridge: Cambridge University Press).

Algra, K., M. H. Koenen, and P. H. Schrijvers (eds.) (1997). *Lucretius and his Intellectual Background* (Amsterdam: Koninklijke Nederlandse Akademie van Wetenschappen).

Algra, K., and D. Runia (eds.) (1996). *Polyhistor: Essays Presented to Jaap Mansfeld* (Leiden: Brill).

Allen, J. (1994). 'Academic probablism and Stoic epistemology', *Classical Quarterly* 44, 85–113.

———— (1997). 'Carneadean argument' in Inwood and Mansfeld (1997), 217–56.

André, J.-M. (1987). 'Les écoles philosophiques aux deux premiers siècles de l'Empire', *Aufstieg und Niedergang der römischen Welt* II 36.1, 5–77.

Annas, J. (1980). 'Truth and knowledge' in Barnes et al. (1980), 84–104.

———— (1990). 'Stoic epistemology' in Everson (1990a), 184–203.

———— (1990a). 'The Hellenistic version of Aristotle's *Ethics*', *The Monist* 73, 80–96.

———— (1992). *Hellenistic Philosophy of Mind* (Berkeley: University of California Press).

———— (1993). *The Morality of Happiness* (Oxford: Oxford University Press).

———— (1996). 'Aristotle and Kant on Morality and Practical Reasoning' in Engstrom and Whiting (1996), 237–58.

———— (1999). *Platonic Ethics, Old and New* (Ithaca: Cornell University Press).

—— (ed.) (2001). *Cicero: On Moral Ends* (Cambridge: Cambridge University Press). With a translation by R. Woolf.

—— (forthcoming). 'Marcus Aurelius: ethics and its background'.

Arthur, E. P. (1983). 'The Stoic analysis of mind's reactions to presentations', *Hermes* 111, 69–78.

Asmis, E. (1989). 'The Stoicism of Marcus Aurelius', *Aufstieg und Niedergang der römischen Welt* II 36.3, 2228–52.

Athanassiadi, P., and M. Frede (eds.) (1999). *Pagan Monotheism in Late Antiquity* (Oxford: Oxford University Press).

Atherton, C. (1988). 'Hand over Fist: the Failure of Stoic Rhetoric', *Classical Quarterly* 38, 392–427.

—— (1993). *The Stoics on Ambiguity* (Cambridge: Cambridge University Press).

Aubenque, P. (ed.) (1991). *Études sur le Sophiste de Platon* (Naples: Bibliopolis).

—— (1991a). 'Une occasion manquée: la genèse avortée de la distinction entre l'"étant' et le 'quelque chose'' in Aubenque (1991), 365–85.

Auroux, S., E. F. K. Koerner, H -J. Niederehe, and K. Versteegh (eds.) (2000). *History of the Language Sciences* (Berlin: Walter de Gruyter).

Ax, W. (1986). *Laut, Stimme, und Sprache* (Göttingen: Vandenhoeck und Ruprecht).

Babut, D. (1974). *La religion des philosophes grecs, de Thales aux Stoïciens* (Paris: Presses Universitaires de France).

—— (1979). *Plutarque et le Stoicisme* (Paris: Presses Universitaires de France).

Backhouse, T. (2000). 'Antipater of Tarsus on false "phantasiai" (PBerol. inv. 16545)', in *Studi e testi per il Corpus dei papiri filosofici greci e latini* 10, *Papiri filososofici, Miscellanea di Studi III* (Florence: Olschki), 7–31.

Baratin, M., and F. Desbordes (eds.) (1981). *L'Analyse linguistique dans l'antiquité classique: I. Les Théories* (Paris: Klincksieck).

Barbour, R. (1998). *English Epicures and Stoics: Ancient Legacies in early Stuart Culture* (Amherst: University of Massachusetts Press).

Barker, P. (1985). 'Jean Pena and Stoic physics in the 16th century', *Southern Journal of Philosophy*, XXIII suppl., 93–107.

Barnes, J. (1978). 'La Doctrine du retour éternel', in Brunschwig (1978), 3–20.

—— (1980). 'Proof destroyed', in Barnes et al. (1980), 161–81.

—— (1986). 'The Logical Investigations of Chrysippus', *Wissenschaftskolleg Jahrbuch* 1984/5 (Berlin), 19–29.

—— (1989). 'Antiochus of Ascalon', in Griffin and Barnes (1989), 51–96.

—— (1993). 'Meaning, Saying and Thinking', in Döring and Ebert (1993), 47–61.

—— (1997). *Logic and the Imperial Stoa* (Leiden: Brill).

—— (1999). 'Linguistics: meaning', in Algra et al. (1999), 193–216.

Barnes, J., M. F. Burnyeat, and M. Schofield (eds.) (1980). *Doubt and Dogmatism* (Oxford: Oxford University Press).

Barnes, J., M. Burnyeat, J. Brunschwig, and M. Schofield (eds.) (1982). *Science and Speculation: studies in Hellenistic theory and practice* (Cambridge: Cambridge University Press).

Barnes, J., and M. Mignucci (eds.) (1988). *Matter and Metaphysics* (Naples: Bibliopolis).

Barney, R. (forthcoming). 'A Puzzle in Stoic Ethics' (forthcoming *Oxford Studies in Ancient Philosophy*).

Barton, T. (1994). *Ancient Astrology* (London: Routledge).

Barwick, K. (1922). *Remmius Palaemon und die römische ars grammatica* (*Philologus* XV Suppl.; Leipzig: Dieterich'sche). Reprint 1967 (Hildesheim: Georg Olms).

—— (1957). *Probleme der stoischen Sprachlehre und Rhetorik* (Abhandlungen der Sächsischen Akademie der Wissenschaften zu Leipzig, Philologisch-Historische Klasse 49.3. Berlin: Akademie-Verlag).

Becker, L. (1998). *A New Stoicism* (Princeton: Princeton University Press).

Bennett, J. (1984). *A Study of Spinoza's Ethics* (Cambridge: Cambridge University Press).

Billerbeck, M. (1985). 'Aspects of Stoicism in Flavian Epic', *Papers of the Liverpool Latin Seminar* 5, 341–56.

—— (1986). 'Stoizismus in der römischen Epik neronischer und flavischer Zeit', *Aufstieg und Niedergang der römischen Welt* II 32.5, 3116–51.

Birley, A. (1987). *Marcus Aurelius: A Biography* (London: Batsford).

Blank, D. (1982). *Ancient Philosophy and Grammar: the Syntax of Apollonius Dyscolus* (Chico, CA: Scholars Press).

—— (1993). 'Apollonius Dyscolus', *Aufstieg und Niedergang der Römischen Welt* II 34.1, 708–30.

—— (1994). 'Analogy, Anomaly, and Apollonius', in Everson (1994), 149–65.

—— (1998). *Sextus Empiricus Against the Grammarians* (Oxford: Oxford University Press).

—— (2000). 'The Organization of Grammar in Ancient Greece', in Auroux et al. (2000), I 400–417.

Bloos, L. (1973). *Probleme der stoischen Physik* (Hamburg: Helmut Buske Verlag).

Bobzien, S. (1986). *Die stoische Modallogik* (Würzburg: Königshausen und Neumann).

—— (1993). 'Chrysippus' Modal Logic and its Relation to Philo and Diodorus', in Döring and Ebert (1993), 63–84.

—— (1996). 'Stoic Syllogistic', *Oxford Studies in Ancient Philosophy* 14, 133–92.

—— (1997). 'The Stoics on Hypotheses and Hypothetical Arguments', *Phronesis* 42, 299–312.

—— (1998). *Determinism and Freedom in Stoic Philosophy* (Oxford: Oxford University Press).

—— (1998a). 'The inadvertent conception and late birth of the free-will problem', *Phronesis* 43, 133–75.

—— (1999). 'Chrysippus' Theory of Causes', in Ierodiakonou (1999), 196–242.

—— (1999a). 'Logic: The Stoics', in Algra et al. (1999), 92–157.

—— (1999b). 'Logic: The "Megarics"', in Algra et al. (1999), 83–92.

—— (2000). 'Wholly hypothetical syllogisms', *Phronesis* 45, 87–137.

Bonhöffer, A. (1890, reprinted 1968). *Epictet und die Stoa. Untersuchungen zur Stoischen Philosophie* (Stuttgart: Frommann).

—— (1894, reprinted 1968). *Die Ethik des Stoikers Epictet* (Stuttgart: Frommann) = Bonhöffer, A. (1996). *The Ethics of the Stoic Epictetus*, trans. W. O. Stephens (New York: Peter Lang).

Boudouris, K. J. (ed.) (1994). *Hellenistic Philosophy* (Athens: International Center for Greek Philosophy and Culture).

Boyancé, P. (1962). 'Les preuves stoïciennes de l'existence des dieux d'après Cicéron', *Hermes* 90, 45–71.

Boys-Stones, G. (2001). *Post-Hellenistic Philosophy* (Oxford: Oxford University Press).

Bramble, J. (1974). *Persius: The Programmatic Satire* (Cambridge: Cambridge University Press).

Brandom, R. (1998). 'Action, Norms, and Practical Reasoning', in Tomberlin (1998), 127–39.

Branham, R. Bracht, and M.-O. Goulet-Cazé (eds.) (1996). *The Cynics: The Cynic Movement in Antiquity and its Legacy* (Berkeley: University of California Press).

Braund, S. (1988). *Beyond Anger: A Study of Juvenal's Third Book of Satires* (Cambridge: Cambridge University Press).

—— (1997). 'A passion unconsoled? Grief and anger in Juvenal, *Satire* 13', in Braund and Gill (1997), 68–88.

Braund, S., and C. Gill (1997). *The Passions in Roman Thought and Literature* (Cambridge: Cambridge University Press).

Bréhier, E. (1910). *La Théorie des incorporels dans l'ancien Stoicisme* (Paris: Vrin).

Brennan, T. (1996). 'Reasonable Impressions in Stoicism', *Phronesis* 41(3), 318–34.

—— (1998). 'The Old Stoic Theory of the Emotions', in Sihvola and Engberg-Pedersen (1998), 21–70.

——— (2000a). 'Reservation in Stoic Ethics', *Archiv für Geschichte der Philosophie* 82 (2), 149–77.

——— (2000b). Review of Algra et al. (1999). *The Cambridge History of Hellenistic Philosophy*, in *Bryn Mawr Classical Review*, 2000.09.11

——— (2001). 'Fate and Free Will in Stoicism', *Oxford Studies in Ancient Philosophy* 21, 259–86.

——— (2003). 'Demoralizing the Stoics', forthcoming in *Ancient Philosophy*.

Brittain, C. (2000). 'Seeing Interesting Things' (unpublished).

——— (2001). *Philo of Larissa: the last of the Academic sceptics* (Oxford: Oxford University Press.

Brody, B. A. (ed.) (1989). *Suicide and Euthanasia* (Dordrecht: Kluwer).

Brunschwig, J. (ed.) (1978). *Les Stoïciens et leur logique* (Paris: Vrin).

——— (1980). 'Proof defined' in Barnes et al. (1980), 125–60.

——— (1984). 'Remarques sur la théorie stoïcienne du nom propre', *Histoire Épistémologie Langage* 6 (Lille: Presses Universitaires de Lille) 3–19. English translation in Brunschwig (1994a), 39–56.

——— (1986). 'The cradle argument in Epicureanism and Stoicism', in Schofield and Striker (1986), 113–44.

——— (1988). 'La théorie stoïcienne du genre suprême et l'ontologie platonicienne', in Barnes and Mignucci (1988), 19–127. English translation in Brunschwig (1994a), 92–157.

———(1988a). 'Sextus Empiricus on the *kritêrion*: The Sceptic as conceptual legatee', in Dillon and Long (1988), 145–75.

——— (1991). 'On a Book Title by Chrysippus: "On the Fact that the Ancients Admitted Dialectic Along with Demonstrations"', *Oxford Studies in Ancient Philosophy*, Supplementary Volume, 81–95.

——— (1994). 'Did Diogenes of Babylon Invent the Ontological Argument?', in Brunschwig (1994a), 170–89.

——— (1994a). *Papers in Hellenistic philosophy* (Cambridge: Cambridge University Press).

——— (1994b). 'On a Stoic Way of Not Being', in Brunschwig (1994a), 158–69.

——— (1994c). 'Remarks on the classification of simple propositions in Hellenistic logics', in Brunschwig (1994a), 72–91.

——— (forthcoming). 'Sur deux notions de l'éthique stoïcienne: de la 《réserve》 au 《renversement》', in G. Romeyer Dherbey and J.-B. Gourinat (forthcoming).

Brunschwig, J., and M. Nussbaum (eds.) (1993). *Passions & Perceptions* (Cambridge: Cambridge University Press; Paris: Editions de la Maison des Sciences de L'Homme).

Brunschwig, J., and G. E. R. Lloyd (eds.) (1996). *Le Savoir grec* (Paris: Flammarion).

Burnyeat, M. F. (1982). 'Gods and Heaps', in Schofield and Nussbaum (1982), 315–38.

———— (ed.) (1983). *The Skeptical Tradition* (Berkeley: University of California Press).

Butts, R. E., and J. Hintikka (eds.) (1977). *Historical and Philosophical Dimensions of Logic, Methodology, and Philosophy of Science* (Dordrecht: D. Reidel).

Caston, V. (1999). 'Something and Nothing: The Stoics on Concepts and Universals', *Oxford Studies in Ancient Philosophy* 17, 145–213.

Cavini, W. (1996). 'Essere ed essere vero – Sull' uso assoluto di *huparcho* nella logica stoica', in Funghi (1996), 141–45.

Cherniss, H. F. (ed.) (1976). *Plutarch: Moralia*, vol. XIII (London: Heinemann; Cambridge, MA: Harvard University Press).

Clarke, K. (1999). *Between Geography and History: Hellenistic Constructions of the Roman World* (Oxford: Oxford University Press).

Codoñer, C. (1989). 'La physique de Sénèque: Ordonnance et structure des "Naturales Quaestiones"', *Aufstieg und Niedergang der römischen Welt* II 36.3, 1779–822.

Colish, M. C. (1985). *The Stoic Tradition from Antiquity to the Early Middle Ages*, 2 vols. (Leiden: Brill).

Cooper, J. M. (1989). 'Greek Philosophers on Suicide and Euthanasia', in Brody (1989), 9–38.

———— (1995). 'Eudaimonism and the Appeal to Nature', *Philosophy and Phenomenological Research* 55, 587–98.

———— (1996). 'Eudaimonism, the appeal to Nature, and "moral duty" in Stoicism', in Engstrom and Whiting (1996), 261–84.

———— (1998). 'Posidonius on Emotions', in Sihvola and Engberg-Pedersen (1998), 71–111.

Cooper, J. M., and J. F. Procopé (eds.) (1995). *Seneca: Moral and Political Essays* (Cambridge, Cambridge University Press).

Couloubaritsis, L. (1986). 'La psychologie chez Chrysippe', in *Aspects de la philosophie Hellenistique*, Entretiens Hardt 32, 99–146.

Craig, E. (ed.) (1999). *Routledge Encyclopedia of Philosophy* (London: Routledge).

Crivelli, P. (1994). 'Indefinite propositions and anaphora in Stoic logic', *Phronesis* 39, 187–206.

Curley, E. (1988). *Behind the Geometrical Method. A Reading of Spinoza's Ethics* (Princeton: Princeton University Press).

———— (ed.) (1985). *The Collected Works of Spinoza*, vol. 1 (Princeton: Princeton University Press).

Darwall, S. L. (1995). *The British Moralists and the Internal 'Ought'* (Cambridge: Cambridge University Press).

Deichgräber, K. (1930). *Die Griechische Empirikerschule: Sammlung und Darstellung der Lehre* (Berlin: Weidmann).

DeFilippo, J., and P. T. Mitsis (1994). 'Socrates and Stoic natural law', in Vander Waerdt (1994a), 252–71.

De Lacy, P. H. (1945). 'The Stoic categories as methodological principles', *Transactions and Proceedings of the American Philological Society* 76, 246–63.

Denyer, N. (1988). 'Stoicism and token reflexivity', in Barnes and Mignucci (1988), 375–96.

Detel, W., K. Hülser, G. Krüger, and W. Lorenz (1980). *'lekta ellipê* in der stoischen Sprachphilosophie', *Archiv für Geschichte der Philosophie* 62, 276–88.

Di Benedetto, V. (1958–9). 'Dionisio Trace e la Techne a lui attribuita', *Annali della Scuola Normale Superiore di Pisa. Serie Lettere, Storia e Filosofia* II 27, 170–210; 28, 87–118.

Dicks, D. R. (1970). *Early Greek Astronomy to Aristotle* (Bristol: Thames and Hudson).

Dillon, J. (1977, revised with a new Afterword, 1996). *The Middle Platonists: A Study of Platonism 80 B.C. to A.D. 220* (Ithaca: Cornell University Press).

Dillon, J., and A. A. Long (eds.) (1988). *The Question of 'Eclecticism'* (Berkeley: University of California Press).

Dilthey, W. (1977). *Gesammelte Schriften* Bd. II: *Weltanschauung und Analyse des Menschen seit der Renaissance und Reformation* 10th ed. (Göttingen/Stuttgart: Vandenhoek und Ruprecht/Teubner).

Dobbin, R. (1991). 'Προαίρεσις in Epictetus', *Ancient Philosophy* 11, 111–35.

——— (1998). *Epictetus, Discourses Book 1*, translated with an Introduction and Commentary (Oxford: Oxford University Press).

Dobbs, B. J. T. (1985). 'Newton and Stoicism', *Southern Journal of Philosophy*, XXIII suppl., 109–23.

Donini, P.-L. (1979). 'L'eclettismo impossibile: Seneca e il platonismo medio', in Donini and Gianotti (1979), 151–274.

——— (1982). *Le scuole, l'anima, l'impero: la filosofia antica da Antioco a Plotino* (Turin: Rosenberg and Sellier).

——— (1994). 'Testi e commenti, manuali e insegnamento: la forma sistematica e i metodi della filosofia in età postellenistica', *Aufstieg und Niedergang der römischen Welt* II 36.7, 5027–100.

Donini, P. L., and G. G. Gianotti (eds.) (1979). *Modelli filosofici e letterari: Lucrezio, Orazio, Seneca* (Bologna: Pitagora Editrice).

Dorandi, T. (1991). *Filodemo: Storia dei filosofi: Platone e l'Academia (Pherc. 1021 e 164)* (Leiden: Brill).

——— (1994). *Filodemo: Storia dei filosofi: La Stoa da Zenone a Panezio* (*PHerc. 1018*) (Leiden: Brill).

——— (1997). 'Lucrèce et les Épicuriens de Campanie', in Algra et al. (1997), 34–48.

——— (1999). '2. Chronology' and '3. Organization and structure of the philosophical schools' in Algra et al. (1999), 31–62.

Döring, K., and T. Ebert (eds.) (1993). *Dialektiker und Stoiker – Zur Logik der Stoa und ihrer Vorläufer* (Stuttgart: Franz Steiner).

Dragona-Monachou, M. (1976). *The Stoic Arguments for the Existence and the Providence of the Gods* (Athens: National and Capodistrian University of Athens).

Dueck, D. (2000). *Strabo of Amasia: A Greek Man of Letters in Augustan Rome* (London: Routledge).

Ebert, T. (1993). 'Dialecticians and Stoics on the Classification of Propositions', in Döring and Ebert (1993), 111–27.

Egli, U. (1986). 'Stoic Syntax and Semantics', *Historiographia Linguistica* 13, 281–306.

Engberg-Pedersen, T. (1990). *The Stoic Theory of Oikeiosis* (Aarhus: Aarhus University Press).

Engstrom, S., and J. Whiting (eds.) (1996). *Rethinking Duty and Happiness: Aristotle, the Stoics, and Kant* (Cambridge: Cambridge University Press).

Erskine, A. (1990). *The Hellenistic Stoa* (Ithaca: Cornell University Press).

Everson, S. (ed.) (1990a). *Epistemology. Cambridge Companions to Ancient Thought 1* (Cambridge: Cambridge University Press).

——— (1990b). 'Epicurus on the truth of the senses', in Everson (1990a), 161–83.

——— (ed.) (1991). *Psychology. Cambridge Companions to Ancient Thought 2* (Cambridge: Cambridge University Press).

——— (ed.) (1994). *Language. Cambridge Companions to Ancient Thought 3* (Cambridge: Cambridge University Press).

——— (ed.) (1998). *Ethics. Cambridge Companions to Ancient Thought 4* (Cambridge: Cambridge University Press).

Fantham, E. (1997). ' "Envy and fear the begetter of hatred": Statius' *Thebaid* and the genesis of hatred', in Braund and Gill (1997), 185–212.

Fehling, D. (1956–1957). 'Varro und die grammatische Lehre von der Analogie und der Flexion', *Glotta* 35, 214–270; 36, 48–100.

Ferrary, J.-L. (1988). *Philhellénisme et Impérialisme* (Rome: École française de Rome).

Festugière, A.-J. (1949). *La révélation d'Hermès Trismégiste*, vol. II: Le Dieu cosmique (Paris: Gabada).

Fillion-Lahille, J. (1984). *Le de Ira de Sénèque et la philosophie stoïcienne des passions* (Paris: Klincksieck).

Finnis, J. M. (1980). *Natural Law and Natural Rights* (Oxford: Oxford University Press).

Flashar, H. (ed.) (1994). *Die Philosophie der Antike*, vol. 4, 2 Die Hellenistische Philosophie (Basel: Schwabe).

Forschner, M. (1981). *Die stoische Ethik: über den Zusammenhang von Natur-, Sprach- und Moralphilosophie im altstoischen System* (Stuttgart: Klett-Cotta).

Fortenbaugh, W. W. (ed.) (1983). *On Stoic and Peripatetic Ethics. The Work of Arius Didymus* (New Brunswick and London: Rutgers University Press).

Foucault, M. (1986). *The Care of the Self = The History of Sexuality*, vol. 3, transl. R. Hurley (NewYork: Random House).

Frede, D. (1982). 'The Dramatisation of Determinism: Alexander of Aphrodisias' *De Fato*', *Phronesis* 27, 276–98.

———— (1990). 'Fatalism and Future Truth', *Proceedings of the Boston Area Colloquium in Ancient Philosophy* 6, 195–227.

———— (1992). 'Accidental Causes in Aristotle', *Synthese* 92, 39–62.

Frede, D., and A. Laks (eds.) (2002). *Traditions of Theology: studies in Hellenistic theology, its background and aftermath* (Leiden: Brill).

Frede, M. (1974). *Die stoische Logik* (Göttingen: Vandenhoeck und Ruprecht).

———— (1980). 'The original notion of cause', in Barnes et al. (1980), 217–49. Repr. in Frede (1987), 125–50.

———— (1983). 'Stoics and skeptics on clear and distinct impressions', in Burnyeat (1983), 65–93. Repr. in Frede (1987), 151–76.

———— (1985). *Galen: Three Treatises on the Nature of Science* (Indianapolis: Hackett).

———— (1986). 'The Stoic Doctrine of the Affections of the Soul', in Schofield and Striker (1986), 93–110.

———— (1987). *Essays in Ancient Philosophy* (Minneapolis: University of Minnesota Press).

———— (1987a). 'The Origin of Traditional Grammar', in Butts and Hintikka (1977), 51–79. Repr. in Frede (1987), 338–59.

———— (1987b). 'Principles of Stoic Grammar', in Rist (1978), 27–75. Repr. in Frede (1987), 301–37.

———— (1990). 'An Empiricist view of knowledge: memorism', in Everson (1990a), 225–50.

———— (1994). 'The Stoic Conception of Reason', in Boudouris (1994), 50–63.

———— (1994a). 'The Stoic notion of a *lekton*', in Everson (1994), 109–28.

———— (1994b). 'The Stoic notion of a grammatical case', *Bulletin of the Institute of Classical Studies* 39, 13–24.

———— (1999). 'On the Stoic Conception of the Good', in Ierodiakonou (1999), 71–94.

——— (1999a). 'Monotheism and Pagan Philosophy in Later Antiquity', in Athanassiadi and Frede (1999), 41–69.

——— (1999b). 'Stoic epistemology', in Algra et al. (1999), 295–322.

——— (1999c). 'Epilogue', in Algra et al. (1999), 771–97.

Funghi, M. Serena (ed.) (1996). *OΔOI ΔIZHΣIOΣ-Le vie della ricerca: Studi in onore di Francesco Adorno* (Florence: Olschki).

Funkenstein, A. (1986). *Theology and the Scientific Imagination* (Princeton: Princeton University Press).

Gabrielsen, V., P. Bilde, and T. Engberg-Pedersen (eds.) (1999). *Hellenistic Rhodes* (Aarhus: Aarhus University Press).

Garrett, D. (1993). *The Cambridge Companion to Spinoza* (Cambridge: Cambridge University Press).

Gerson, L. P. (1990). *God and Greek Philosophy. Studies in the Early History of Natural Theology* (London: Routledge).

Geytenbeek, A. C. van (1963). *Musonius Rufus and Greek Diatribe* (Assen: Van Gorcum).

Giannantoni, G. (ed.) (1981). *Lo Scetticismo Antico* (Naples: Bibliopolis).

Gill, C. (1983). 'Did Chrysippus understand Medea?', *Phronesis* 28, 136–49.

——— (1988). 'Personhood and personality: the four-*personae* theory in Cicero, De Officiis I' *Oxford Studies in Ancient Philosophy* 6, 169–99.

——— (ed.) (1995). *Epictetus, The Discourses, Handbook, Fragments*, translated by Robin Hard (London: Dent).

——— (1997). 'Passion as madness in Roman poetry', in Braund and Gill (1997), 213–41.

——— (ed.) (1997a). *Marcus Aurelius, Meditations*, translated by R. Hard (Ware: Wordsworth).

——— (1998). 'Did Galen understand Platonic and Stoic thinking on emotions?', in Sihvola and Engberg-Pedersen (1998), 113–48.

——— (2000). 'Stoic Writers of the Imperial Era', in Rowe and Schofield (2000), 597–615.

Glucker, J. (1978). *Antiochus and the Late Academy. Hypomnemata* 56 (Göttingen: Vandenhoek und Ruprecht).

Goldman, A. (1977). 'Discrimination and perceptual knowledge', *Journal of Philosophy* 73.20, 771–91.

Goldschmidt, V. (1953). *Le système stoïcien et l'idée de temps* (Paris: Vrin).

——— (1972). '*huparchein* et *huphestanai* dans la philosophie stoicienne', *Revue des Etudes Grecques* 85, 331–44.

Goldstein, B. R., and A. C. Bowen (1983). 'A New View of Early Greek Astronomy', *Isis* 74, 330–40.

Göransson, T. (1995). *Albinus, Alcinous, Arius Didymus* (Göteborg: Acta Universitatis Gothoburgensis) = *Studia Graeca et Latina Gothoburgensis* LXI.

Görler, W. (1994). 'Fünftes Kapitel: Älterer Pyrrhonismus. Jüngere Akademie. Antiochus aus Askalon', in Flashar (1994), 717–989.

Gosling, J. (1987). 'Stoics and *akrasia*', *Apeiron* 20, 179–82.

Gould, J. B. (1970). *The Philosophy of Chrysippus* (Albany, New York: State University of New York Press).

Goulet, Richard (ed.) (1989). *Dictionnaire des philosophes antiques* (Paris: Centre National de la Recherche Scientifique).

Goulet-Cazé, M.-O. (1996). 'Religion and the Early Cynics', in Branham and Goulet-Cazé (1996), 47–81.

—— (ed.) (1999). *Diogene Laërce: Vies et doctrines des philosophes illustres* (Paris: Le Livre de Poche). Translation of Book 7 by R. Goulet.

Graeser, A. (1971). 'A propos ὑπάρχειν bei den Stoikern', *Archiv für Begriffsgeschichte* 15, 299–305.

—— (1978). 'The Stoic categories', in Brunschwig (1978), 199–222.

—— (1978a). 'The Stoic theory of meaning', in Rist (1978), 77–100.

—— (1991). 'Stoische Philosophie bei Spinoza', *Revue Internationale de Philosophie* 45, 336–46.

Graver, M. (2000). 'Philo of Alexandria and the Origins of the Stoic *Propatheiai*', *Phronesis* 44, 300–25.

Greenspan, P. (1988). *Emotions and Reasons* (New York: Routledge).

Griffin, M. T. (1976, paperback edition with Postscript 1992). *Seneca, A Philosopher in Politics* (Oxford: Oxford University Press).

—— (1986). 'Philosophy, Cato, and Roman Suicide', *Greece and Rome* 33, 64–77, 192–202.

—— (2000). 'Seneca and Pliny', in Rowe and Schofield (2000), 532–558.

Griffin, M. T., and J. Barnes (eds.) (1989). *Philosophia Togata* (Oxford: Oxford University Press).

Griffith, M., and D. J. Mastronarde (eds.) (1990). *Cabinet of the Muses. Essays on Classical and Comparative Literature in Honour of Thomas G. Rosenmeyer* (Atlanta: Scholars Press).

Grimal, P. (1989). 'Sénèque et le Stoïcisme Romain', *Aufstieg und Niedergang der römischen Welt* II 36.3, 1962–92.

Haakonssen, K. (1996). *Natural Law and Moral Philosophy* (Cambridge: Cambridge University Press).

Hadot, I. (2001). *Simplicius: Commentaire sur le manuel d'Epictète, tome 1* (Paris: Les Belles Lettres).

Hadot, P. (1969). 'Zur Vorgeschichte des Begriffs "Existenz", ὑπάρχειν, bei den Stoikern', *Archiv für Begriffsgeschichte der Philosophie* 13, 115–27.

—— (1987). 'Théologie, exégèse, révélation, écriture, dans la philosophie grecque', in Tardieu (1987), 13–34.

—— (1995). *Philosophy as a Way of Life*, translated by M. Chase with Introduction by A. I. Davidson (Oxford: Blackwell).

Hahm, D. E. (1977). *The Origins of Stoic Cosmology* (Columbus: Ohio State University Press).

Hampshire, S. (1951). *Spinoza* (London: Penguin). Reprinted with revisions 1962.

Hankinson, R. J. (1987a). 'Evidence, externality, and antecedence', *Phronesis* 32, 80–100.

—— (1987b). 'Causes and empiricism', *Phronesis* 32, 329–48.

—— (1990). 'Saying the phenomena', *Phronesis* 35, 194–215 (critical notice of von Staden 1989).

—— (1991). 'Galen's anatomy of the soul', *Phronesis* 36, 197–233.

—— (1991). 'A purely verbal dispute? Galen on Stoic and Academic epistemology', *Revue internationale de Philosophie* 45, 267–300.

—— (1993). 'Action and passion: affection, emotion, and moral self-management in Galen's philosophical psychology', in Brunschwig and Nussbaum (1993), 150–83.

—— (1994). 'Galen's theory of causation', *Aufstieg und Niedergang der römischen Welt* II 37.2, 1757–74.

—— (1996). 'Cicero's rope', in Algra et al. (1996), 185–205.

—— (1997). 'Natural criteria and the transparency of judgment: Philo, Antiochus, and Galen on epistemological justification', in Inwood and Mansfeld (1997), 161–216.

—— (1998a). *Cause and Explanation in Ancient Greek Thought* (Oxford: Oxford University Press).

—— (1998b). *Galen: On Antecedent Causes* (Cambridge: Cambridge University Press).

—— (1998c). *The Sceptics* (London: Routledge).

—— (1999). 'Explanation and causation', in Algra et al. (1999), 479–512.

—— (forthcoming). 'Academics and Pyrrhonists', in C. Shields (ed.), *The Blackwell Guide to Hellenistic Philosophy*.

Heintz, W. (1932). *Studien zu Sextus Empiricus* (Halle: M. Niemeyer)

Henrichs, A. (1974). 'Die Kritik der stoischen Theologie im PHerc. 1428', *Cronache Ercolanesi* 4, 5–32.

Hicks, R. D. (ed.) (1925). *Diogenes Laertius: Lives of Eminent Philosophers* (London: Heinemann; Cambridge, MA: Harvard University Press).

Hijmans, B. L. (1959). *Askêsis: Notes on Epictetus' Educational System* (Assen: Van Gorcum).

Hine, H. M. (ed.) (1996). *L. Annaeus Seneca: Naturalium Quaestionum Libros* (Stuttgart and Leipzig: Teubner).

Hochstrasser, T. J. (2000). *Natural Law Theories in the Early Enlightenment* (Cambridge: Cambridge University Press).

Hope, V. (ed.) (1984). *Philosophers of the Scottish Enlightenment* (Edinburgh: Edinburgh University Press).

Horst, P. W. van der, and J. Mansfeld (1974). *An Alexandrian Platonist against dualism* (Leiden: Brill).

Hoven, René (1971). *Stoïcisme et Stoïciens Face au Problème de l'Au-delà* (Paris: Société d'Edition Les Belles Lettres).

Huby, P., and G. Neal (eds.) (1989). *The Criterion of Truth* (Liverpool: Liverpool University Press).

Ierodiakonou, K. (1990). *Analysis in Stoic logic* (Diss. London, London School of Economics).

—— (ed.) (1999). *Topics in Stoic Philosophy* (Oxford: Oxford University Press).

Ildefonse, F. (1997). *La naissance de la grammaire* (Paris: Vrin).

Inwood, B. (1984). 'Hierocles: theory and argument in the second century A.D.', *Oxford Studies in Ancient Philosophy* 2, 151–84.

—— (1985). *Ethics and Human Action in Early Stoicism* (Oxford: Oxford University Press).

—— (1991). 'Chrysippus on Extension and the Void', *Revue internationale de philosophie* 45, 245–66.

—— (1993). 'Seneca and Psychological Dualism', in Brunschwig and Nussbaum (1993), 150–83.

—— (1995). 'Review of *The Morality of Happiness*', *Ancient Philosophy* 15, 647–65.

—— (1995a). 'Seneca in his philosophical milieu', *Harvard Studies in Classical Philology* 97, 63–76.

—— (1995b). 'Politics and paradox in Seneca's *De beneficiis*', in Laks and Schofield (1995), 241–65.

—— (1998). Review of Becker (1998), *Apeiron* 31, 293–308.

—— (1999). 'Rules and Reasoning in Stoic Ethics', in Ierodiakonou (1999), 95–127.

—— (2000). 'The Will in Seneca the Younger', *Classical Philology* 95, 44–60.

—— (2002). 'God and Human Knowledge in Seneca's *Natural Questions*', in Frede and Laks (2002), 119–57.

Inwood, B., and P. Donini (1999). 'Stoic ethics', in Algra et al. (1999), 675–738.

Inwood, B., and L. Gerson (eds.) (1997). *Hellenistic Philosophy: Introductory Readings*, Second edition (Indianapolis: Hackett).

Inwood, B., and J. Mansfeld (eds.) (1997). *Assent and Argument: Studies in Cicero's Academic Books* (Leiden: Brill).

Ioppolo, A. M. (1980). *Aristone di Chio e lo stoicismo antico* (Naples: Bibliopolis).

—— (1981). 'Il concetto di "*eulogon*" nella filosofia di Arcesilao', in Giannantoni (1981), 143–61.

Irwin, T. H. (1986). 'Stoic and Aristotelian conceptions of happiness', in Schofield and Striker (1986), 205–44.

—— (1996). 'Kant's criticisms of eudaemonism', in Engstrom and Whiting (1996), 63–101.

—— (1998). 'Socratic paradox and Stoic theory', in Everson (1998), 151–92.

—— (forthcoming). 'Stoic naturalism in Butler', in Miller and Inwood (forthcoming).

Jagu, A. (1989). 'La morale d'Epictète et le christianisme', *Aufstieg und Niedergang der römischen Welt* II 36.3, 2164–99.

James, S. (1993). 'Spinoza the Stoic', in Sorell (1993), 289–316.

Janko, R. (2000). *Philodemus: On Poems I* (Oxford: Oxford University Press).

Johnston, D. (2000). 'The Jurists', in Rowe and Schofield (2000), 616–34.

Jones, A. (1999). 'Geminus and the *Isia*', *Harvard Studies in Classical Philology* 99, 255–67.

Jones, C. P. (1978). *The Roman World of Dio Chrysostom* (Cambridge, MA: Harvard University Press).

Joyce, R. (1995). 'Early Stoicism and Akrasia', *Phronesis* 40, 315–35.

Kahn, Charles (1973). *The Verb Be in Ancient Greek* (Dordrecht: D. Reidel).

—— (1988). 'Discovering the will: from Aristotle to Augustine', in Dillon and Long (1988), 234–59.

—— (1997). 'Greek Philosophy and Religion in the Sisyphus Fragment', *Phronesis* 42, 247–62.

Kamtekar, R. (1998). *ΑΙΔΩΣ* in Epictetus', *Classical Philology* 19, 136–60.

Kidd, D. (1997). *Aratus: Phaenomena* (Cambridge: Cambridge University Press).

Kidd, I. G. (1978). 'Philosophy and science in Posidonius', *Antike and Abendland* 24, 7–15.

—— (1989). '*Orthos Logos* as a criterion of truth in the Stoa', in Huby and Neal (1989), 137–50.

Klauser, T. (ed.) (1950–). *Reallexicon für Antike und Christentum*, 18 vols. (Stuttgart: Hiersemann).

Kneale, W., and M. Kneale (1962). *The development of logic* (Oxford: Clarendon Press).

Korsgaard, C. M. (1996). *The Sources of Normativity* (Cambridge: Cambridge University Press).

Kristeller, P. O. (1984). 'Stoic and Neoplatonic sources of Spinoza's Ethics', *History of European Ideas* 5, 1–15.

Labarriere, J. L. (1993). 'De la "nature phantastique" des animaux chez les Stoïciens', in Brunschwig and Nussbaum (1993), 225–49.

Lafollette, H. (ed.) (2000). *The Blackwell Guide to Ethical Theory* (London; Malden, MA: Blackwell).

Lagrée, J. (1994). *Juste Lipse et la restauration du stoicisme* (Paris: Vrin).

Laks, A., and M. Schofield (eds.) (1995). *Justice and Generosity* (Cambridge: Cambridge University Press).

Lallot, J. (ed.) (1997). *De la construction* (Περὶ συντάξεως), 2 vols. (Paris: Vrin).

Lamberton, R., and J. J. Keaney (eds.) (1992). *Homer's Ancient Readers: The Hermeneutics of Greek Epic's Earliest Exegetes* (Princeton: Princeton University Press).

Lang, H. S. (1998). *The Order of Nature in Aristotle's Physics: Place and the Elements* (Cambridge: Cambridge University Press).

Lapidge, M. (1973). '*archai* and *stoicheia*: A Problem in Stoic Cosmology', *Phronesis* 18, 240–78.

Lasserre, F. (1966). *Die Fragmente des Eudoxos von Knidos* (Berlin: Walter de Gruyter).

Ledbetter, G. (1994). 'The Propositional Content of Stoic Emotions', in Boudouris (1994), 107–13.

Lesses, G. (1999). 'Content, Cause, and Stoic Impressions', *Phronesis* 43, 1–25.

Linke, K. (1977). *Die Fragmente des Grammatikers Dionysios Thrax* (Sammlung griechischer und lateinischer Grammatiker 3) (Berlin: Walter de Gruyter), 1–77.

Lloyd, A. C. (1971). 'Grammar and metaphysics in the Stoa', in Long (1971), 58–74.

―――― (1978). 'Emotions and Decision in Stoic Psychology', in Rist (1978), 233–46.

―――― (1978a). 'Definite propositions and the concept of reference', in Brunschwig (1978), 285–96.

Lloyd, G. (1994). *Part of Nature: Self-Knowledge in Spinoza's Ethics* (Ithaca: Cornell University Press).

Lloyd, G. E. R. (1975a). 'A Note on Erasistratus of Ceos', *Journal of Hellenic Studies* 95, 172–5.

―――― (1975b). 'Alcmaeon and the early history of dissection', *Sudhoffs Archiv* 59, 113–47; repr. in Lloyd (1991).

―――― (1991). *Methods and Problems in Greek Science* (Cambridge: Cambridge University Press).

Long, A. A. (1967). 'Carneades and the Stoic *telos*', *Phronesis* 12, 59–90.

―――― (1970/71). 'The logical basis of Stoic ethics', *Proceedings of the Aristotelian Society* 71, 85–104. Repr. in Long (1996), 134–155.

―――― (ed.) (1971). *Problems in Stoicism* (London: Athlone Press).

―――― (1971a). 'Language and Thought in Stoicism', in Long (1971), 75–113.

―――― (1974/1986). *Hellenistic Philosophy: Stoics, Epicureans, Sceptics* (1974, London: Duckworth; repr. 1986 London/Berkeley/Los Angeles: University of California Press).

—— (1975/1976). 'Heraclitus and Stoicism', *Philosophia* (Yearbook of the Research Center for Greek Philosophy at the Academy of Athens) 5/6, 132–153. Repr. in Long (1996), 35–57.

—— (1978). 'The Stoic distinction between truth and the true', in Brunschwig (1978), 297–316.

—— (1982). 'Astrology: Arguments pro and contra', in Barnes et al. (1982), 165–92.

—— (1983a). 'Greek ethics after MacIntyre and the Stoic community of reason', *Ancient Philosophy* 3, 184–97. Repr. in Long (1996), 156–78.

—— (1983b). 'Arius Didymus and the exposition of Stoic ethics', in Fortenbaugh (1983), 41–65. Repr. in Long (1996), 107–33.

—— (1985). 'The Stoics on World-Conflagration and Everlasting', *Southern Journal of Philosophy* XXIII Suppl., 13–58.

—— (1988). 'Socrates in Hellenistic philosophy', *Classical Quarterly* 38, 150–71. Repr. in Long (1996), 1–34.

—— (1989). 'Stoic eudaimonism', *Proceedings of the Boston Colloquium in Ancient Philosophy* 4, 77–101. Repr. in Long (1996), 179–201.

—— (1990). 'Scepticism about Gods in Hellenistic Philosophy', in Griffith and Mastronarde (1990), 279–91.

—— (1991). 'Representation and the Self in Stoicism', in Everson (1991), 102–20.

—— (1992). 'Stoic Readings of Homer', in Lamberton and Keaney (1992), 41–66. Repr. in Long (1996), 58–85.

—— (1996). *Stoic Studies* (Cambridge: Cambridge University Press).

—— (1999). 'Stoic psychology', in Algra et al. (1999), 560–84.

—— (2002). *Epictetus: a Stoic and Socratic guide to life* (Oxford: Oxford University Press).

Long, A. A., and D. N. Sedley (1987). *The Hellenistic Philosophers* (Cambridge: Cambridge University Press).

Longrigg, J. (1975). 'Elementary Physics in the Lyceum and Stoa', *Isis* 66, 211–29.

Lutz, C. E. (1947). 'Musonius Rufus: "The Roman Socrates"', *Yale Classical Studies* 10, 3–147.

Lynch, J. P. (1972). *Aristotle's School: A Study of a Greek Educational Institution* (Berkeley: University of California Press).

MacIntyre, A. (1981). *After Virtue* (London: Duckworth).

—— (1988). *Whose Justice? Which Rationality?* (Notre Dame: University of Notre Dame Press).

Maconi, H. (1988). 'Nova non philosophandi philosophia', *Oxford Studies in Ancient Philosophy* 6, 231–53.

Mansfeld, J. (1979). 'Providence and the Destruction of the Universe in Early Stoic Thought', in Vermaseren (1979), 129–88; repr. in Mansfeld (1989), I 129–88.

—— (1986). 'Diogenes Laertius on Stoic Philosophy', *Elenchos* 7, 297–382.

—— (1989). *Studies in Later Greek Philosophy and Gnosticism* (London: Variorum).

—— (1991). 'The idea of the will in Chrysippus, Posidonius, and Galen', *Boston Area Colloquium in Ancient Philosophy* 7, 107–45.

—— (1992). *Heresiography in Context – Hippolytus' Elenchos as a Source for Greek Philosophy* (Leiden: Brill).

—— (1999). 'Theology', in Algra et al. (1999), 452–78.

Mansfeld, J., and D. Runia (1997). *Aëtiana* I (Leiden: Brill).

Mates, B. (1953). *Stoic logic* (Berkeley: University of California Press).

Menn, S. (1999). 'The Stoic Theory of Categories', *Oxford Studies in Ancient Philosophy* 17, 215–47.

Meyer, B. F., and E. P. Sanders (eds.) (1983). *Jewish and Christian Self-Definition, Vol. 3, Self Definition in the Greco-Roman World* (Philadelphia: Fortress Press).

Mignucci, M. (1988). 'The Stoic Notion of Relatives', in Barnes and Mignucci (1988), 129–221.

—— (1993). 'The Stoic *Themata*', in Döring and Ebert (1993), 217–38.

—— (1999). 'Logic: The Stoics: Paradoxes', in Algra et al. (1999), 157–76.

Miller, J., and B. Inwood (eds.) (forthcoming). *Hellenistic and Early Modern Philosophy* (Cambridge: Cambridge University Press).

Mitsis, P. (1999). 'The Stoic Origin of Natural Rights', in Ierodiakonou (1999), 153–77.

Moles, J. L. (1978). 'The career and conversion of Dio Chrysostom', *Journal of Hellenic Studies* 98, 79–100.

—— (1983). 'The date and purpose of the fourth kingship oration of Dio Chrysostom', *Classical Antiquity* 2, 251–78.

—— (1990). 'The kingship orations of Dio Chrysostom', *Papers of the Leeds International Latin Seminar* 6, 297–375.

Moore, J., and M. Silverthorne (1984). 'Natural sociability and natural rights in the moral philosophy of Gerschom Carmichael', in Hope (1984), 1–12.

Moore, G. E. (1903). *Principia Ethica* (Cambridge: Cambridge University Press).

Morford, M. P. O. (1991). *Stoics and Neostoics: Rubens and the Circle of Lipsius* (Princeton: Princeton University Press).

Morrison, D. (1992). 'The Taxonomical Interpretation of Aristotle's *Categories*: A Criticism', in Preus and Anton (1992), 19–46.

Most, G. W. (1989). 'Cornutus and Stoic Allegoresis: A Preliminary Report', *Aufstieg und Niedergang der römischen Welt* II 36.3, 2014–65.

Mueller, I. (1979). 'The completeness of Stoic propositional logic', *Notre Dame Journal of Formal Logic* 20, 201–15.

Müller, R. (1947). *Die Stoische Grammatik* (Diss. Rostock, unpubl.).

Mygind, B. (1999). 'Intellectuals in Rhodes', in Gabrielsen et al. (1999), 247–93.

Natali, C. (1996). 'Lieux et écoles du savoir', in Brunschwig and Lloyd (1996), 229–49.

Neugebauer, O. (1964). Review of W. H. Stahl, *Roman Science*, *American Journal of Philology* 85, 418–23.

—— (1975). *A History of Ancient Mathematical Astronomy*, 3 vols. (Berlin: Springer-Verlag).

Nock, A. D. (1933). *Conversion* (Oxford: Oxford University Press).

Nuchelmans, G. (1973). *Theories of the proposition: Ancient and medieval conceptions of the bearers of truth and falsity* (Amsterdam: North-Holland).

Nussbaum, M. (1993). 'Poetry and the Passions: Two Stoic Views', in Brunschwig and Nussbaum (1993), 97–149.

—— (1994). *The Therapy of Desire* (Princeton: Princeton University Press).

Oestreich, G. (1982). *Neostoicism and the Early Modern State* (Cambridge: Cambridge University Press).

Osborne, M. J. (1981–3). *Naturalization in Athens* (Brussels: Paleis der Academiën).

Osler, M. J. (ed.) (1991). *Atoms, Pneuma, and Tranquillity* (Cambridge: Cambridge University Press).

Palladini, F., and G. Hartung (eds.) (1996). *Samuel Pufendorf und die europäische Frühaufklärung* (Berlin: Akademie Verlag).

Penelhum, T. (1985). *Butler* (London: Routledge).

Pinborg, J. (1975). 'Classical Antiquity: Greece', *Current Trends in Linguistics* 13, 69–126.

Pingree, D. (1997). *From Astral Omens to Astrology: from Babylon to Bîkâner* (Rome: istituto italiano per l'Africa e l'Oriente).

Pohlenz, M. (1938). 'Zenon und Chrysipp', *Nachrichten der Akademie der Wissenschaften in Göttingen* 1.2, 173–210.

—— (1948). *Die Stoa: Die Geschichte einer geistigen Bewegung*, 2 vols. (Göttingen: Vandenhoeck und Ruprecht).

Preus, A., and J. P. Anton (eds.) (1992). *Essays in Ancient Greek Philosophy 5: Aristotle's Ontology* (New York: State University of New York Press).

Price, A. W. (1994). *Mental Conflict* (London: Routledge).

Rackham, H. (ed.) (1931). *Cicero: De Finibus Bonorum et Malorum* (London: Heinemann; Cambridge, MA: Harvard University Press).

Randall, J. H., Jr. (1962). *The Career of Philosophy*, 2 vols. (New York: Columbia University Press).

Reesor, M. E. (1954). 'The Stoic concept of quality', *American Journal of Philology* 75, 40–58.

—— (1957). 'The Stoic categories', *American Journal of Philology* 78, 63–82.

—— (1972). '*Poion* and *poiotês* in Stoic philosophy', *Phronesis* 17, 279–85.

Reydams-Schils, G. (1999). *Demiurge and Providence: Stoic and Platonist Readings of Plato's Timaeus* (Turnhout: Brepols).

Rieth, O. (1933). *Grundbegriffe der stoischen Ethik* (Berlin: Weidmann).

Rist, J. M. (1969). *Stoic philosophy* (Cambridge: Cambridge University Press).

—— (ed.) (1978). *The Stoics* (Berkeley: University of California Press).

—— (1983). 'Are You a Stoic? The Case of Marcus Aurelius', in Meyer and Sanders (1983), 23–45, 190–2.

—— (1989). 'Seneca and Stoic orthodoxy', *Aufstieg und Niedergang der römischen Welt* II 36.3, 1993–2012.

Rochberg-Halton, F. (1988). *Aspects of Babylonian Celestial Divination: The Lunar Eclipse Tablets of Enûma Anu Enlil*. Archiv für Orientforschung Beiheft 22 (Horn: F. Berger).

Rochberg, F. (1998). *Babylonian Horoscopes*. Transactions of the American Philosophical Society 88.1. (Philadelphia: American Philosophical Society).

Romeyer Dherbey, G. (dir.), and J.-B. Gourinat (ed.) (forthcoming). *Les Stoïciens* (Paris: Vrin).

Rorty, A. (1996). 'The two faces of Stoicism: Rousseau and Freud', *Journal of the History of Philosophy* 34, 335–56.

Rosenmeyer, T. (1989). *Senecan Drama and Stoic Cosmology* (Berkeley: University of California Press).

Rowe, C., and M. Schofield (eds.) (2000). *The Cambridge History of Greek and Roman Political Thought* (Cambridge: Cambridge University Press).

Russell, D. A. (1992). *Dio Chrysostom, Orations VII, XII, XXXVI* (Cambridge: Cambridge University Press).

Rutherford, D. (1999). 'Salvation as a state of mind: the place of *acquiescentia* in Spinoza's Ethics', *British Journal for the History of Philosophy* 7, 447–73.

Rutherford, R. B. (1989). *The Meditations of Marcus Aurelius: A Study* (Oxford: Oxford University Press).

Salles, R. (2001). 'Compatibilism: Stoic and Modern', *Archiv für Geschichte der Philosophie* 83, 1–23.

Sambursky, S. (1959). *The Physics of the Stoics* (London: Routledge and Kegan Paul).

Sandbach, F. H. (1971a). '*Phantasia Katalêptikê*', in Long (1971), 9–21.

—— (1971b). '*Ennoia* and *Prolêpsis*', in Long (1971), 22–37.

—— (1975). *The Stoics* (London: Chatto and Windus).

—— (1985). *Aristotle and the Stoics* (Cambridge: Cambridge Philological Society).

Sartre, J. P. (1933). *Esquisse d'une théorie des émotions* (Paris: Éditions Scientifiques Hermann).

Saunders, J. (1955). *Justus Lipsius: The Philosophy of Renaissance Stoicism* (New York: Liberal Arts Press).

Scaltsas, D. (ed.) (forthcoming). *Zeno of Citium and his Legacy* (Larnaca).

Schenkeveld, D. (1990). 'Studies in the History of Ancient Linguistics III: The Stoic *TEXNH ΠΕΡΙ ΦΩΝΗΣ*', *Mnemosyne* 43, 86–108.

Schneewind, J. B. (1996a). 'Kant and Stoic Ethics', in Engstrom and Whiting (1996), 285–301.

—— (1996b). 'Barbeyrac and Leibniz on Pufendorf', in Palladini and Hartung (1996), 181–9.

—— (1997). *The Invention of Autonomy* (Cambridge: Cambridge University Press).

Schofield, M. (1980). 'Preconception, Argument, and God', in Schofield et al. (1980), 283–308.

—— (1983). 'The Syllogisms of Zeno of Citium', *Phronesis* 28, 31–58.

—— (1984). 'Ariston of Chios and the unity of virtue', *Ancient Philosophy* 4, 83–96.

—— (1988). 'The Retrenchable Present', in Barnes and Mignucci (1988), 329–74.

—— (1991). *The Stoic Idea of the City* (Cambridge: Cambridge University Press), Repr. (1999) with new epilogue.

—— (1999a). 'Social and political thought', in Algra et al. (1999), 739–70.

—— (1999b). 'Morality and the law: the case of Diogenes of Babylon', in Schofield (1999c), 160–77.

—— (1999c). *Saving the City* (London: Routledge).

Schofield, M., M. Burnyeat, and J. Barnes (eds.) (1980). *Doubt and Dogmatism. Studies in Hellenistic Epistemology* (Oxford: Oxford University Press).

Schofield, M., and M. Craven Nussbaum (eds.) (1982). *Language and Logos: Studies in Ancient Greek Philosophy presented to G. E. L. Owen* (Cambridge: Cambridge University Press), 315–38.

Schofield, M., and G. Striker (eds.) (1986). *The Norms of Nature: Studies in Hellenistic Ethics* (Cambridge: Cambridge University Press/Paris: Editions de la Maison des Sciences de L'Homme).

Schubert, A. (1994). *Untersuchungen zur stoischen Bedeutungslehre* (Göttingen: Vandenhoeck und Ruprecht).

Scott, W. R. (1900). *Francis Hutcheson* (Cambridge: Cambridge University Press).

Sedley, D. (1982). 'The Stoic criterion of identity', *Phronesis* 27, 255–75.

—— (1985). 'The Stoic theory of universals', *Southern Journal of Philosophy* XXIII Suppl., 87–92.

—— (1989). 'Philosophical allegiance in the Greco-Roman world', in Griffin and Barnes (1989), 97–119.

—— (1993). 'Chrysippus on Psychophysical Causality', in Brunschwig and Nussbaum (1993), 313–31.

—— (1999). 'Stoic physics and metaphysics', in Algra et al. (1999), 382–411.

—— (1999a). 'The Stoic-Platonist Debate on *kathêkonta*', in Ierodiakonou (1999), 128–52.

Seidler, M. (1981). 'Kant and the Stoics on the emotional life', *Journal of Philosophical Research* 7, 1095–1149.

—— (1983). 'Kant and the Stoics on suicide', *Journal of the History of Ideas*, 429–53.

Sharples, R. W. (1975). 'Aristotelian and Stoic conceptions of necessity in the de fato of Alexander of Aphrodisias', *Phronesis* 20, 247–74.

—— (1983). *Alexander of Aphrodisias On Fate* (London: Duckworth).

—— (1986). 'Soft Determinism and Freedom in Early Stoicism', *Phronesis* 31, 266–79.

—— (1996). *Stoics, Epicureans, Sceptics: an introduction to Hellenistic philosophy* (London: Routledge).

Sharvy, R. (1983). 'Aristotle on Mixtures', *Journal of Philosophy* 80, 441–48.

Shields, C. (1993). 'The Truth Evaluability of Stoic *Phantasiai*: *Adversus Mathematicos VII*', *Journal of the History of Philosophy* 31, 242–46.

Sihvola, J., and T. Engberg-Pedersen (eds.) (1998). *The Emotions in Hellenistic Philosophy* (Dordrecht: Kluwer).

Slote, M. (1999). 'Moral psychology', in Craig (1999).

Sluiter, I. (1988). 'On *ê diasaphêtikos* and propositions containing *mallon/hêtton*', *Mnemosyne* 41, 46–66.

—— (1990). *Ancient Grammar in Context: Contributions to the Study of Ancient Linguistic Thought* (Amsterdam: Vrije Universiteit Press).

Solmsen, F. (1961). 'Greek philosophy and the discovery of the nerves', *Museum Helveticum* 18, 150–97.

Sorabji, R. (1980). *Necessity, Cause, and Blame* (London: Duckworth).

—— (1983). *Time, creation, and the continuum* (London: Duckworth).

—— (1993). *Animal Minds and Human Morals* (London: Duckworth).

—— (ed.) (1997). *Aristotle and After*, Bulletin of the Institute of Classical Studies Supplement 68 (London: Institute of Classical Studies).

—— (2000). *Emotion and Peace of Mind: From Stoic Agitation to Christian Temptation* (Oxford: Oxford University Press).

Sorell, T. (ed.) (1993). *The Rise of Modern Philosophy* (Oxford: Oxford University Press).

Spanneut, M. (1962). 'Epiktet', in Klauser (1962), vol. 5, 599–681.

——— (1973). *Permanence du Stoicisme de Zénon à Malraux* (Gembloux: Duculot).

Steinmetz, P. (1986). 'Allegorische Dichtung und allegorische Deutung in der alten Stoa', *Rheinisches Museum* 129, 18–30.

——— (1994). 'Die Stoa', 'Viertes Kapitel: Die Stoa', in Flashar (1994), 491–716.

Stewart, M. A. (1991). 'The Stoic legacy in the early Scottish enlightenment', in Osler (1991), 273–96.

Striker, G. (1974). *Kritêrion tês aletheias. Nachtrichten der Akademie der Wissenschaften in Göttingen*, Phil.-Hist. Kl. 2 (Göttingen).

——— (1980). 'Sceptical strategies', in Barnes et al. (1980), 54–83.

——— (1981). 'Über den Unterschied zwischen den Pyrrhoneern und den Akademikern', *Phronesis* 26, 353–69 (English version in Striker (1996a), 135–49.

——— (1986). 'Antipater, or the art of living', in Schofield and Striker (1986), 185–204. Reprint in Striker (1996a), 298–315.

——— (1987). 'Origins of the concept of natural law', *Proceedings of the Boston Colloquium on Ancient Philosophy* 2, 79–94. Repr. in Striker (1996a), 209–20.

——— (1990). 'The problem of the criterion', in Everson (1990a), 143–60.

——— (1991). 'Following nature: a study in Stoic ethics', *Oxford Studies in Ancient Philosophy* 9, 1–73. Repr. in Striker (1996a), 221–80.

——— (1996a). *Essays on Hellenistic Epistemology and Ethics* (Cambridge: Cambridge University Press).

——— (1996b). 'Plato's Socrates and the Stoics', in Striker (1996a), 316–24.

——— (1997). 'Academics fighting Academics', in Inwood and Mansfeld (1997), 257–76.

Stroux, J. (1912). *De Theophrasti Virtutibus dicendi* (Leipzig: Teubner).

Tardieu, M. (ed.) (1987). *Les Règles de l'interprétation* (Paris: Cerf).

Taylor, C. (1989). *Sources of the Self* (Cambridge, MA: Harvard University Press).

Taylor, C. C. W. (1980). 'All perceptions are true', in Barnes et al. (1980), 105–24.

Taylor, D. J. (1986). 'Rethinking the History of Language Science in Classical Antiquity', *Historiographia Linguistica* 13, 175–90.

Thomas, L. (2000). 'Moral Psychology', in Lafollette (2000), 149–62.

Tieleman, T. L. (1996). *Galen and Chrysippus on the Soul: Argument and Refutation in the de Placitis Books II–III* (Leiden: Brill).

Todd, R. B. (1976). *Alexander of Aphrodisias on Stoic Physics: A Study of the De Mixtione with Preliminary Essays, Text, Translation, and Commentary* (Leiden: Brill).

—— (1985). 'The Title of Cleomedes' Treatise', *Philologus* 129, 250–61.

—— (1989). 'The Stoics and their cosmology in the first and second centuries A.D.', *Aufstieg und Niedergang der römischen Welt* II 36.3, 1365–78.

Tomberlin, J. E. (ed.) (1998). *Language, Mind, and Ontology*, Philosophical Perspectives 12 (Malden, MA: Blackwell).

Toomer, G. J. (1975). 'Hipparchus on the Distances of the Sun and Moon', *Archive for History of Exact Sciences* 14, 126–42.

Trapp, M. B. (1997). 'Philosophical sermons: The "Dialexeis" of Maximus of Tyre"' *Aufstieg und Niedergang der römischen Welt* II 34.3, 1945–76.

—— (1997a). 'On the *tablet* of Cebes', in Sorabji (1997), 159–78.

van der Eijk, P. J. (2000). *Diocles of Carystus: a collection of the fragments with translation and commentary* (Leiden: Brill).

van der Waerden, B. L. (1952). 'Das grosse Jahr und die ewige Wiederkehr', *Hermes* 80, 129–55.

Vander Waerdt, P. A. (ed.) (1994a). *The Socratic Movement* (Ithaca: Cornell University Press).

—— (1994b). 'Zeno's *Republic* and the origins of natural law', in Vander Waerdt (1994a), 272–308.

Vermaseren, M. J. (ed.) (1979). *Studies in Hellenistic Religions* (Leiden: Brill).

Versnel, H. S. (1990). *Ter unus: Isis, Dionysos, Hermes. Three Studies in Henotheism* (Leiden: Brill).

Von Staden, H. (1975). 'Experiment and experience in Hellenistic Medicine', *Bulletin of the Institute of Classical Studies* 22, 178–99.

—— (1989). *Herophilus: The art of medicine in early Alexandria* (Cambridge: Cambridge University Press).

Vlastos, G. (1972). 'The Unity of the Virtues in the *Protagoras*', *Review of Metaphysics* 25, 415–458. Repr. in Vlastos (1973), 221–69.

—— (1973). *Platonic Studies* (Princeton: Princeton University Press).

—— (1983). 'The Socratic elenchus', *Oxford Studies in Ancient Philosophy* 1, 27–58. Reprint in Vlastos (1994), 221–69.

—— (1994). *Socratic Studies* (Cambridge: Cambridge University Press).

West, M. L. (1999). 'Towards Monotheism', in Athanassiadi and Frede (1999), 21–41.

White, M. J. (1985). *Agency and Integrality: Philosophical Themes in the Ancient Discussions of Determinism and Responsibility* (Dordrecht: D. Reidel).

—— (1986). 'Can Unequal Quantities of Stuffs Be Totally Blended?', *History of Philosophy Quarterly* 3, 379–89.

—— (1992). *The Continuous and the Discrete: Ancient Physical Theories from a Contemporary Perspective* (Oxford: Oxford University Press).

Williams, B. (1985). *Ethics and the Limits of Philosophy* (London: Fontana).

Wilson, M. (1997). 'The subjugation of grief in Seneca's *Epistles*', in Braund and Gill (1997), 48–67.

Wollheim, R. (1999). *On the Emotions* (New Haven: Yale University Press).

Zeyl, D. (ed.) (1997). *Encyclopedia of Classical Philosophy* (Westport, CT: Greenwood).

Zierl, A. (1995). *Alexander von Aphrodisias, Über das Schicksal* (Berlin: Akademie Verlag).

LIST OF PRIMARY WORKS

This list does not pretend to be complete. Works that appear rarely are, for the most part, detailed where they occur; works judged to be common and familiar to the presumed readers of this volume are not indicated. Abbreviations, particularly where they are not standard, are indicated below.

Aëtius. *Placita* included in *Doxographi Graeci* (see later reference), pp. 265–444.

Albertus Magnus. *Opera Omnia*, B. Geyer (ed.) (Münster: Aschendorff, 1960).

Alexander Aphrodisiensis. *De fato* [*On Fate = Fat.*], R. W. Sharples (ed.) *Alexander of Aphrodisias On Fate* (London: Duckworth, 1983).

——— *De mixtione* [*On Mixture = Mixt.*], R. B. Todd *Alexander of Aphrodisias on Stoic Physics: A Study of the De Mixtione with Preliminary Essays, Text, Translation and Commentary* (Leiden: Brill, 1976).

——— *In Aristotelis Analyticorum Priorum librum I commentarium* [*On Aristotle's Prior Analytics = In Ar. An. pr.*], M. Wallies (ed.) *Commentaria in Aristotelem Graeca* [= *CAG*] II, i (Berlin: Reimer, 1883).

——— *In Aristotelis Topicorum libros octo commentaria* [*On Aristotle's Topics = In Ar. Top.*] M. Wallies (ed.) *CAG* II, ii (Berlin: Reimer, 1891).

——— *Scripta Minora* II, 2, I Bruns (ed.) (Berlin: Georg Reimers, 1892).

Apollonius Dyscolus [= AD]. *De adverbiis* [= *Adv.*], *De pronominibus* [= *Pr.*], R. Schneider (ed.) *Grammatici Graeci* 2, 1 (Leipzig: Teubner, 1878; repr. Hildesheim: Olms, 1965).

——— *De constructione* [= *Synt.*], J. Lallot (ed.) *De la construction* (Περὶ συντάξεως), 2 vols. (Paris: Vrin, 1997).

Apuleius. *De interpretatione* [*On Interpretation = De int.*], P. Thomas (ed.) (Leipzig: Teubner, 1908).

Aquinas, Thomas. *In Decem Libros Ethicorum Aristotelis ad Nicomachum Expositio*, R. M. Spiazzi (ed.), 3rd edn. (Turin: Marietti, 1964).

Boyle, R. *A Free Enquiry into the Vulgarly Received Notion of Nature* (1686), E. B. Davis and M. Hunter (eds.) (Cambridge: Cambridge University Press, 1996).

Butler, J. *Works of Joseph Butler*, J. H. Bernard (ed.), 2 vols. (London: Macmillan, 1900).

Cicero. *Academica* [*Academics* = *Acad.*], O. Plasberg (ed.) (Leipzig: Teubner, 1922).

—— *De divinatione* [*On Divination* = *Div.*], *De fato* [*On Fate* = *Fat.*], R. Giomini (ed.) (Leipzig: Teubner, 1975).

—— *De finibus bonorum et malorum* [*On Ends* = *Fin.*], L. D. Reynolds (ed.) (Oxford: Oxford University Press, 1998).

—— *De natura deorum* [*On the Nature of the Gods* = *ND*], W. Ax (ed.) (Leipzig: Teubner, 1933).

—— *De officiis* [*On Duties* = *Off.*], O. Plasberg and W. Ax (eds.) (Leipzig: Teubner, 1949).

—— *Tusculanae disputationes* [*Tusculan Disputations* = *Tusc.*], T. W. Dougan and R. M. Henry (eds.) (Cambridge: Cambridge University Press, 1905–1934).

Clement (Clemens Alexandrinus). *Stromateis* [*Miscellanies* = *Strom.*], O. Stählin, L. Früchtel, and U. Treu (eds.) (Berlin: Akademie-Verlag, 1960).

Cleomedes. *Cleomedis Caelestia* (*Meteora*) [= *Cael.*], R. Todd (ed.) (Leipzig: Teubner, 1990).

Diocles. *Diocles of Carystus*, Volume 1: Text and Translation, P. J. van der Eijk (ed.) (Leiden: Brill, 2000) (= vdE).

Diogenes Laertius [= DL]. *Vitae Philosophorum* [*Lives of the Philosophers*], H. S. Long (ed.) (Oxford: Oxford University Press, 1964).

Dionysius Thrax. *Dionysii Thracis Ars grammatica* [= DT], G. Uhlig (ed.) *Grammatici Graeci* I, 1, 3 (Leipzig: Teubner, 1883; repr. Hildesheim: Olms, 1965).

—— *Scholia in Dionysii Thracis Artem grammaticam* [*Scholia on Dionysius Thrax* = DT Sch.], A. Hilgard (ed.) *Grammatici Graeci* I, 3 (Leipzig: Teubner, 1901; repr. Hildesheim: Olms, 1965).

Duns Scotus. *Duns Scotus on the Will and Morality*, A. B. Wolter (ed.) (Washington: Catholic University of America Press, 1986).

Epictetus. *Dissertationes ab Arriano digestae* [*Discourses* = *Diss.*], *Enchiridion* [*Manual* = *Handbook* = *Ench.*], H. Schenkl (ed.) (Leipzig: Teubner, 1916).

Eusebius. *Praeparatio evangelica* [*Evangelical Preparation* or *Preparation for the Gospel* = *Pr. ev.*], K. Mras (ed.), 2 vols. (Berlin: Akademie-Verlag, 1954–56).

Galen. *De causis continentibus* [*On Sustaining Causes* = *Caus. cont.*] M. C. Lyons, K. Kalbfleisch, J. Kollesch, D. Nickel, and G. Strohmaier (eds.) *Corpus medicorum Graecorum, Suppl. orientale* II (Berlin: Akademie-Verlag, 1969).

—— *Galeni de Placitis Hippocratis et Platonis* [*On the Doctrines of Hippocrates and Plato* = *PHP*], P. H. De Lacy (ed.) *Corpus Medicorum Graecorum* V 4, 1, 2 (3 vols.) (Berlin: Akademie-Verlag, 1978–84).

—— [*Outline of Empiricism*], fr. 10b in K. Deichgräber *Die Griechische Empirikerschule: Sammlung und Darstellung der Lehre* (Berlin: Weidmann, 1930).

Gellius. *Noctes Atticae* [= *NA*], P. K. Marshall (ed.) (Oxford: Oxford University Press, 1968).

Grotius, H. *De jure belli et pacis* [= *JBP*], W. Whewell (ed.), 3 vols. (Cambridge: Cambridge University Press, 1853).

Herophilus. *Herophilus: The Art of Medicine in Early Alexandria*, H. von Staden (ed.) (Cambridge: Cambridge University Press, 1989) (= vS).

Hierocles. *Elementa Moralia* [*Elements of Ethics*], G. Bastianini and A. A. Long (eds.) in *Corpus dei Papyri Filosofici Greci e Latini*, pt. I vol. 1**: Autori Noti (Florence: L. S. Olschki, 1992).

Hippocrates. *Oeuvres Complètes d'Hippocrate*, vol. 6, É. Littré (ed.) (Amsterdam: Hakkert, repr. 1962).

Hume, D. *A Treatise of Human Nature* (1739), L. A. Selby-Bigge (ed.) (Oxford: Oxford University Press, 1888).

Hutcheson, F. *On Human Nature*, T. Mautner (ed.) (Cambridge: Cambridge University Press, 1993).

Lactantius. *Divinae institutiones* [*Divine Institutes* = *Div. inst.*], P. Monat (ed.) (Paris: Éditions du Cerf, 1973–).

Leibniz, G. W. 'On Nature Itself' in L. E. Loemker (ed.) *Philosophical Letters and Papers*, 2nd edn. (Dordrecht: Reidel, 1969), 498–508.

—— 'Opinion on the Principles of Pufendorf' in P. Riley (ed.) *Leibniz: Political Writings*, 2nd edn. (Cambridge: Cambridge University Press, 1988), 64–75.

Marcus Aurelius. *Meditations*, J. Dalfen (ed.) (Leipzig: Teubner, 1987).

Origen. *Origen: Contra Celsum*, H. Chadwick (ed.) (Cambridge: Cambridge University Press, repr. 1965).

Philodemus. *De pietate* [*On Piety* = *Piet.*], D. Obbink (ed.) *Philodemus: On Piety*, pt. 1 (Oxford: Oxford University Press, 1996).

—— *De signis* [*On Signs* = *Sign.*], P. and E. De Lacy, *Philodemus, On Methods of Inference* (Naples: Bibliopolis, 1978²).

Plutarch. *Adversus Colotem* [*Against Colotes* = *Col.*], *De communibus notitiis adversus Stoicos* [*On Common Conceptions* = *Comm. not.*], *De*

Stoicorum repugnatiis [*On Stoic Self-contradictions* = *St. rep.*], M. Pohlenz and R. Westmann (eds.) (Leipzig: Teubner, 1959).

—— *De virtute morali* [*On Moral Virtue* = *Virt. mor.*] W. R. Paton, M. Pohlenz, and W. Sieveking (eds.) (Leipzig: Teubner, 1929).

Posidonius. *Posidonius: Volume I, The Fragments* [= EK], L. Edelstein and I. G. Kidd (eds.) (Cambridge: Cambridge University Press, 1972). Kidd, I. G. (1988) *Posidonius II. The Commentary*, 2 vols. (Cambridge: Cambridge University Press).

Praxagoras. *The Fragments of Praxagoras of Cos and His School*, F. Steckerl (ed.) (Leiden: Brill, 1958).

Ptolemy. *Tetrabiblos*, W. Hübner, post F. Boll and Ae. Boer (ed.) *Claudii Ptolemaei Opera quae exstan omnia*, III, 1, *ΑΠΟΤΕΛΕΣΜΑΤΙΚΑ* (Stuttgart/Leipzig: Teubner, 1998).

Pufendorf, S. *Les Devoirs de l'Homme et du Cityoen*, trans. J. Barbeyrac, 4th edn., (Amsterdam: Pierre de Coup, 1718).

Pufendorf, S. *De jure naturae et gentium* [= *JNG*] (Amsterdam: Hoogenhuysen, 1688). Trans. C. H. Oldfather and W. A. Oldfather (Oxford: Clarendon Press, 1934).

Seneca. *Ad Lucilium epistulae morales* [*Letters* = *Ep.*], L. D. Reynolds (ed.) (Oxford University Press, 1965).

—— *De beneficiis* [*On Benefits* = *Ben.*], F. Préchac (ed.) (Paris: Les Belles Lettres, 1972).

—— *De ira* [*On Anger*], in *L. Annai, Senecae Dialogorum Libri Duodecim*, L. D. Reynolds (ed.) (Oxford: Oxford University Press, 1977).

—— *Naturales quaestiones* [*Natural Questions* = *NQ*], H. H. Hine (ed.) (Stuttgart/Leipzig: Teubner, 1996).

Sextus Empiricus [= S. E.]. *Adversus mathematicos* [*Against the Professors* = *M*], *Pyrrhoneae hypotyposes* [*Outlines of Pyrrhonism* = *PH*], H. Mutschmann and J. Mau (eds.) (Leipzig: Teubner, 1912–1954).

Simplicius. *In Aristotelis Categorias Commentarium* [*On Aristotle's Categories* = *In Ar. Cat.*], K. Kalbfleisch (ed.) *CAG* VIII (Berlin: Reimer, 1907).

—— *In Aristotelis Physica Commentaria* [*On Aristotle's Physics* = *In Ar. Phys.*] H. Diels (ed.) *CAG* IX–X (Berlin: Reimer, 1882–95).

Spinoza. *The Collected Works of Spinoza*, Vol. 1, E. Curley (ed.) (Princeton: Princeton University Press, 1985).

Stobaeus. *Anthologium* [*Eclogae* = *Ecl.*], C. Wachsmuth (ed.) (Berlin: Weidmann, 1884, reprinted 1958).

Suarez, F. *Opera Omnia*, C. Berton (ed.), 28 vols. (Paris: Vivès, 1866).

—— *The Metaphysics of Good and Evil According to Suarez*, J. J. E. Gracia and D. Davis (eds.) (Munich: Philosophia Verlag, 1989).

COLLECTION OF TEXTS

Döring, Klaus (1972). *Die Megariker* (Amsterdam: Brüner).

Dox. Gr.: Diels, H. (repr. 1965). *Doxographi Graeci* (Berlin: Walter de Gruyter and Associates).

FDS: Hülser, K. (1987–88). *Die Fragmente zur Dialektik der Stoiker*, 4 vols. (Stuttgart: Frommann-Holzboog).

LS: Long, A. A., and D. N. Sedley, eds. (1987). *The Hellenistic Philosophers* (Cambridge: Cambridge University Press).

SVF: Arnim, H. von (1903–5). *Stoicorum Veterum Fragmenta*, Vols. 1–3 (Leipzig: Teubner); Vol. 4 (1924), indexes, by M. Adler (Leipzig: Teubner).

GENERAL INDEX

PASSAGES INDEX